Fruitlands

Also by Richard Francis

*Transcendental Utopias: Individual and Community at Brook Farm,
Fruitlands, and Walden*

*Ann the Word: The Story of Ann Lee, Female Messiah, Mother of the Shakers,
The Woman Clothed with the Sun*

*Judge Sewall's Apology: The Salem Witch Trials and the Forming of an
American Conscience*

Fruitlands

THE ALCOTT FAMILY AND
THEIR SEARCH FOR UTOPIA

by

RICHARD FRANCIS

YALE UNIVERSITY PRESS | NEW HAVEN AND LONDON

For information about this and other Yale University Press publications, please contact:

U.S. Office: sales.press@yale.edu   yalepress.yale.edu
Europe Office: sales@yaleup.co.uk   www.yalebooks.co.uk

Set in Arno Pro by IDSUK (DataConnection) Ltd
Printed in the United States of America

Library of Congress Cataloging-in-Publication Data

Francis, Richard, 1945–
    Fruitlands: the Alcott family and their search for utopia / Richard Francis.
      p. cm.
    ISBN 978-0-300-14041-5 (cl: alk. paper) 1. Fruitlands (Harvard, Mass.)—History. 2. Alcott, Amos Bronson, 1799–1888—Family. 3. Utopias—Massachusetts—Harvard—History—19th century. 4. Communal living—Massachusetts—Harvard—History—19th century. 5. Transcendentalism   (New England)   I. Title.
    HX656.F78F73   2010
    307.7709744′3—dc22

                                                                         2010019705

A catalogue record for this book is available from the British Library.

10 9 8 7 6 5 4 3 2
2014 2013 2012 2011 2010

Contents

List of Illustrations

Plate section

This book is for

Will, Sam, Zac, and Eli

Helen

Jo

my own family

Introduction

ABOUT THIRTY MILES west of Boston there is a pleasant country lane called Prospect Hill Road, alongside which are plump suburban houses with cars in their driveways, basket ball hoops, sheltering bushes and trees. At a certain point on the west side of the road, the land falls away and a huge view opens up—the prospect of Prospect Hill. A driveway snakes down with a scattering of buildings on each side of it. The far one, a deep red clapboard farmhouse, is situated about two-thirds of the way down the slope, tucked into a shallow dell. Beyond it the valley bottoms out into an intervale, as it is technically known, a low-level tract of land by a river, the Nashua River in this case. The view stretches for miles to a couple of far mountains, Wachusett and Monadnock, the intervening land mainly forest with occasional scars from highways, a military base, a prison. But it is still a beautiful place. Standing on the slope of Prospect Hill in the summertime is like being on the shore of a vast green lake.

In 1843 an odd assortment of people assembled at that remote farmhouse (none of the other buildings were there then) to begin an experiment in living. This is the story of one of history's most unsuccessful utopias ever—but also one of the most dramatic and significant.

In 1842 Bronson Alcott, a forty-two-year-old out-of-pocket philosopher in a state of deep depression, was funded by his friend Ralph Waldo Emerson to go to England on a morale-boosting trip. Over at Ham, in Surrey, a group of Englishmen had set up a community called Alcott House in his honor.

Both Alcott and his English admirers believed that the Garden of Eden would return if only people avoided meat, cheese, milk, eggs, tea, coffee, and alcohol, preferably living on water and fruit. The English contingent also thought that a new generation of perfected humans could be born if sexual intercourse became entirely devoid of lust and passion. Alcott, however, was happily married and already the father of four daughters (one of whom was the future author of *Little Women*).

Nevertheless two of the Englishmen, Charles Lane and Henry Wright, decided to go back to America with him to set up a utopian experiment in New England. Lane's ten-year-old son William (product of a previous unhappy marriage) came too. They crammed into the Alcotts' family home in Concord, and then the following summer everyone moved out to the farmhouse off Prospect Hill Road, which they named Fruitlands. Here, with a handful of other followers, they tried to live a self-sufficient life, eating their own produce and wearing homemade linen clothes (one of them believed in wearing nothing at all, in imitation of Adam and Eve).

Soon tension developed on all fronts. Alcott and Lane liked to go on "penniless pilgrimages," taking rides across country without paying for them, in an effort to gather new recruits—they had a tendency to do this just when demanding farm work needed to be done, leaving it to the women and children. The farm chores themselves were made more difficult because the community disapproved of using animals to plow the ground and prohibited the use of manure. There were arguments about money (since the Alcotts did not have any, Lane had to pay for everything). The leaders accused each other of being tyrannical. There was despair about their inability to attract recruits to their austere way of life (the community peaked at thirteen members). One member left because Fruitlands was not spiritual enough; another found the regime too tough (she was thrown out for eating a piece of fish, at least according to one account); another—the nudist—decided it was not tough enough and left to be more abstemious elsewhere. Above all,

Abigail Alcott realized that Lane's beliefs threatened her marriage and devalued her role as a mother. Soon a battle developed between the two for the possession of her husband. As a savage winter began, she hatched a plan with her brother to bring Fruitlands to an end.

Despite their eccentricity, many of the Fruitlanders' ideas ring bells today. They thought pollution and environmental damage could destroy civilization; they intuited the interconnectedness of all living things, and had an inkling of ecology long before the science had been invented; they were passionately opposed to slavery, and supported women's rights; they believed in civil disobedience, and espoused anarchism. Their experiment is a blend of outmoded and surprisingly modern ways of thinking about the world. Above all it is a very human story of misunderstanding and jealousy, in which a group of idealists end by trying to destroy each other.

Fruitlands was one of a number of utopian communities that were being established in New England at that time. The year previously the Northampton Community for Association and Education had been set up about forty miles from the Fruitlands site on the western edge of Massachusetts; at about the same time the Hopedale Community was established about thirty-five miles to the southwest. These experiments, like Fruitlands itself, advocated abolitionism and temperance but ultimately were not simply a product of particular grievances or issues. They reflected large-scale political and social unease running through both Europe and America, giving rise to the Chartist movement in Britain, for example, and in due course manifesting itself in the repeal of the Corn Laws and, on the European mainland, the revolutions of 1848. The broad impulse behind the American experiments was a reaction to the industrial revolution and the rise of cities, with their consequent social injustice, poverty, and environmental deterioration—developments that had taken place later in the U.S.A. than on the other side of the Atlantic but which were making themselves felt by the 1840s.

The Americans indulged in their community building with particular relish, the example of the Puritan plantations and townships still comparatively fresh in their minds. There were longer-established institutions too, even closer at hand. The Shakers had settled both in Harvard village, the township to which Fruitlands belonged, and in Shirley, just a few miles west. These were religious organizations rather than reforming ones, established by the followers of Ann Lee, the eighteenth-century female "messiah," and devoted to the worship of God through dance and song, cultivating the land, and producing simple and beautiful furniture. Though Fruitlands was not a religious community as such, its members were influenced by Shaker austerity and its prohibition of sex, its advocacy of women's rights, and its farming practices.

There was an affinity of a different kind between Fruitlands and the most famous community of its day, Brook Farm. This utopia had been established in West Roxbury, now part of urban Boston but in those days a pleasant rural location just to the west of the city, and like Fruitlands it was the product of the Transcendentalist movement that had originated in the region in the 1830s.

New England Transcendentalism had its roots in a religious controversy. The Calvinism of the colonial Puritans had gradually given way to Unitarianism, a nondogmatic and inclusive form of Christianity that was essentially the product of empirical philosophy and Enlightenment values. The Unitarians held that the message of the gospels appealed to basic decency and commonsense, but because of their Lockean belief that evidence was needed to underline faith, their creed at that period was pared down to one irreducible point: a belief in the authenticity of the gospel miracles. God broke the laws of nature briefly to prove he existed: it is just what a logical Supreme Being *would* do.

However, a number of Unitarian ministers and other thinkers, among them Ralph Waldo Emerson, George Ripley, and Bronson Alcott, came to the conclusion that belief in miracles was an unnecessary concession to the supernatural: the Christian message was true because it was true, and didn't need any evidence to substantiate it. From one point of view they can be seen as more rationalistic than their opponents; from another, as more mystical. As Emerson put it, "the very word Miracle, as pronounced by the Christian churches, gives a false impression: it is Monster. It is not one with the blowing clover and the falling rain." The New England Transcendentalists believed that Christ was not endowed with supernatural gifts but was a man like other men, except that he had lived a perfect life, and thereby set an example which we can follow. It is not surprising therefore that this movement gave birth to two utopian experiments—three, if one includes Thoreau's later community of one, when he lived in his hut for two years beside Walden Pond.

George Ripley abandoned his ministry (as did Emerson and others) and he and his wife Sophia set up Brook Farm in April 1841. Though it began in a small way, it expanded rapidly and by the time of the founding of Fruitlands had around a hundred members. It represented an attempt to abolish social division and injustice, and to reconcile manual and mental work. This meant two things essentially: cutting across class boundaries, so that manual workers lived cheek by jowl with those traditionally regarded as their social superiors; and allowing intellectuals—including the man of letters Nathaniel Hawthorne, who was a member during the first year—to live a more balanced life, with healthy work on the land acting as a counterweight to mental activity. Fruitlands shared this ambition but differed from its rival in other respects, particularly in terms of its scale.

Lane and Wright were English Transcendentalists rather than New England ones, disciples of an obscure British educationalist and philosopher called James Pierrepont Greaves, who gathered a small group of acolytes around him in London in the 1830s. Greaves had imbibed his Transcendentalism from German philosophy via the mediation of Samuel Taylor Coleridge. Like his American counterparts he believed that there was a coherent underlying structure to the world, and that if one lived one's life correctly, one could participate in that universal harmony.

In his earlier days Greaves had worked with the Swiss educational reformer Johann Pestalozzi; over on the other side of the Atlantic, Bronson Alcott ran a famous experimental school in Boston for several years in the mid-1830s. Greaves came to hear of it, and made contact with him, thus triggering a transatlantic cross-fertilization of ideas that ultimately led to Lane and Wright joining forces with Alcott in Massachusetts to conduct their experiment in living a good life.

Nevertheless the Fruitlands community insisted on thinking of itself as a family, though what they meant by that word, and indeed whether they all meant the same thing, was to be its major bone of contention. Did "family" refer simply to a small group of people or to a biological entity? Should Fruitlands be seen as a paradigm, offering itself as an example in living to other households, or should it be regarded as part of a process, as a group that would swell inexorably? In the midst of all this uncertainty ten-year-old Louisa May Alcott was keeping a diary and recording some of the experiences that would lie behind the great celebration of family life she would publish nearly thirty years later.

One thing the Fruitlanders did agree on: diet was the key to a good life. They were vegans a century before the term was invented. They were even uneasy about the process of cooking, and one member of the community, Samuel Bower, insisted on eating only raw food, including beans and grain. They would not wear wool or cotton (the latter because it was the product of slavery), and they tried to avoid leather.

Tracking the sources of these prohibitions takes us in two different directions. On the one hand, the Fruitlanders looked backward, toward the story of the Garden of Eden in the book of Genesis. For them that myth had literal truth, depicting a world in which human beings were at one with nature, pristine, and innocent. The Fall had taken place because our original parents had eaten the wrong food. Ergo, if this dietary slip-up could be rectified, the Garden would be reinstated, and people would become perfect once more.

For most of us nowadays this seems simplistic, to say the least. We are separated from the Fruitlanders' belief in a lost but retrievable golden age by all the big complicating ideas that have overtaken Western culture since their day, by Darwinism, Marxism, Freudianism; their optimism hardly stands up against tragedies like the American Civil War (less than two decades away from their experiment), not to mention the world wars of the twentieth century. But of course the Fruitlanders were reacting to traumas and upheavals of their own. Indeed, as with other utopian experiments in that place and time, one of the impulses behind their community was the anti-slavery movement itself.

Alcott had taken part in abolition meetings in Boston in the late 1830s. He was very much involved, along with his brother-in-law Samuel May, in the strategic discussions which led to a refusal to endorse government injustice and violence, a consequent belief in withholding taxes and, ultimately, in taking up an anarchist stance. When Lane joined Alcott he too embraced abolitionism and became an advocate of anarchism. The two men refused to pay their poll tax in order to get sent to jail several years before Henry David Thoreau famously committed the same act of civil disobedience. They believed that by stepping out of the political and administrative structure of their society they would discover another system to supplant it, one that had been lost to us as a consequence of the Fall but was still available, just out of sight.

When we come to explore the other trajectory of their thinking, it turns out that they have more in common with us than we might have imagined. Their obsession with living an uncorrupted life at one with their surroundings contained within itself an intuition of twin preoccupations of our own time, ecology and environmentalism. They were deeply concerned with the danger of environmental degradation and pollution, the harm that it represents for people and for the world itself. This awareness was linked to their sense that all phenomena were interlinked, that life can be seen as one force running through a multitude of differing manifestations.

Obviously this belief can be related to romantic pantheism of a Wordsworthian kind, but because the Fruitlanders were practical (in their own way) the idea tends to move from the abstract and mystical to the concrete and literal. They treated the landscape around them as a single phenomenon, of which they themselves were a component. Indeed on one occasion they attracted the incredulity (and mirth) of fellow-Transcendentalists by roundly attacking the love of Nature because it represented an aesthetic distancing between human beings and the world in which they found themselves. Their gropings towards an apprehension of ecological science, like their act of civil disobedience, were taken forward over the next few years by their friend and admirer Thoreau.

In another respect their attitudes seem a world away from ours—in their view of sex. Lane was, it is fair to say, opposed to it, and Bronson Alcott followed his lead for a time. There could not be an outright prohibition, of course, because the human race needed to reproduce. This part of the Fruitlands credo was derived from the theories developed across the Atlantic, in the Greaves circle. The danger of sexual passion was that it made a couple turn inward towards each other, and therefore lose their engagement with the human predicament as a whole. More particularly, sexual intercourse could have the effect of passing on spiritual imperfections from one generation to the next. Sexual activity had to be carefully regulated and controlled in order not to let such flaws creep into the process. It must be passionless and only undertaken when the couple concerned have undergone physical and mental discipline that would give the maximum chance of producing perfect offspring. Because of the difficulty of achieving the requisite level of chilly disinterest, in practical terms it was best to defer the whole issue and avoid sex altogether.

This taboo was inevitably a cause of tension, first among the English Transcendentalists, and then among the Fruitlanders themselves. At the heart of the story is a dramatic variation on the love triangle, as Abigail Alcott and Charles Lane began to fight for possession of Bronson Alcott. Their conflict was perhaps the principal reason why the experiment was so short-lived.

The community moved into the farmhouse off Prospect Hill Road on June 1, 1843; it dispersed the following January. However, the Alcotts, the Lanes, and Wright had started living together as one household, in Concordia Cottage in Concord, during the October of 1842, and endeavored to conduct their lives according to the principles that would underlie Fruitlands itself, so the experiment can be seen as lasting over fourteen months altogether. The small town of Concord had claims to be a kind of utopia in its own right, as the name the Alcotts gave to their cottage implied. They had moved there from Boston in April, 1840 in order to be near Emerson. Thoreau lived there too, with his parents and sister, and after leaving Brook Farm, Nathaniel Hawthorne arrived with his wife in 1842. It was a place top-heavy with philosophers and literary men, and within easy reach of Boston and the intelligentsia there. At the same time it was a rural community of farmers and a self-contained village, creating very much the sort of juxtaposition of laborers and intellectuals that Brook Farm was endeavoring to achieve. Moving the fifteen miles or so further west to Fruitlands represented an attempt to give a harder empirical edge to these aspirations, to engage with the land itself, and to attempt to define the basic component of a redeemed society, the lowest common dominator of perfection.

The fascination of utopia is that it represents an attempt to live out ideas, to live deliberately, to use Thoreau's memorable adverb. The tension between ideal and real, which affects the lives of all of us, is particularly sharp and clear in this context. There is always a counterpoint between a narrative—by turns tense, painful, and comic, and sometimes all three at once—and the high-minded philosophizing to which the participants were addicted. The fact that a relatively small group was involved makes the drama—for them as players and for us as audience—particularly vivid and intense. The strongest and most fundamental relations are at stake and in conflict: those between husband and wife, between parents and children, between friends and allies, between individuals and the community.

Everything has to be re-examined and redefined: what it is to be a lover, a companion, a child, a woman, a man; the best way of living in a house, engaging with the land, participating in a community; whether one should try to influence others by force of example, by engaging in dialogue, or by putting pen to paper; the relative desirability of staying at home or traveling, and if electing to do the latter, the best way to proceed, whether on foot or taking advantage of modern means of transportation, the railroad and the steamboat; the extent to which it is possible to be self-sufficient and to refuse to participate in the mechanisms of society (including voting and using money).

For the Fruitlanders nothing could be taken for granted. Perhaps this above all gives them their fascination to this day: they insisted on looking at the world with fresh eyes.

My interest in Fruitlands dates back to two years I spent as an American Council of Learned Societies' Fellow at Harvard University. In 1997 this resulted in a book, *Transcendental Utopias: Individual and Community at Brook Farm, Fruitlands, and Walden.* Two chapters of it concerned the Fruitlands experiment, and at the time I felt I had dealt sufficiently with the topic. I went on to write two more nonfiction works, a biography of Ann Lee (1736–1784), the English founder of American Shakerism, and another of Samuel Sewall (1652–1730), the only one of the nine judges at the Salem witch trials to admit in public that there had been a terrible miscarriage of justice, and to ask forgiveness from God and his community. But in fact I was not straying very far from my interest in Fruitlands. Some of the most significant and dramatic episodes of Ann Lee's life took place in the small village of Harvard (not to be confused with the university of that name)—the very place where Fruitlands would be established seventy years after Ann Lee left it. And Samuel Sewall was the ancestor of five of the members of the Fruitlands community, the great-great-grandfather of Abigail Alcott, and (with one more "great") of her four daughters.

My earlier account of the community was fundamentally analytical and abstract, an exploration of the assumptions that fused together Transcendentalist and utopian beliefs. Its argument was that the three great experiments of the Transcendentalist movement all depended on a conception of the serial repetition of all phenomena, and that the different scales of the communities—large Brook Farm, family-sized Fruitlands, solitary Thoreau in his hut by Walden Pond—simply reflected different theories as to what the basic building block of the ideal society might be. I pursued my philosophical quest by hopping blithely from one utterance to another of the philosophers concerned, moving from the inception of Fruitlands to its demise, and back again, in my two chapters dealing with the community.

A few years ago it began to dawn on me that this approach, while it had its merits, did not tell the whole story. In fact, it did not tell the story at all. The biographies I have written since, as well as my other career as a novelist, have made me realize there is a meaning implicit in the very structure of a narrative. And this is particularly true of utopian experiments, where people choose to act out theories and principles in their daily lives. It also struck me that the Fruitlands enterprise, because it was so short-lived, could be monitored month by month, week by week, even at times day by day.

When I began this book I was a little worried that it might develop a tendency to become over-reliant on its predecessor for intellectual capital, rather as Bronson Alcott himself depended on relatives and friends for financial backing. As it turns out, I am surprised at the extent to which this has not been the case. Of course there are moments when I revert to a point I made before, or when I make use of particular materials for the second time. But while I don't repudiate my previous analysis, it now seems to me to have been located primarily in my own head, representing my particular take on what happened. I was of course covering much more ground overall than I do here—Fruitlands had to be dealt with in fewer than eighty pages. In the present book, by contrast, I have the space to portray events as the participants experienced, discussed, and wrote about them. My own reactions inevitably become part of the story, but my intention has been to show how Fruitlands was essentially a drama in which a particular group of people interacted with each other, intellectually and emotionally: it is that interaction which gives the experiment its fullest significance.

This book is in fact a collective biography, which leads to one small technical problem. Of the cast of characters involved, five are called Alcott (and two Lane). Normally I try to maintain some degree of detachment from my subject by using his or her surname, but that is hardly practical here. I have no inhibitions about using the first names of the children involved, but that still leaves Bronson and Abigail Alcott, and I can hardly refer to them both as Alcott, while at the same time it is cumbersome always to use two (or even three) names for each of them. I therefore usually call Mrs. Alcott, Abigail, hoping that readers will not accuse me of being patronizing or sexist (in the cases of Margaret Fuller and Elizabeth Peabody I have no hesitation in referring to them as Fuller and Peabody when appropriate). As a matter of fact Mrs. Alcott was usually known in her family as "Abba," but that seemed a step too far. The formality of her full first name is less intrusive, particularly as she followed the custom of the time in calling her own husband "Mr. Alcott."

My wife and I first went to the Fruitlands Museums many years ago and still remember with gratitude the hospitality we were shown by the then director and his wife, the late Pat and Clio Harrison, and their daughter Anthea. It was a great pleasure to renew our acquaintanceship with that beautiful place, and I am deeply indebted to all the staff there for encouragement and support, in particular to Michael Volmar, the curator. Mike provided access to the Fruitlands archives, and one lunchtime took us on a wet and bug-ridden walk round the archaeological remains of the Lovejoy house. Following our visit he was on the receiving end of a host of queries, which he has dealt with promptly and with good humor. He also read the manuscript of this book and corrected a number of mistakes. The former director of education for the Museums, Laurie Butters, also gave me advice and help.

I am grateful to Susan Halpert and the staff of the Houghton Library, Harvard University, where the bulk of the Alcott family's manuscripts are kept, to Kimberly Reynolds and Sean Casey of the Rare Books and Manuscripts Department of the Boston Public Library, to Maggie Collins at the Bath Spa University Library, to the British Library and to the Widener Library of Harvard University, and to Robert Bell of the Wisbech and Fenland Museum. Thanks too, to the British Academy for a research grant, and to my colleagues at Bath Spa University for study leave. I am also indebted to Joel Myerson, scholar of Transcendentalism, to my friend Victor Gray, to my children William and Helen, my agent Caroline Dawnay, and my editor Phoebe Clapham, for all their help, encouragement, and support.

My wife Jo did the research side by side with me and was involved at every stage, as she always has been.

PART 1

The Seed

1

To Reproduce Perfect Men

IN 1834 AMOS BRONSON ALCOTT arrived in Boston with his wife Abigail and their two small daughters, Anna and Louisa. He was a schoolteacher, at a time when formal qualifications were not needed for the profession, which was just as well, since he didn't have any. He was a tall, lanky man, with fair hair and rather horsey features, restless and impulsive, with an extraordinary gift for talking.

Alcott came from a struggling farm in Wolcott, Connecticut, and was born in 1799, the oldest of a family of eight children.[1] He left school at thirteen but read widely under the influence of his cousin William, later a doctor and dietician. He was particularly addicted to *Pilgrim's Progress*, which became a central text of his life. At seventeen he went on a peddling expedition to the Deep South, and over the next five years embarked on five such trips in all, sometimes alone, sometimes with his brother Chatfield or his cousin William. Then he became a schoolteacher back in his home state of Connecticut. He discovered the doctrines of the Swiss educator Johann Pestalozzi in a series of English pamphlets and enthusiastically adopted his theories, describing the use he made of them in articles for the *American Journal of Education*. As a result he attracted the attention of Samuel May, a minister and educator from Boston who was living in Connecticut at the time.

Alcott's first visit to Boston was in 1828 where he set up a school with the help of an introduction from Samuel May. He also wooed and wed May's sister Abigail. The Mays were a prominent local family, some members of which unsurprisingly took the view that Abigail was marrying beneath herself.[2] Her father Joseph May had made—and lost—a large fortune as a merchant and subsequently devoted much of his life to charitable causes. On her mother's side Abigail, known as Abby or Abba, was related to Boston "aristocracy," like the Quincys—one of whom had just become the president of Harvard University—and the Sewalls. Abigail herself was the great-great-granddaughter of Samuel Sewall, one of the nine judges who presided over the Salem witch trials in 1692. He was the only one to apologize publicly for the miscarriage of justice, and was distinguished throughout his life by his hostility to slavery, and his advocacy of the rights of Native Americans. Abigail was dark, almost swarthy in complexion, contrasting sharply with her fair-skinned husband. She was twenty-nine when they married on May 22, 1830, quite old for that period, but she had been engaged previously to a cousin who had died.[3]

The couple went off to Pennsylvania where Alcott ran a couple of schools in Germantown and Philadelphia. All his forays into teaching were characterized by original ideas and energetic execution; none of them lasted long. Now the Alcotts came back to Boston to try their luck again.

Alcott had already evolved a revolutionary technique. Pestalozzi had advocated teaching the child rather than the subject, building on the pupil's own observations, and relating educational progress to psychological and intellectual development. Alcott went a step further, basing his whole strategy on the Socratic method, whereby the teacher asks questions to elicit truths that the child already knows, was born knowing, in an apparent reversal of the normal pattern. Alcott had the journals produced by the children he had taught in Pennsylvania as a demonstration of the effectiveness of his approach. He showed them to a young woman he and his wife had known since their early married days in Boston, four years previously. She was Elizabeth Palmer Peabody, one of three talented sisters who would make their own marks on the New England artistic and intellectual scene.

Thirty-year-old Elizabeth Peabody was a teacher too. Though like Abigail she came from a more prominent background than Alcott's, she had one thing in common with him: as a woman she also lacked formal educational qualifications. Nevertheless, she had become a formidable intellectual through her own efforts, with encouragement from such local dignitaries as John Kirkland, the Harvard president preceding Abigail's relative Josiah Quincy, and the university's professor of divinity, Andrews Norton. She was fluent in classical languages and was well versed in philosophy and theology.

Reading the children's journals, Peabody was astonished by what Alcott had achieved in Philadelphia, and immediately began helping him to set up a school in Boston. In due course she would become his (unpaid) teaching assistant and, more importantly, his Boswell, recording the actual content of his lessons and publishing them in 1835 in a book entitled *Record of a School*.

The two found what they wanted in the newly built Masonic Temple overlooking Boston Common, on the corner of Tremont Street and Temple Place. They were able to rent a sixty-foot-long room with an enormous gothic window. At the beginning of her *Record*, Peabody describes how Alcott arranged the room for his teaching. He had a desk specially made for him and positioned opposite the window. It was ten feet wide and shaped in a curve. Behind the desk a cast of Christ was "made to appear to scholars just over the teacher's head," hovering above his fair hair like a halo.[4] The juxtaposition tells us a lot both about Alcott himself, and the philosophical and religious movement stirring in Boston at this time, in which he would play a central part.

That movement became known by the cumbersome name of New England Transcendentalism, and resulted from a dispute within the ranks of the Unitarians, Boston's dominant creed. Unitarianism at that time was doctrinally liberal, but Andrews Norton and other leading theologians argued that the authenticity of the gospel miracles was the sticking point: without a belief in *them*, it would not be a religion at all. The miracles were the means used by the divinity to make his existence known to humankind. Disaffected ministers like George Ripley, Theodore Parker, and Ralph Waldo Emerson argued that individuals had direct access to God in any case. Christ was not a supernatural being but simply an—or rather *the*—exemplary individual. "One man," Emerson would say in the Divinity School Address he gave at Harvard a few years later, "was true to what is in you and me." There had been no miracles, no hocus-pocus serving to establish a gulf between humankind and the Almighty, and calling into existence, as with a wave of a magician's wand, a force to override or defy nature itself. Miracles were unnecessary anomalies: the word was a "Monster," Emerson would tell the class of graduating Unitarians.[5]

This was primarily a home-grown Boston debate. Alcott, brought up in in Connecticut, had been baptized into the Episcopal Church in any case. But under the influence of Coleridge, and through him German philosophy, he had made his own way to the Transcendentalist position, and now based in Boston he joined in the debate with enthusiasm. His view was that apparent miracles were in fact the product of laws not yet understood. "The wonderful cures wrought by Jesus," he wrote in his journal "were wrought in accordance with the action of certain immutable laws, *organic, and spiritual.*" Characteristically, he added, "*The philosophy of the miracles of Christ—this is my aim.*"[6] The bas-relief of Christ, hovering over Alcott's head, acted as a Divinity School Address in miniature, his own equivalent, in the language of classroom furbishment, of Emerson's vibrant claim "that God incarnates himself in man, and evermore goes forth anew to take possession of his World."

When teaching, Alcott arranged the children in chairs in a semicircle in front of his semicircular desk, one curve beyond another, like ripples spreading outward. It was an arrangement that would be imitated by his admirers, so in a sense the ripples kept on spreading. Peabody's *Record* provided the agency for that process, and gives us an account of the actual content of Alcott's lessons.

One of them, unsurprisingly, focused on Wordsworth's "Ode on Intimations of Immortality from Recollections of Early Childhood," a poem which proclaims that children are born with a visionary perception of the world which they gradually lose as they grow up.[7] This analysis underpinned Alcott's whole approach to teaching, and indeed his philosophy. In effect it involves a psychological adaptation of Transcendentalist theories, explaining both why they are true and why their truth is not always perceived. Children are born with the ability to see beyond, that is to be aware of a larger struc-ture to the world than adults, one that unites all phenomena with each other and with the divinity—but they slowly lose this faculty of perception as they grow older.

Going through the poem with his class, Alcott got to the line "Heaven lies about us in our infancy" and at this point shut the book in order to transfer the poem's issues to the children themselves. He asked each one

RECORD

OF

CONVERSATIONS ON THE GOSPELS.

View of Mr. Alcott and the Children conversing.

CONVERSATION I.
IDEA OF SPIRIT.

EVIDENCE OF CONSCIOUSNESS.
Introduction. — Method. — Sentiment of Spirit.
I. METAPHYSICAL AND PSYCHOLOGICAL FACTS.
1. Testimony of External Senses, — Their Office ; Fruits.
2. Testimony of Internal Senses, — Their Office ; Intuition of Spirit ; Analysis of Functions and Offices ; Terms.

Introduction.   MR. ALCOTT. WE are now going to speak of the Life of Christ. If any of you are interested to understand how Jesus came into this world ; and lived ; and acted ; and went back to God ;

1

Opening page of Alcott's *Conversations with Children on the Gospels*, showing the Temple School's classroom layout

what he or she understood by the word *birth*. Some children said that the soul itself actually formed the body, while others suggested that the body was made as a sort of container, in order to have the soul placed in it. Alcott explained that he inclined to the first opinion. He wrote in his journal at about this time: "Body is Spirit at its circumference. It denotes its confines to the external sense."[8] A body is the external configuration of the human soul—the soul taking its place in the world. All his life he would be fascinated by the notion that there is a meeting point between the spiritual and material domains.

In his lesson, Alcott moved on to a consideration of the meaning of the word *pulp*. It surrounds the seed as the body surrounds the soul, enabling it to germinate into new life. The seed needs both soil and light to grow, both material and spiritual nourishment. But if it probes too deeply into the ground it will lose its capacity to flower, and will become "an earthly, dark thing, a root." In another lesson, Alcott discussed the word *yelk* (the old form of *yolk*). It too "was the food by which the germ of life was nourished into the power of forming a body that might individualize it." From here his mind took an imaginative leap. "He said that the earth (perhaps) was the yelk by which souls were nourished or born into a consciousness of the spiritual life."[9] The world is an egg, with our soul the aspiring dot of life inside it. Alcott would be committed for the rest of his life to the notion that the soul's growth and development was determined, at least to a degree, by the nature of the nourishment it receives from its material environment.

When Peabody's book was published in the summer of 1835, Alcott became a celebrity. Several of the most influential families in the area were sending their children to him (his intake had risen to thirty); visitors came regularly to sit on his classroom sofa, covered in green velvet.[10] Most importantly of all, he caught the attention of Ralph Waldo Emerson.

At this time Emerson was in his early thirties (he was born in 1803). After graduating from Harvard he had become a schoolteacher and then returned to study for the Unitarian ministry at the Divinity School. He took up an appointment at Boston's Second Church in 1829, and married his first wife Ellen. He was distraught when she died of tuberculosis just two years later. At this period he became disillusioned with his role in the church, believing that he was taking his congregation through dead forms (that of the communion service in particular), and in 1832 he resigned his ministry. He then went on a European tour where he met Thomas Carlyle, who became his life-long friend. On his return to America he made a natural transition from preaching to lecturing, and began to earn a living by giving public talks on a wide variety of topics, many of which he later wrote up as essays and published. He had in fact been giving a course of lectures—on the uses of biography—in the very building where Temple School was housed.[11]

He read the *Record* and was so impressed that in October 1835 he invited Alcott out to the home in Concord he now shared with his second wife Lydia (known as Lidian, and sometimes Queenie). Concord was a village twenty miles to the west of Boston that within the next few years (partly thanks to Emerson and to Alcott himself) was to become the center of New England intellectual life.

At the end of the visit Emerson noted down a comment Alcott had made. "Every man, he said, is a Revelation, and ought to write his Record, but few with the pen. His book is his school, in which he writes all his thoughts."[12] Emerson's later experience would lead him to agree—he became impatient at Alcott's clumsiness with the pen when compared with the exhilarating fluency of his conversation. But Alcott was sliding over a paradox, because while his school may have been a book in itself, it had also been transformed into a literal one through Elizabeth Peabody's reporting. All his life Alcott would be preoccupied with whom or what was immediate or near: family, pupils, friends, and community; but while he wanted to transform the microcosm, he believed in the interconnectedness of everything, and therefore expected this transformation to ripple out into the big wide world beyond.

This confusion about whether the school was a book, or a book was the school, led ultimately to disaster. What Alcott now had in mind was a sequel to the *Record*, one which would deal with a cutting-edge subject, the children's interpretation of the gospels. This topic would enable them to make a direct contribution to the religious ferment currently taking hold of Boston. Alcott was confident that his pupils could actually shed light on the issues under scrutiny. "To *investigate the Consciousness of Childhood*, as to the *Life of Christ*, is to bring as *Evidence of Christianity* all that belongs to the *Young Being*," he claimed in his journal. "As the elements and germs of humanity are all to be found in *the common ground of our Being* even in the first stages of its terrestrial existence, I feel that this attempt . . . will be the herald of a future Investigation, based on the *Facts* and *Principles* which shall be its blessed Fruits."[13]

As this project developed, Peabody began to have doubts. She thought that by harping on about his pupils' perceptiveness, and getting them talked about by the whole city, Alcott was liable to injure "their modesty and unconsciousness" (that is, he was making them self-conscious).[14] She objected to the fact that in this follow-up book he wanted to name the children rather than leave their contributions anonymous. In a perceptive criticism of the Socratic method, she complained that Alcott led the minds of his pupils and that she had "heard them questioned out of their opinions" by him. Even worse, she realized that he had begun to revise her reports of classroom conversations to make them more striking and pertinent.[15] The book was beginning to override the school.

Another problem was that Alcott was becoming converted to the ideas of the diet reformer Sylvester Graham. He and Abigail attended a series of lectures he gave in Boston early in 1836. Graham was a fellow product of Connecticut, just five years older than Alcott. He had a similarly impoverished upbringing, having worked on farms and in a mill and acquired an education in bits and pieces, but in due course had become an influential and controversial writer and lecturer.[16] He was in Philadelphia during Alcott's time there, and Alcott's cousin William was a follower of his doctrines. Graham's path seemed to be running parallel with Bronson Alcott's, particularly since the latter had come to believe that the nature of the soul must be partly determined by the nutriment it receives from the world it is born into.

Graham advocated vegetarianism, including eating coarse brown bread made to his own recipe (avoiding additives), and he was an important figure in the current temperance movement. What this meant, as Alcott excitedly explained in his journal, was that Graham too had realized that physiology was an index of spirit.[17] He was providing a basis for Alcott's own claim that body was spirit at its circumference, establishing, in his dietary rules, the connection between two apparently separate elements. It is one thing to say that spirit informs and determines body; but the converse is equally important: body can define spirit. If the world is the yolk to be consumed by the soul, then the soul is dependent for its structure on the quantity and nature of the specific nutriments provided. In fact, Graham claimed, body can gain the upper hand and thwart spirit completely.

Graham was a showman. In one of his lectures he appeared in front of the audience looking restless and ashamed, and told them he would be unable to do himself justice that evening. He explained he had sunk to the level of a brute. "I yielded to temptation," he confessed, "and ate a slice too much of bread!" Graham bread it was (of course), but even that wholesome substance, taken in excess, would distort the spirit–body balance. "Look at me," he asked his audience, "at my exhilaration—all arising, let me assure you, from one extra slice of bread." Salvation therefore is essentially a practical matter, a question of how you organize yourself in relation to the physical world. "I should have known better," Graham said sadly, "I did know better."[18]

Graham's lesson was transferred very directly to Alcott's classroom. How long can babies keep their "spiritual faces"? he asked the children. One boy replied that it took quite a while for eating and drinking too much to take all the good out of them.

> *Mr. Alcott*: And then what changes take place?
> *Francis*: They begin to look dull.
> *Mr. Alcott*: And the brow comes down, and the head grows out back, instead of growing high towards heaven, and the hands begin to scratch, and there is quarrelling.

People revert to apes squabbling in the jungle, in a back-to-front version of what would become the theory of evolution a couple of decades later.

"Spirit is the body builder," Alcott told the children, "Temperance is the body preserver; Self-indulgence is the body waster." If the spirit fails "to govern the matter in which it lives according to God's will, the body shall waste and decay prematurely." If a child eats a large meal, he or she will become cross; similarly, robbers and murderers usually overindulge before going out to commit their crimes. And the physiological consequences can last through the generations: "Sometimes an evil produced in a body by intemperance may sleep in a son . . . but burst out again in a grandson."[19] Overeating and drinking can act like original sin, condemning generations yet unborn. Indeed, eating what should not have been eaten *was* the original sin.

Peabody was now lodging with the Alcotts. She thought that these dietary views were cranky, and told Alcott so. This spin on the mind–body problem was not an essential product of the Transcendentalist debate; neither Elizabeth Peabody nor most of the other members of the Boston intelligentsia felt the need to go down the same path, though Graham had a large popular following. Nevertheless the position rose logically enough from Emerson's allegation that miracles were monstrous because they were not "one with the blowing clover and the falling rain." If the task was indeed to achieve oneness with clover and rain, with the phenomenal world, then the act of eating provided—almost literally—an interface. But this was not a point of view Peabody was able to accept. She and Alcott had a row and she rushed off to her bedroom.[20]

But worse was to come. If the problem of evil could be solved by the correct manipulation of the material world, then redemption would follow. This was a reversal of traditional Puritan pessimism about the possibility of earning salvation. As Alcott's cousin William would put it, obedience to natural laws is "a means of lifting us toward the Eden whence we came." In his introduction to *Conversations with Children on the Gospels*, Alcott baldly claimed "It is the mission of this age . . . to reproduce Perfect Men."[21] The verb is significant: birth itself is the moment when spirit and body first interact. In other words, reproduction takes its place alongside digestion as a bodily process with spiritual implications. Sex was a topic that had received some attention in the *Record*; in the *Conversations* it became of central importance.

One day when Elizabeth Peabody could not attend the Temple School, her sister Sophia took her place and recorded the belief of six-year-old Josiah Quincy (son of the then president of Harvard University) that babies resulted from "the naughtiness of other people"—not in fact so much a theory of reproduction as a slightly foggy version of the doctrine of original sin.[22] When she saw it, Peabody foresaw disaster in tightly buttoned Boston. Some parents had already got wind that Alcott's classes were taking on dangerous topics and were thinking of removing their daughters from the school. Since everyone knew that Peabody was Alcott's amanuensis, she would be implicated in any scandal. As she put it in a later letter to Alcott, "you as a man can say anything: but I am a woman."[23] She argued with him for days about the issue, and confided her fears in letters to her other sister Mary, whose advice was for her to leave the household and the Temple School. Before a decision had been made, an extraordinary and disturbing event took place.

One day in July 1836, Alcott suddenly came into Peabody's room and began to attack her views. At first she had no idea what he was talking about. Then he referred to a remark about "poor men's bills." A horrible suspicion began to dawn on Peabody. Her sister Mary had used that very phrase in a letter to her just a week or two before. She confronted Alcott with this, but he blustered, saying Mary had also made the comment to Abigail in person the previous winter.

Before the matter could be resolved, Peabody had to go out to an engagement. When she got back there was a note waiting for her. The contents confirmed her worst fears about what had happened. One can still feel the shock waves as Peabody explained it to Mary: "Mrs. Alcott came into my room & looked over my letters from you & found your last letter to me & the one to Sophia & carried it to Mr. Alcott—& *they have read them.*"

Mary had said in her letter that she didn't trust Alcott to allow the new book to be "honestly printed." She wanted her sister to block its publication, which would mean, she had told her, that he could then concentrate on making a success of the school, and on paying off the local tradesmen. That was where the reference to poor men's bills had come from—she had been referring to the Alcotts' chronic failure to settle their accounts, a habit that they would continue for most of their lives, one which caused Abigail much anguish, and which made them deeply unpopular in the various communities in which they lived (though for Alcott it always seemed to be water off a duck's back).

The next morning Peabody announced that her relations with Alcott were at an end. Her privacy had been violated; even worse, she was being held to account not for her own opinions but her sister's. At that point both Alcotts confronted her. Abigail took it for granted that what Mary had said in her letter, Elizabeth must think too—in itself an insult to a woman as intellectually independent as Peabody would be all her life. Abigail predicted "eternal damnation"; this correspondence amounted to the greatest crime she had ever heard of. When Peabody tried to defend herself Alcott criticized her tone of voice, and went on to make extraordinary assumptions about what she must have previously written to her *other* sister Sophia. Apparently Sophia had (somewhat disloyally) reported to him that people would assume, from Elizabeth's words, that he, Alcott, was a "thief & a murderer."

When Peabody accused the two Alcotts of a breach of honor, they told her she had no right to speak the word, since in their opinion she was guilty of so much worse.[24]

It is hard to relate Bronson Alcott's attempt to silence the person who had made his school famous with the inspiring teacher who encouraged his pupils to express their own thoughts, and to record them in journals. The paradox is central not just to Alcott's own attitude to the nature of the personality but to that of the New England Transcendentalists in general. One can get a handle on it by looking at his lesson on the word *spot*, as described by Peabody in the *Record*. The class considered how souls born innocent became spotted as time went on—by disobeying conscience or parents, becoming enraged, or (of course) eating too much. Then the question arose as to whether Alcott understood the characters of the children. Some thought he did, others not. "This led to a consideration of the evil of secretiveness, and the beauty and advantage of transparency." A "character," by which was meant a person's public identity, ought to be synonymous with the nature of that person. By the logic of this argument, if Alcott did not understand the characters of some of the boys, that wouldn't be a failure of perception on his part but evidence that they were concealing their own evil tendencies.[25]

Unspotted equals *transparent*: that is the key to this discussion. At just this time, Emerson was writing a little book on *Nature* and describing an ecstatic experience he had had while splashing his way through snow puddles on a common—perhaps Boston Common itself, where Alcott liked to walk too, and to take his pupils during recess. "Standing on the bare ground,—my head bathed by the blithe air and uplifted into infinite space,—all mean egotism vanishes. I become a transparent eyeball; I am nothing; I see all; the currents of the Universal Being circulate through me; I am part or parcel of God."[26]

The phrase "transparent eyeball" was as open to ridicule as some of Alcott's own writings would prove to be. One of the Transcendentalists, Christopher Cranch, drew a cartoon of it, showing a large eyeball positioned, as if it was a head all by itself, on top of a short body and a pair of spindly legs.[27] In one way this missed the point, because the eyeball should be invisible rather than gigantic, but in fact Cranch understood the gist. All that is left in Emerson's description is the eye itself, perched on legs rather as the newly invented camera was supported on its tripod; there is no actual person involved to interpret and make individual what the eye is seeing. In this mystical moment it is not merely "mean egotism" that vanishes but any sort of particularity altogether. Both the world and the perceiver of that world seem to become transparent simultaneously.

Of course we are not dealing here with daily experience but a moment of rapture. But the fact remains that if our essential nature, before it is corrupted

Christopher Pearse Cranch's illustration of Emerson's "Transparent Eyeball"

by worldly business, is to resemble Christ, then not only are we potentially perfect, we are also all alike, lacking individual identities. As Emerson would put it in his essay on "Self-Reliance" a few years later, "persons themselves acquaint us with the impersonal."[28]

When he came to sit on the green velvet sofa at the Temple School, Emerson saw what he felt was empirical proof of this claim. He was hugely impressed by little Josiah Quincy, who had "something wonderful and divine in him." When a child perceives a truth, Emerson claimed as a result of his visit, "he is no more a child. Age, sex, are nothing."[29] Little Josiah had entered the realm of the impersonal, and in doing so had ceased being little; for that matter had ceased being Josiah. The movement in which Alcott was becoming a leading player was hostile to the very notion of the private person.

There is an obsessive explicitness at the heart of Transcendentalism. Alcott didn't make his pupils keep journals in order to give them access to some personal space but rather so that he could look at them himself—even show them to the world at large, just as he showed his own journals to family and friends, and published parts of them when he could. He didn't want people to have their own stories to tell—he wanted them to be open books, a different matter entirely. Over the years he would show no inhibition about altering or censoring the journals and letters of his wife and daughters. Meanwhile Emerson used his own journals as a source of public lectures. "Secretiveness, Mr. Alcott thought, was naturally connected with selfishness," Peabody reported, "and frankness with generosity."[30] The very privacy of private correspondence was enough to put her in the wrong.

Peabody had no choice but to leave the school and her lodgings. A third daughter had been born to the Alcotts a year before, and they had christened her Elizabeth Peabody. Now they altered her middle name to Sewall. It was a fitting end to a sorry episode, prioritizing family over outsider. Peabody had provided Alcott with unpaid support and by recording his lessons had been the instrument of his fame; she had been a friend as well as a co-worker, and had taken up residence with the family. Then the Alcotts teamed up against her and made it impossible for her to stay. Seven years later, at the time of Alcott's second great experiment, the Fruitlands community, this exact pattern of behavior would be repeated.

Peabody continued to do what she could to rein Alcott in, and in fact succeeded in persuading him to relegate Josiah's contribution on the reproductive process to a footnote. But her fears were vindicated. The first volume of *Conversations with Children on the Gospels* came out in December 1836, the second the following February. Andrews Norton, Unitarianism's leading spokesman, called the book "one third absurd, one third blasphemous, one third obscene." "Filthy and godless jargon," said the press.[31] The generous-spirited Elizabeth Peabody rallied to her former colleague's defense. "It is but . . . humanity towards Mr Alcott . . . who has a family dependent on the success of his school,—that we frown upon exaggerated and one-sided and panic-striking strictures upon his book, such as have appeared in many of the late papers," she told the *Christian Examiner*.[32]

It was to no avail. The parents removed their children in droves. Only a handful (including Josiah's parents) stayed loyal for a time. "The City press, pulpit, State Street and the mob call roundly at 'the school master and his Book,'" Alcott wrote.[33] Moreover, like some kind of reverse Midas, Alcott had managed to achieve debts of around $6,000, an astronomical sum, despite apparently having had several years of local success—and this against a background of a financial crisis that hit Boston's banks in early 1837. By April 13 his library had been auctioned off for $994. "Ideas are costly," he wrote sadly.[34] What was left of his school was transferred to the basement of the Temple building.

But in the fall of 1837 a letter arrived from England, completely out of the blue. It was from a certain James Pierrepont Greaves. Alcott had no idea who he was, but a ripple from Temple School had traveled across the Atlantic Ocean, against all odds. Greaves's letter began: "Believing the Spirit has so far established its nature in you, as to make you willing to co-operate with itself in Love-Operations, I am induced, without apology, to address you as a friend and companion in the hidden path of Love's most powerful revelations."[35]

It is a strange approach, one that might bewilder or alarm a lesser man, but in fact it was uncannily attuned to Alcott's wavelength. Spirit is invoked as an impersonal and overarching force that manifests itself in individual people. Two years previously Alcott had described the same phenomenon in his journal: "Body . . . individualizes, defines Spirit, breaks the Unity into Multiplicity and places under the vision of man parts of the great Whole which, standing thus separate, can be taken in by the mind."[36] But if these broken pieces are aware of that fact (as Alcott obviously is), then they can refer back to the spirit and use it to connect with other aware individuals. Greaves and Alcott may not ever have met each other, but they can be friends and companions through its "hidden path." That odd technical term, "Love-Operations," seems to anticipate modern methods of communication, like the Internet.

Greaves had become aware of Alcott's work through the unlikely agency of Harriet Martineau. She was a British intellectual in her thirties who would ultimately come to be regarded as the first female sociologist. She had already written a well-received series of pieces exploring such topics as political economy, taxation, and the Poor Law when she visited the United States a couple of years previously and duly sat herself upon the Temple School's green velvet sofa. But she completely disapproved of Alcott's whole approach and said so in her book, *Society in America*, published in 1837, and adding its weighty criticism to the vituperation being heaped on the head of the "self-styled philosopher," as she contemptuously called him. "Harriet Martineau took the bread out of the mouths of my family," Mrs. Alcott complained.[37]

Martineau was appalled at the notion that "spirit makes body" and at the way Alcott "presupposes his little pupils possessed of all truth in philosophy and morals." She herself had no sense of smell or taste, and was so deaf she had to use a large ear trumpet. Perhaps because she had learned the hard way to value the input of the senses, the grip they give you on surrounding reality, she was scathing about what she regarded as Alcott's cavalier attitude towards them. Aware herself of missing so much sensory data, she utterly rejected the value of transparency. The blind, deaf, and dumb, she declared, would not receive proper support if able-bodied people are told that "the interior being of these sufferers is in a perfect state, only the means of manifestation being deficient."[38]

But Greaves himself was immune to any such considerations. For him the Temple School books represented an exciting confirmation of his own ideas, and his reaction was to offer himself to Alcott as a sort of John the Baptist. He was even prepared to cross the Atlantic to meet him.

It would be reassuring for anyone in a time of vilification and failure to discover a coincidence of views from so far away, but there was a special bonus in it for Alcott, since he believed that the human condition, properly understood, made such parallels inevitable. Greaves's approach didn't just provide him with an ally but seemed to offer actual proof that Alcott's deepest vision of how things were structured was accurate. Perhaps the school had not been wasted effort after all but was simply part of a larger plan that was unfolding. Perhaps it had done its work by transmitting its message all the way to Greaves's residence in Burton Street, in London. As Greaves himself put it in his letter: "The Unity himself must have his divine purposes to accomplish in and by us, or he would not have prepared us as far as he has."[39]

Greaves's letter arrived in the second week of October. It must have cheered Alcott up because he then wrote a clunkily humorous letter to Emerson describing his woes. He compared himself to Diogenes, the philosopher who lived in a tub. Alcott could barely pay rent on his own "tub" (Cottage Place, it was called) and therefore, as the tub told him in tub-language, "thou . . . standest in great danger, sirrah, of ejectment with all they [sic] tublings streetwise." But he consoled himself by imagining an alternative prophetic voice telling him, "Perchance thy farm is sown already." He concluded by hinting that he might respond to a call from foreign parts: "Take passport then, my Psyche, and run on thy errand."[40]

In the light of which, it might seem strange that Alcott didn't reply to the letter for eighteen months, particularly as he painstakingly copied it out in full, in his best handwriting, in his journal.[41] The explanation is that Greaves was writing to him about a school that had ceased to exist. Despite the portentous opening, much of his letter is taken up with a series of practical questions about the experience at Temple School. Question 20, for example (there are twenty-nine in all), is: "Do the Girls make greater progress under you than the Boys, and are they more grateful for the results?", while number 28 asks: "Do you consider the mode in which you have fitted up your school room as very beneficial?" It would have been painful indeed to try to answer such questions now that the experiment which engendered them had collapsed.

In November 1837 Alcott wrote in his journal that Greaves's notice of him was "a fact more important than any which has transpired since the opening of my career as an educator."[42] It was a pity, then, that it had come just as his career as an educator, at least of children, was coming to an end.

Nevertheless cross-fertilization had taken place across an ocean, and the seed of Fruitlands had been planted.

Now I Know What Thought Is

AT ABOUT THE TIME Alcott was conversing on the gospels at the Temple School, a young British intellectual by the name of George Henry Lewes was regularly attending a discussion group in a London tavern situated in Red Lion Square. Eventually, Lewes would become an important literary critic and philosopher (as well as the partner of George Eliot), and he was attracted to this gathering because it discussed philosophical matters.

It was a group of characters who could have stepped straight out of the pages of *Pickwick Papers*: a bookstall owner, a watchmaker, a sonneteer, a cobbler, an anatomist. One of them, James Pierrepont Greaves (who looked rather like Mr. Pickwick himself, with a round, benevolent face) didn't seem to belong in this habitat at all since he drank only water, didn't smoke, and lived almost entirely on raw fruit and vegetables. To Lewes he appeared to be floating above the proceedings on his own private cloud. Exasperated by this serene inscrutability, Lewes asked him to drop down a ladder so he could join him. Not possible, Greaves replied: Lewes hadn't yet been phenomenized. He went on to explain: "I am what I am, and it is out of my *Iamity* that I am phenomenized."

These incomprehensible words must have dropped through the pub atmosphere like pebbles plinking into a well. There was a stunned silence as the group digested the word "Iamity"; then an explosion of laughter.[1]

Greaves arrives in our presence, as he did in Alcott's, fully formed. There are no surviving manuscripts that can shed light on his external and, more significantly, internal experiences and development, and most of his publications were brought out after his death for the benefit of a tiny circle of followers and consist of strings of assertions made in letters or journal entries, with almost no autobiographical content.[2]

He was born in 1777 (twenty-two years before Alcott), and inherited a drapery business, but it failed during the Napoleonic wars, leaving him with debts he struggled for years to repay. As in the case of Alcott after the collapse of the Temple School, the trauma of failure seems to have put him off regular work. In 1817 he had a mystical experience. That was the year of publication of Coleridge's *Biographia Literaria*, and the two events were obviously connected. Coleridge's book was instrumental in providing the source for Greaves's Transcendentalism, just as it was for Alcott. Greaves's doctrine of "Iamity" is derived from the famous sentence in which the poet defines the primary imagination as "the living power and prime agent of all human perception . . . a repetition in the finite mind of the eternal act of creation in the infinite I AM."[3]

Greaves's soul had up to that moment been "wantful, lustful," and "working actively in lower regions," but now it became "receptive of Spirit from the higher elements."[4] The result was a vegetarian diet and a sudden interest in the doctrines of the Swiss educational reformer Johann Pestalozzi. Already the concerns that would in due course connect Greaves with Alcott were falling into place: reception of spirit, diet, education.

Pestalozzi had been born in 1746. He established a school in Burgdorf in 1799, and published an important book on education shortly afterward. He advocated relating the content of teaching to the pupil's development, his most famous aphorism being "The role of an educator is to teach children, not subjects." In 1805 he moved to Yverdun, on Lake Neuchatel, and over the next years his school there attracted attention from worthies and intellectuals from all over Europe. In 1818 Greaves arrived in Yverdun, and took up residence in Pestalozzi's home for several years. Neither man spoke the other's language and they would salute each other with a kiss, "as somewhat customary in the country." Greaves seems to have acted as a kind of valet for the disheveled maestro, a post he was hardly fit for, being fairly disheveled himself. When necessary he would tiptoe along in the middle of the night, spirit Pestalozzi's tatty clothes away, and put a new set in their place.[5]

By the mid-1820s Greaves was back in London, acting as secretary of the Infant School Society, an organization set up by Robert Owen ten years previously. One glimpse of him during this period: he showed an interested party around some of the schools then took him home for a dinner consisting, to the man's dismay, solely of sopped toast and sugar.[6] Later his diet would become more rigorous even than that. In 1828 he lost his job through the influence of an evangelical element that had risen to power in the Society, rather as Alcott would lose his school through the hostility of religious conservatives in Boston. For most of his subsequent life Greaves seems to have lived with the help of handouts from friends, exactly as Alcott would.

In the early 1830s Greaves was living with his sister, near Stroud in Gloucestershire. The battle over the Reform Bill was in full swing, and he tried his own hand at practical socialism, attempting to alleviate the hardship of local unemployed weavers by setting them to work for the public good—building roads, for example—in exchange for tokens that could be used to buy necessaries (presumably funded by his sister and friends). This experience wasn't a success and taught him, according to a later disciple, that "no circumstances, however good, could effect the regeneration or reformation required by society"; instead, "*another nature*, of a higher order, must come into play."[7] In other words there was no point in trying to reform the present dispensation of society. The only solution was to replace it altogether.

Later in the 1830s Greaves settled in London, in due course moving into 49 Burton Street, St. Pancras, where he presided over weekly meetings of the London Aesthetic Institute (otherwise known as the Syncretics) and began to gather around him a group of disciples whom Emerson would in due course describe (and gently mock) in an article on "English Reformers." The most important of them were all men drawn, like Greaves himself, from the world of business and trade rather than from the professional and educated class.

One of them, William Oldham, had been a maker of fur hats but, like Greaves, had come upon bad times and even been imprisoned for debt. Oldham met Greaves in about 1834, rapidly became a vegetarian (in retrospect his fur hats must have been anathema), abandoned the use of "verbal prayers," and committed himself to what he called, in Greavesian terminology, "a more practical and being religion." Greaves's influence extended to Oldham's marriage and in 1837, at the age of forty-seven, he separated from his wife and moved into Burton Street to be with his master.[8]

From Alcott's point of view, the most important member of the group would turn out to be Charles Lane, who had first met Greaves in the 1820s. As in the case of his master we know tantalizingly little about Lane's early life. He had been born in 1800 (a year after Alcott) and was a commercial journalist who tracked commodity prices in his own listings bulletin, the *London Mercantile Price-Current*. Despite being at the hub of the business world, he was an educational idealist and life-long vegetarian (plagued by the fact that most of his male relatives were butchers). Like Oldham he had had an unhappy marriage which had led to three years of painful litigation following his separation from his wife. He had a son, William, who had been born in 1832 (the same year as Louisa May Alcott).[9]

Several of Greaves's followers began as supporters of Owenism, one being his most important correspondent, Alexander Campbell, while another was Samuel Bower, whose path, like Lane's, would in due course cross with Alcott's. Bower believed strongly that a utopian transformation of society was possible, even imminent, and in the 1830s published several pamphlets on the subject. In *The Peopling of Utopia* he was dismissive of radical proposals like universal suffrage and attacks on capitalism because they would antagonize vested interests. Like Greaves, then, he believed there was no point in meddling with the status quo. Utopianism was different because each community could function without threatening the outside world, depending solely for its influence upon the "demonstrable nature and superiority of truth."[10]

Henry Gardiner Wright was another Greavesian who would soon play a significant part in Alcott's life. He began as an usher at a boarding school in Chipping Ongar, but in due course found himself working as a clerk for Messrs. Green, Wilson, and Burton, tea importers, of Upper Thames Street. He came across Greaves because one of his employers, Thomas Green, happened to be a member of the Burton Street circle and introduced his young employee into it.[11]

Wright's description of his first encounter with the master gives a good idea of the impact Greaves had on those around him in this late phase of his career (he was around sixty by this time). The occasion was a sort of soirée. As he walked in, the young man (he was in his early twenties) was pole-axed by Greaves's appearance. "There he sat with an eye—oh! How shall I describe that eye to you? . . . this eye—'twas unfathomable—in it your own ethereality might float forever unimpeded . . . Oh! the wonders of that eye . . ." In his raptures he sounds like Melville's Ishmael in *Moby-Dick*, discoursing on the enigma of the white whale: "But the eye—oh, that marvellous eye; mystery, God, Fathomlessness, were written upon it."[12] Charles Lane also waxed lyrical about "the flash from his singularly bright eye . . . those penetrating orbs were not employed to scan body, but were as well inlets as outlets to soul." Greaves's followers were equally under the spell of his voice, "those delicious tones, trembling occasionally on the verge of treble."[13]

Greaves was interrogating a couple of admiring ladies on the nature of music when Wright first saw him. One participant, a certain Mrs. G., eventually lost her grip on the discussion altogether. "My opinion is," she announced despairingly, "that you are all pretty nearly alike unintelligible."

Despite the discussion's inaccessible profundity, Greaves's summing-up seems a trifle lame. "All music is an inspiration," he asserted. "The true musician is deeply inspired in a double manner, and all his compositions are expressions, often imperfect, of the eternal melody and harmony." Wright, though, was bowled over by these generalizations. "When I retired to bed that night, I exclaimed, 'Now I know what thought is, and never till now.' "[14] Even at this distance in time you can sense the need of a man thirsty for education and guidance, a man doing a small job in a big city, wanting intellectual purchase on the world.

For Mrs. G., Greaves's thoughts were unintelligible; for followers like Wright, they were life-changing. For Alcott, they would serve to underline the truth of his own ideas, and give them an apparent direction for future success. There would be the shock of recognition, and then a heady sense of gathering momentum. Greaves was a kindred spirit. He and his circle could make Alcott's dreams come to fruition. But ultimately it would prove that the very coincidence of the two men's ideas was disastrous. Greaves's philosophy was a seductive mirror image, reflecting and enforcing Alcott's own ambiguities and confusions.

What Greaves offered his disciples was a new world—or rather an old one, a world that had been lost. At the heart of his philosophy, as of Alcott's, was a vision of the Garden of Eden. And at the heart of that story was the consumption of an apple. For years Greaves had been living mainly on raw fruit and vegetables. "Boil an orange," he demanded, "and what is it worth?" The answer: nothing. "All that is Spirit and Spiritual is drawn out of it by the fire, and a lifeless gross mass remains."

This veganism, as we would now call it, actually allows us to eat living things: to incorporate life, therefore, quite literally. "In fruits, in uncooked vegetables, the vital force is operating."[15] By contrast, butchery is not only cruel, it involves the physical absorption of dead matter. So, to a lesser degree, does cooking. "Essence and esse [the Latin for "to be," or, in this case, "being" or "life force"] are fled—only the coarsest materiality remains." Both butchery and cooking involve manipulating the world instead of simply being within it. "Evil comes when the hunger spirit too much impresseth its own form on the thing that it eateth," Greaves tells us, "so it cannot receive the free spirit of the thing eaten to appease its hunger."[16]

The hunger spirit impresses its own form by killing or by cooking, or both in succession. This is inappropriate because it means acting on the external world instead of accepting it for what it is—instead of being simply a part of it. Adam and Eve in the Garden weren't content with taking what was being freely given them. As a result of imposing their will on the environment, by wanting to know rather than simply be, by eating of the forbidden fruit, they brought death into the world. They lost the "free spirit"; betrayed the vital force.

Adam and Eve were undone through what appears to be a thoroughly vegan act: eating a raw apple. But an apple, properly considered, possesses a dual identity, like humankind itself. "*An apple* is some middle double thing, related to the heaven and the earth . . . to the spirit for its life, and the universe for its existence."[17] Ultimately eating the fruit of the Tree of

Knowledge implies the knowledgeable manipulation of the environment, the dark arts of butchery and cooking. But the problem is solved by eating of the Tree of Life rather than that of Knowledge. Just as it caused the Fall, the apple can provide redemption. "The love germinating esse to the apple is in the core," Greaves asserts, "the core is its home, the home of Love, its central abode. Internal authority must be in the inmost soul, which is its core, or heart, as the life is in any fruit core whatsoever." Bread and water are also acceptable—boiled bread, at least, because it has had no direct contact with a flame. They provide "non-combustible conditions" which check the sin in the soul, unlike meat which causes its consumers "to reap the FLAMING consequences."[18]

But this severely limited diet had to be taken in moderation. Greaves was as strict on that topic as Sylvester Graham was, over in America. The two men were united in their tendency to take moderation to excess. Greaves believed that the metabolism became efficient over time in extracting benefit from tiny amounts of the right sort of food. "A very little food will suffice," he claimed, "when the digestive power acts so strongly, as to unlock the spirit that is confined within the food consumed . . . The more substance taken in, the less spirit given out by digestion. The less substance taken in, the more spirit got out, and the more civilisation."[19]

Greaves celebrated when his friend Alexander Campbell lost weight (and thereby gained spirituality): "I am glad you are less stout and lighter than you were; nothing can be better for you than to become more and more immortal in soul; and less and less mortal in body." The advice is reminiscent of the story of the donkey that had just learned to do without food altogether when it died. As he grew older Greaves admitted that he had paid a price for the way of life he had chosen for himself. "I have so ardently sought immortality," he told Campbell, "that I have, in some degree, neglected mortality, and now, at 63 years of age, discover that (with respect to mortality) I have committed an error, and I am a double fact to all about me."[20]

In his later years he suffered from arthritis and a chronic hernia and presided over followers in his house at 49 Burton Street wearing an old gray dressing gown. "We require of such a figure that he should be robed," claimed Charles Lane, loyally transmogrifying the dressing gown into something altogether more stately and Grecian, and so performing on an abstract level the function of valet to guru, as Greaves himself had done many years before.[21]

Two of the people who fell under Greaves's spell were sisters, Sophia Chichester and Georgiana Welch. They lived in Ebworth Park, near Stroud, close to the scene of the experiment he had conducted with out-of-work weavers—which they had undoubtedly helped to fund. They were wealthy women and their financial backing was to prove important in the final phase of Greaves's career. Greaves had the effect of rejigging the very grammar of their relationship with the world. "Mr Greaves is . . . very diligent in leading us into a more universal state of thinking & speaking," they exclaimed enthusiastically, "especially to remember the Antecedent, & let it always be the Nominative and to keep ourselves in the accusative, and in the subjunctive position, as Neuter grounds."[22] Charles Lane remarked that in Greaves's hands, "Terminologies were rent asunder, and by this flexible and fluent pouring in of an essential meaning to any phraseology, he . . . was preserved from sinking into the narrowness and miserable fixedness of a verbal philosophy."[23] In short, he made words mean what he wanted them to. Alcott shared this need to escape from the "miserable fixedness" of inert language and to catch thought on the wing.

What Greaves taught the two sisters was that the Antecedent (the state of being before the Fall) should be the determining factor of existence. If our life is seen as a sentence, that blessed state must be the subject of that sentence, with ourselves as the object. We should endeavor to live not in the world-as-it-is but in the would-be world, in the world of the paradise that was lost but is waiting in the wings to be found again. This is the world of the ideal rather than the immediate: the world of the "subjunctive position." As for the final phrase, "neuter grounds," it suggests that passivity is the way to achieve this subjunctiveness. But it also implies gender, or rather the absence of it. There is another consequence of the story of the Tree of Knowledge, apart from the implications for diet. As a result of eating the fruit of the tree, Adam and Eve became conscious of their nakedness, and covered their private parts with fig leaves. Sex became sin.

The issue of sex was to cause great conflict and trauma, both within the ranks of the English Transcendentalists, as Greaves and his followers became known, and in their interactions with the New England Transcendentalists during the short life of the Fruitlands community. Adam and Eve produced offspring who inherited their parents' guilt: original sin was passed down through history, from generation to generation. How, then, can we escape from it and get back in touch with the Antecedent? It's a question as old as Christianity itself.

Greaves remained a bachelor all his life, but it was hardly practical to rule marriage out altogether. Greaves's account of how a courtship should be conducted makes clear what a dangerous undertaking it was. "Marriages unblessed by the Divine-marriage awaken the root-evil," he remarked ominously, "the dark fire-source, which engenders ungodliness, erroneousness, and weakness."[24] The phrase "root-evil" calls to mind Alcott's warning to the children in his class that if a seed was planted too deeply in the ground, it would become "an earthly, dark thing, a root." The reference to the "fire-source" also suggests a connection between sex and cooking.

The way to avoid the root-evil, Greaves explained to Campbell, was for the "woman, with the love in her feelings," to "win the man's affections," while "the man, with his wisdom, must exercise and direct the woman's understanding." While he believed the sexes were equal—equal in original guilt, equal in potential—Greaves couldn't escape certain contemporary assumptions about gender differences and roles. The man is the source of wisdom, the woman of feelings. Their courtship dance has to be a long-drawn-out process. "The man and the woman ought to be betrothed, and live together until the prophetical union is consolidated, as well as the metaphysical; and at a given state, when the woman demands it, not the man, the physical marriage should take place."[25]

Metaphysical first, physical second: it's a way of ensuring that a new reality comes into being based on the ideal. "In no case are passions to be allowed to enter the affair," Greaves told Campbell sternly. Enjoying sex would be as great an error as relishing a hearty meal. "Exterior excitement," he warned, "must be avoided at all costs."[26] Greaves was taking very much the same line as Sylvester Graham over in the States, who opposed extramarital sex because it was too stimulating but ruled that marital sex was acceptable (as long as it only happened once a month) because the parties are so well "accustomed to each other's body" that "their parts no longer excite an impure imagination." You have to find sex boring in order to be allowed to have it at all. William Oldham would take an even more austere line, asserting that sex every two or three years should be quite enough to achieve "*holy* and *divine* ends"; anything more would be "the downward road and of the devil."[27]

We find more details of Greavesian courtship ritual in a booklet written by Henry Gardiner Wright in 1840 called *Marriage and its Sanctions*. It should last a "term of years" and be characterized by considerable austerity. "Luxury must be surrendered" and "wintry cold" braved, at least by the "tender sex." Not only that, but "exercises must be gone through to conditionate the evolution and education of all the muscles"; to top it all, "poetry must be cultivated." The passive voice is all-pervasive. This is a world in which virtue is achieved by *not* doing things; only thus, like Jesus (Wright tells us) may we "*be Goodened* with Good."[28] The tortured phrasing is there to emphasize that good is something that happens to you just so long as you have created the right conditions. Vegetables are not merely to be eaten; they are to be imitated.

Even the sexual act, when it is finally permitted, has no element of assertion in it. There's to be nothing so thrusting as planting a seed. Instead, Greaves informed Campbell, passivity rules—for both the genders involved. "The two uniting parties must be considered not as seed but as ground; and as is the ground, so will the seed flourish."[29] The parents must give birth to a new generation; their offspring cannot inherit their natures, because that inheritance would include original sin. Therefore Greaves modifies the traditional husbandry metaphor to suggest preparation of the soil rather than planting of the seed.

For any farmer or gardener, preparing the ground is likely to involve the application of manure, but this is not at all what Greaves is advocating. Dung is historical; it is a compacted embodiment of the past. "It is not the *land* on which the dung is cast that has made the dung, but it is the *receptive of it*" [i.e. land is just the recipient of the dung]. The betrothed couple have to become new ground, not soil contaminated by the legacy of the past. In his journal, meditating on this topic, Greaves made one of his daring sideways leaps: "I *dung* that land, I *dislike* that man."[30] Somehow the two actions, dunging and

disliking, are held in balance with each other; they are two parallel manifestations of the same mistaken stance towards the world, just like eating meat
or cooked food. "By cooking we . . . feed on the physical and the excremen-
titious . . . The bowels are extended beyond their proper size, and the digestive power has rather to digest corruption than Spirituality."[31] In short,
cooked food is manure.

The point is that dung, in whatever form, "has been made in another place
of other elements; in the same way dislike is made and cast upon some
body or thing . . . *dung is cast upon the land*."[32] This comparison is central to
Greaves's thinking and would influence the structure and course of the
Fruitlands experiment in more ways than one. Dung involves transference,
from one place (and time) to another; so does dislike. It is the here-and-now
that provides the secret of harmony, the living moment. Meat, cooked food,
manure, dislike—are all forms of baggage, the baggage of the past.

Greaves's imagination is far more preoccupied with mating an individual
to the universe as a whole than with dealing with an interaction between two
people. "Man can only provide a good transmutation for his own identic
atom," he tells us, "by a most intimate union with the Infinite." Each person has
to remember that he or she is the center of existence—hardly the recipe for a
happy marriage. "A circle says, I am what I am, and no reasoning will make me
into a square or an oval. The centre is in an unalterable position."[33] Once this
centeredness has been achieved, its reverberations can extend outward indefinitely. Indeed Greaves's vision is far more consonant with vegetable propagation than with human methods of reproduction—charged particles drifting
through the air like pollen or spores. "The smell arising from the spiced Island,"
he claims, "at the distance of some hundred miles, is a fact which will show the
transmutation and circulation of elementary particles in a *living state*."[34]

Wright continues this tendency to regard human reproduction in
gardening terms when he talks in his booklet of the "one great end" as being
"the propagation and perfection of a beautiful and god-like race." It sounds
like a system of eugenics when put so baldly (as does Alcott's intention to
"reproduce Perfect Men"). But we are a long way from achieving that
outcome. When you come to inspect small babies, you discover that far from
having the passive perfection of vegetables, "infancy is born almost all
animal." And pregnant women are almost as bad as their offspring. The

"tempers that women exhibit during the time of child-bearing," Wright decided, "are referable to the activity of the universal law in the foetus, struggling to overcome the deforming conditions with which she supplies it."[35] Instead of being "pure birth," a blissful transition to a perfected generation, pregnancy was a struggle and babies were greedy little animals. The Greavesian philosophers peered down in dismay from their fluffy white clouds at the bloody contingencies of the life force, at the mess of generation.

It is probably fair to say that English Transcendentalist thought was entering a muddled stage at about the time the master read the records of Alcott's teaching and detected a kindred spirit. That same year, 1837, Greaves published *Three Hundred Maxims for the Consideration of Parents in Relation to the Education of their Children* in which his readers are told to respect the authority of the child's perception: "Let not the child study *your* doings, but study the *child's* doings with respect to the inner mover" (Maxim 22). The precept expresses an Alcottian faith that an infant comes into the world with an uncorrupted spirit—as Maxim 31 puts it: "The child sees life and action in the whole of nature, and this is not a dream of childishness, but the consciousness of the *in*-forming spirit."[36] That is to say, the spirit that provides you with information is also the spirit that forms you. As usual, Greaves quarries language for truth.

At the same time Greaves was worried that the sex act was liable to corrupt its offspring and transmit original sin from one generation to the next, so that even small children would carry its stigma. When Campbell came to edit Greaves's letters to him, he wrote an introduction in which he made the point that during his later years his master moved from a belief in the efficacy of education—"outside work"—to a sense that "the sacred relationship of mother and child is of secondary importance to the prior Being state of the parent."[37] It is almost literally the chicken and egg dilemma: Does the child redeem the adult, or the adult redeem the child?

As a Pestalozzian involved in the infant school movement, Greaves had believed, like Alcott, in education as the way to escape the legacy of the Fall. But as time went on, he became convinced that the key lay in the act of generation itself. In other words, while he could accept that a child could be father to the man, he became increasingly worried about the father's (and mother's) capacity to produce a properly qualified child in the first place. "As

Being is before knowing and doing," he explained, "education can never repair the defects of birth."[38]

Despite this wobble at the very heart of Greaves's otherwise serene system, the late 1830s saw the great practical experiment of his life get underway. He began planning his own educational experiment as soon as he encountered the Alcott books, and it was inaugurated a year later. The example of the Temple School, and more particularly the ideas that lay behind it, gave him a new access of confidence, a sense that others had already grappled with the problems he was addressing. "The Americans at Boston," he would tell Campbell, "are more alive to man's fall in his constitution than we are; we seem to have lost sight of what he is by a mis-birth."[39] Ironically, Alcott's very failure to respond to his overture for more than eighteen months may have helped Greaves's own enterprise get off the ground, because he didn't have to cope with dispiriting news of the Temple School's collapse. Wright's enthusiasm, too, no doubt played an important part, along with the slightly tenuous experience of pedagogy gleaned from his time as an usher at a school in Chipping Ongar. The two sisters of Ebworth Park, sustaining their idealism and their commitment to a subjunctive position in which the would-be world would become accessible again, put up the necessary money.

Wright explained that the school arose out of a discussion in the Greaves circle on the vexed subject of free will. Sadly, "the false birth" of the individual precludes "the manifestation of pure humanity," but even in the worst cases "there is yet a germ of Spirit within, that is found flickering."[40] The task of the school would not be to rectify what is wrong but to keep that germ alive. In fact, Wright reflected his own master's ambiguity about the role of education and the state of the infant mind. He saw his task as to enable the first years of the child's life to "be passed over without depravation," a view that suggests that children are born innocent and then liable to corruption by a fallen world. At the same time, he also believed the school had to overcome the "depravity of birth," and "awaken the purer nature in the infants," which implies the opposite view.

A suitable building was found at Ham Common, near Richmond, and rented for £28 a year. Though close to central London, Ham was still a village, with a population of about 1,400 people. The house came with four acres of land, an important asset given the convergence of gardening and educational theory that lay at the heart of Greavesian thought.

Greaves himself remained at 49 Burton Street. He was sixty-one and his poor health probably prevented him from taking an active part. In any case his role was to be the calm mystical center of a vortex of idealism. Lane continued to work on his commodities periodical in London. The two Greavesians entrusted to get the new enterprise off the ground were Henry Gardiner Wright, who was to take charge of the school, and William Oldham, who would be responsible for practical matters.

Wright's sister came along too. In his original letter Greaves had asked whether Alcott found that girls learned faster and were more appreciative of their lessons than boys. Nevertheless he believed that males monopolized the understanding, while females were left in charge of the feelings, and this distinction became part of the philosophy of the school. As Wright expressed it in a later prospectus, the "grace and loveliness of the girl" can relieve the "asperities" of the boy, while the girl in turn needs "the advantages of intellectual activity, which is to be found characteristically only in the opposite sex."[41] Given this emphasis on the contribution of the two sexes, the school was committed to co-education, and therefore it was clearly wise to have a woman on the staff, particularly because the pupils were to be residential, and the institution was being seen as a community as well as a school. Wright's sister made possible a balance of the sexes without the danger of love or marriage. It must have seemed to Greaves that his school would be safe from any sexual threat.

The experiment commenced in July 1838. It was called Alcott House.

3

A Joy in a Winding Sheet

ALCOTT WAS IN LIMBO. For a time he held a class in a small room in the basement of the Temple building, and then in his lodgings. "A few children come daily to my house," he said, "but that does not give me a school." In addition he conducted public "Conversations." He would borrow or rent a room for the evening, sell tickets, and talk with his audience on matters of philosophy or morality. His family was close to destitution, and he felt intellectually isolated. "Few men know me, fewer listen to me. I seem to be of small account."[1]

In the early summer of 1838 he sent Emerson a mountainous manuscript called *Psyche: An Evangele* on the development of his third daughter Elizabeth, who was then three. His observations of infant development were buried in a mass of general philosophizing, much of it revealing similar contradictions and muddle to that apparent in the work of the Greavesians. Sin can be passed down from parent to child—"His own uncleanness doth flow in their corporeal members"—while at the same time "a Family is the heaven of the Soul."[2] It was almost 347 closely written manuscript pages long, and full of high-flown empty rhetoric. "Tis all stir and no go," Emerson told him (apologizing for using language usually related to sexual fiasco), thereby putting paid to any hopes Alcott might have had of making a career as an author. "It lamed me," he confessed after hearing this verdict, "it made me blind and dumb. I had music in my soul but no voice."[3]

The English connection was a consolation. Since his own school had vanished into thin air, it was comforting to discover he was being embodied in bricks and mortar at Alcott House, though still he could not summon up the courage to respond to Greaves's letter. In June 1838 William Oldham wrote to him on behalf of the master, pointing out that he had been waiting for ten months for a reply, and the following October Greaves himself wrote again, sending him books and pamphlets from his own circle and asking for more copies of the two books on the Temple School to distribute to interested parties at his end, whetting Alcott's appetite for contact but still not triggering a reply.[4]

One day in early February 1839, Alcott had an argument with his wife. She complained that entries in his journal describing her were caricatures (his custom being to show his diary to friends and relatives). He hoped he hadn't done her an injustice. "She was one of the facts to be noted in the history of my domestic life," he told her, a tepid verdict that reveals the degree to which he regarded family life as a project or experiment. Abigail said she would have to use her scissors on some passages one day. Indeed, hundreds of pages have been cut out with scissors from the journals of this period. The manuscript contains the scars as well as the records of Alcott's mental state and of his relationship with his wife. Her journals and letters, as well as those of the children, would also in due course be edited and censored by him.

On February 5th he was asked to buy a joint at the butcher's. His family still ate meat at this time, but Alcott had been a vegetarian for four years or so, and he asked for the wrong cut. The butcher, he decided, was aware of his mistake. He was being taken for a ride but couldn't summon up the confidence to protest, so went back to teach his tiny class while the butcher's boy delivered the meat.

Abigail summoned him "to survey the strange flitch as it lay on the kitchen table." Alcott blustered. It had been a fool's errand. How could he be expected to know one bit of flesh from another? What did he have to do with butchers? The simple solution was never to send him on such an errand again. Butchers were liable to be swindlers, given "their carnal code of practice"; it went with the territory.[5] (This argument would be used over at Ham Common several years later, when the Greavesians suggested that butchers, and even meat-eaters, should be banned from serving on juries because of their inevitable enthusiasm for capital punishment. In this respect, Ham was an unfortunate address.[6])

Finally Alcott lost his temper and sense of proportion. "Death yawns at me," he exclaimed in his diary, "as I walk up and down in this abode of skulls . . . The death-set eyes of beasts peer at me and accuse me of belonging to the race of murderers." Suddenly he is possessed by the very thing he has repudiated. "Quartered, disembowelled creatures on suspended hooks plead with me. I am a replenisher of grave yards. I prowl, amidst other unclean spirits and voracious demons, for my prey."[7]

He is picturing how it might feel to be implicated in the butchery of animals. But the writing teeters on the verge of hysteria (in fact ten pages of the manuscript journal are torn out following this entry). There is a drastic failure of Transcendental optimism, Alcott feeling himself trapped in the horrors of the material world. He was aware that there were two sides to his personality. A month later, having written an optimistic letter to his mother, he explained that for the moment, "the fore-face of my Janus is most vivid." He had told her that he expected to make a living from his Conversations and that the "future looks bright and encouraging," adding "so you can see I am still the same Hoper that I have always been."

He also announced that "a young Hoper is on his way." Abigail was pregnant again, and he was sure their fourth child would be a boy. But just for a second the mask slipped and the happy Janus face gave way to its tragic opposite. "Yet strange, that grief should bear him to me, is it not?" he asked, presumably thinking about the fact that the baby was conceived in the aftermath of his school's collapse.[8]

On April 6th, just three weeks after Alcott wrote this letter, Abigail gave birth to a boy. He lived only a few minutes. "Gave birth to a fine boy full grown perfectly formed but not living," she wrote in her diary. "Mysterious little being!! Oh for that quickening power to breathe into its nostrils the breath of life . . . No!"[9]

In August 1841, sixteen months later, Alcott turned to the page of his journal where he had transcribed his letter announcing Abigail's pregnancy and added a chilling codicil: "—But my thrill of Hope proved a pang of grief—a true son of its mother—a Joy in a Winding Sheet." Here is the dark side of the happy family that would one day be immortalized by Louisa— and that was partly the product of Alcott's own propaganda. In the very letter copied into his journal he had done his bit to build the mythology, presenting old Anna Alcott as the archetypal American mother: "I fancy you sitting there in your rocking chair, in your cleanest, whitest, Sunday cap, and spectacles well polished, reading, or perhaps talking . . . about your children, declaring that they are the kindest, best children that ever a mother had, and wondering why it is so."

The reason of course is that "they have one of the kindest and best of mothers."[10] To call a dead baby the true son of its mother represents a savage reversal of such inheritance, particularly since Alcott is likely to have read the description of Abigail's own pain in her journal. Just a couple of weeks after his letter to his mother, Alcott had celebrated sex and reproduction in a passage that is as frank and explicit as it is lyrical:

> Fluids form solids. Mettle is the Godhead proceeding into the matrix of Nature to organize Man. Behold the creative jet! And hear the morning stars sing for joy at the sacred generation of the Gods![11]

A week later the Alcotts' baby came into the world unequipped for survival. If parents were ultimately responsible for generating perfect men, they must be to blame for the birth of imperfect, or unviable, ones. Alcott was indeed, in Greaves's words, one of those men of Boston aware of the consequences of a "mis-birth." In a strange passage written shortly after the bereavement Alcott argues that bile, traditionally equated with choler, is in fact unnatural (Jesus didn't have any, apparently). This strange piece of biology shifts the blame for the baby's death squarely on to Abigail, and Alcott slips into hysteria and paranoia again. "So a mother, in a fit of rage, poisons the fountain at which her child draws sustenance, and he dies, slain by her choler," he wrote in his journal. "Beware of the bilious temperament. It is of the family of demons, insane, rabid."[12]

From the beginning of their relationship both Alcott and his wife had been aware of the difference in their temperaments. "He is moderate,"

Abigail told her brother Samuel when she announced her engagement, "I am impetuous—He is prudent and humble—I am forward and arbitrary. He is poor—but we are both industrious."[13] Perhaps the references to Alcott's prudence and industry were over-optimistic, but she was perfectly aware that their marriage would be based on the attraction of opposites. Alcott had his own swings of emotion, but he usually showed a serene exterior; Abigail was turbulent and subject to outbursts of temper. She associated these differences with the contrast in their coloring. Their daughter Louisa took after her both in complexion and temperament. "Louisa is a true blue May," Abigail claimed, "or rather *brown*."[14]

It is ironic that when he did succumb to rage, Alcott should demonize his wife for exactly that tendency. There is no way of knowing if Abigail read these passages in his journal: it is disturbing to think she might have done.

Perhaps it was this tragedy that finally caused Alcott to reply to Greaves's overture, on April 26, 1839. The delay was caused by the collapse of his school, he said, hostility from pulpit and press, and betrayal by some he had "deemed my best friends," all of which meant he had "no other than words of grief to impart." He was now going to establish a *"Ministry of Talking"* in order to "prepare the way for demonstrating the principles of human culture."[15]

Three days later he went off to visit Emerson in Concord, the aim being to move there in due course. Abigail couldn't see how he was going to earn a living (the village had only about 700 inhabitants at this period, plus perhaps twice that number living in its rural outskirts). Alcott applied his own maddening logic: "Neither do I see with the eyes of sense; but I know that a purpose like mine must yield bread for the hungry and clothe the naked, and I wait not for the arithmetic of this matter."[16]

The arithmetic of earning a living never managed to add up for Alcott so perhaps it was as well that he didn't wait for it. The nearest he got to being practical was to consider how to make an impact on the larger world from the seclusion of an individual life. He evolved a theory which coincided with Greaves's belief that elementary particles could circulate for hundreds of miles, just as the perfumes from the Spice Islands could waft across the oceans. The atmosphere is the product of all the planet's souls; therefore a redeemed individual could spread his or her virtue everywhere: "Like ocean, it tumbles round the world, and stirs the whole mass of fluid air."[17] This oceanic possibility was probably as close to a business plan as Alcott ever got.

During the few days he spent on this visit to Concord, Alcott found himself attending concerts and having discussions both with fellow Transcendentalists (he and Emerson rode over to Waltham to talk to Sarah Ripley, who with her husband George would found the utopian community of Brook Farm), and with the Concord villagers themselves.[18] It was a—perhaps *the*—classic New England township, with mainly white clapboard houses picturesquely clustered together and surrounded by fields and woodland, with the Sudbury and Assabet rivers joining to form the Concord River, and a village pond, Walden, a mile or so from the town. Concord played a famous part at the beginning of the Revolutionary War, when Paul Revere rode out to warn its citizens of the approach of the British and there was a battle at the town's north bridge. Emerson had written his "Concord Hymn" just three years previously:

Here once the embattled farmers stood
And fired the shot heard round the world.[19]

This visit gave Alcott a sense of new possibilities emerging, of shifts and stirrings in society at large, of the coalescing of new perspectives. Later in the year his teaching methods were the subject of an essay by one of the English Transcendentalists, J.A. Heraud. "America . . . already possesses such a miracle of a school master," Heraud enthused.[20] Charles Lane wrote a letter of "love and encouragement," and Greaves sent books and articles.[21] Alcott must also have felt in the swing of things because of playing an active role in the Transcendental Club which had been established in 1836. This was an informal group consisting of those involved in the philosophical and religious upheavals of the time, usually meeting at each other's houses in the Boston area. Besides Alcott and Emerson, members included Orestes Brownson, Christopher Pearse Cranch (who had drawn the cartoon of Emerson's transparent eyeball), Frederick Henry Hedge, George and Sophia Ripley, Elizabeth Palmer Peabody, and Margaret Fuller, another formidable product of home-based female education. The club's name was bestowed by others; as far as the members were concerned they were simply an informal group. As Hedge put it, "there was no club in the strict sense . . . only occasional meetings of like-minded men and women."[22] Nevertheless, in 1839 the Transcendental Club decided to publish a journal, with thirty-year-old Margaret Fuller as editor, and Alcott provided its title, the *Dial*.[23]

In the spring of 1840, the decision was finally made to move out to Concord. "I have been among the 'sceptical,'" Abigail told her brother Samuel, "and he still thinks me almost impotent in faith." She was impressed by his patient endurance: "There is a reality here, which does not show itself all on the surface."[24] They rented the Hosmer Cottage, with an acre and three quarters of land, for a dollar a week, and promptly renamed the place Concordia.[25] Alcott was a lover of *Pilgrim's Progress*, and the choice reflected his need to see life in allegorical terms (though they also called the house Dove Cottage as a tribute to Wordsworth's dwelling of that name).[26] Concordia was surrounded by Concord, implying that process of outward transmission that the physical layout of the Temple School classroom had established, semicircle after semicircle, rippling as far as Surrey. Charles Lane in fact had just published an article describing a lesson by Henry Gardiner Wright which clearly followed the template of the Temple School, right down to classroom furnishings and a large gothic window.[27] Perhaps that defunct enterprise was indeed tumbling in oceanic fashion around the world. In July 1837 Emerson had gone to Providence, Rhode Island, to open a new school established by one Hiram Fuller, and was taken aback to discover that both the classroom design and the lessons followed the lines established by Alcott; now the blueprint had crossed the Atlantic.[28]

But there was no plan to establish a school at Concordia or Concord. Instead Alcott filled his letters and journal entries with metaphors of planting and harvesting, except that now he was able to ground them in the actual daily work he was undertaking. "Labour is, indeed, sweet," he assured his brother-in-law, and it "invests man with primeval dignity."[29]

Abigail went singing round their new home, she was so pleased with it, but (Emerson told fellow-Transcendentalist Margaret Fuller) the very popularity of his decision to move to Concord was making Alcott nervous.[30] He already had experience of knowing that it was just when things seemed to be going well that disaster was likely to strike.

The first issue of the *Dial* was published in July 1840. It included a sequence of "Orphic Sayings" by Alcott, sentences or short paragraphs of gnomic wisdom in the spirit of the "Orphic Sayings" of Goethe (as translated and published by one of the Transcendentalists, James Freeman Clarke, in 1836).[31] In one of his own, Alcott talks of the need to find a spiritual calculus in order to identify the center and circumference of the universe. In effect this is the mission of the sequence as a whole. The universe is a locked door, and each saying a key to try it in turn, its serrated edge intended to engage with the intricate ins and outs of that big everything into which Alcott methodically pushes it.

Alcott's sayings are often obscure and lumbering ("The poles of things are not integrated: creation globed and orbed"), lacking the pithy precision of good aphorisms, the pungency that Emerson could give his formulations ("Trust thyself: every heart vibrates to that iron string."[32]) Alcott expresses his hostility to democracy—"multitudes ever lie"—and asserts his faith that a spiritual harvest will come just when—just because—it is needed: "The hunger of an age is alike a presentiment and pledge of its own supply . . . When there is a general craving for bread . . . bread is even then growing in the fields." In Saying XII on the subject of temptation he also affirms the Greavesian doctrine of prior being:

> Greater is he, who is above temptation, than he, who, being tempted, overcomes. The latter but regains the state from which the former has not fallen. He who is tempted has sinned; temptation is impossible to the holy.[33]

This is a repudiation of the Lord's Prayer itself, of the very heart of Christian morality. Here we see the quest for a lost Eden that was implicit in Alcott's educational theories and practice and that would underlie the Fruitlands experiment. Redemption or reform as we commonly understand the words weren't on his agenda; he had no interest in mending what had been broken.

The real task was not to earn forgiveness by being forgiving ourselves, nor to expiate or overcome the Fall, but to jettison history altogether. Meeting Carlyle a couple of years later, Alcott concluded that the great man's melancholy was caused by his career as an historian, "the miming giant overmastered by the ghosts he evoked from their slumbers."[34] Alcott wanted to re-establish the state of affairs that prevailed before the Fall ever took place, before history even began; to achieve, like Sophia Chichester and Georgiana Welch over in Stroud, a "subjunctive position"; to take his place in the would-be world of the Antecedent. The English Transcendentalists were alert to the significance of Saying XII and when, eighteen months later, they started their journal *The Healthian* ("A Journal of Human Physiology, Diet, and Regimen"), they used its first sentence as an epigraph to each issue. The press and public in New England were not so impressed. "The Boston Post expressed the feeling of most readers," remarked Emerson, "when it said of his Orphic Sayings that they 'resembled a train of 15 railroad cars with one passenger.' "[35]

Meanwhile utopia was in the air. George Ripley and his wife Sophia spent their summer holiday at Brook Farm in West Roxbury, just outside Boston, and decided it was the ideal site for a community that would unite mental and physical labors. They wished to break down class barriers by arranging things so that all their members, even literary ones like Nathaniel Hawthorne, did their share of manual work. And this process would mean that each individual would live a fulfilling and balanced life, rather as Alcott (lacking the social agenda) was trying to do in his own person in Concord. Indeed Alcott had played a part in helping to formulate plans for Brook Farm at a convention of radical thinkers that took place in Groton, Massachusetts, in August.[36]

Ripley invited Emerson to join the community. Emerson refused but felt guilty, and consequently formulated a more modest plan of his own. The Alcotts (there were six of them now, with the birth of Abigail May in July) would move in with him and his family, along with a young Irish boy, Alexander McCaffery, in whom Emerson had taken an interest. Emerson also planned to inform the servants they should eat at the same table as the rest of the household. He told Margaret Fuller of these intended arrangements when she visited him in December. She regarded them as "a plan most unpromising, but for the nobleness of motive, in my friend."[37]

Emerson addressed the current ferment, along with his own ambiguous feelings about it, in his lecture on "Man the Reformer," which he gave in Boston a month later, on January 25, 1841. "Not a kingdom, town, statute, rite, calling, man, or woman, but is threatened by the new spirit," he told his audience, "the demon of reform." The use of words like "threatened" and "demon" give a sense of Emerson's own reservations about the ferment. He was of course himself one of the central figures in the whole Transcendentalist movement, but his take on the upheaval was always on a philosophical or literary level. When he saw the world afresh it was a mystical experience, one of those heightened moments that Wordsworth called "spots of time," not the vision of a future social ordering.[38] The problem with buying a farm as the solution to current woes, he went on to claim, is that it involves operating the very economic mechanisms that prevail in society, so betraying the epiphanic nature of utopia. "To earn money enough to buy one [a farm] requires a sort of concentration toward money, which is the selling himself for a number of years," he told his audience, "and to him the present hour is . . . sacred." But "a man should have a farm or a mechanical craft for his culture," he conceded, contradictorily. "We must have an antagonism in the tough world for all the variety of our spiritual faculties, or they will not be born."

An antagonism in the tough world: it's a phrase that evokes Alcott's own experience. Emerson gives his friend's austerity the heroic remoteness of another time and place when he goes on to praise the Caliph Ali and his "Temperance Troops": "His diet was barley bread; his sauce was salt; and oftentimes by way of abstinence he ate his bread without salt. His drink was water." Pretty much the menu in Concordia, and perhaps Alcott too would be in the vanguard of a new faith that was about to sweep the world: "The fact, that a new thought and hope have dawned in your breast," Emerson told his audience, "should apprise you that in the same hour a new light broke in upon a thousand private hearts."[39]

Despite the unhelpful ridicule Alcott's first contribution to the *Dial* had generated, its editors kept faith with him. Late in 1840 Margaret Fuller asked Emerson to encourage him to produce another batch, which was duly published in the issue for January 1841 and which attracted even more mockery than its predecessor. "Ever the true putty fast-sticketh," claimed the *Knickerbocker*, a New York literary journal contributed to by some of the leading writers of the day, in a parody of Alcott's assertive and anachronistic style.[40] At about this time he came across the *Plain Speaker*, edited by George Clarke, William Chace, and Christopher Greene in Providence, Rhode Island (where there was a school based on his own prototype), and taking up the causes of abolition, women's rights, and radicalism generally. Alcott wrote a letter for its second issue, a baffled and cornered man hitting out wildly: "My Breast is a-glow with Fires, and I would send my shafts abroad to kindle and enlighten," he claimed. "And surely there is fuel for a general conflagration!"[41]

Emerson's mini-utopia came to nothing. "I cannot gee and haw in another person's yoke," Abigail Alcott announced. "I know that everybody burns their fingers if they touch my pie," she added, perhaps remembering the terrible conflict with Elizabeth Peabody (the Alcotts also turned down an invitation to live in a house provided by Abigail's brother Samuel). Moreover, the Irish boy, Alexander McCaffery, went off to New Jersey, and Emerson's servants, having a more traditional outlook than their master (or perhaps intuiting that he was traditional at heart) refused point blank to eat with the family at table, so the plan failed at the first hurdle. Margaret Fuller was pleased. She told Emerson that the most the experiment could have been was an "instructive blunder," and nailed precisely his preferred stance of interested detachment. "Let others cook the *potage*," she told him, "and you examine the recipe."[42]

The recipe for *potage*, as far as Alcott was concerned, would take very little examining. He proudly affirmed his diet in an entry in his diary for May 19, 1841, later published in the *Dial*: "Our wine is water,—flesh, bread,—drugs, fruits."[43] He almost writes a manifesto for the Fruitlands experiment, now just two years down the road. He wishes to be self-sufficient, not merely in order to avoid the fruits of oppression but so as to achieve "entire independence"— in other words to sever his ties with the fallen world. At about this time the reformers associated with the *Plain Speaker* invited him and his family to join a utopian experiment of their own, Holly House in Providence, and Abigail actually went there to try it out for a few days but came to the same verdict she had given on Emerson's previous proposal. Alcott contented himself with writing another torrid letter to the *Plain Speaker* attacking partial reform and looking forward to a "Final renovation of Humanity."[44]

"This Beast named Man," he claimed in his journal, "has yet most costly tastes, and must first be transformed into a very man, regenerate in appetite and desire, before the earth shall be restored to fruitfulness, and redeemed from the curse of his cupidity." The word "regenerate" here doesn't simply mean reformed but, in the most literal sense, generated in a new way. As a result farm toil would become elegant and attractive, and farms metamorphose into gardens. We now think of farming as the original impetus behind civilization, marking the transition from the hunter-gatherer lifestyle, but for Alcott, in his pre-Darwinian world, the garden was the original human environment.

He goes on to broach the subject of manure. "The soil, grateful then for man's generous usage, debauched no more by foul ordures, nor worn by cupidities, shall recover its primeval virginity, bearing on its bosom the standing bounties which a sober and liberal providence ministers to his need,—sweet and invigorating growths, for the health and comfort of the grower."[45] This resounding sentence owes an enormous debt, consciously or unconsciously, to one in Sylvester Graham's *Lectures on the Science of Human Life* which had come out two years previously: "It is probably true that the new soil, in its virgin purity, before it becomes exhausted by tillage, and debauched by the means which man uses to enrich and stimulate it, produces most, if not all, kinds of vegetables appropriate for human aliment, in a more perfect and healthy state, than any soil which has been long under cultivation, can be made to do."[46]

The shared phrasing in the two passages, with those references to debauchery and "primeval virtue," has the effect of linking the relinquishment of manure to sex, morality, and health. Greaves too was vehemently opposed to the use of manure, and made an equation between sexual intercourse and appropriate preparation of the soil. Emerson was quite right to talk about the simultaneous flooding in of new light. Perhaps he wasn't so right about the desirability of antagonism from the tough world, at least from Alcott's perspective. The tough world was not there to be confronted, but to be transcended. He was a Transcendentalist, after all.

Alcott, Graham, and Greaves shared a faith that Eden could be made accessible once more, through the adoption of the correct formulae for husbandry, diet, and reproduction. We can be freed from the coils of our earthly inheritance, released from the prison of the past, and find anew a perfect way—not a good or an effective or a desirable way, but a perfect way—of interacting with our surroundings and each other. There is a fierce literalness and absolutism about this proposal.

The Ripleys founded their community at Brook Farm in the spring of 1841. By early autumn Alcott was reaffirming his belief that "reform begins truly in individuals." The transformation is then conducted outward through a series of ever-enlarging social groups that already lie to hand, "the simplest ministries of families, neighbourhoods, fraternities." The process, Alcott asserts, will be "quite wide of associations, and institutions"—such as the deliberately contrived community of Brook Farm. "The true reformer initiates his labor in the precincts of a private life . . . and makes it . . . a tendency towards perfection of being."

Perfection will be achieved when the individual becomes "a primeval creature" once more, "in his original estate on earth, in harmony with nature, the animal world, his fellows, himself, his creator." For the aged Unitarian divine William Ellery Channing, Alcott was already well on the way. "Mr. Alcott, hiring himself out for day-labor, and at the same time living in the region of high thought, is, perhaps, the most interesting object in our Commonwealth," he reflected, as if observing a rare animal in a zoo.[47] Alcott's day-labor consisted of cultivating his garden, traveling to Boston and other local communities to give his Conversations, and chopping wood for his neighbors for a dollar a day.

Ironically, just as Alcott was becoming an individual icon in Massachusetts, his institutional namesake in England was relaunching itself as an even more highly structured community than Brook Farm, at least in its initial phase. A Concordium, its leaders decided to call it. This renaming was not in any sense a repudiation of their connection with Alcott—his own address was now Concordia, Concord, so the new letterhead was if anything a further act of homage. In any case the English Transcendentalists retained the name Alcott House for the building itself.

Like Brook Farm the inhabitants of the Concordium would "unite the desirable intelligent vivacity of urban intercourse and rural quiet." Just as Alcott was making himself a "primeval creature," they would establish a "primitive home": there was the same deep atavism, the same tropism towards Eden. But even as they formalized their community, the Greavesians were aware of their own master's reservations about such structures. "No human association can be the progress cause!" they proclaimed in their prospectus, but then went on, "Though when founded on the spirit-progress-law, it may represent the cause in harmonious consequences."[48]

Either Greaves himself is speaking here, or his followers have got him off to a tee. The main peculiarity of this language lies in its lack of adjectives. The sentence gives all its material equal weight, so that the nouns lie side by side like seals basking on a beach, none becoming subordinate to its fellows. The reasoning resembles the old Puritan doctrine of justification, according to which a sinner cannot earn salvation through living a good life but by leading a good life can show that salvation has already been bestowed by God. An association cannot be the engine of progress, but by coming into existence can show that progress is at work. If people are agents of "prior being" they cannot be credited with their own volition, with free will—or even with their own identity.

The school was a vital component of the community, and education was to be part of the daily experience of all the members. Half an individual's waking hours were to be spent on "individual improvement," while the remaining eight were given over to "productive industry." Like Alcott over in Massachusetts, they would all be combining day-labor with high thought. Like Alcott too, they espoused the elegance of gardening rather than the strenuousness of agriculture. "The land will be . . . apportioned to the purposes of recreation, exercise, study, the raising of food, fuel, and, as far as possible, all articles for dress, so that all the produce required may be obtained from the estate." Despite the demands of a subsistence economy, "recreation" comes top of the list. As a result of this program, "as soon as individuals have grown up and passed their whole educative career in accordance with the universe law, they will not from mere instruction and consideration, but from being, spontaneously manifest in triune harmony the love-wisdom-power from which *their* being is derived."[49]

So education is necessary but it is "being" that will do the trick; and being will be generated "spontaneously." George Holyoake, a historian of cooperatives who visited the Concordium, explained that its "only experiment . . . consisted in standing still in a state of submission to the Spirit until it directed them what to do." That spirit could well manifest itself through the voice of the Concordium's autocratic ruler, a sort of pope—indeed he was to be called the pater, "every probationer and member recognizing in the Concordist father an entire undivided authority in all matters whatsoever, without limitations of time." There were no down or feather mattresses; only water to drink; the diet would consist of fruit and vegetables "chiefly uncooked by fire," though (hopefully) "often it may be prepared and combined novelly, and in a superior way with reference to its homogeneous qualities."

"The inmates were scrupulously clean, temperate, transcendental … repudiated even salt and tea, as stimulants, and thought most of their guests who ate their cabbage uncooked," reported Holyoake. "They practised abstinence from marriage, and most things else." All in all, he concluded, "their cardinal doctrine was that happiness was wrong."[50]

Just as this list of thou-shalt-nots was coming into being, Henry Gardiner Wright managed to flout its central prohibition.

In the spring of 1841, Sophia Chichester sent her parlor maid, a young woman called Elizabeth Hardwick, to Wright to be trained as a teacher. It was only a year since he had published his pamphlet on *Marriage and its Sanctions*, where he had listed so many sanctions that marriage became practically impossible to achieve, at the very least involving stressful callisthenics and exposure to climatic extremes, as well as poetry. Despite all this, the two young people fell in love, and secretly married later that year while attending Robert Owen's Rational Society Congress in Manchester. It wouldn't be the last time that Wright failed in his commitment to orthodox Greavesianism.

His master was appalled. "Thank God I can close my room door and lay me down in peace to die," he exclaimed. Wright was "woman-bewitched" (beneath all the high-minded praise of woman's capacity for relieving the asperities of the male gender, there was a good dose of misogyny in Greavesian sexual theories). In revisiting the Garden of Eden, the mystical philosopher had avoided the canard about Eve being to blame for humankind's Fall, but he had no doubt who was to blame for Henry Gardiner Wright's. Elizabeth Hardwick was the villain of the piece. She had set her cap at the two eligible bachelors of Alcott House, cynically deciding that if she didn't get the one she would trap the other. "Elizabeth has won the game, she has the odd trick and Mr Oldham has been fairly beaten by the young gambler; out of the two she has made sure of one."

The claustrophobic maleness of the Burton Street group, and the extremeness of Greaves's reaction to this marriage, suggest that his account was hardly likely to be fair. "The Ham school is fairly in the ground, in the dust," he claimed mournfully. It would not recover if manipulative women had anything to do with it. "It may be risen, but not by any thieves."[51]

Over in Concord's Concordia, at almost exactly this time, Mrs. Alcott had a rather different take on the gender conflict. Exhausted at having to keep her family on the go in the face of her husband's depression and failure to provide, she wrote in her journal for August 1841, "Why are men icebergs when beloved by ardent nature and surrounded by love-giving and life-devoted beings. Why so much take, take: so little Give! Give! Women are certainly more generous than men. Man receives, enjoys, argues, forsakes. Man reasons about right. Woman feels right. Love is with her instinctive, eternal. With man it is pastime and passion."[52]

Greaves's fears proved groundless. Alcott House did rise again. Henry Wright offered to resign and suggested that Alcott should be asked to take his place. Greaves thought that might be a good idea but knew there would be a problem in raising money to bring him across the Atlantic.[53] Instead, Charles Lane lessened his ties with his periodical and business affairs, and took a larger part in running the Concordium. Despite his disgrace, Wright continued to work in the school, though he grumbled about "opposition in spirit from those nominally coadjutant."[54] At the end of 1841, Greaves himself went over to Ham—not to take an active part but because his health was more frail than ever. He was in great discomfort from the combination of rheumatism and his hernia, and he wanted to try the water cure that had been newly introduced in the community. Even Elizabeth Wright, promptly pregnant, got her regular dousing of cold water, up to just a few hours before delivery.[55]

Back in New England, Bronson Alcott was again sticking his head over the parapet. Like most of the New England Transcendentalists, he was a member of the abolitionists, led in Boston by William Lloyd Garrison, who edited the antislavery newspaper, the *Liberator*. Both Alcott and his brother-in-law Samuel May were friends of Garrison's, and supported his uncompromising stance on the issue. In 1838 Garrison's antislavery movement had spawned a Peace Convention in which the nonresistance stance of the abolitionists had been codified into a more broadly based movement that asserted it was unlawful to bear arms and to use retaliative punishment. Alcott and Samuel May were signatories of the code. A worried correspondent wrote to

Garrison's *Liberator* pointing out that in effect this meant subscribing to a "No-Government Theory." The Peace Convention spawned an annual series of meetings of the Non-Resistance Society in Boston and on September 21, 1841 Alcott joined Samuel May as one of the main speakers. "They make a virtual declaration of independence from the government," reported the press, "they will pay it no taxes, except on compulsion—they will hold no office under it, civil or military—they will not even serve as jurors in courts of justice, and they will not appeal to those courts to redress any wrongs they may suffer."[56]

Some Transcendentalists—Emerson, for example—made a distinction between a mystical communion of solitaries and the practical interactions of sublunary existence, but in any attempt to make a coherent social model from Transcendental beliefs anarchism was the logical solution. And Alcott saw himself as discarded by society; small wonder that he should reject it in return. Entire independence, as he put it, was his objective. Anarchism would inform his actions over the next years, provide the basis of his utopian experiment, and unite him with Charles Lane.

In Concordia things were turning rather grim, as they so often did for the Alcotts. Abigail's father died early in 1841, leaving her one-seventh of his estate, roughly $2,000. The terms of his will specified that the money was for her "sole and separate use, without the control of her husband or liability of his debts." Abigail, volatile as usual, failed to understand that this was a sensible precaution (given her husband owed $6,000, which would have swallowed the whole legacy), and took enormous offense, claiming it meant her father hadn't loved her. Alcott's creditors challenged the will anyway, and the money was put in escrow, where it remained for another four years.[57]

The Alcotts' indignation is understandable in the light of their poverty. We get a glimpse of how things stood in late November 1841 when Abigail's aunt by marriage, Hannah Robie, came to visit. Miss Robie knew what to expect at Concordia. She was about to have her period, so took some necessary precautions. "As it was time for me to expect a headache, I did not dare to go to Concord without carrying tea and coffee and cayenne pepper—and a small piece of cooked meat, in case my wayward stomach should crave it; which last article was a little piece of *à la mode* beef." She arrived at the cottage after dark and the family didn't hear her approach, so she let herself in. Alcott and Abigail and their four children, Anna (aged ten), Louisa (nine), Elizabeth (six), and baby Abby (one) were sitting around the table, consuming their meager evening meal of bread and water. "I would rather live on acorns the next ten years with those who are free to live and die for their principles, than be compelled to conform to the world,—all of whose ways are so fallen," Abigail had written in her journal a couple of months before. She leapt to her feet, overjoyed at her friend's appearance. "O you dear creature!" she cried, "you are the one I should have picked out of all the good people in Boston. How thankful I am to see you."

The children were delighted too. There was an air of desperation in the warmth of the welcome.

Miss Robie produced a parcel. It had been sent along by Mrs. James Savage, mother of two of the pupils at the Temple School (some parents still remained loyal). Alcott looked on "like a philosopher" while the parcel was unwrapped to reveal a bundle of clothes. "There," he said to Abigail, "I told you that you need not be anxious about clothing for the children; you see it has come as I said." He had no doubt been taking his usual line, that "when there is a general craving for bread . . . bread is even then growing in the fields." But when the two women were alone together, Abigail confided that "things had got pretty low." As she talked about her husband's disappointments, she was overwhelmed with pity for him and had a "good crying spell," before pulling herself together for her guest.

The Alcotts were living on coarse brown sugar, bread, potatoes, apples, squashes, and simple puddings. Somehow Hannah Robie couldn't bring herself to nibble on her private store, so the *à la mode* beef went to waste. The only indulgence she couldn't pass up was tea, though Alcott told Abigail she was wrong to prepare it for her. There was an argument about milk. Alcott wanted the family to dispense with it altogether, but Miss Robie said baby Abby needed it. The Alcotts had just started living on two meals a day so the children could take what was saved along to a poor family who were living in a "hovel" near by. Years later this commitment was recalled in *Little Women*, when the March girls give their Christmas breakfast to the indigent Hummels. Rather touchingly *Little Women* has Marmee bundling up used clothing for them, just as Mrs. Savage had for the Alcotts themselves. When Hannah Robie went along to visit the real-life starving family, she discovered that Alcott had already been there twice before, cutting wood for them.[58]

On December 6th Alcott received yet another blow. He had previously submitted selections from his journal for 1841 for publication in the January 1842 issue of the *Dial*, but was told that there was now no room in that number, and publication would have to be postponed until the April issue. He wrote a bitter little introduction to his extracts, claiming he had more or less lost interest in them in any case, and pointing out that "the Dial prefers a style of thought and diction, not mine." The mockery his "Orphic Sayings" had attracted came back to him. "Nor can I add to its popularity with its chosen readers," he admitted sadly. "A fit organ for such as myself is not yet, but is to be."[59] He had prepared a new batch of "Orphic Sayings" for publication (they were smuggled in as part of the journal extracts). "Great is the man whom his age despises," one of them went, "for transcendent excellence is purchased through the obloquy of contemporaries; and shame is the gate to the temple of renown."[60]

The word "shame" gives some inkling of how he felt about the collapse of his school (there is a punning reference to it in "the temple"), his lack of success in print, his failure to provide for his family. It was "my winter of discontent," Alcott said. "Every avenue to honest and worthy employment is closed against me."[61] Even his role as an icon could be called into question. On January 6th, Margaret Fuller gave a warning to her brother Richard. "You can visit Mr. Alcott sometimes with profit," she told him, "but keep your eyes open and steady to look at him on all sides."[62]

On January 19, 1842 Abigail Alcott wrote to her brother Samuel, thanking him for passing on $10. On fine days, she told him, Mr. Alcott chops wood, and also spends time teaching the girls. Mr. Emerson has brought him an elegant cloak, which she was putting away until next winter. For the moment his old orange one "seems to suit the color of his condition better." An admirer in Providence, Mr. Barker, has offered to build him a cottage to the value of $1,500, along with five acres of land, for the purpose of establishing a utopian community. But Barker wants to see a plan, a blueprint for the good life. Abigail doesn't feel up to producing any such thing: she doesn't think her husband is able to either. He is on a different plane from these Providence sympathizers—all his thoughts are directed at his admirers in England. But his family holds him back. It is a tension we see time and again—family commitment on the one hand, a desire to encounter and transform the world as a whole on the other. Abigail thinks she could live on wood chippings from the logging her husband is doing in order to "effect his emancipation from physical wants."

Years later Alcott changed "his" to "this," trying to save face by suggesting that Abigail was proposing a solution for the family as a whole rather than just the rescue of her husband. But her concern is all for him. "He will not long survive this state of things," she tells her brother, "if his body don't fail his mind will." She goes on to diagnose what we would call paranoia. "He experiences at times the most dreadful nervous excitation[,] his mind distorting every act however simple into the most complicated and adverse form—I am terror-stricken at this." She would even rather see him die than have his great spirit laid low in this fashion.

But usually, she tells Sam, hope preponderates. Mr. Alcott "feels sure that the dawn of his day is not far below the horizon." Perhaps they should go from Concordia to Providence after all (shades of *Pilgrim's Progress* again). "More hereafter," she concludes.[63]

A month later, an extraordinary thing happened, one of the most amazing events in a life that seems to brim with them. Alcott's philosophy, that just when things got bad, providence would wave its wand and they would get better again, that absurd, unlikely, loser's philosophy, was vindicated.

On January 29, 1842, Emerson lost his five-year-old son Waldo. It was a terrible blow for a man who regularly described himself as cold and detached and who was sometimes accused of being aloof by others (including Alcott) but who consistently showed deep love and loyalty to his family and friends. This paradox was perhaps the result of a conflict between the impulses of his heart on the one hand, and on the other the espousal of a philosophy that asserts the primacy of the impersonal totality—coupled with a taste for a reflective existence in the quiet of his study.

"My boy, my boy is gone," Emerson wrote to his aunt, Mary Moody Emerson. "My darling & the world's wonderful child . . . has fled out of my arms like a dream." Writing to Margaret Fuller, he asked, "Shall I ever dare to love anything again. Farewell and Farewell, O my Boy!"

The answer to his anguished question, however, was—yes. Unlike his friend, bereavement didn't tempt him into the blame game. "And now how art thou, Sad wifey," he wrote to Lidian. "Alas! Alas! That one of your sorrows, that our one sorrow, can never in this world depart from us!" Their sorrow was a shared one. And three weeks to the day after the tragedy, Emerson wrote to Alcott:

> It seems to me . . . you might spend the summer in England and get back to America in the autumn for a sum not exceeding four or five hundred dollars. It will give me great pleasure to be responsible to you for that amount; and to more, if I shall be able, and more is necessary.[64]

Emerson was comfortably off, at least compared with the Alcotts, though not a rich man, and this was a very generous offer. Despite, or perhaps because of, his own sorrow, he was able to remember his friend's bafflement, indeed despair, at the frustrations of his life, and provide him with the means and opportunity to deal with them. Perhaps he would not have made the gesture if he had been aware of the Alcottian perspective on such losses as his. In her journal a couple of months later Abigail Alcott talks of the great mortality of children in Boston that winter. "Waldo Emerson and many other interesting children have been rudely torn from our midst by disease." It is all down to a neglect of the doctrines of Sylvester Graham, however, and therefore "I cannot offer sympathy to these dear suffering Mothers,—for I see so much culpable neglect of the means of living, feeding, clothing, bathing, exercise, sleeping."[65]

Alcott responded at once to Emerson's offer, writing the same day to ask his youngest brother Junius to come and stay with Abigail and the family while he was gone. Junius was only twenty-four, living with their mother in Oriskany, New York, and admiring his brother from afar. "My good wife is humane and social," Bronson assured him. This was Alcott's big chance to go where he was appreciated. "These Englishmen have manifested a true interest in my objects, and I seek them with hope—sure of their friendship and aid." His good wife put a brave face on it but wasn't quite as enthusiastic about the arrangement as he was.[66] "Wife, children and friends are less to him than the great idea he is seeking to realize," she told her diary. "How naturally man's sphere seems to be in the regions of the head—and woman's in the heart and affections."[67]

On March 6th Alcott was in Boston, visiting friends to tell them about his English trip. "How grateful is sympathy to his solitary soul," Abigail wrote, adding, "he wanders too [sic] and fro on the face of the earth not like Satan to destroy but to seek and save mankind."[68] It is rather disturbing that she has to remind herself that he is not being Satanic in his perambulations. One of the friends Alcott visited was Margaret Fuller, though her sympathy was guarded, to say the least. She had respect and admiration for some of his qualities, but at some deep level she distrusted him. Alcott seemed to feel the need to "make a clean breast on't," she told Emerson, the "it" presumably being all his manifold failures to date. He gave her a history of his mental state over recent months. He looked on his own conduct during the last year with more disapproval than at any other time of his life. He had sunk into moodiness and musing which eventually intensified till he "found himself on the borders of frenzy."

He had been rescued from this despair by "the magnanimity of a friend." The thought of that made him weep "a plenteous shower of gracious tears." He started telling her about his hopes and schemes at this point, while she listened skeptically. She was clearly worried that by making his investment in Alcott's prospects, Emerson would get his fingers burned. "I felt after he had talked out this ne[w] phase to a dozen people," she warned, "it would have done its work, and truth be left unembodied as far as depends on him."[69] It was the usual criticism. Alcott could talk a good line, but it was beyond his capabilities to make things actually happen.

Still, the trip to England was duly arranged. Junius moved into Concordia as requested to help with the family. "Here are my wife and children," Alcott told him, "my house, library, friends, garden, (and acre if you desire it) all at your profit or service, and you can read, meditate, labour or converse, as you incline."[70] Given he had found it impossible to make the set-up work himself, it's not easy to understand how he thought his brother could. But he had become a Hoper once more.

In return for all this apparent largesse, Junius wrote his brother an ode:

> Go noble brother
> Enrapt in God and God enrapt in thee
> Leave this thy country this the boasted free

And plow old oceans rolling tumbling wave
To meet the living man the just the brave . . .[71]

Alcott's belief in transmission by means of oceanic tumbling was about to be
realized literally.

On May 6th Alcott left Concordia for Boston and the good ship *Rosalind*,
"furnished by his friend Emerson with all the means to accomplish his voyage
and visit to England," as Abigail wrote in her journal. "Noble friend!" she
added.[72] Her husband was thinking on the same lines. The following day he
wrote her a graceful and loving letter: "More than ever as I leave this friend do I
feel the more deeply the worth of this friendship; it is the highest prize (but one)
in Life's Lottery in which I have been the lucky, taking the great ones—a wife,
whose worth I am living to appreciate the more and more, and this unparalleled
friend." He thought that by showing him that he was loved, the voyage would
reclaim him "from the injustice of that bigotry into which I was fast falling."

He had transmogrified from being on the borders of frenzy to believing
himself one of the lucky in the space of a mere three months. "My passage is
paid," he reminded Abigail gleefully. There were ten sovereigns in his red
pocketbook along with a bill of exchange for £20, and other amounts were
secreted in his trunks. He itemized this new-found wealth with a miser's—or
indigent's—care.

He showed the same eye for detail in respect of his provisions. The fine
loaves Abigail had cooked for him were in the steward's storeroom, along
with a jar of applesauce. "The apples and crackers are accessible at any
moment," he told her.[73] If fruit was the key to redemption, it was essential to
be able to get hold of it at short notice, particularly when exposed to all the
dangers of "old oceans rolling tumbling wave."

Luckily Alcott was unaware of a transaction taking place on shore. A
lawyer called Manlius C. Clarke went to call on Elizabeth Peabody. He
explained that he had acquired 750 unbound copies of *Conversations with
Children on the Gospels*, and was going to sell them as waste paper to a trunk
maker for the sum of $50.[74] Future transatlantic passengers might be stowing
their luggage in cabin trunks lined with the compacted residue of Alcott's
first great experiment, while he set off to inaugurate the second.

4

Fabling of Worlds

THE VOYAGE LASTED THREE weeks (it was a period of transition in transatlantic crossing—vessels had steam engines generating 400 horsepower or so, as well as sails).[1] As the *Rosalind* made its way past the Newfoundland Banks, Alcott led a Conversation on reform. He must have let his dreams of utopia carry him away because his fellow passengers thought at first he was simply spinning pleasing fables. But by persevering, Alcott was able to make them believe in the concreteness of his proposals (so he thought), enacting on an intellectual level the very journey he was making on an elemental one, and achieving conversational landfall: "Before we closed I succeeded in taking firm and vigorous root in the solid terra firma of reality."[2]

The "Cottage bread," baked in Concordia, lasted the best part of ten days. The steward scalded and sugared his applesauce so it remained edible even longer. As for the apples themselves, several were still sound by the time the ship glided into the English Channel. He had given some to other passengers. "Apples I shall henceforth always recommend to all my friends who may try this Brine."

The *Rosalind* arrived off the English coast, "in this fairie water," on May 30, 1842. A waterman came aboard; several others hove into view. "It seemed like meeting neighbors to see these bluff hearty persons, and hear them speak in their rude brogues." Like so many Americans, Alcott felt that in arriving in England for the first time he was returning to a place where he belonged, another enactment in small of the Eden project. Sure enough that evening, after he went late to his berth, he found his mind teeming with possibilities: "Troops of gentlest, fairest, sublimest thoughts usurped my brain all night, I slept not, but was planting Edens—fabling of worlds—building kingdoms and men—taking the hands of friends and lovers—of wife and babe . . ."[3]

On Sunday June 5th, Alcott took a steamer up the Thames to central London, lodged at the London Coffee House, and walked out to see the sights. St. Paul's, it seemed to him, was an emblem of what was wrong with Christianity. It stood so high above the multitude they could not hear its message. "Christendom mortar and stone—its Christ a Ghost and its Priests ossified at the heart."

Two days later, on the Tuesday, he cashed in his bill of exchange and then went off to see if he could find Charles Lane at his office in Liverpool Street. It's easy to imagine his feelings on that summer morning. Here he was in London, with money in his pocket (for once), about to meet the group of philosophers and utopians who had admired, and been influenced by, him during the last few dark years when he seemed to be regarded with contempt by many in his own country. Lane would take him to James Pierrepont Greaves himself, the man with an "influence not unlike that of Jesus"—the man whose ideas strangely meshed with his own.[4]

Sure enough Lane was sitting at his desk, and was delighted to see him. But he had some dreadful news.

Greaves, the very man Alcott had come over an ocean to see, had died on March 11th, breathing his last at the exact hour, Alcott realized (smudging the dates slightly), "when the Divinity moved me to visit." Junius's ode had celebrated his brother's journey across the ocean "to meet the living man the just the brave," but sadly the living man had been dead for some weeks by the time the *Rosalind* set sail.

Nevertheless Greaves's work lived on, as the *Healthian* pointed out, describing the dead man's belief that "there subsists an eternal, sensibly realizable connection between the human soul and Deity; that God ever impregnates it with new seeds of love, intelligence, and virtue; that the development of these seeds is, consequently, an awakening of divine nature in humanity." This wasn't simply an obituary; it was an agenda. "The fostering influences best adapted for such an evolution are the object to be contemplated in all societarian arrangements."[5]

It may have been Lane himself who penned these words. Certainly Alcott could be in no doubt that the magical rapport between his own ideas and those of the English Transcendentalists was still intact. Here in the reaction to Greaves's death was that familiar imagery of seeds and planting—except of course that it wasn't imagery at all, it was the same process of propagation as in the vegetable world but taking place on the spiritual level. The connection between the human soul and the deity was eternal, but it was also "sensibly realizable"—that is to say, it was tangible, as tangible as those very apples Alcott and his fellow passengers had munched so happily while they sailed across the "Brine." There were "societarian arrangements" to investigate and pursue. That afternoon, he and Lane went over to Ham.

It was "like returning home after the absence of a few days, so familiar, companionable, was all about me." He was three thousand miles from anywhere he had ever been before. His sense of déjà vu was proof in itself of the validity of Transcendentalist perspective, providing a powerful example of the repetitive inner structure of things. Henry Wright was a "younger disciple of the same Eternal Verity," and Alcott found that sitting in on the school Wright ran with his new wife "seems like being again in the Temple."[6] It was called the Alcott House School, after all.

If anything, the English Transcendentalists had produced "a purer version of the same scripture a brighter revelation of the same Divine Idea in thought and act." Greaves had believed that the "Americans at Boston" possessed more grasp of humankind's true predicament than his own immediate circle could; excited and flattered by his reception at the Concordium, Alcott was only too ready to return the compliment to the English at Ham. "England is in advance of America in the province of thought and action wherein I have dwelt so long, and with so little company to cheer me in my work." In "the culinary department," domain of Mrs. Wright, "a most happy, sensible and affectionate person," the Concordium echoed Alcott's own dietary practices, and (almost unimaginably) achieved a greater austerity than that of Concordia: "The living [i]s simpler even than ours," he told Abigail.[7] So keen was he to make his two spiritual dwellings, on their different sides of the Atlantic, indistinguishable from each other that in one letter to Abigail he referred to the cottage in Concord as "that Concordium," while in another to his daughters he described Alcott House as "another Home—another Concordia."[8]

Everywhere he detected the lingering influence of James Pierrepont Greaves. "I am not bereft of his presence and society," he claimed. "I write these lines, while sitting on the couch from where he was borne to the village cemetery, and on the table where he was wont to delineate his mystic thoughts." The disposition of furniture had been an important part of the Temple School's achievement, providing a physical scaffolding for spiritual intercourse. Now Alcott sat himself on the couch where Greaves's body had lain, wrote at the desk his counterpart had used. He was doing all he could to find again the exact place in the world occupied by his fellow mystic, to reconstruct his viewpoint. He didn't feel despondent at the bereavement. The whole point about Greaves's philosophy was its optimism. "He was the Prophet of the deepest affirmative Truths, and no man ever sounded his depths."[9]

That may have been true, but in his disciple Lane Alcott discovered a man who could give Greaves's formulations a sharper edge and a more practical spin, without, however, quite solving some of their underlying paradoxes and clearing up all the loose ends. Lane was an energetic, assertive man of forty-two, just a year younger than Alcott. The one photograph we have of him, taken much later in life, shows a strong, rather hard-looking face, with not a hint of a sense of humor. He looks every inch the tough Victorian businessman, as befits the editor of a journal monitoring commodity prices. But at the same time, he was an idealist who envisaged the total replacement of society by a new utopian ordering. A year previously he had written an essay called "The Third Dispensation," originally as the preface to the translation of a work on the theories of the French utopian thinker Charles Fourier but reprinted as a free-standing pamphlet that same year by Pestalozzi Press, the Alcott House printers. Alcott pasted a copy of it into his autobiographical collections for 1842, so reading it was obviously a seminal part of his experience that summer.[10]

Lane identifies the three dispensations as family or tribal, national, and association. On the face of it this chimes in with Alcott's own notion that society's transformation begins with the family and seeps out to the larger community and thence to the world as a whole. However Lane didn't quite see it like that—for him each stage superseded the one before. We are currently in the second dispensation, awaiting the final one, now due. Unfortunately the familial perspective has not been successfully cast off and is breaking society down into cliques and factions. True, in the essay Lane does make use of an analogy drawn from the family structure, and this may have lulled Alcott into a false sense of security. "In a family," Lane says, "the children are born one after the other, links in the generative chain, but," he goes on to say, "they are not consequences one of another, but each separately and distinctly is the consequence of a separate act in the parents."

The fact that he talks of a sibling sequence rather than successive generations through time reflects Greavesian skepticism about the frequency and sustainability of pure reproduction. Lane is explaining away the fact that history consists of fits and starts rather than consistent amelioration, that "alternate links of gold and iron succeed each other." The point is that each of history's phases is referable back not to the one before but to "an antecedent generative causant, from which all flow."[11] It's a doctrine that can free enlightened members of each generation from the heritage of its predecessor. One dispensation doesn't follow another as cause and effect, but rather represents a new influx of the eternal spirit on humankind.

Alcott had a very different view, though he may not have realized it. He was fascinated by the sibling relationships of his own children, the fact that they were so different from each other in character. Six years previously he had recorded the baptism of his (then) three children, Anna Bronson, Louisa May, and Elizabeth Peabody. But the occasion made him think about the way names persist through history. "Our genealogy is inscribed on the appellations of our children," he mused. Just as a name can persist through history, so can the spirit persist through the generations: "the spirit's ancestry finds embodyment in terrestrial parentage."[12] The result is that it is possible to track the record of souls through time—almost the diametrical opposite of Lane's point. As it happened each of his children had not merely a surname inherited from Alcott himself, but a middle name referring back to other ancestral lines—except for Elizabeth, of course, until the row with Elizabeth Palmer Peabody had allowed him to fix that anomaly and change his daughter's middle name to that of Abigail's distinguished ancestors, the Sewalls, affirming historical continuity in her case too.

Over the next few days Alcott became increasingly disillusioned with the English at large, or at least with Londoners. They all looked "bestial and ferocious," he decided. Each of them was like an animated castle, surrounded by defensive walls, equipped with the instruments for attack. "Every Englishman is a walking fortification—organized of blood, he believes in the necessity of spilling it."[13] But while he was falling out of love with the British in general, Alcott—unaware of the faultline that underlay the concept of family—was falling more and more in love with the community he had found at Ham. Alcott House did not merely reflect his values and principles but provided a pattern of living that he would take back with him and which would act as the basis for life at Concordia and subsequently at Fruitlands.

Members rose early—at five-thirty in the summer months—had a cold shower, and dressed. The women wore no corsets and the men wore blouses made of brown Holland or cotton ("similar to the dress worn by Tolstoi," as one member recalled later), checked shirts without neckcloths, and white trousers. They didn't wear hats but had their hair long instead (as well as sporting beards). They began the day by working in the gardens for an hour. These consisted of four acres, and provided the fruit and vegetables for the community. The gardener, Scott, was kind and benevolent, and particularly loved his orchard. According to H.S. Clubb, who joined the community the spring after Alcott's visit, "he felt as though every tree was a part of his own soul, and that he was so wrapped with them that their growth was promoted by his own mental influence being thrown into each tree, that there was, in fact, a close relationship existing between himself and the trees he planted."[14] Like Alcott, Scott cultivated an inward as well as an external garden, fusing myth and actuality. Samuel Bower, author of several pamphlets on utopia, and a chronicler of the development of the Concordium—as well as becoming, in due course, a member of the Fruitlands community—saw man as the superintendent of nature, with the task of preserving "unbroken the harmonic relationship between the things seen and unseen."

Needless to say, manure was not used. According to Bower it would affect the weather itself. "The bright sun is dimmed on its rising when first the vapours ascend from the dwellings of man—the atmosphere, thickened and darkened by the noxious mists exhaling from unnaturally decomposed matter, obscure its beams." Bower goes on to assert that no form of life, not even a fly, should be killed because each is an integral part of the totality of things. However extreme this position may seem, it points to modern ways of thinking about the relationship between pollution and climate change (not to mention the influence of methane gases from livestock), and about the vulnerability and interdependence of nature; above all, it represents a groping towards an ecological perspective—tendencies which would continue in the thinking of the Alcott House group on both sides of the Atlantic.

Bower imagines an "ingenious speculator" replying to his assertion in the following terms: "Then we must stay our hand from attacks even upon vegetable life, and never cut a cabbage or dig a potatoe." Quite right, replies Bower, unexpectedly. "It is probable, that in his more elevated state, man will never do either; the food conditions of his purer life will be found in those fruits of trees, shrubs, and plants which give off their produce periodically without interfering in any manner with life."[15] It is the logical culmination of Greaves's point about incorporating the living essence of the apple. If you cut a cabbage or lift a potato you kill the plant itself, just as you kill an animal in order to eat its meat. But pluck an apple, and you leave the tree intact and healthy.

We don't have the austere menu prepared by Mrs. Wright. In any case she gave birth in mid-July and her position as cook was taken over by a man called Robert Aitkin. Under his regime, breakfast consisted of porridge, strawberries or other fruit in season, and wholemeal bread prepared according to Sylvester Graham's recipe, with one innovation: the addition of raisins.[16]

After breakfast members went to work (industries and chores included tailoring, printing, shoemaking, blacksmithing, and baking as well as gardening) or to the school, as teachers or scholars, or indeed both. The school offered languages, writing and drawing, maths and sciences, music, dancing, domestic economy, gardening. The children had lunch at noon, the adults at one, a meal consisting of potatoes, asparagus, cauliflower, and other produce in season. More work in the afternoon, then time for reading or writing before the evening meal at six, like the midday one except for the addition of "filberts, almonds or raisins, and apples." Then members went for a walk or enjoyed the garden.[17]

It was Alcott's own way of life, only in a more orderly and communal form. And despite his earlier belief that perfection should spread outwards from the individual to the world at large via the structures—family, neighborhood—already in place, he was rapidly seduced by the utopia in which he found himself. For years he'd felt alone and unappreciated, and here was a community that revered him as a person and whose members lived their lives according to parallel beliefs. It must have seemed to him to have a reassuring concreteness after his time living on speculation and hope. As he had insisted in his Conversations on the *Rosalind*, what appears to be fable can turn out to be reality. That grounding, after all, was essential if the Garden of Eden were to be planted again. Henry Wright, for example, had a remarkable ability, more astounding than his own, to achieve intellectual landfall. "What I have dreamed and stammered, and preached and prayed about so long," Alcott claimed modestly, "is in him clear, definite; it is life, influence, reality." But the Concordium as a whole shared these qualities. It was lively; it represented interpenetrating influences across the Atlantic; it manifested itself in an actual house and place. Alcott reckoned there were more than thirty children at the school, mostly aged between three and twelve.[18]

A utopian future was within reach. In one of his pamphlets, *The Peopling of Utopia*, Samuel Bower explained that the new dispensation could be brought into being without causing any harm to the social fabric around it (just as a fructivore could satisfy his bodily needs without the need to kill anything). Word would be spread through the newspapers and journals as well as by modern methods of travel, he pointed out in *A Sequel to The Peopling of Utopia*. The railway was not simply an instrument of communication but a model for utopian economics. It had been established in 1830, and succeeded simply because it was a manifest improvement on the use of roads. As a result, after a mere eight years, forty million pounds was invested in it. In the same way, a community established in 1840 could demonstrate that the way of life it offered was superior to that of conventional society. Following the same incremental law, this meant that by 1848, "500,000 persons would be living in communities, and there would have been expended for that purpose forty millions, or £80 for each person." In fact, Bower went on to claim, he thought the real figure for community membership by 1848 was more likely to be in the region of five million. Heady stuff for Alcott the Hoper to think about.

Bower concluded his sequel to utopia by making a comparison that must have seemed prophetic. Who would choose to cross the Atlantic by sailing boat when they could use one of the new steam-powered vessels instead? Somehow communitarianism and travel to America ended up in the same sentence:

> The great business, then, of the age is to form communities; when that shall have been done the people can no more refuse to avail themselves of that social improvement than can they who have occasion to cross the Atlantic now expose themselves to the risk and delay of a passage by even a "liner," when it is equally in their power to embark in a steam-ship, with the prospect of a much more speedy termination to the voyage.[19]

Alcott was a utopian American who had come to England for inspiration. This necessitated some rejigging of traditional mythology. The original European colonization of America was perceived as a repudiation of the past in order to fashion a New World, a westward journey to build a city on a hill. But Alcott had found inspiration by sailing east. "Brighter days are dawning on us," he told Abigail, "are, indeed, risen—to me here in this East, and shall appear soon on your horizon." However, though inspiration might come from England, its transmission and ultimate fulfillment would involve another westward journey, following the course of the sun. Henry Wright, he said, cherished hope of "making our land the place of his grand experiment in human culture."[20]

The early European settlements in New England were known as plantations, and Alcott eagerly latched on to the implications of the word. "It is not in Old, but in the New England, that God's Garden is to be planted, and the fruits matured for the sustenance of the swarming nations," he told his brother Junius, the task being to achieve "a new plantation in America." He became even more rapt in a letter to his cousin. By this time William Alcott, who was a year older than Bronson, had published a number of books, mainly on the benefits of a vegetarian diet (in years to come he would also produce dire warnings about the dangers of overexcitement in courtship, very much in accordance with Greavesian—and Grahamite—ethics.) His books, Bronson announced, were available in the Alcott House library. "Our freer, yet far from freed land is the asylum, if asylum there be, for the hope of man," he continued. "There, if anywhere, is that second Eden to be planted, in which the divine seed is to bruise the head of Evil, and restore Man to his rightful communion with God, in the Paradise of Good,—whereinto neither the knowledge of Death nor Sin shall enter; but Life and Immortality shall then come to light, and man pluck wisdom from the tree of life alway."[21]

He was less over the top to Junius but nevertheless reasserted his faith in the efficacy of hope, proclaimed in the "Orphic Sayings" though contradicted (apparently) by their rude reception. "The heart's visions shall all be realized . . . I will hope ever even against all hope, for only in hope is the reality of life." "Real," "realize," "reality" beat like a pulse through the letters he wrote home during his first months away, as he celebrated the way the abstract could become concrete; that ideas could take form in the material world; that utopia could be grounded in physical locations.

Even Greaves's death could be seen as making a positive contribution. Alcott was hostile to the use of manure just as Greaves had been, but still death could make new possibilities germinate. The picture he drew was not of composting but traveling to richer ground, drifting over the Atlantic like pollen or spores released into the atmosphere, just as Greaves had envisioned when he wrote of elementary particles wafting across space like the scents from the Spice Islands. "My visit here has been most timely," Alcott told his brother (somewhat pragmatically). "Mr. Greaves on whom our friends leaned for support has just been withdrawn from them, and the ties that bound them to England are all loosened, and they can never transport themselves so well to a more fertile soil."[22]

It was one thing for Alcott to settle into the inevitably welcoming environment of Alcott House; quite another to go along to Cheyne Row in Chelsea and call on Thomas Carlyle. But his trip had been funded by Emerson, and Emerson was anxious that his friends should meet each other.

Emerson and Carlyle had been friends since 1832. Indeed, Emerson had written an introduction to the American edition (1836) of Carlyle's first major work, *Sartor Resartus*, which in its struggle to assert faith—an "Everlasting Yea"—in the face of a mechanistic world, had an influence on the development of New England Transcendentalism. In 1837 Carlyle had established himself as a major historian with the publication of *The French Revolution* in three volumes.

The relationships he had with Alcott and Carlyle drew on two different sides of Emerson's own character. Carlyle tapped into his tough-minded, witty, skeptical intelligence, Alcott into the idealistic mysticism that lay rather uneasily alongside it, sometimes, as far as lectures and essays were concerned, within the scope of a single paragraph. Emerson wrote a letter of introduction to Carlyle which urged him to forget anything he had heard about Alcott before making up his mind about him, in particular to ignore any writings to which his name was attached. He continued to feel uneasy about the meeting, writing on July 1st, "My friend Alcott must . . . have visited you before this and you have seen whether any relation could subsist between men so differently excellent."[23] Sure enough Alcott had made his visit just six days previously.

Carlyle saw a man "with long lean face and figure, with . . . grey worn temples and mild radiant eyes." Alcott saw a man in "a dark hour," whose "every merriment had madness in it." He found Carlyle's devotion to history self-destructive, his own ambition being to re-establish the world as if history had never happened in the first place. In Carlyle's words, he was "all bent on saving the world by a return to acorns and the golden age." Carlyle was hardly likely to be impressed by Alcott's enthusiasm for the Alcott House group or his reverence for their dead leader. "I knew old Greaves myself," he told Emerson later, "and can testify that few greater blockheads (if 'blockhead' may mean 'exasperated imbecile' and the ninth-part of a thinker) broke the world's bread in his day." He did his best to dredge up some affection for Alcott, for Emerson's sake. "He comes to me like a veritable Don Quixote, whom nobody can even laugh at without loving."[24]

In July Alcott visited Carlyle again and stayed the night; this time the two men quarreled outright. "He the Cynic," Alcott complained, "and I the Paradise-Planter." In the morning, Carlyle sent out for some strawberries for Alcott's breakfast. To his horror, Alcott put them on his plate along with potatoes, so that "the two juices ran together and fraternized." The Concordium prospectus published the year before had proclaimed that fruit and vegetables should be "combined novelly," but the novelty appalled Carlyle (who in any case suffered from chronic gastric problems). He couldn't eat any breakfast himself, but instead "stormed up and down the room."[25]

Carlyle and Alcott were about as compatible as the contents of Alcott's plate. In Alcott's opinion Carlyle consumed the past and was being consumed by it in turn—"there lay smouldering in him a whole French Revolution." For Carlyle it was vegetarian Alcott who was trying to bite off more than he could chew. "What a view must a man have of the universe," he remarked to Emerson, "who thinks 'he can swallow it all', who is not double and trebly happy that he can keep it from swallowing him!"[26] He catches exactly the totalizing aspiration of the radical Transcendentalist, as well as Alcott's confidence that diet could provide a way into the second Eden, just as it had created a miserable exit from the first.

Carlyle was the embodiment of the past; Alcott House of the future. On July 6th that future was discussed in a public meeting held there and enthusiastically advertised in the *Morning Chronicle* the day before: "An open meeting of the friends of human progress will be held tomorrow . . . for the purpose of considering and adopting means for the promotion of the great end." A. Bronson Alcott, Esq., would take the chair at three o'clock and again at seven, the invitation proclaimed.[27]

As it turned out, the friends of human progress numbered "some sixteen or twenty of us assembled on the lawn at the back of the house." This slightly disappointing turnout did nothing to dampen the utopian fervor, however. Language itself, in true Greavesian fashion, was being born anew. "When a word failed in extent of meaning," Lane claimed in his account of the meeting, "we loaded the word with new meaning." If they had adhered to the established meaning of a word, their perspective would simply repeat that of the past. By redefining words, an escape from history was possible. "The word did not confine our experience, but from our own being we gave significance to the word . . . a word is a Proteus that means to the man what the man is."[28] In the *Union* magazine a couple of weeks later he advocated the replacement of literature's "fine words" with the "being" quality of spoken language. "The old black spirit may have its antiquated black letter; the new white spirit will have its new white type."[29] This chimed exactly with Alcott's disillusionment with the printed word as a result of Emerson's reaction to *Psyche* and the public ridicule of his "Orphic Sayings" as well as with his belief that Conversations and letter writing were the appropriate media for the transformation of the world. "The thoughts and desires of men wait not thereby the tardy and complex agencies of booksellers' favour, printer's type, reader's [sic] chances," he had told his journal, "but are sped forthwith far and wide, by these nimble Mercuries."[30]

Three papers by three different speakers were delivered. It is not known for certain who gave which, though a guess can be made that the first, "Reformation," was delivered by Wright, the second, "Transition," by Lane, the last, "Formation," by Alcott. In a sense it is beside the point to assign individual authorship, because common cause was being made. By the same token, despite the advertisement, no one acted as chair. This was Alcott's own decision. "Mr A. Bronson Alcott of Boston, U.S., was invited to preside, but, faithless in the authority of Chairs or Presidents, he was not formally appointed, and the company proceeded to business in good order, based on the spontaneous feeling in each."[31]

The first paper argued that political and social activism only attracted the hostility of the authorities, so that individual reform was the way forward. The second gave a more radical spin to that argument, advocating an opt-out from the political and religious establishment altogether, anarchism in effect. "We, therefore, ignore human governments, creeds, and institutions," the speaker declared, "we deny the right of any man to dictate laws for our regulation, or duties for our performance; and declare our allegiance only to Universal love, the all-embracing Justice."[32]

The third paper tackled the most vexing question of all: How do you get there, from here?

It is the old problem: "The Generation of a new race of persons is demanded." Alcott, if it was he, produced a crackling list of paradoxes to illustrate the problems associated with birth, "the most sacred, the most profane, the most solemn, the most irreverent, the most godlike, yet possibly the most brutal of acts." Birth is the moment when the most fundamental conflict of humankind is played out, "the point on which God and Devil wage most irreconcilable warfare." Perhaps it is appropriate to see the struggle in these medieval terms, with good and evil being personified, since morality as such hardly comes into it. The real issue here is that of cause and effect. Words can be loaded with new meaning, but they need new men to load them, and where are the new men to come from? If our present civilization is corrupting, then any would-be utopians born within it will find their endeavors are corrupt too.

The answer was one new-minted at Alcott House: emigration to America. Society as presently constituted invades all the basic human relationships—so the trick is to go elsewhere, "to select a spot whereon the new Eden may be planted, and man may, untempted by evil, dwell in harmony with his Creator, with himself, his fellows, and with all external natures." Providence has ordained that this spot should be New England, "the field wherein this idea is to be realized in actual experience." That insistent thrum of reality once more, of actuality, of experience. Alcott and his colleagues may have lived deep inside their own heads, but they never stopped scrabbling at the solid world beyond. New England was only a solution, however, provided one bought into the old mythology that it was genuinely new, that America was a place without a history, without a government, without a society even. Perhaps, in his revulsion at old English oppression and his enthusiasm for the enthusiasts at Ham, Alcott temporarily convinced himself that was the case. "We propose not to make new combinations of old substances," he explained, "the elements themselves shall be new." A "better body shall be built up from the orchard and the garden" (no mention of farming) and as a result an "unvitiated generation and more genial habits shall restore the Eden on Earth."[33]

In short, Eden will be rediscovered in America. A century and a half previously Abigail Alcott's great-great-grandfather, Samuel Sewall, had made exactly the same case, arguing that America would be the location for the New Jerusalem, and providing a famous evocation of its beauties:

As long as any Salmon, or Sturgeon shall swim in the streams of *Merrimack*; or any Perch, or Pickeril, in *Crane Pond*; As long as any Cattel shall be fed with the Grass growing in the Medows, which do humbly bow down themselves before Turkie-Hill; As long as any Sheep shall walk down upon *Old Town Hills*, and shall from thence pleasantly look down upon the River *Parker*, and the fruitfull Marishes lying beneath; As long as any free and harmless Doves shall find a White Oak, or other Tree within the Township, to perch, or feed, or build a careless Nest upon; and shall voluntarily present themselves to perform the office of Gleaners after Barley-Harvest; As long as Nature does not grow Old and dote; but shall constantly remember to give the rows of Indian Corn their education, by Pairs: So long shall Christians be born there; and being first made meet, shall from thence be Translated, to be made partakers of the Inheritance of the saints in light.[34]

Now Alcott, homesick for his family, was also evoking the pastoral beauties of America. "Be loving little girls," he wrote to his daughters, "and grow more fair with every day, and when I come to see my Garden plot, then shall the flowers all blooming scent the fields around my lot . . ."[35]

When Emerson got to hear that Alcott had convinced the leaders of Alcott House that America offered the prospect of Eden, he was horrified, and put pen to paper at once.

5

Rembrandt's Pot

THE IDEA THAT BRONSON ALCOTT had sold a utopia in Massachusetts to a bunch of Englishmen shook Emerson to the core—particularly because he felt implicated in the potential disaster, as it was he who had sent the paradise planter across the brine in the first place. What was happening was the rabid transmission of the reforming zeal he had just described in the *Dial* in his "Lecture on the Times": "They bite us, and we run mad also."[1] He therefore wrote a letter which he insisted Alcott should show to Wright and Lane. In it he said that while the Englishmen might safely trust Alcott's theories, "they should put no trust whatever in his statement of facts."[2] Rather charmingly he had complete confidence that Alcott would show his admirers a piece of paper telling them how utterly unreliable he was.

Emerson confided his worry to Abigail, as tactfully as possible. "Mr. Emerson," she noted in her journal, "was greatly apprehensive that Mr. Alcott had dipped his pencil in Rembrandt's pot of gay coloring, and that his friends would find themselves in a barren field with no sun to cheer them." She herself took a more robust approach. We all have free will, she argued, and having chosen "the pioneer whose faith beheld the rising star," it was a matter of following him to "the Gate of Delivery."[3]

She was not free from doubt herself, however. In early July she visited an old mansion house that had been fitted up in Concord for Nathaniel Hawthorne. It contained the "sweetest arrangement" of "Etruscan vases" and "antique flower-stands" made from the old roots of trees; overall, a "scene of enchantment" that made her restive about her husband's "ideas of beauty" and the cramped domestic arrangements she had to cope with. "We have always been too crowded up. We have no room to enjoy that celestial privacy which gives a charm to connubial and domestic intimacy." This train of thought led her to admit "I am enjoying this separation from my husband."[4] It was pleasant, she realized, to have his voice conveyed through the written word for a while rather than to listen to him directly—somewhat contradicting her husband's whole philosophy of communication.

Nothing meanwhile could dampen Alcott's hopes. On August 2nd he wrote her a letter bubbling with plans. It was time to catch the packet back to Boston. Mr. Wright would come with him, and his wife and baby (only two weeks old) would embark later. Or maybe it would be better if Wright, too, delayed until next spring. The same for Lane: that would give time to sort everything out on both sides of the Atlantic. Wright was "an accomplished educator." He would begin his labors with the Alcott girls—and they would serve as the nucleus of the new institution.[5] After the failure of his Temple School he was prepared to let Wright take over that most vital of tasks rather than do it himself.

But there is an inconsistency here. It was the usual problem, the influence of generation on the one hand, that of education on the other. The Alcott girls were young, but they had all actually been born. The critical moment of generation was over in their case. Back in Concord even Abigail Alcott had begun to wonder if the die of personality was already cast by the time of birth. On her own birthday, July 26th, Junius took her and the children for a ride along the river in his little boat *Undine*. While they were bobbing along she told her daughters how much they meant to her, and then the theme of birthday made her start pondering about Louisa, the most difficult of the four. Abigail had suffered from depression while carrying her, "which accounts to me for many of her peculiarities and moods of mind," a diagnosis that corresponded with Henry Wright's analysis of the pitfalls of pregnancy (and with her husband's strident accusation that she was responsible for the stillbirth of their son). Louisa was liable to "the greatest volatility and wretchedness of spirit—no hope, no heart for anything, sad, solemn, and desponding." Despite all this, Abigail's overall verdict was positive: "Fine generous feelings, no selfishness, great good will to all, and strong attachment to a few."

Perhaps a certain amount of inconsistency could be swallowed by utopia. "God can make our very contradictions harmonize with his solemn ends," she wrote in her journal.[6]

Alcott's optimism, meanwhile, was based on his belief that a community could be lifted off the ground with the minimum expense. "It needs no costly apparatus, no expensive outlays; its apparatus and resources are the gifts and graces of its subjects." Indeed, he saw it as a kind of justification, celebration even, of the poverty he and his family had experienced over the years; the community, like a medieval monastery, would make "obvious to all, the sublimity of worldly indigence." Once again he had to juggle astronomy to show how the impetus for this brave new world came partially from the despised old one, in both a personal and geographical sense. "From this darkness that well-nigh swept my Sun from the heavens, rises my Genius again in this East, and I return to my own land to dwell in its rising light."[7] Lane was bowled over by his high spirits. In the *Union* magazine on August 1st he wrote: "The Yankees are famous fellows for going ahead, as everybody knows." Somehow he had managed to pick up the traditional view of Americans as can-do people from the most unlikely embodiment of that quality ever minted. "There is nothing that they cannot do as well as, and better, if they choose, than any other nation under the sun," he proclaimed happily.[8]

Perhaps the greatest puzzle of the whole Fruitlands episode is why Charles Lane, who gives every impression of being a shrewd operator, should have been willing to leave Alcott House, which was already established on principles he endorsed, and which was being run in an orderly way, to go off to America to live in cramped quarters in the hope that a community could be set up over there. Part of the explanation obviously lay in Alcott's eloquence, just as Emerson had feared. Lane had been sold the traditional picture of America as the New World, a place where pioneers can set about the task of building civilization from scratch—but of course there is an uncomfortable paradox in the very conjunction of "traditional" and "new." However business-like, Lane was susceptible to charisma, as he had already proved by becoming a disciple of Greaves in the first place.

The other factor was obviously the chicken-and-egg problem intrinsic in the English Transcendentalists' take on reproduction. The notion of an "unvitiated generation," composed of the pristine elements to be found in the wilderness on the other side of the Atlantic, as outlined in Alcott's paper on "Formation" given at the meeting on July 6th, seemed to present a solution to that problem. New bodies could be conceived in that new place, bodies that could serve as the outward manifestation of unsullied spirits.

This vision comes from a view of human propagation that denies married love; indeed that is most comfortable in thinking of reproduction in vegetable terms. But just as Abigail's concern about the size of Concordia Cottage was a straw in the wind, there was, in her husband's letter of August 2nd, a passionate uxoriousness, clearly heightened by being homesick. The night before, Alcott had visited a domestic household for the first time since his arrival. "This is the first Family, beautiful in its simplicity & purity, that I have seen in England." He tried to persuade them to emigrate: "I said my best for Concord, and may yet have them as neighbors." Back at Alcott House he read letters from Abigail and Emerson and then composed a poem to relieve his loneliness:

Unmated, lone, divorced, man cannot be:
Woman's the flesh wrought from his living side;
Through all her veins his purple currents run,
From every wave his fluent forms emerge;
Embracing her, himself he doth embrace—
Narcissus imaged in Love's mimic stream.[9]

Scant consolation in some ways, if Abigail was nothing more than his second self. Patently untrue, anyway, as Alcott himself would have acknowledged in another mood (if anyone was his second self, it had been the late James Pierrepont Greaves). The notion was probably derived from Lane— in a piece called "The True Life" which Alcott pasted into his scrapbooks, Lane claimed that "the spouse is an expansion and enlargement of one's self, and the children participate of [sic] the same nature."[10] Perhaps this narcissism, obviously derived from the account of Adam's rib, was Lane's way of abolishing the idea of a wife altogether. Nevertheless the next morning Alcott announced that Abigail was his "Queen at Concordia"; when he arrived back they would take their wedding vows all over again. "This few months Divorce," he told her, "is the sacrement [sic] of our Espousals—this Absence an Invitation of Guests to our Wedding—that meeting the Bridal ring at our reunion—those Children our chaplet of Loves."[11] What his fellow utopians, Lane in particular, might think at discovering that their role in America was to be guests at Bronson and Abigail's renewal of marriage vows, he doesn't predict. Over in Concordia at just about this time Abigail spotted a steamship announcement in a newspaper and penciled the word "Come!" against the sailing date of August 4th.[12]

Despite his homesickness Alcott wasn't quite ready yet. On August 11th a long-standing admirer of Greaves called R.W. Birch visited Alcott House, gave its eponymous hero a £10 note, and invited him up to Derbyshire.[13] Before leaving for the north, Alcott wrote to his wife again, explaining that Lane and his son would be coming with him to America after all, along with a brother of Wright's and a certain Miss Parsons. Abigail was slightly taken aback when she received this letter on September 4th. She had expected him back by then, and the proposed entourage gave her food for thought. "May I keep my mind and judgment unbiased!" she told herself fervently.[14]

Meanwhile Alcott had gone off to Derbyshire to acquire books and demonstrate the importance of generation—as he perceived it—by exploring his family tree. Again, if Lane was aware of this motive, he should have taken it as a warning. On arriving back at Alcott House, Alcott edited the September issue of the *Healthian* and then on September 7th members held a "property convention." "The Parliament will commence at 3 o'clock," they announced, "but your presence at an earlier hour will be esteemed. A simple repast of vegetables will be provided at half-past 1 o'clock."

Some idea of the scope of the discussion is apparent from a letter to Alcott written after the event by a woman called Sophia Dobson, who had been in the audience. "Do you intend to do without government?" she asked. She herself felt it was reductive to see government only as a protector of property. Her own opinion was that "there is a heart to everybody, and surely there should be one to society." She had not quite decided whether she agreed that property owning should be abolished altogether. She also wondered about clothing. "Of course you intend to simplify clothing as well as food,—do you think you can do this to such an extent as to put it in the power of every man to fabricate his own?—I doubt whether this be feasible—besides which would not this cause a great waste of time and labour?" She was also disturbed by one of Lane's more radical suggestions: "Mr Lane said he wants to abolish ships and railroads—that seems to me unreasonable."[15]

It was now firmly decided that these extremely radical ideas would be best fulfilled in America. Lane and Wright would definitely come back with Alcott (Mrs. Wright and the baby remaining behind, and no further mention of Miss Parsons). About this time a Mr. Bennett from Switzerland visited, and slipped Alcott another £10 note, clearly the going rate for an encounter with the impoverished genius. It is worth noting that it had the buying power of around £770 today.[16] Mr. Birch of Derby kindly sent Alcott some china objects, a Cupid in a bed of flowers and a figurine with the theme of "Goodnight Mother."[17]

Abigail, meanwhile, went to check out another couple of properties. The Hosmer place at Stowe wasn't big enough "to accommodate so large a family," she decided, and though she would like to be nearer Boston, she felt it might be wise to find somewhere more remote from neighbors. Meanwhile, the Codman farm in Lincoln was large, but "I dare not dwell long on any place till I have seen the persons." Given that the money to pay for a large property could not possibly come from the Alcotts themselves, that was probably a wise decision. Again there is a background hum of anxiety. "My children, I am sure, must be benefited," she told herself, and "if *they* are, surely then am I not injured." "I live, move, and have my being in them," she had written in her diary a couple of months previously.[18]

Still, she scrubbed Concordia Cottage in preparation for the arrival of her husband and his new friends. "The lord of our house and life shall find that his servants and lovers have not slept or idled during his absence from the field of labor," she told her journal, apparently without satirical intent.[19]

Over in Ham, Alcott and Lane were boxing up Greaves's books to bring with them to the States. A meeting of the Health Association took place on September 19th at the perhaps inappropriate venue of the Leathersellers'

Building at London Wall. There was a big crowd since it was Alcott's last public appearance before he left the country. Lane told the audience that "it is a man's duty, by eating, to build up a holy body; it is the true object in marriage to generate a holy family," while Alcott explained that "all disease originates in the soul—the body but reports the state of the soul: the diseased have sinned"—a bald restatement of the doctrine that caused his wife to seem so unsympathetic about the death of little Waldo and so many other children in the Boston area.[20] A year or two previously Alcott had calmly told Henry James Sr., father of the novelist and an important member of the Boston intelligentsia in his own right, that he himself had never sinned.[21]

Just over a week later, on September 28th, Alcott, Lane, and Henry Gardiner Wright, together with Lane's ten-year-old son William, embarked on the ship *Leland*, the only passengers to have state room berths, as Alcott gleefully noted later, forgetting in this instance the sublime nature of worldly indigence.[22] They had brought a sack of oatmeal and one of corn with them, and their steward baked them a loaf every day. The ship's cook made sure he didn't pollute their food with meat grease.[23]

The *Dial* prepared to greet the new arrivals. Its October issue featured a piece by Emerson on "English Reformers" as well as Lane's debuts in the magazine: a rather conventional essay on Cromwell (hero and man of action who ultimately failed to follow through) and the first installment of a long two-parter on Greaves. In his article Emerson surveyed the blizzard of material Alcott had sent him from Ham. "Here are Educational Circulars, and communist Apostles; Alists; plans for Syncretic Associations and Pestalozzian Societies, Self-supporting Institutions, Experimental Normal schools, Hydropathic and Philosophical Associations, Health Unions and Phalansterian Gazettes, Paradises within the reach of all men, Appeals of Man to Woman, and Necessities of Internal Marriage illustrated by Phrenological Diagrams."[24]

"These papers have many sins to answer for," Emerson added, seeing the earnest to-ing and fro-ing on the part of the English reformers as insectile and pointless. Of course he is leading up to a big "but" in which he identifies what is praiseworthy in their ideas—he could hardly do otherwise, with his friend's return imminent. Nevertheless, throughout the piece there is an undercurrent of humor which he knew Alcott was unlikely to spot. Implicit in the whole tone and stance of the article is a suggestion that all this tumultuous enthusiasm is po-faced and lacking in irony or self-awareness, that it represents a simplistic or naive approach to existence.

His brief survey of Greaves's life is a case in point:

> His active and happy career continued nearly to the seventieth year, with heart and head unimpaired and undaunted, his eyes and other faculties sound, except his lower limbs, which suffered from his sedentary occupation of writing. For nearly thirty-six years he abstained from all fermented drinks, and all animal food. In the last years he dieted almost wholly on fruit.[25]

It's telling how innocent-looking phrases—"nearly to the seventieth year," "except his lower limbs," "In the last years"—can subvert the apparently respectful recapitulation of a life of programmatic abstention intended to nourish, if that's the word, both body and spirit. By contrast, in his own essay on Greaves, Lane talks the language of a disciple, like Wright before him. Spending time with his mentor made "white days in the mind's calendar," he claimed. What Emerson picked up on was a weakness of the legs; what Lane saw, by contrast, was a man "bestriding the narrow world of literature like a colossus."[26]

Emerson treated Lane with respect in his piece. He knew of course that he would be having to deal with him in person shortly, but he also suspected that Lane had an intellectual rigor denied to his colleagues, including Alcott. He quoted enthusiastically and at length from "The Third Dispensation," struck by the way Lane wrestled with the vexed issue of cause and effect, the difficulty that "the external arrangements indispensable *for* the evolution of the Uniting Spirit can alone be provided *by* the Uniting Spirit."

Lane had illustrated this problem by explaining that it feels as though we are in an endless circle that has split into two halves (like a schoolboy's marble which has broken in two down the middle), so that each of them is spinning independently of the other. One half contains the "spiritual or theoretic world," the other the actual one, "a life of self-falseness and clever injustice." The former comprises a "set of principles," a static and consistent law; the latter, the contingencies, chaos, and blind alleys of human civilization as it has unfolded over the generations.[27]

Emerson himself had seen this problem in terms of a distinction between the stable world of nature and the volatile one of history. On the one hand there are the "rats in the wall, . . . the lizard on the fence," on the other the "village-tale" of history. "What does Rome know of rat and lizard?" he asked at the end of his essay on "History," published in 1841.[28] This corresponds with the Alcott group's vision of a perfect and abiding Garden of Eden from which humankind has been exiled and to which it will at last return. In his first "Orphic Saying," Alcott had shown how the very name he had given the *Dial* reflected the task of transcending time, as the heart learns to move in harmony with spiritual revolutions rather than post-lapsarian ones:

> Thou art, my heart, a soul-flower, facing ever and following the motions
> of thy sun, opening thyself to her vivifying ray, and pleading thy affinity
> with the celestial orbs. Thou dost
> > The livelong day
> Dial on time thy own eternity.[29]

None of the Transcendentalists could have intuited what was in store less than twenty years down the line—that instead of the temporal blossoming into the eternal, Darwin would heal the divide between nature and history by showing how nature itself was historical.

Emerson was less enthusiastic about Lane's suggestion as to how the two halves of the human circle were to be reunited. The Englishman's solution ultimately lay in "True Harmonic Association," in other words, the establishment of a utopian community. Emerson wasn't convinced. In his opinion, Lane "more justly confides in 'ceasing from doing' than in exhausting efforts at inadequate remedies."[30] Opting out of civilization's discontents was one thing; opting into a homemade paradise quite another. What Emerson had not taken on board at this stage was that the community when it came into being would show little sign of making exhausting efforts at inadequate remedies—that it would lay itself open to the charge of doing very little, indeed of going to the very verge of "ceasing from doing."

It wasn't clear when Alcott, Lane, Lane's son William, and Wright would finally turn up. They were expected on a daily basis for weeks. The Emerson household felt some uneasiness about what was approaching them across the Atlantic Ocean. Emerson's wife Lidian, for one, saw the voyagers as a threat to the Concord community rather than as a promise of redemption, proclaiming "loudly" on October 5th that "they shall not come into the good town," as if they were the vanguard of an invading army.[31] Meanwhile Abigail Alcott herself had cause to fear and resent the prospective landfall. Her brother Charles was staying at the cottage while she helped him try to sort out his life; now "both he and Junius must be displaced immediately for Mr. Wright," she told her other brother Samuel— another example of the ongoing struggle between the claims of family and those of community. "*They* can be only temporary sojourners," she adds bitterly, "as he is to be a permanent inmate." For her it was "a further abundance of care which I am to meet fearlessly and faithfully."[32]

The group finally arrived on October 20th. The *Leland*'s captain took Lane and Alcott (state room passengers, after all) ashore in his own boat. They walked around for a few hours, making visits and getting their land legs again. They had a meal in a Graham house, one of a number of establishments that had sprung up to offer refreshment in accordance with the dietician's theories. Lane, expert on prices, noted that the water and bread were provided free as long as you bought something else.[33] Then they journeyed to Concord—"With my friends, to my friends," Alcott serenely explained, giving ballast to this optimism by adding that Lane had brought £450 with him, money gained in the very heart of the commercial system he himself so despised since it had been earned by the *Price-Current*'s sharp-eyed monitoring of the going rate of every commodity imaginable.[34] The sum was the equivalent of $2,160, enough to fund a small community. Alcott had gone to England with Emerson's money, and come back with Lane's.

Junius, despite his impending eviction, enthusiastically bought into the trio's mission statement, playing with the paradoxes of old and New England, of past and future paradise, as he announced that the idealists had come to America "indulging the Hope that here in this *new* England a new (old) Eden shall be instituted worthy the instalment and reinstalment of Humanity to its design and destiny."[35] Abigail overcame her doubts: "Husband returned, accompanied by the dear English-men, the good and the true. Welcome to these shores, this home, to my bosom!"

Two days later, the household were taking a walk together when Louisa, then nine, asked, "Mother, what makes me so happy?"

Abigail welled up, unable to reply. The answer she wanted to give was Alcott's safe return, the "gentle sympathy" of these new friends, the embrace of nature, allegiances that rippled outwards from their biological family unit to the totality of the world. She was relieved when Lane answered for her, no doubt offering the child a cool analysis of the mechanics of happiness. After all, Emerson had quoted him in the current issue of the *Dial* as claiming that "it is when the sympathy with man is the stronger and the truer, that the sympathy with men grows weaker." No bosoms there. "Mr. Lane does not confound society with sociableness," Emerson had pointed out, always ready to approve a loner's stance despite his own tendency towards kindness and friendship.[36]

The party from England shoehorned themselves into Concordia cottage; Junius returned to his mother in Oriskany Falls in New York State. He had completed his task of replacing his brother during the English trip, but even Alcott, in the midst of his triumphant return, was aware of the paradox that a beloved family member was being displaced by idealists from far away. "I parted with you with sincerest grief," he told him, looking forward to a "joyful reunion" in the future.[37]

In effect the experiment ultimately known as Fruitlands now began, since the little group in Concordia immediately began to try to live according to their values, and thereby inaugurate a new society. The seed was planted. But from the very beginning there was uncertainty about the nature of the plant they were trying to grow.

PART 2

The Fruit

6

Hesitations at the Plunge

UTOPIA HAD BEEN INAUGURATED at Concordia Cottage. Emerson gave the travelers a cautious welcome. He was impressed by the thousand books they had brought with them, a combination of the Alcott House library and purchases Alcott himself had made in London and Derbyshire, but a little appalled by the unrelenting mysticism of their contents. "We shall scarcely need the moon any longer o' nights," he told his brother William, imagining the mass of cabalism giving off a phosphorescent glow.

Emerson also noted with some alarm that the collection included "9 or 10 volumes of Mr. Greaves's MSS, & some casts & prints of him & others." A few weeks later he explained to Margaret Fuller that the English Transcendentalists needed to outgrow their master's influence. Greaves practiced "Spiritualism from an armchair," he explained, perhaps thinking about that weakness in the great man's legs; moreover, any five sentences Greaves wrote were as good as any other five—for which reason, he confessed, he himself had read very few of them.

From the start he saw something overweening in the English visitors. In bringing their books, their Greaves memorabilia, and their "wonderful selves, they hardly believe that they have left anything behind them in England." But given this sense of superiority to the rest of their native country, Emerson suspected they would soon pick fault with America as well. Their egos were as fragile as Sèvres porcelain or tropical fruit; "the least non-reception of them in the thought & heart of those to who they come makes cruelty, futility, & confusion."[1]

True, Lane was convinced that America offered the best environment for utopian experiment. In an article penned shortly after his arrival he explained that it was a place where "perhaps every modal search for happiness has had a trial," adding that the publication of the *Dial* spoke well for the opportunities of spiritual discovery there. He had the pleasant sensation, he claimed, that America could be the source of "new psychical supplies" as well as physical plenty.[2] But it didn't take long for Emerson's suspicion to be confirmed, as the Englishmen took it upon themselves to explain America's deficiencies to him. Emerson's irritated response was, "Yea, but not in America only, but in the Universe ever since it was known, just this defect has appeared."[3]

He checked of course that Alcott had been as good as his word and had shown the Alcott House contingent the letter explaining that any practical suggestions he might make should be given a wide berth, as if he were some sort of utopian Typhoid Mary. The Englishmen were able to reassure him on that point. But it wasn't just a matter of establishing that Alcott had not victimized them: the larger question was whether they were victimizable in the first place, whether they could be gulled by or subordinated to another's will. Or, and this was obviously Emerson's main fear, whether they themselves would try to make victims out of other people. "Will you waste my time?" he wondered, "or, are you afraid I shall waste yours?" If both parties remained wary about being taken over by the other's agenda, then fine, "we shall agree like lovers."[4]

What particularly annoyed Emerson about them was a combination of analysis and vagueness, their inability to maintain concentration and attention. Even the relatively hardheaded Lane, he decided, showed this tendency. "When he has anatomized the evil, he will be called out of the room, or have something else in his head. Remedied it will never be."[5] Nevertheless, within days of the arrival of Alcott's party, Emerson was inviting Lane and his son to stay in his house for some weeks.

Obviously the immediate plan was to relieve the overcrowding in Concordia Cottage. In his opinion Lane had a sharper intelligence than his two colleagues, and he imagined how weary he must get at being closeted all the time with Alcott and Wright, "who cannot chat, or so much open the mouth on ought less than A New Solar System & the prospective Education in the nebulae." Enjoying the quiet of his own study as he did, Emerson was appalled at the thought of that endless gabble. "All day, all night they hold perpetual Parliament."[6] He was running a risk, of course, in offering the pugnacious Lane his hospitality—his "powers of conversation are so superior, that they tempt him continually to a little play for victory." Nevertheless, Emerson believed that "alone, man to man, he is found a very sincere, conscientious person."

But Emerson had a hidden motive too, as he later explained to Margaret Fuller. He was hoping to disrupt the utopia at the very moment of its inception. The real point was to thwart Lane's desire to re-establish the Garden of Eden by re-enacting, on a limited scale, humankind's subsequent expulsion from it. The idea was to use his house as "a sort of cooling furnace, or a place where he might be partially corrupted & fitted for the grossest realities of the Yankee land." The grossest realities would of course include square meals, apples from the forbidden tree. Emerson was intending to engage in diet warfare.

It didn't work. Lane "tried us for one day or two, & fled again." "Mr. Emerson's food is *too good* for my simplicity," Lane wrote to Oldham, back at Alcott House. "A month of it, I think, would finish me." He decided to visit Emerson sparingly, and always between meals.[7]

As the reformers explained their ideas, Emerson grew more and more appalled. He was beginning to regret his investment in the English adventure. What he had wanted was for Alcott just to be Alcott, living an exemplary life in a cottage, supported by admirers, including of course himself. There was no way Alcott was capable of making a success of the grand schemes he was promoting. A harsh note begins to enter Emerson's response. "But for a founder of a family or institution, I would as soon exert myself to collect money for a madman."[8]

Indeed, at times he began to succumb to slightly paranoid fantasies. He wanted to be rid of the lot of them. Perhaps they would all die. Equally, they might succeed in their plans—same result, they'd be out of his hair. One solution would be for them to simply take what they wanted. Or maybe convert others. It didn't matter what they did, in fact, just so long as they left him alone. They might be rude to him: fine, that would give him an excuse for breaking all ties. What Emerson needed, what the whole world needed, was that at all costs these reformers should "cease to hang there in the horizon, an unsettled appearance, too great to be neglected, & not great enough to be of any aid or comfort to this great craving humanity."[9]

It is a wonderful image of the deep disturbance in the atmosphere caused by the men on a mission, a dark cloud gathering over the "good town" of Concord. As Edward Emerson would later remark in a footnote to his edition of his father's diaries, "Mr Emerson was human . . . And his journal had to be his safety-valve now and then."[10]

Emerson accepted that a great change was afoot. Many voices were calling for union and the effect would be to renovate institutions and bring drudgery to an end. "But not in the way these men think, in none of their ways." Despite the perpetual parliament in the hothouse of Concordia Cottage, true union would be silent and separate. In one of the essays he had published the previous year, Emerson had described the Over-Soul, "the eternal One," a principle that unites humankind and indeed all things.[11] True union, ironically both silent and separate, is in fact in place already. It always has been, though only fitfully glimpsed. Ultimately his central interest was in such glimpses, in the experience of epiphanies like the one he had had himself while splashing through snow puddles on the Common. Any change would be a matter of authenticating and respecting an individual's capacity to have such visions.

From this perspective, the various schemings of the utopians seemed to him not merely redundant but a kind of betrayal. He made a distinction between the ideal on the one hand, this overarching connecting structure, and the sublunary domain of practical and pragmatic affairs on the other. "You may associate on what grounds you like," he reflected, "for economy, or for good neighborhood, for a school, or for whatever reason, only do not say that the Divine Spirit enjoins it. Do not gloze & prate & mystify."

Since he was himself a financial sponsor of his old friend, he was particularly indignant about Alcott's tendency to gloss over financial realities. "Here is our dear, grand Alcott says you shall dig in my field for a day & I will give you a dollar when it is done, & it shall not be a business transaction! It makes me sick." In an extract from the journals Alcott had published in the *Dial* only a few months earlier (at the very time in fact when he was packing to go to England at Emerson's expense), he had claimed that he was seeking "entire independence" and that if only he wasn't held back by poverty, he would already have achieved it. In other words, to feel free of economic and commercial imperatives, he needed to have profited by that very system (as he was now about to do by proxy, via Lane's earnings). When he talks in this vein Alcott seems to be endorsing a middle-class suburban version of the good life at a price, rather than a genuinely radical vision of a new social order (though suburbanism too needed to be invented, and in time he would play his part in inventing it).

For Emerson this was all the product of delusion, of a process of self-mystification. "Let us not 'say no, & take it'," he advised sharply, with pithiness born of impatience.[12] But despite his deep reservations, he did what he could to help his friends spread their proposals to the community at large. The Transcendental Club had become rather moribund but on November 7th he wrote to various members asking them to a meeting at his house to hear from "Messrs. Lane, Wright, & Alcott, who promise to unfold as far as they can their idea of a true social institution."[13]

How clear a picture they were actually able to give of their plans is hard to tell. Margaret Fuller alertly identified the basic twofold thrust of their Eden project in a letter she wrote Emerson the next day. She clearly resented the fact that Emerson seemed to be acting as a kind of surrogate proselytizer, spending time and energy on a cause not his own: "I suppose we poor private friends must not expect to hear from thee, dear Waldo, till it shall have been finally settled how many generations must live on 'vegetables.'" That was one half of the Alcott–Lane–Wright agenda: reform through diet. Its hoped-for end-product, as Fuller pointed out, was that man would "finally be reinstated in his birthright and walk the market place fair, strong, and pure as the Archangel Michael." But at the same time, the unregenerate world would have to be taught how to achieve redemption.

What worried Fuller was how long all this transformation of the world would take. "Alas, alas!" she exclaimed, the "poor privates"—those friends of Emerson choosing to remain uninvolved—were likely to be " 'left sitting', as the Germans phrase it, for a long time."[14]

She is clearly jealous that Emerson is busy with the arrivals at the expense of his other friends, herself in particular (she was deeply attracted to him). His absorption in their plans, as she saw it, removed the distinction between public and private, between friendship and society. Her fears were in fact unfounded, as this distinction was exactly the one Emerson was so at pains to maintain. Nevertheless her analysis went to the heart of one of the problems that would undermine Fruitlands. Were intimate relationships (particularly the whole concept of family) to be invoked simply as metaphors for communal bonding; was the notion of a distance between one's personal and public life to be discarded?

It is true that in certain respects the English Transcendentalists spoke very directly to Emerson, however suspicious he may have been about them generally. In the second part of his piece on Greaves, postponed until the January 1843 edition of the *Dial*, Lane quotes his master: "We must agree together in some third if we are to act together; it is not two but three who are to make the two, and that which unites them."[15] This number-juggling (one plus one equals three) is uncannily similar to Emerson's own account of the mechanism of conversation. "In all conversation between two parties, tacit reference is made as to a third party, to a common nature." That third party or common nature Emerson calls the "Over-Soul." "I feel the same truth how often in my trivial conversation with my neighbours," Emerson remarks, "that somewhat higher in each of us overlooks this by-play, and Jove nods to Jove from behind each of us."[16] Earthly dialogue proves to be just a manifestation of heavenly monologue.

Perhaps Fuller regrets the way two become three, and chatty neighbors transmogrify into Jove (the three proving just to be one, after all). But of course Emerson himself draws a different conclusion from this number-juggling than the enthusiasts at Concordia Cottage were doing, in their perpetual parliaments. For him the presence of the Over-Soul guaranteed the relevance of silence and separateness. The structure was in place; you didn't have to rush out to build it. Fuller had in fact no need to fear losing sight of him in a mob of reformers.

As for Lane, Alcott, and Wright, they were indeed determined to spread the word about their plans in the last months of 1842. A glimpse of them in action can be found in the pages of a book by Mary Gove Nichols, a radical and reformer in her own right who lectured to women on anatomy, and campaigned against the wearing of corsets. *Mary Lyndon or, Revelations of a Life: An Autobiography* is sometimes regarded as a novel, but is actually just what it so insistently says on the title page, with certain liberties taken here and there. It was published without further authorial attribution so that the title can be regarded as the writer's nom de plume rather than as belonging to an invented narrator. Actually she was quite heavy on names. Her maiden name was Sergeant; she had been unhappily married to a man called Gove; and eventually became Nichols when she married her second husband. She was Mary Gove during the period when her path crossed with that of the Concordians.

Mrs. Gove would have met them when they visited Lynn, Massachusetts, where she lived, some time in the November of 1842. In her book, however, she presents the encounter at an outdoor summer party, so that nature is at hand to be pontificated upon, and the "beautiful food" espoused by the reformers (she too was a follower of Graham's doctrines) could be contrasted with picnic tables piled up with "stuffed hams boiled, roast chickens, sausages, and minced pies, and other horrors compounded of the corpses of animals."

Gove was not impressed by Lane, or "Mr. Lang" as she calls him. She described him as "a tall, hard, Scotch-looking man," an image of grimness that seems to get some support from the one photograph we have of him, taken late in life. For Mary Gove, the problem with Lang/Lane was that he "looked as though he was appraising the oaks for shipping, measuring the sap in the maple trees, and calculating the number of pounds of sugar it would make." This impression may have resulted from her awareness that Lane had been the editor of the *Price-Current*. "Such a commercial countenance hardly fitted the idea of communism," she complains.

He spoke eloquently, however—his lecture "rang clear and beautiful as a silver bell" and almost convinced her, despite her suspicions. Alcott (Mr. Mooney, she pointedly called him) was "another bland, kindly communist, who rejoiced now in having Mr. Lang's help in converting refractory Americans to a creed containing much love and no money."

But Henry Gardiner Wright was a different matter altogether, as events were to prove, much to Lane's and Alcott's chagrin. In the book he is called

Mr. Lynde, a name that all but merges with that of the author's alter ego, Mary Lyndon, who sure enough falls for his charms at once. "His face was fair and beautiful like a babe's," she noted raptly; "his complexion was the rose and lily shining through a skin that was a transparent medium of a hereditary scrofula." Only infatuation could convert a skin disease into a romantic asset. And the clincher: "His collar was turned over *à la Byron*."[17]

It is therefore Mr. Lynde who transmits the utopian impulse to Mary, but her way of explaining how this happened sheds light on the assumptions of all the utopians from Concordia Cottage. The harmony generated by a guitar or violin, the narrator claims, can have the effect of making particles of wood from the instrument bond with the surface of the concert building's very walls. (In fact it's likely that Gove took this theory not from Wright but from Lane, who was an accomplished violinist and who would use musical analogy to describe the utopian impulse in an article he wrote a couple of years later.) The same process is true of souls, Gove/Lyndon explains: they can send their virtues outward just as Aeolian harps or orchestras can. After all, she points out, we have no difficulty in accepting that disease—"the small-pox, the plague, and more vital evils"—is transmitted in a parallel fashion. "There is a soul of evil and death in every plague particle that exhales from this human body"; indeed, "half the people we meet radiate more or less a death-sphere," she adds, unintentionally anticipating the language of science fiction. But by the same token, "there is a loving life flowing from the pure in heart; and there is healing in the touch of love and sympathy."[18] James Pierrepont Greaves himself could not have put it better. She has come extraordinarily close to propounding a theory of viral transmission, given that her era had not yet discovered how diseases are communicated.

Gove's imagery goes some way towards reconciling the two main tenets of the utopianism being promulgated by the inhabitants of Concordia Cottage. The individual can be redeemed through diet (just as Lynde/Wright's scrofulous skin was transformed into the rose and the lily as a result of his consumption of "beautiful food"). Then this spiritual health can be transmitted outward to society at large by means of a beneficent form of "plague particle." In this way it would be possible to blend passivity and activism, to allow oneself to be invaded by the goodness of nature, and to pass on the reward through busy commingling with one's fellows.

Which is just what Lane, Alcott, and Wright were doing as fall gave way to winter. They held Conversations on "Community Life," not merely in Gove's home town of Lynn but also in Boston, Providence, and Dedham, as well as in Emerson's house. They also took their message to the rival establishment of Brook Farm, where not everyone was impressed. One of the members, James Burrill Curtis, described their visit in a letter written in early November. "They are men of some virtues, I don't doubt," he told his father, "but they have a many great faults, exclusiveness, spiritual pride, egotism, & a certain supercilious supervisory peeping that I do not like."[19]

In the same period Alcott and Lane went to inspect the Codman place in Lincoln with a view to purchasing it for their experiment. A man called Thomas Davis visited them and discussed the possibility of investing some money—along with contributions from Lane, Emerson, and Abigail's brother Samuel May—to get the project off the ground.[20] Such practical negotiations emphasized for Emerson the materialism he feared lay at the heart of this version of Transcendentalism, and in mid-November he had a long and searching discussion with Alcott about his plans.

Alcott explained (using the impersonal passive to absolve himself from any financial responsibility) that "there should be found a farm of a hundred acres in excellent condition, with good buildings, a good orchard, & grounds which admitted of being laid out with great beauty; and this should be purchased & given to them, in the first place."

"You ask too much," Emerson told him. The simple fact of the matter was that anyone, given such advantages, would find it easy enough to live the good life. The trick was to achieve the same thing in adversity (to make something positive from "antagonism in the tough world," as he'd put it in his lecture on "Man the Reformer" a couple of years previously). A farm built out of poverty and toil would be a different matter entirely.

"But," replied A., "how is this to be done, how can I do it who have a wife and family to maintain?"[21]

It is hard to avoid interjecting, at a distance of over a century and a half, that he hadn't in fact made much of an attempt at maintaining his wife and family during the five years that had passed since the collapse of the Temple School. Indeed, Mrs. Gove perhaps hit the nail on the head when she reversed the Alcott predicament, claiming that Mr. Mooney's "ultimate providence . . . was an excellent wife, who clothed and fed him as a baby, and reverenced him as a divinity."[22]

Emerson answered Alcott bluntly. "He was not the person to do it, or he would not ask the question." The Spirit, he pointed out, doesn't demand land or exemption from taxes. On the contrary, "it manages . . . to occupy and enjoy all land, for it is the law by which land exists." Greaves had made exactly this point a few years previously. "These richly wooded Hills are mine—I enjoy their beauty," he claimed contentedly while looking at the countryside near Stroud, "exempt from the injurious cares of their legal owner." And a few years later Thoreau would claim in similar vein that without actually buying a farm he nevertheless "retained the landscape, and . . . have since annually carried off what it yielded without a wheel-barrow."[23] Emerson sadly summarized the problem as he saw it: "Their whole doctrine is spiritual, but they always end with saying, Give us much land & money." The true achievement would involve not acquisition but attitude. "I know the spirit,—*by its victorious tone.*"

As so often, Emerson concluded by trying to give the utopians the credit due to them. It is a powerful thing to make an act of commitment off one's own bat rather than to be edged forward by society, and this was the achievement of "our three adventurers." However, "the deductions to be made from each are the hesitations at the plunge, the reserves which they still make and the reliances & expectations they still cherish on the arm of flesh, the aid of others."[24]

Mrs. Gove gives a harsher account of these deductions and reserves. "How would he get a title to the land if he denied human government, and the right of any to own the soil?" one of the people attending the picnic asks Mr. Mooney. His reply, according to her, was that "His wife did not agree with him, and she could take a deed of a farm, in trust for a community."[25]

In the end, Emerson found it hard to withhold his blessing from earnest endeavor, however inconsistent and indeed hypocritical it may have appeared to him. A few days after his conversation with Alcott, he wrote to Frederick Henry Hedge, a Transcendentalist living in the midwest, that Alcott, Lane, and Wright "talk of buying a farm in these parts to realize their high ideals" and added: "May they prosper."[26]

7

The Mind Yields, Falters, and Fails

OUR THREE ADVENTURERS, Emerson called the utopians from Concordia Cottage. But there was another adult living in those cramped confines, as well as five children. What of Abigail Alcott?

Lane and Wright claimed to be impressed by American womanhood. "The greatest interior advantage which they observed in our community over theirs was in the women," Emerson reported. "In England the women were quite obtuse to any liberal thought; whilst here they are intelligent & ready."[1] It is a distinctly backhanded compliment, particularly given the insufferably patronizing tone—and one of those Englishwomen apparently obtuse to liberal thought was Elizabeth Wright, left alone so soon after her wedding to cope with a small baby. But the point must have reverberated through the years because we can detect after-echoes in the Camp Laurence picnic in *Little Women*, where comparisons are made between English and American girls. "Young ladies in America go to school more than with us," says the "starched-up Englishwoman"; "Young ladies in America love independence," announces old Mr. Brooke.[2] Certainly the adventurers were coming into contact with intelligent and confident women: Elizabeth Peabody, Margaret Fuller, and Mary Gove among them, though none of these proved to be exactly "ready" in their sense of the word. And of course

Abigail Alcott was also perfectly capable of forming strong opinions of her own.

On November 28th, Alcott wrote to his brother Junius, telling him that plans were afoot to establish their community. Two more couples, he hoped, would join them, but none of the women he expects to be involved in the enterprise merit a mention by name. "It looks now, as if we should take the place [Lincoln Farm]: ourselves, Lane, Wright, Robbins and wife, Greene and wife making our present family." And almost in the same breath as he sketches out this extended structure, he asserts that he is very much preoccupied with his own family—a typical Alcottian switch from one perspective to its alternative, probably caused on this occasion by the thought that the following day would be the birthday he shared with his daughter Louisa (she would be ten and he forty-three). He reiterates his thanks to Junius for all he did for the family during his own absence, talks of the children's gratitude, and asks Junius to give his regards to their mother. He doesn't, though, make a single mention of Abigail.[3]

The next day he wrote a letter to Louisa, as was his custom on their birthday, combining genuine affection with a slightly tiresome, detailed, and repetitive homily on the importance of behaving well (he was always worried about Louisa's wildness and passion). "The good Spirit comes into the Breasts of the meek and loveful," he told her, while "anger, discontent, impatience, evil appetites, greedy wants, complainings, ill-speakings, idlenesses, heedlessness, rude behaviour, and all such, drive it away." He concludes by asserting that as long "as she and her sisters come more and more into the presance [sic] of this spirit, shall we become a family more closely united in loves that can never sunder us from each other."[4]

Abigail would of course have seen this letter or listened to it being read out—it was part of the birthday ritual in the Alcott household. At some point that day she took time out from the festivities to make a long entry in her journal, giving her own take on daily life in the cottage and subverting her husband's high-minded epistle by laying claim to every one of the evils he listed. They were presumably sins to which Alcott thought Louisa was particularly prone. But Abigail identified strongly with her daughter, their shared "brown" coloring suggesting a shared temperament. By taking her faults upon herself she is acting as a mother in the teeth of the abstract idealism of the men in the household.

It is not the good spirit who is being driven away, Abigail claims—she herself is, into a form of internal exile while in the very bosom of her family. Circumstances, she begins, "most cruelly drive me from the enjoyment of my domestic life." While her husband is proclaiming his commitment to family, she expresses her own alienation from Concordia. The prevailing mood there is grim and humorless, she finds, and every time she makes a joke ("I am prone to indulge in occasional hilarity"), she is "frowned down into stiff quiet and peace-less order" ("ill-speakings"; "heedlessness"; "rude behaviour"). The atmosphere in fact is suffocating and she looks back wistfully to her five months of freedom while her husband was in England ("complainings"). She is tired of a monotonous diet of coarse bread and water, and the apples they have to eat are too hard for her teeth ("evil appetites"; "greedy wants"). At the same time she hates cooking so much that she'd rather do without; and she is desperate for a vacation ("idlenesses").

All in all it is the entry of a desperate woman, full of "anger, discontent, impatience." She comforts herself with the thought that the set-up in the household is in a transitional state, and that a change will be as good as a rest. "So I wait, or rather plod along, rather doggishly." But in the meantime she is actually afraid of losing her sanity. "The mind yields, falters, and fails."

Just as, consciously or unconsciously, she deconstructs her husband's ponderous advice to Louisa, so too does she take apart the condescending judgments she was hearing on the subject of female obtuseness versus relative intelligence and readiness. Abigail must have been exposed to the party line on this matter just like Emerson (and Louisa), and she makes one of gender warfare's counter-attacks. "They all seem most stupidly obtuse," she says of the men in her household, because they refuse to understand "the causes of this occasional prostration of my judgment and faculties." Unless they see what they are doing, it might be too late for her to recover or for them to atone for "this invasion of my rights as a woman and a mother." Clearly the battle lines are being drawn. She is defending not just her gender but her maternal role, which she senses will be undermined in the new dispensation.

After Abigail's death Louisa and Alcott read her journal. Louisa wrote "Poor dear woman!!" over this whole passage. Alcott meanwhile crossed out the word "all" in "They all seem most stupidly obtuse" and replaced it by "friends," implying that only Lane and Wright were to blame, not himself. It rather proves Abigail's point about the invasion of her rights as a woman—even the source of her pain could be retrospectively edited.

Abigail's conclusion: "Give me one day of practical philosophy. It is worth a century of speculation and discussion."[5]

The next day, serenely ignorant of what Abigail had just entered in her journal, Lane put pen to paper to write to his friend William Oldham, now in charge of Alcott House. It's a report from a different planet. "Mr and Mrs Alcott have made me very comfortable," he explains. He had a bedroom study with a cheerful fire; Wright brought his desk in sometimes so they could work side by side. The dwelling that was unbearably cramped to Abigail seemed quite spacious to Lane. Downstairs there was a parlor where the children had lessons or played. The community ate in a room beyond it. The cottage had carpets and mats which kept them warm and quiet.[6] The reason he communicates these apparently petty details of their lives is because he wants to make clear that the utopian experiment has already begun. Some years later Thoreau would explain in his book *Walden* that he went to the woods because he wanted to live "deliberately," and that adverb describes just what the Concordians are doing.[7]

Lane sees the way of life they have already established as the blueprint for an enterprise on a grander scale. True, the members are in a "transitional" state, as Abigail remarked—even after the move to Fruitlands they would still be on the lookout for more desirable premises. But transition is in fact a part of the utopian program, as had been established in the second of the addresses at the Alcott House meeting for friends of human progress the previous June. "In all respects," Lane told his friend, "we are living or trying to live as we should in a larger community."

Perhaps it was the thought that a larger structure would make the family metaphor redundant which led him on to a consideration of Abigail Alcott. "Mrs. A. has passed from the ladylike to the industrious order," he claimed airily, "but she has much inward experience to realize." Lane clearly has no qualms about shaping Abigail Alcott to fit the utopian structure. "Her pride is not yet eradicated," he tells Oldham, rather as though she were a horse needing to be broken in. The problem is basically that "her peculiar maternal love blinds her to all else"; he loftily claims solidarity with her plight by asking "whom does it not so blind for a season?"[8] (One could answer that rhetorical question with the name of Henry Gardiner Wright, since parenthood had not been allowed to stand in the way of his American adventure.) After little more than a month together, tensions among the inhabitants of Concordia Cottage have already been ratcheted up. A few weeks more, and the whole structure of the community would begin to crack under the strain.

Nevertheless, from the point of view of some of the Concord villagers the English arrivals were a breath of fresh air. "We find the English men very agreeable," Prudence Ward told her brother George in early December, after she and her mother took tea with them at a Mrs. Brooks' (not that they would have drunk any tea) and subsequently entertained them at their lodgings. "We are all agreed in liking to hear Mr. Lane talk," she explained, though at the same time she feared George himself would find the newcomers "clean daft; for they are as like Mr. Alcott in their views as strangers from a foreign land can well be."[9]

Emerson, though, took much the same view as Abigail did on the oppressive atmosphere of the cottage. "Men of aim," like Charles Lane, would invariably be able to control those who lacked it; but nevertheless, Emerson reminded himself, "there will always be singing-birds."[10] The Concordia philosophy failed to allow for gratuitous beauty. And the enthusiasts took for granted that any audience would be hostile, so immediately went on the attack themselves.

Nevertheless, after a Conversation on the subject of "The Family" at "our good Mrs. B's" (perhaps the same Mrs. Brooks who had entertained Prudence Ward and the Englishmen to tea), Emerson decided that despite his "provoking and warlike" manner Lane was pretty impressive after all, so quick-witted and articulate that it was a delight to hear him. But the reason he gives for this verdict is an interesting one. Emerson was not only able to speak and write ironically; he could listen ironically as well. Lane repudiated the world of business—he "rails at trades and cities"—yet is clearly its product. And this very heritage has provided a "toughness and solidity of experience" that makes him entertaining and shows up Alcott's words, by contrast, as "pale and lifeless." Emerson always admired the shrewd and hardheaded: he welcomed exactly that stance of appraising oak trees and calculating the yield of sugar maples that Mrs. Gove found so lamentably "Scotch" in spirit, and so incompatible with "communism" (and of course he counted a hardheaded Scotsman, Thomas Carlyle, as one of his closest friends).

Another irony: Emerson left the party full of high spirits because he hadn't himself spoken a single word. That was his way of enjoying a conversation, or at least a Conversation. One wonders if the other participants, or perhaps one should say, the participants, were aware of just how complex Emerson's silence could be. Saying nothing was one way of dealing with overassertiveness. Another, he decided, would be to ask: "Shall there be no more cakes and ale? Why so much stress?"[11]

There were certainly no cakes and ale to be found at Concordia. In December, Alcott recorded that a "stricter Pythagorean diet and discipline" prevailed in the cottage, though perhaps surprisingly, "also music and dancing."[12] As early as December 4th Abigail was claiming that as a result of a diet of fruit, bread, and a limited intake of water, her health wasn't what it ought to be. "I have not been able to detect where the error lies," she admitted. The problem was that different physiologists gave differing advice. She resolved that she would try living on fruit, vegetables, and only a small amount of bread—which sounds pretty much like what she was doing already. As the month wore on she felt worse and worse.[13]

Meanwhile the menfolk of the cottage were off in Boston holding one Conversation after the other ("admission by ticket"). "Mr. Alcott and his new allies make some little stir," Margaret Fuller remarked. Indeed, Alcott had not lost his ability to incite the anger of the Boston public. A Conversation on "Childhood" scheduled for the Marlborough Chapel was prevented by a mob, and had to be hurriedly transferred to Ritchie Hall.[14]

This combination of intense evangelizing and frugal living would be maintained for the next year. But by December 24th Abigail had had enough, for the moment at least.

Louisa May Alcott would one day become, like Dickens, one of the literary architects of the nineteenth-century family Christmas, where snow lies thick outside and hearts are warm within. In the light of that subsequent achievement it is interesting to note how many of her own childhood Christmases went seriously awry. Christmas 1842 certainly did, as would the one the following year.

On Christmas Eve Abigail Alcott left the cottage to stay with her relatives in Boston, taking Louisa with her, as well as William Lane (perhaps she hoped that his absence would awaken fatherly feelings in Lane).[15] "Left Concord to try the influence of a short absence from home," she explained in her journal.

"My duties for the past three months have been arduous and involved." (So much for all those Conversations on the subject of The Family.) Christmas Day for her, and presumably for Louisa too, was "anything but merry"—and they weren't the only ones, because by this point Henry Wright's commitment was seriously beginning to falter.[16]

The day after Christmas, Alcott wrote to his brother Junius, explaining that as soon as the snow melted, Mr. Lane would be buying a farm and they could then make "a demonstration of a truer life under more favorable conditions." However, he admitted, it wasn't clear whether Mr. Wright would actually join in. Moreover Abigail couldn't be relied on either. "Abba is in some respects quite unequal," he explained. But having dismissed her so readily he must have promptly recalled what she was actually like, adding: "but in others very potent as you know." He explained that she had taken Louisa off to Boston and was likely to be gone for some weeks. "I hope distance and absence from Home and cares will restore her," he explained, hardly an endorsement of the values of that capitalized institution.

Strangely, though, he goes on to claim that he himself is "very happy both in present and prospect." Charles Lane, he says, "is near to me, and now I have the best substitute for yourself at [my] fireside." It is a suggestive tableau, Alcott and Lane cozying up together by the Concordia hearth, while Abigail was off in Boston and Henry Wright was thinking of abandoning the experiment altogether.[17]

Two days later two more Concordians were in Boston. Emerson's friend Ellery Channing, nephew of the great divine, reported back that he saw "Messrs. English Mystics there, in their fur caps and collars."[18] (His eyes must surely have deceived him about the material involved, given the refusal of Messrs. Mystics to make use of animal products.) Wright was in Boston to give a lecture on the subject of education, that topic about which his expertise had been so admired by Alcott just six months before. But this time Lane at least was not impressed. "Our friend H.G.W has fallen away from what he knew and what he saw most terribly," he wrote to Oldham, "and even the most superficial observers can find it out." As a result "his public audiences are not affected in the way in which they should be."[19]

Among the public audience, however, was Wright's admirer, Mary Gove, who asked a question. This led to a discussion to which the famously pugnacious radical Orestes Brownson made a contribution—only to be over-thrown by, of all people, Abigail Alcott, who had turned up for the occasion and laid into him with vigor. Lane was extremely impressed by her perform-ance. She "took him in hand and spoke like an inspired woman and quite elec-trified the audience."[20] Perhaps she was getting those months of oppression out of her system. It must have done the trick, because on New Year's Eve she returned to the cottage, having been away only one week after all.

Meanwhile matters were coming to a head with Henry Wright. Lane felt that Alcott was paying the price of putting pressure on him to come with them across the Atlantic rather than waiting till later. Wright complained about Alcott's *"iron despotic order"* and on the evening of December 30th the three men sat down to try to thrash things out. Alcott, rather proving Wright's point, took it upon himself to list his disorderly habits, his love of food, and his general unsteadiness of purpose. Wright complained that Lane was undermining his ability to teach by his very presence. Lane's own diagnosis was that Wright was not able to handle "the simplicity and order to which affairs were coming," particularly in relation to diet. Potatoes were not a vegetable that lent itself to the Greavesian regime of raw food, but as the next best thing they were eating them cold, which Wright found hard to bear. "No butter nor milk, nor cocoa, tea, nor coffee—nothing but fruit, grains and water was hard for the inside," Lane conceded, while poor Wright's outside was equally troubled by "regular hours and places, clearing up scraps, etc."[21]

It must have seemed a sad decline. Eighteen months before, in a pamphlet he wrote in March 1842 and entitled *What, When, Where, and How; or, Subjective Education*, Wright had endorsed the Greavesian notion "that cooking impoverishes the food," continuing with the reversal of normal values so beloved of the Burton Street/Alcott House contingent: "It may indeed happen that impoverished being [sic] requires impoverished food; but in a progressive education, the advancing enrichment of being will demand the food adjusted to plenitude . . . an uncooked diet of fruit, pulse, and roots is the most advanced, and evidence of the highest progress."[22] In short, plenitude is plenty of not much, eaten raw. Now, faced with the "plen-itude" of Concordia and potatoes eaten cold, he had fallen at his own hurdle and yearned after "impoverished food."

Emerson describes the reaction of his wife Lidian, or Queenie, as he often called her, to this regime and to the po-faced manner in which it was proclaimed and defended. "Queenie makes herself merry with the Reformers who make unleavened bread, and are foes to the death to fermentation," he wrote in his journal at about this time. Their affirmation of simplicity in diet seemed to her to betray nature's complexity. "Queenie says, God made yeast as well as wheat, & loves fermentation just as dearly as he loves vegetation, that the fermentation developes the saccharine element in the grain, & makes it more palatable & more digestible." The reformers had a sentimental attachment to the concept of purity: "They wish the 'pure wheat' & will die but it shall not ferment." ("Alas for the unleavened bread! alas for the unleavened wit!" Emerson's friend Ellery Channing would exclaim a few months later.) Emerson concluded this entry by evoking an interaction between humankind and the environment that is harsher and more dangerous than Greaves and his followers could imagine but is comprehensive precisely for that reason: "Earth Spirit, living, a black river like that swarthy stream which rushes through the human body is thy nature, demoniacal, warm, fruitful, sad, nocturnal."[23]

Mary Lyndon depicts the crisis on a less elemental and heroic level. Lynde/Wright is rebuked by the other two men "for taking a little cream upon his 'mush,' " and complains in turn about Lang/Lane's despotism in relation to coiffure. "It is your taste to have your hair cut very close," Lynde tells Lang. "It is my wish to wear my hair rather long, to take some pains, in curling it with a wet brush, for though its waves and rings are entirely natural, its appearance is improved by art." In the one photograph we have of Wright, a certain artfulness in the matter of waves and rings is indeed evident, though the question of improvement is debatable.[24] Mary Gove obviously admired the effect, however. And on January 3rd Wright left Concordia to go to stay with her in Lynn.[25]

It is impossible to establish the basis on which they cohabited. In her book, Gove depicts Lynde living with Mary for six months. It's the happiest time of her life, though the relationship is regarded as deeply improper and attracts a great deal of condemnation from the community at large.[26] With her lectures on female anatomy, her battle against tight corseting, and her later espousal of the doctrine of free love, it is easy to picture flagrant defiance of Greavesian notions of chastity (Wright's second in a row). And yet, of course, the prim and proper Sylvester Graham had lectured on anatomy; corseting was being attacked by no less a respectable authority than the Registrar for Births and Deaths for England ("The higher mortality of English women, by consumption, may be ascribed partly . . . to the compression preventing the expansion of the chest, by costume"); and the doctrine of free love was evolved later on in collaboration with her second husband and was directed at the oppression of loveless marriages, like her first one to Gove, rather than at advocating promiscuity as such. Moreover in April 1842 she had received the congratulations of the *Boston Quarterly Review* for a lecture explaining how masturbation leads to the lunatic asylum, so sexual permissiveness should not be assumed.[27]

Wright used his experience on the *Healthian* to help her with her own periodical, *The Health Journal and Independent Magazine*, and introduced her to the mysteries of hydrotherapy. He was short of funds and kept contacting Lane to persuade him to give him one third of the value of the library of mystical books they had brought out from England, an almost allegorical example of that habit of putting a price tag on highmindedness that Emerson was always complaining about.[28]

Meanwhile Abigail Alcott was being eased back into her place in Concordia. On New Year's Day Alcott wrote her a letter telling her to "Relinquish all selfwillfulness. Be willing to be used as He shall direct." He himself had accomplished just this resignation: "I am in the hands of a holy Destiny that shall make me be, and do, better and wiser than I can do for myself." If Wright wasn't adhering to Greavesian orthodoxy, at least Alcott still was, advocating passivity—though wrapped incongruously inside an imperative: "Be willing to be used."[29]

For the time being, Abigail was so willing. On January 4th she confided to her journal, "I am quite absorbed in my mental condition—felt since my return from Boston an unusual quietude—less tenacious of my rights or opinions." There might seem to be a hint of surrender here, but for her the transformation had the dignity of religious renewal: "I do believe that the miracle is about being wrought," she added. But there was a price to be paid. "To be truly quickened into spiritual life one must die a carnal death."[3]

8

The Little Wicket Gate

ON JANUARY 16, 1843, ALCOTT did something strange, even by his standards. He got himself sent to jail.[1] Or rather, being Alcott, he tried to get himself sent to jail but didn't quite succeed.

His plan was to opt out of state control by refusing to pay the poll tax. As we saw in Chapter 3, the antislavery agitation that provided the original impulse of the movement had broadened into a belief that to pay taxes meant endorsing government violence, as expressed in the maintenance of a militia and the prosecution of wars, and from there it had ballooned into a repudiation of the judicial process itself—in effect to an anarchist position. So Alcott's gesture was in accordance with the principles of the Non-Resistance Society, of which he was a leading member, along with Samuel May. But he may also have been influenced by an acquaintance of his, Joseph Palmer, who would in due course become closely involved with the Fruitlands community. The two men had met at a convention of so-called "come-outers" at Groton, Massachusetts in 1840. The "come-outers" derived their name from II Corinthians 6:17: "Wherefore come out from among them, and be ye separate, said the Lord, and touch not the unclean thing; and I will receive you." This provided a credo not only for abolitionists but for potential utopians as well. George Ripley conceived Brook Farm at the convention, and Adin Ballou founded the Hopedale Community shortly after attending it.

Palmer came from the memorably named No Town, near Fitchburg, and was famous for having a beard at a time when men rarely did. As a result he was known to all and sundry (including Alcott and Lane) as the Old Jew. One of the local ministers once asked him, "Palmer, why don't you shave and not go around looking like the devil?"

"I have never seen a picture of the ruler of the sulphurous regions with much of a beard," he replied, "but if I remember correctly, Jesus wore a beard not unlike mine."

Some years previously he had been attacked by four men who tried to shave his beard off. In the scuffle he stabbed two of them in the leg with his jackknife. As a result he was tried for "unprovoked assault" and fined $10, along with court fees and a bond to keep the peace in the sum of a swingeing $700 (the best part of $20,000 in today's terms). He refused to pay and was committed to jail, where he was consistently ill-treated. Eventually his imprisonment became an embarrassment to the authorities, who offered to waive the bond if only he would pay his fine and depart. His reply was: "If I aint [sic] a safe person to have my Liberty I ought not to go out. And I am willing to stay in confinement til [sic] I am." Finally the judge who had sentenced him came to the prison to plead for him to leave, and showed him a letter from his aged mother asking him to come home. Only then, after fifteen months in jail, did Palmer relent and pay his fine.[2]

Perhaps influenced by this example of stubborn principle, which in the end had reversed the balance of power between judiciary and alleged miscreant, Alcott had tried to get himself into jail the year before, but the tax-collector at the time couldn't quite bring himself to imprison him for the princely sum of $1.50 (for which he would receive a tiny commission of one cent on the dollar), so paid it instead. Rather than bringing down the government, "only the humblest instrument of the State was subdued"—that is the tax collector himself, who had by his action been forced to declare "the law was too base for him to execute." That was Lane's analysis, in a letter to Garrison's *Liberator*.[3]

The tax collector in 1843, Sam Staples (who was also Concord's sheriff), was less ready to be subdued than his predecessor. Lane would use what happened next as the starting point for a whole series of letters—articles in effect—expounding his political philosophy, contributions that go a long way to establishing his input to the ideology of the Fruitlands community.

"This year, a collector was appointed, who could execute the law," he explained grimly, "and although no doubt it went hard with him to snatch a man away from his home, from his wife, from the provision and education of his little children, in which latter he found Mr. Alcott serenely engaged, he nevertheless did it."

Lane pictured the tax collector witnessing "with his own eyes" Alcott getting his things together in preparation for indefinite imprisonment, "the little hasty preparations to attend him to the jail, the packing up of a few personal conveniences to ward off the inclemencies of the season." The collector refused to be deflected from his purpose by the poignancy of all these arrangements. "And yet, with no higher authority than the general warrant in his pocket, which, without particular investigation, trial, or inquiry, hands over the liberty of every townsman to his discretion, he took a fellow-citizen, an unoffending man, to a long confinement."

But once Sheriff Staples had delivered Alcott to the prison, both men's plans went awry. Strangely, the jailer "appeared to be not at home," so Staples went off to find him while the prisoner waited.[4] Lane omits to mention that Alcott in fact took advantage of the hiatus to go off for a meal with Thoreau and himself before returning to the jailhouse to face the music.

Thoreau was just twenty-five at this time, the son of a pencil manufacturer and the only one of the place's great talents to have been born in Concord. After studying at Harvard he returned to the little town and like so many of the Transcendentalists set up a school, in company with his brother George. He gave it up when his brother died in 1842. By this time he had fallen under Emerson's spell, contributing articles to the *Dial* with his encouragement, and indeed living with him and his family. He had moved into his house in April 1841, at the very time the Alcotts had decided not to join in Emerson's utopian plan themselves, so in a sense he represented the afterglow of that intention. He acted as literary assistant, children's tutor, handyman, and gardener. "He is as ugly as sin," Hawthorne wrote in 1842, "long-nosed, queer-mouthed and with uncouth and rustic, though courteous manners." Hawthorne had just moved to Concord with his wife Sophia (sister of Elizabeth Peabody) and they had invited this strange-looking personage to dinner (after which Thoreau sold them a boat he had built himself). As far as Hawthorne could make out, Thoreau seemed to "lead a kind of Indian life among civilized men—an Indian life, I mean, as respects the absence of any systematic effort for a livelihood." He believed Emerson was merely indulging Thoreau by giving him odd jobs about the house.[5] All in all, it is hardly surprising that Thoreau and Alcott became close friends for the rest of their lives.

After Alcott left the meal table, Thoreau and Lane decided that it might be incumbent upon the two of them to "agitate the state" in the matter of his imprisonment. In fact Lane went off to take up his pen immediately, beginning his letter to the *Liberator*. Meanwhile, back at the lockup Staples announced that he couldn't hold Alcott any longer (so much for the long confinement). It turned out that the tax had been paid in the meantime. When asked who had obliged, Staples named "a gentleman who may be regarded, and who would willingly be regarded, as the very personification of the State."[6] The distinguished lawyer and politician Samuel Hoar (known as Squire Hoar), one of Concord's leading citizens and friend of Emerson, had in fact paid the tiny sum owing. Hoar was himself a man of liberal views, dedicated to the antislavery cause, and renowned for his generosity.[7]

When the news reached Lane he became as indignant about Alcott's release as he had been about his arrest. His work-in-progress was being forced around a somewhat anticlimactic corner—which, it must be said, he managed to negotiate without losing any of his polemical momentum.[8] Thoreau's attitude to the news was a good deal more relaxed. That evening he was attending a lecture on "Peace" by a Mr. Spear ("ought he not be beaten into a ploughshare?" Thoreau wondered—perhaps the same could be suggested of the fiery Lane) when the newly liberated Alcott reappeared. "When, over the audience, I saw our hero's head moving in the free air of the Universalist Church," Thoreau told Emerson, "my fire all went out, and the State was safe as far as I was concerned."

Thoreau's sister asked Sam Staples what he thought Alcott's motives were. The sheriff replied, "I vum, I believe it was nothing but principle, for I never heard a man talk honester."[9]

That principle was of course nonresistance to the State. In his letter, Lane (sounding rather like a 1960s hippy) expressed his antagonism to "power and might" as opposed to "peace and love," and claimed that if the full amount of tax paid were returned to the payer the following day in the form of bread it would still be "a sacred duty in every man" to oppose it, because the process itself would be a manifestation of "brute force."[10] (Squire Hoar took precisely the opposite view, content to pay even unfair taxes, since "the money might as well go in this way as in any other."[11])

The oppositional stance Lane was advocating seems more like resistance than nonresistance. True, it involves not-doing rather than doing, but as his pugnacious tone suggests, the whole point is to confront authority. Thoreau may have claimed that his fire had gone out, but in fact he had also refused to pay his poll tax for 1842, and indeed continued to withhold it during the years following. However he was not arrested until 1846 when he had a similarly mock-heroic experience in confronting the power of the state.[12] Sam Staples let him out after one night in jail, claiming "he was mad as the devil when I turned him loose."[13] His essay on the event would become one of the most famous and influential documents of New England Transcendentalism, admired by Tolstoy and ultimately influencing Mahatma Gandhi's anticolonial protests in India, and Martin Luther King's civil rights strategy in sixties America, as well as inspiring the Beats and hippies. Thoreau's own title for his piece, "Resistance to Civil Government," would reverse the misleading negative; and the one applied to the essay by posterity, "On the Duty of Civil Disobedience," also carried with it the notion of confrontation.

Lane visualizes the state as a collective and malignant consciousness on the lines of the Big Brother George Orwell would depict a century later, aware of Alcott's refusal to pay his tax and fiendishly bent on searching out any flaw in his character or situation in order to sabotage the gesture. "Probably the authorities anticipated that if they showed a rigid determination to enforce this old monstrous system," Lane explained, "a weakness would be discovered somewhere; that domestic attractions would be too potent; that wive [sic] or friend would interfere." Such speculations clearly reveal Lane's own concern about the influence of domestic attractions on Alcott's resolve. However, in this case he had held firm and, disappointed in their evil plan, the authorities' "courage failed." The only move they could make when Alcott called their bluff by being willing to go to prison was to switch strategies and refuse to let that happen. According to this scenario, by paying the arrears to keep a fellow townsman out of jail, Samuel Hoar himself became Big Brother, "the very personification of the state."[14]

The other version—ironically, Thoreau's own sister's version—undermines this grandiloquence by simply recording that revealing "vum," catching the small-town homeliness of it all, the local sheriff scratching his head over the eccentric behavior of one of the village's intellectuals and in fact admiring him for his integrity. Staples' pause for thought suggests that the authorities had no malign agenda ready to hand, that they hadn't devised any particular strategy to foil Alcott—indeed, that the picture Lane paints of the state as a tightly organized, omniscient, highly focused system was a fantasy. As far as Staples was concerned, Alcott might as well have been shadow-boxing. What was at stake was not the future of governance in America but the payment of the sum of $1.50. Nevertheless, one of the *Liberator*'s subheaders for Lane's letter was "Dawn of Liberty."[15]

It is of course a fundamental principle of utopian thought that large effects can be produced by apparently small causes. Applied to the status quo rather than to the prospective spread of utopia itself, however, this model can seem like a symptom of paranoia. Thus Lane claims citizens will eventually shudder at the tyranny to which they submit, "for greater oppressions than any they have thrown off, have grown from smaller beginnings."

What is missing from Lane's analysis is a clear vision of the non-governed state. Just as theories of the afterlife give us a better picture of the horrors of hell than the delights of heaven, so utopian proposals are often more eloquent on the abuses of the present than the pleasures to come. All Lane can say is that public opinion has "not yet perceived that all the true purposes of the corporate state may as easily be carried out on the revolutionary principle."[16]

The day before Alcott's adventure, Abigail set up a domestic post office in the cottage. "I thought it would afford a daily opportunity for the children, indeed all of us, to interchange thought and sentiment," she wrote in her journal. Part of its purpose was to defuse the tensions that tended to arise in the hothouse atmosphere. "Had any unhappiness occurred," she went on, "it would be a pleasant way of healing all differences and discontents."[17]

In *Little Women*, Louisa credits Laurie, the boy-next-door, with this invention. Jo reveals him sitting in a closet during the deliberation of the girls' secret society, the Pickwick Club, and he takes on the identity of Sam Weller. His contribution to the proceedings is a mailbox he has made by adapting a birdhouse situated between their gardens. "Letters, manuscripts, books, and bundles can be passed in there; and, as each nation has a key, it will be uncommonly nice, I fancy."[18] His use of the word "nation" is suggestive. Perhaps Louisa is remembering that the purpose of their original domestic mail service was to cross the transatlantic divide that had become evident within the narrow confines of Concordia. A mailbox might be a mechanism for relieving tension, but its very existence implies a sense of distance between the correspondents.

Despite this device Abigail continued to feel that she couldn't get all her worries out in the open. After the post office had been in operation a week she reported that it had been effective in lessening conflict between the children but confessed that she was oppressed by debts and was being "beset by men to whom we are owing small sums of money." Alcott, unsurprisingly, had told her that nothing could be done except let them wait. He always seemed to have a remarkably guilt-free attitude to his creditors. "I have expressed my mind very explicitly," Abigail told her journal, "and yet I have not said all I feel, for I do not know how to do it advisedly." The mailbox obviously didn't cure all ills. She went on to confide that they had been discussing the move to a house and farm, but "there is not that unanimity of opinion which it seems to me ought to prevail before consistency of action."

Her phrasing was prophetic: unanimity leads to consistency—and of course, the opposite is true too.

Life in the cottage wasn't all bad. At least one of her complaints, that she was left to do all the cooking, was being addressed. Alcott had been "learning to prepare our meals" and had devised a method of doing so. In fact, the day before there had been a visit from their landlord, Edmund Hosmer, along with six of his children, and everyone "partook of a simple dinner which Mr. Alcott had neatly prepared in the morning: an oatmeal pudding, apples, bread, and nuts" (simple indeed). Moreover, Lane gave music lessons and the children were learning to dance. With this thought, she cheered up. "Our days pass very agreeably in the interchange of light labors and serene enjoyments."[19]

Lane's letter to the *Liberator* must have caused a few ripples, because on January 28th he issued an amendment. There had been a typographical error, he explained (unconvincingly): the word "revolutionary" had been printed instead of "voluntary" in the phrase "revolutionary principle." It is hard to visualize how a typo could have been responsible for such a radical change —and radical it was, making people fear that "violent proceedings are recommended or contemplated." Not at all, Lane explained. The new arrangements he was advocating could only be brought into the world "by kind, orderly and moral means." But in one sense "revolution" was the right word after all because it suggested "a something on the other side of the moral wheel."[20]

There must also have been some complaint that he had gone off-message by interpreting Alcott's gesture not merely as an attack on slavery but as the first step toward a new world order. This was a common grievance of abolitionists who wished to deal with the specific evil of slavery rather than philosophize about the state of society in general. But if the whole system was replaced, Lane explained, then slavery would vanish along with all other abuses. In fact, anything less would leave ex-slaves simply becoming wage-slaves, like Irish laborers. "Why then should we aim alone at the mere modification, when with as much ease we might carry the whole question?"

At this point he introduces a metaphor drawn from the Alcott family's favorite book, *Pilgrim's Progress*, but replacing the journey toward heaven with one toward paradise on earth: "This, Sir, is the little wicket gate, by which we must enter the straight and narrow way which leads to universal liberty."[21]

In this context the image suggests utopian transition rather than revolutionary upheaval. Implicit are two ideas close to Alcott's heart, not to mention those of the other Transcendentalists, including the Brook Farmers— and of course Thoreau. Just as Alcott anticipated Thoreau's actual arrest, so Lane laid out in his letters to the *Liberator* what would become the main arguments of Thoreau's great essay. The first is the notion that large, indeed all-embracing, changes can result from small local endeavors. As Thoreau would put it in "Resistance to Civil Government," "It is not so important that many should be as good as you, as that there be some absolute goodness somewhere; for that will leaven the whole lump." The second is that the perfected and redeemed world is already out there, waiting for us, mapped out. At the end of his essay Thoreau anticipates "a still more perfect and glorious State, which . . . I have imagined, but not yet anywhere seen."[22]

On January 30th, two days after sending off his second letter to the *Liberator*, Lane sat down and wrote another, to be posted in Abigail's mailbox—indeed, addressed to Abigail herself. He tries to explain the misunderstanding that has arisen between them, and in doing so provides a rather different picture of the connection between the individual and the totality than the one produced for the *Liberator*. "In coming to this hospitable land," he told her, trying to seem a grateful guest, "I hoped to enact only a fractional part of some larger work." He was evoking a large upheaval of which a particular person was just a component—a fraction. "If it be ordained otherwise," he said, putting a brave face on it, "I am happy."[23]

This sheds a new light on his partial retraction of the word "revolution." Perhaps oral communications can have their own sort of typo, just like newsprint—those excited discussions with Alcott in England had given Lane a sense that enormous forces were already in motion on the other side of the Atlantic. Now he was actually here their project suddenly seemed small-scale and domestic.

On February 1st he made use of the household postal service again, with another letter to Abigail. "I confess I do not see my way very clearly," he told her. A fog seemed to have descended on that "straight and narrow way" he claimed lay just beyond the narrow wicket gate. "Had I been aware of the real state of things here," he admitted, "the probability is that I should not have come." He was aware that this sounded very much as if he was accusing Alcott of misleading him, hardly the best way of defusing the tensions marring Concordia, so he immediately tried to reassure her. "Yet no one has deceived me nor do I think I have deceived myself." His expectation, he went on (craftily implying modest ambition), was to "fill some very subordinate part in a large affair." Time for the stiff upper lip again. "I cannot say I feel disappointed that it is otherwise and that we are left to work our way in comparative solitude."

Lane was aware he had veered between small-scale utopianism and large-scale revolution. He puts out a conciliatory hand to Abigail: "I join with you in the passive mood," he tells her, falling back on Greavesian orthodoxy, "let it no longer be a mood but a permanence." And to show that he was prepared to be content with the little rather than the big, with the utopian rather than the revolutionary, with the passive rather than the aggressive, he adds,

"Wafers are but small things but they will serve as introductions to the new order."[24]

The wafers in question were slivers of gummed paper, used for sealing the letters in the domestic post office, a humble version of the sealing wax and stamps used for proclamations and legal documents. They had improving aphorisms on them, like cracker mottoes or Chinese fortune cookies. Louisa later quoted examples of those used at Fruitlands:

Vegetable diet and sweet repose. Animal food and nightmare.
Pluck your body from the orchard; do not snatch it from the shamble.
Without flesh diet there could be no blood-shedding war.[25]

On the same day that Lane dropped his peacemaking epistle into the domestic mailbox, Alcott posted one of his own, grandly dated "Feb 1, Cottage Concordia," and addressed to "The Young Inmates of the Cottage while supping around Its Hearth." The most beautiful thing in the world, he tells them, "is a pure and happy; a kind and loving family." The letter paints a picture of domestic bliss, "a house where peace and joy and gentle quiet, abide always . . . where every hand is quick to help, every foot swift to serve, every eye to catch the wishes, and every ear, the wants of the other." This, he announces, is "the Jewel—the pearl of priceless cost . . . 'Tis Heaven and Earth in substance."

Lane seems to fear diminishment in accommodating himself to the domestic scale; Alcott, however, in a flight of lyrical enthusiasm, actually manages to achieve apotheosis as Concordia Cottage becomes paradise itself. "Come then, my Children, and abide in this imperishable mansion which I would prepare for you." And in case they miss this conflation of himself with the Almighty, he signs himself "Your Ascended Father."[26] Three years previously, his daughter Anna had explained in her diary that "I like to read about Jesus because he is so good," adding "Father is the best man in the world now." Alcott would have agreed with that verdict. On one occasion Henry James Sr. had asked him whether he had ever claimed to be the Resurrection and the Life, and he had replied, "Yes, often."[27]

Alcott must suddenly have remembered that he wasn't a father— ascended or not—to one of the children, young William Lane, and he therefore added further, more down-to-earth titles, "Your Present Friend, and Careful Provider," though his claim to the second of them is distinctly dubious.[28]

There is ambiguity in the stances of both male leaders of the Concordia household, but unfortunately the symmetry it reveals is one of opposition. Lane wistfully aspires towards "revolutionary" upheaval while convincing himself that he is not disappointed with comparative solitude; Alcott mystically celebrates the family structure before reminding himself that it already extends outward to include others to whom he is not related. Lane is uneasily trying to reconcile himself to an exemplary mode of utopian transformation, whereby a small group provide a model to imitate; Alcott is doing his best to allow for transmission outward from the family to a larger association.

Nevertheless, for the moment concord did indeed seem to take hold in Concordia. On February 3rd Alcott used the domestic post office to write to his daughter Anna, congratulating her on her developing maturity (she was nearly twelve) and claiming that "the Cottage never seemed to me in a more lively and improving state than just now."[29] In a letter to Parker Pillsbury, abolitionist and editor of the *Herald of Freedom* (which like the *Liberator* was publishing Lane's letters) he returns to the figure of Janus, this time using it not to represent different aspects of himself but to refer to himself and Lane as if they were two aspects of the same identity.[30] And as though to drive the point home, on February 15th he gives his version of the image of the wicket gate that Lane had appropriated from Bunyan in a letter to an unknown correspondent: "The entrance to paradise is still through the strait gate and narrow way of self-denial."

In this letter Alcott goes on to outline their plans. "First, to obtain the free use of a plot of land"—his careful language demonstrating exactly the evasiveness that so annoyed Emerson, avoiding sordid verbs like "buy" or "rent"—and there to live by a subsistence economy, "independently of foreign aids." He becomes a little coy on the question of recruits. Certainly he does not approve of associations "of human beings for the purpose of making themselves happy by . . . improved outward arrangements alone."[31] This was a reference to Brook Farm, which by this time was prospering, with perhaps a hundred members living in buildings scattered over gently rolling countryside.[32] Brook Farm was intent on creating a balance between physical and mental labor, but the school was an important part of the endeavor and the number of children and young people gave a youthful tone and buoyancy to the proceedings. Emerson later described it as a "perpetual picnic," and while this is a little unfair, there was certainly a merry-go-round of parties, masquerades, and concerts, interspersed with more serious episodes when Margaret Fuller came to stay and conducted Conversations, or the farm demanded hard labor. There was a Graham table available at mealtimes for the vegetarians among the members, but all in all it was a relaxed, non-doctrinal establishment, with a broad spectrum of members and tolerating a range of views and degrees of utopian commitment, without the sort of puritanical consensus that prevailed—or was being enforced—at Concordia.[33]

Should Lane and Alcott "attract parties" toward them, their community would have no taint of the materialistic (unlike Brook Farm). This would be achieved by pre-harmonization, consociation with the universal spirit, and conformity with the "state of being." Greavesian terminology is technical and vague at the same time, handily providing the space ambiguity requires. Individual men and women might be attracted, Alcott explains, but so might families with children; one way or another this process may contribute to human regeneration "and the restoration of the highest life on earth."[34]

The whole letter glides from the little to the big, from the material to the ideal, from the individual to the associative (nodding towards the family as it goes), from Alcott's allegiances to Lane's perspective, without confronting any of the issues that arise en route.

A few days later Lane and Alcott performed a double act, a Conversation in Emerson's house covering the topics of prophecy and nature. The weather was bad, few people turned up, and Emerson himself was absent on a lecture tour, but Lidian Emerson enjoyed it thoroughly. Lane accused Thoreau of a love of nature, in which aberration he was apparently being supported by Elizabeth Hoar, daughter of the squire (that personification of the state), and by Lidian herself. Lidian pleaded not guilty. According to Lane, loving nature was a vice worse than the grossest sin. In the latter case the sinner would inevitably become aware of the magnitude of what he had done; but love of nature was a refined vice that would not be addressed; those who succumbed to it would inevitably be the last to enter the kingdom of heaven.

On the face of it, this argument seems ludicrously over-the-top, but it has the extremeness that comes from following a particular train of thought to its logical conclusion. The story of the Fall is one of alienation from nature. By eating the apple of knowledge, humankind were excluded from nature's garden and forced to view it from a distance. In short, an aesthetic delight in nature is a manifestation of our original alienation from it. Thoreau's reply was that Lane and Alcott did not know what they were talking about because they did not appreciate nature in the first place. Alcott explained they were beyond "mere material objects, and were filled with spiritual love and perception (as Mr. T. was not)." Lidian thought the whole discussion was hilarious.[35]

The day after his attack on nature-lovers, Lane sat down to write another letter to the *Liberator*. His original protest about Alcott's arrest had now modulated into a decision to write a coherent series of pieces on the subject of "A Voluntary Political Government," a kind of anarchy for beginners, explaining that the business of a nation could in fact be carried on "if it were left to the free judgment in every individual to support it or not."[36] In this letter, the first of the newly defined set, Lane deals with the issue of the protection of persons and property. This is at present achieved by terror and retribution, despite the fact that the "head of the decapitated murderer will not fit the shoulders of any murdered brother." Lane manages to slide Alcott's arrest by Sam Staples into his consideration of extreme penalties, almost as if Alcott had faced the prospect of execution himself. The "wild and lawless red man" would not have treated Alcott so badly—indeed would even leave personal assaults and murder unavenged (Lane offers no anthropological evidence for this assertion). Untaught Irishmen and Scottish highlanders (obviously considered more savage by "Scotch"-looking Lane than Native Americans), even they, would probably have drawn the line at trying to punish "the most meek, inoffensive and well-disposed of the community."[37] As it was in the interests of everybody to protect persons and property, this would happen without the compulsory and coercive mechanisms of the state, though Lane doesn't go into how.

The following day, February 21st, Lane sat down to write a long letter to William Oldham, back at Alcott House (he didn't actually finish it until March 1st). If his piece in the *Liberator* deals with dystopia, this letter gives the opposite side of the coin. It provides, in almost excruciating detail, an hour by hour summary of a day in Concordia. Superficially it resembles one of those letters from friends or relatives who take it for granted you wish to know every smidgeon of their lives. But here detail is the very point. The large-scale generalizations of the *Liberator* articles are appropriate for, indeed reflect, the power structures to which Lane is objecting. By contrast the minutiae of daily life in a specific location suggest an empirical and lived alternative. Concordia is an exercise in replacing the faulty society Lane has been describing; what he is giving his colleague in England is a blueprint for utopian living. Perhaps, too, he is trying to convince himself that this is indeed the way to transform society.

The household begins to stir with the dawn. Alcott goes downstairs, lights the fire, baths the baby, and prepares breakfast. William (who shares his father's chamber) lights the little fire in their room. Everybody has a strip-wash in icy water (often having to break through an inch of ice in order to pour it, only to have it freeze again around the rim of the bowl). Then they dress and at seven or seven-thirty they sit round the fire in the living room and have breakfast. Each Concordian has a red napkin, and "one who is Ganymede on the occasion" hands around water, unleavened bread, apples, and potatoes. Meanwhile they converse on "some domestic Pythagorean topic."

At just after eight, Abigail goes up to the Lanes' room to tidy it while Lane shoulders his violin and gives a music lesson. Abigail likes singing, so when she comes down she joins in. At nine Lane goes off to his room to write "in God-like quiet" until the midday meal. Downstairs, between nine and ten, Alcott gets in water and wood, and lays out the classroom for the children. The children play or do their homework, while "Mrs. A. sees to her functions" (a rather lofty vagueness here). Alcott begins teaching at ten. If the children are studying quietly, he slips away to bake bread. In any case he always gets the midday dinner ready and they eat it at one o'clock, this time sitting at the table (except on Sundays when they take their places around the fire again). It's basically the same menu as breakfast.

Then they all relax until two. At that time William and Anna come to Lane for an hour's French, with Louisa joining them at three for a geometry lesson. At four the girls sew or play, while William digs a path through the snow or fetches more wood. It was a particularly cold winter, and William clearly had to do a substantial share of the work for a ten-year-old. He is the most elusive of the children at Concordia and Fruitlands. Louisa, the same age, and Anna, slightly older, would both write diaries the following year (the other two girls, Elizabeth and Abby May, were only seven and two respectively at this time). William may have written one too, but it has not survived. There are few other references to William receiving lessons, and several to him working, so one forms an impression that this silent member of the community had to act as if older than his years, though the two other older children would also do their share of the chores in due course.

While his son is shoveling snow, Lane returns to his writing, or perhaps goes into the village for letters and to read the newspapers. He might visit Lidian Emerson (her husband still being away lecturing), or Thoreau, who is currently a stand-in editor for the *Dial*. Supper is at six-thirty, again around the fire. Then the domestic post office is opened. If there is a lamp available the contents are read—but usually there isn't, because they will not use animal oil and it is very difficult to get hold of candles. It's an odd picture: the Concordians sitting with letters in the dark, wondering what they've said to each other.

The evening concludes with Lane on the violin again, and the household singing and dancing. At eight o'clock the children go to bed. The adults converse in the flickering firelight while Abigail settles to her knitting and Alcott peels the potatoes for tomorrow's breakfast. At nine or so, they go up too.

At this point in the letter Lane provides a sketch. From the left, we have Mrs. A., Anna (12), Louisa (10), Elizabeth (6 – actually she was 7), C.L., W.L., Mr. A, and the baby.[38]

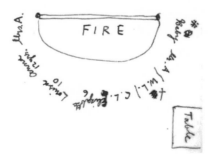

The Concordia Hearth, as depicted by Charles Lane

It might seem extraordinary that a serious-minded middle-aged man should send such an illustration to another serious-minded middle-aged man on the other side of the Atlantic. But this is the picture of the heart of the utopian structure, the engine room of change in the community they have built for themselves. It resembles the illustration of the Temple School classroom showing the semicircle of students sitting in front of their teacher. Years later, in *Little Men*, Louisa would superimpose those two frames of reference when she describes how the schoolboys were seated for Mr. Bhaer's Sunday evening talk: "Nat thought it seemed more like a great family than a school, for the lads were sitting in a wide half-circle round the fire." [39] Mary Gove described the utopian impulse rippling outward like the sound waves from an Aeolian harp, a guitar, or a violin (just as Lane bonded the household with his own playing, at the beginning and end of the day). This little illustration can be seen as the first ripple of such a pulsation: domestic warmth, represented by the fire, being transmitted outward to the Concordians and then further, by means of the letter, across the Atlantic to the world at large.

While the sketch gives us a moment of harmony in the lives of the Concordians, it also embodies the ambiguities and tensions that were already making themselves felt. It seems to be identifying a fundamental social unit, but what exactly does that consist of? We have a deeply domestic scene, but there are two families present. The image subverts the very domesticity it purports to represent. [40]

This is exactly the problem Emerson puts his finger on, in a journal entry from around this time. He is thinking in fact of Brook Farm, not Concordia, but what concerns him is the whole nature of utopian transmission. "The Brook Farm Community," he writes, "is an expression of the theory of impulse." This theory is put into practice by "several bold and consistent philosophers." The whole process is odious because it radiates outward infinitely. The utopian "wish to obey impulse is guarded by no old, old Intellect or that which knows metes and bounds." [41] Lane has provided an image of this tendency. The impulse at Concordia has already transcended domestic metes and bounds.

Towards the end of his letter, Lane's tone changes. Alcott, he says, "cannot part from me," a remark that suggests Lane has thought about leaving Concordia and the Alcott family. However, Alcott himself is "too sincere and valuable" to be abandoned, and in any case if they stick to their principles they can achieve their goals; "but rents, debts and mortgages would destroy us." He is obviously getting worried about Alcott's finances.

Oldham must have previously told Lane that Concordia could recruit members of the Concordium if Lane contributed the cost of their passage. But Lane took a dim view of the present incumbents of Alcott House. "I think we shall not be much aided by their presence," he told Oldham. "Understand we are not going to open a hospital." He goes on to make a rather suggestive point. "We are more Pythagoreans than Christs, we wish to begin with the sound rather than to heal the sick." Christ was engaged in the process of rectifying the wrongs of the world, with redeeming sinners. Alcott, as we have seen, preferred those who had never sinned to those who had come back into the fold. Both he and Lane were engaged in a neo-Platonic quest to rediscover a lost perfection, not to make the world around them a better place. Their austerity obviously had Puritan ancestry but it was not at the service of mortification or self-punishment; it was a recipe for establishing an ideal relationship with the environment. They were imbued with the imagery of Genesis but not much concerned with most of the paraphernalia of Christianity, including its moral system.

Lane concludes his letter (perhaps suddenly homesick) with an emotional outburst: "My God, dear Oldham, how I wished to give you an affectionate embrace when I read your vivid description of the selfish torrent opposed to you!"[42] We don't know what Oldham had told him, but he was now sharing power at the Concordium with a man called William Gilpin who had a reputation as a hardliner—like Lane himself, ironically. One of the members of the community, H.S. Clubb, later remembered Gilpin "with a rather wild expression in his eyes," never smiling or giving a word of encouragement. He wanted the inhabitants of the Concordium to learn to see in the dark like animals, so forbad lights. Not much difference from Concordia there, but Gilpin also tried to take his community to a further extreme by imposing a rule of silence, requiring the members to use sign language.[43]

Abigail Alcott was as worried as Lane about rent and debts, and on March 6th she went over to Lexington to discuss such matters with her brother Samuel. He was a loyal source of support, regularly sending them small amounts, though as a Unitarian minister he was hardly a wealthy man himself. He had stood many times on the same platform as Alcott, arguing the cause of nonresistance, but now a certain impatience showed through. This time he could not help them, and he didn't understand why Alcott was not able to support his family without making demands of his friends. "They have to labor," he pointed out to Abigail. "Why should not he?"

Abigail confessed that it was a difficult question to answer. Perhaps time would tell. She was aware, like her brother, like Emerson too, that her husband's stance could be seen as hypocritical. "His unwillingness to be employed in the usual way produces great doubt in the minds of his friends as to the righteousness of his life," she noted in her journal, "because he partakes of the wages of others occupied in this same way."[44]

The following day, March 7th, Lane sat in his room and wrote two very substantial pieces, once again dealing virtually simultaneously with the wrongs of society in another article for the *Liberator*, and providing a detailed narrative of what was right with Concordia in a long letter to Junius Alcott. Perhaps some guilt at the eviction still lingered, because he expressed the wish that Junius could be the ninth member of their company (Wright having sacrificed his claim). If this overture were accepted, Lane's need to expand the community could be rewarded without challenging Alcott's family loyalties. Lane explained that he was busy writing for the press, while Alcott "has been our chief baker, cook, teacher &c, entering personally and actively into all the mysteries of unleavened bread, boiled potatoes, turnips, parsnips, apples and all the best materials for building up the human statue divinely." Even Abigail has made some painful progress. Perhaps others would join them, but he wasn't sanguine about many of their neighbors taking "the straight and narrow way of self-denial."

This itinerary does not get any more attractive for being repeated so often, but Lane tries to claim it has its own rewards: after all, "mere existence, always designed a blessing, should be to man a joyous state." And—perhaps gritting his teeth—a small community living the true life is better than a large one in false harmony. "Brazil pebbles are very clear transparent stones, but they are not diamonds."

Lane told Junius he would like his advice about spending one or two thousand dollars, "the little cash I have collected from my London toils ... to redeem a small spot on the planet." They need an orchard, wood, a house; they want to be able to cultivate the land without using animals; and it was necessary to keep in touch with the world of "mind and letters." He then goes on to provide an account of a day in the life at the cottage, hour by hour, just as he had for Oldham. Each well-spent interval was another facet of the utopian diamond; the sketch he had drawn for Oldham could perhaps be seen as the jewel itself.

It is a discipline of abstinence, he tells Junius. "We are learning to hold our peace, and to keep our hands from each other's bodies," he says, adding strangely, "the ill effects of which we see upon the little baby." It sounds as if he means that they are avoiding arguments, and that Mr. and Mrs. Alcott are abstaining from sex—an issue that will arise again at Fruitlands itself. It is hard to construe the remark about two-year-old Abby May, but it seems to suggest, cruelly, that in her case the generative process has not been up to scratch. This is one of those moments, like Abigail's comment about the death of little Waldo Emerson, when we are reminded of the uncompromising principles behind Concordia.

Lane concludes by formally inviting Junius to join them, if he can make arrangements for his mother's care—perhaps just for one summer, though a year would be better. In a postscript, Alcott reiterates the invitation, though also the caveat that their mother needs his brother's attention. He hopes, rather vaguely, that she too will be able to come over some day "on a visit at least." The family might be a jewel of priceless cost, but sometimes its obligations are best delegated or deferred.

The letter was sealed with a green wafer asserting "Temperance is the herald of holiness."[45]

The same day he wrote to Junius, Lane provided the second installment in his series of sweeping assessments of society's wrongs for the *Liberator*. He begins by noting gleefully that an assassination attempt has been made against Robert Peel, the very man who had invented the modern police force twelve years previously: proof positive that the existence of the police is more likely to cause crime than prevent it. As far as property entitlement is concerned, courts and laws thrive on its uncertainties. He would rather trust his neighbors to be his jury if he were involved in a dispute, since a voluntary court would inevitably be superior to an instituted one. People claim that laws are there to protect the weak against the strong, but they are actually formulated and enforced by the strong rather than the weak, and the strong will inevitably uphold their own interests.

He goes on to picture circle upon circle, extending outward. Around the government of the strong are those who most resemble it. These people, like the government itself, spend their time being acquisitive. Beyond this circle are further circles which "adopt the grasping system in modes less nice and refined than those of the inner circle." And so on, "until a class is generated who exercise their organs of secretiveness in another mode, not more dishonest, and prey upon the classes who have generated them"—criminals, in fact. Their existence gives the inner circles the opportunity to put on a show of virtue and morality, despite the fact that they are ultimately tarred with the same brush. Once again Lane seems to look forward a century to the work of George Orwell, who would talk in *Animal Farm* of looking from man to pig and from pig to man, though Lane fastens on a different creature. "All the other classes of cormorants," he writes, "join in prosecuting this last class of dark feathered birds, and occasionally cage them, so that they may learn to be more wary and clever in their plans."[46]

The rippling circles remind us of Mary Gove's description of the utopian transmission of sound waves or, more particularly, the malign alternative to this process, whereby plague particles exhale from the "death sphere" of "a soul of evil and death." Emerson looked in horror at the way Brook Farm's impulses could ripple outward for ever, odiously lacking metes and bounds. Lane looks at the status quo's power structure with an exactly parallel distaste.

9

The Principle of Inverse Ratio

OVER IN LONDON CARLYLE had read the second part of Lane's *Dial* essay on that "blockhead" Greaves, and on March 11th put pen to paper to warn Emerson he should keep "a rather strict outlook on Alcott and his English Tail . . . Bottomless imbeciles ought not to be seen in company with Ralph Waldo Emerson."[1] He didn't need to worry, since Emerson was hardly likely to be seduced. He had his fear of the utopian impulse to keep him at a distance, after all, not to mention a sense of humor. At about this time he produced a surreal account in his journal of an incident that had just taken place in Concordia:

> The history of grasshoppers said the Reformer has never been written. Mamma said the child they have begun again![2]

Emerson's son Edward later glossed the entry as follows: "Louisa Alcott, or one of her sisters, was sent by her mother to find out whether the philosophers had desisted from their speculations and got to some needed task, and came in with this hopeless report."[3]

Abigail had hoped to cut through the gabble and get some help around the house because she was once again feeling ill (the extra austerity of her diet having done her no good) and was aware of relying too much on the daughter to whom she was closest. She sent Louisa a letter via the household post office on March 12th. "I might be a sick but a loving mother," she told her, "looking to my daughter's labours for my daily bread", but "you and I have always liked to be grouped together."[4]

Meanwhile the philosophers continued with their speculations. In the third of his series of letters on "A Voluntary Political Government," penned on March 27th, Lane pointed out that the heart of the social and political system lay not in the central government but at the other end of the structure altogether. "The town meeting," he claimed, "to the external eye the mere circumference of the wheel, is the very centre of it, the axle upon which it revolves, and the power which imparts its motion."[5] A few years later, in *Walden*, Thoreau would picture a device called a Realometer which as its name implied would measure degrees of reality and enable the user to find a *"point d'appui,"* a point of leverage which could shift the world, a bedrock "below freshet and frost and fire, a place where you might found a wall or a state."[6] In a political sense the town meeting could provide that purchase on the social structure. But its members are not aware of this possibility and instead of engaging with communal and local matters, town meetings mainly content themselves with transferring responsibility elsewhere, by electing representatives to other organs of government or by raising taxes to hire individuals and organizations to cater for the community's needs.

Education was a case in point. The evil of raising money for a national school system was amply demonstrated by the fact that a man (i.e. Alcott) could be sent to jail (more or less) for failing to pay his portion. "The true school," Lane asserts, "is doubtless the parental home." This seems a rationalization for the fact that having been involved respectively in two pioneering educational experiments, the Temple School and Alcott House, Alcott and Lane were simply teaching their children at home in Concordia. As for those children whose parents are too irresponsible or ignorant to provide such teaching for their children—well, they don't bother to send them to the state's schools anyway. There is no point in being coercive. If education is conducted on a local level, the negligent will be awakened to their failings by their concerned neighbors.

Similar arguments apply to certain other subjects. Roads would be maintained more effectively if they were paid for by those who actually made use of them. The poor would be treated more sensitively by the informal interventions of local people than by the chilly charity of the poorhouse. Lane concludes by announcing that in his next piece he will consider the consequences of "a total absence of the citizens from the ballot box." He reminds his readers of Pythagoras's saying, "avoid the bean." This referred to the custom of voting by placing a bean in a vase (it was important to clear this matter up, as he and Alcott were both self-declared Pythagoreans, but at the same time dependent on beans for part of their austere diet).[7]

About this time the evil of being a nature lover came up again in a Conversation, along with a list of other taboo objects of desire, but Emerson himself was present on this occasion and he was having none of it. He summarized the argument that took place. Alcott and Lane "did not like pictures, marbles, woodlands, & poetry; I liked all these & Lane & Alcott too, as one figure more in the various landscape." Nature included the grasshopper philosophers whether they liked it or not. In a sense this argument missed the point, which was that they felt that loving nature reinforced one's distance from it. But somehow Emerson's hearty affirmation makes their attitude seem like logic-chopping.

He was conscious of having bested them too emphatically—after all, his preferred mode of argument was silence. "And now," he asked them, "will you not please to pound me a little, before I go, just by way of squaring the account, that I may not remember that I alone was saucy." Alcott, pacifist that he was, refused to take the bait and "contented himself with quarreling with the injury done to greater qualities . . . by the tyranny of my Taste." Very soft pounding, admitted Emerson. "And so I departed from the divine lotus-eaters."[8]

The lotus-eaters in fact saw themselves as practical men, at least compared to Greaves. Over in England the Alcott House contingent were starting a new magazine, the *New Age and Concordium Gazette,* and on March 31st indefatigable Lane wrote a letter for its inaugural issue (it didn't in fact get printed until the second number came out on May 13th; the transatlantic packets only sailed once a month in the low season). He grandly announced the plan of buying land in "an attempt to aid man's emancipation." If their master Greaves had come to America as he had intended, no doubt something important would have come of it. Without him their endeavors would be less striking and intellectual but perhaps more permanent. The truth of the matter (and here was a barb aimed at the apostate Wright) was that "most of Mr. Greaves's auditors were sad backsliders." Though "most sincere and real in being, Mr. G. was, in few respects only, a practical man." Lane and Alcott would inevitably work more slowly but to "make a successful appeal to the human race," he tells his former colleagues, "it is necessary to build up bodies, flesh and blood, bricks and timber, fields, gardens, orchards—an entire life."[9]

He might not have been able to accept that he was a figure in the landscape in the Emersonian sense, but in an ecological rather than aesthetic one he is doing exactly that, seeing human beings as indivisible from their surroundings. In its way this is a remarkably prescient environmental perspective, and one which explains and validates his hostility to nature lovers.

If it was true that Greaves was "in few respects only, a practical man," what about his spiritual successor, Bronson Alcott? This is a problem Lane confronted in a long article entitled "A. Bronson Alcott's Works," published in the April 1843 edition of the *Dial*. Alcott's endeavors had met with very little success, after all, at least until that geographical paradox of English recognition of American possibility. "Alcott, almost utterly neglected by contemporaries, must seek a truer appreciation beyond the great waters; and in the quietest nook in Old England behold the first substantial admission of his claim to be considered the exponent of a divinely inspired idea."[10]

True, neglect is a fate common to geniuses generally, but it brings to the fore the issue that had been plaguing Lane ever since his arrival in America and his disappointment that change was not as imminent as he had expected. If Eden is permanently available, why can't one enter it immediately? The English Transcendentalists might have been appreciative of Alcott's "annunciation to mankind," but they had failed to act on it. "The gates of Eden were temptingly in view," Lane explained, but "the ultimate abode was not entered." The Greavesian set "were personally too aged and too unexecutive," he decided.[11]

The issue obviously relates to the one that had troubled the Greavesians from the beginning, instantaneous reform by means of perfected birth versus the longer process implicit in education. Much of Lane's article inevitably concerns teaching, and the same problem surfaces within the topic itself.

The records of Alcott's conversations with children could hardly have caught the excitement of the original moment, that spontaneous interaction of inspiring teacher and inspired children. "Any one, who has attended a public meeting, and has afterwards read a printed report of it in the newspapers," Lane points out, "will have experienced the insufficiency of any recital in inputting a semblance of the life and creative energy in the original."[12]

Alcott himself frequently expressed his frustration at the impossibility of catching the word on its wing. "Thoughts rising spontaneously in the mind, and taking the warm life, and radient [sic] with the light, of the inspired mood of the moment, refuse to reappear in their original freshness and beauty," he wrote sadly in a journal entry of 1839. Memory's pictures "are ever of the dead, not of the living." Both men yearned for the "white type" that Lane had envisaged in his *Union* article the previous year, invisible print capable of capturing the corresponding invisibility—and evanescence—of the spoken word.[13]

Now, in his Alcott article, Lane again attempts to describe the problem of seizing the present. Using almost the same terminology as Alcott's own journal entry of three years previously, he says that "Of the radiant sun at noon, while we say it is, it is not." (Less than a decade later Melville would talk in *Moby-Dick* of the "ungraspable phantom of life.") But while generation happens in a "*flash,*" so quickly that we cannot measure the time it takes, gestation is a process that unfolds gradually.[14] There are in short two timescales, and both play their part. Lane is talking here of how an idea gets itself realized, but his argument applies equally well to (of course) a plant, to the birth of a person, and to the inauguration of a new ordering of society. It is an analysis that vindicates Alcott's lack of success to date. He has planted the seed; it just hasn't blossomed yet.

This extended study of his career to date must have been balm to Alcott's soul. Moreover, on April 1st, Abigail found a flattering passage about her husband in "The Hall of Fantasy," a skit by Hawthorne, and glued it into her diary. Hawthorne was a reclusive and introspective man, preoccupied by the enduring power of historical evil and the question of guilt, concerns that kept him well apart from the Transcendentalist ethos. Nevertheless, in a small community like Concord he could hardly avoid becoming friendly with Emerson and Alcott, as far as his instinct for privacy allowed—in due course he would even buy a house from Alcott. Though he satirized the Transcendentalists in his story "The Transcendental Railroad," he was in a more generous mood here, like Lane confronting—and solving—the problem of Alcott's ineffectualness (though he deleted this passage when the skit was published in book form). "Perhaps his misty apparition may vanish into the sunshine," Hawthorne conceded, but there was no need to worry because "his influence will have impregnated the atmosphere and be imbibed by generations that knew not the original apostle of the ideas which they shall shape into earthly business."[15] Once again we have an act of fertilization followed by a long slow unfolding of earthly business. Alcott himself could hardly have put it better (he might well have put it worse).

It is, of course, a tantalizing business, to have influence with no authorship attached, but that goes with the Transcendental territory. Pondering on the fact that some of the children's contributions to the Record and Conversations come across as a bit too sophisticated to be believable, Lane made the point in his Alcott article that even if they were sometimes just "echoing the teacher's mind," it hardly mattered as long as the ideas themselves were the right ones.[16] There is no copyright in truth.

Ellery Channing, merriest of the Concord set, couldn't bring himself to read the Dial's Alcott panegyric by the "illustrious professor of Poh." He feared the journal was being swamped by puritanical ideas. "A magazine written by professed drunkards," he told Emerson, "gentlemen who eat nothing but beef steaks,—and believers in Original Sin,—must be the thing for me."

Perhaps he had also come across Hawthorne's praise of Alcott, because he professed the hope that the author of Twice-Told Tales would resist the Concordia Cottagers' onslaught of temperance and abstemiousness, and instead maintain his commitment "to strong drinks and strong meats, and above all to the gentle art of angling,—a true disciple of the pimple-cheeked Walton." Hawthorne must never let himself "simmer in horrid bathos" or sell himself "body and soul, for twelve volumes of Greaves manuscripts . . . fit only to be sold at the shops of second-hand booksellers, or to enjoy their existence as wrapping literature."[17]

Theodore Parker had a calmer but equally indignant reaction. He was one of the leading figures in the Transcendental movement, and had a strong commitment to abolition and social justice. In certain respects this would qualify him as an ally of Lane and Alcott (he had none of Emerson's literary detachment), but precisely because of his engagement with causes he was impatient of their trust in a dietary solution to the world's problems. The two were full of "new notions," he told a correspondent, but "at present they do nothing but *abstain from eating flesh.*"[18]

Not quite fair, because the Professor of Poh at least was still busy with his political philosophizing for the *Liberator.* On April 17th Lane penned the next installment of his series, this time dealing with state-level government, commerce, manufacture, and communications. Broadly speaking he was set against all of them. As far as he was concerned, the whole apparatus of state government could be swept away at once, without loss. As things were, it devoted its energies to solving problems it had itself created. The speaker of the Massachusetts legislature had just been elected at a cost of $15,000. As usual Alcott's martyrdom is dragged into the argument. To pay for this folly "sane and honest men are to be sent to jail, terrified, coerced, or cajoled." And because of the labyrinthine nature of state economics, the amount raised to cover this expenditure would in fact amount to $50,000 (or to reckon it another way, more than 30,000 imprisoned, terrified, coerced, and cajoled Alcotts, each owing $1.50).

But even while going into hock to cover such debts, the state was handing out money to finance public projects like railroads and canals. If such systems are worth establishing, then it will be in the interest of private capitalists to invest in them themselves without assistance from the authorities. He personally doesn't see the point of building modern forms of transportation at all. (It must have been an earlier formulation of this view that put the wind up Sophia Dobson, when Lane and Alcott spoke at the Property Convention at Alcott House.) Such "so called improvements . . . are no real advantage to human welfare."

As far as Lane is concerned, "if science could enable us in one month, to compass all the sea and land on the globe, we should compass no more virtue or happiness."[19] (He doesn't mention the fact that Alcott compassed the sea to find English recognition and that the two of them then made use of a modern steam packet to sail toward their American destiny.) Here, as in so many cases, Lane's argument will flower again (more brightly) several years later in the words of Thoreau: "We are in great haste to construct a magnetic telegraph from Maine to Texas; but Maine and Texas, it may be, have nothing important to communicate."[20] Samuel Bower, as we saw, was happy to compare the potential of utopia with the development of the railroad. Lane is much more skeptical about the benefits of such inventions. His position here reveals the extent to which his view of a brave new world actually represented a reaction against modern life on the grounds that it erodes the commitment of individuals to the here and now.

In short, implicit throughout Lane's article is a utopian conception of self-sufficiency, of perfecting the specific, the immediate, and the local, of curing the ills of the whole by engaging with the part that lies to hand—that commitment he had made somewhat reluctantly in his letter to Mrs. Alcott. "If you would have your work done, do it," he says in his *Liberator* piece. "If you would not have it done, set some one else about it."[21] Tantalizingly, though, he avoids spelling out what exactly is on his agenda. There is a paradox here, since this kind of evasion seems related to that very abrogation and delegation of responsibility he is condemning. It turns out that his affirmation of free-market economics throughout the letter has been a kind of devil's advocacy. "My endeavor," he explains, "has been to meet the public world where it now stands, and to show that on principles even no better than those now recognized, the world could go on very well without a government." There is another solution to the problem of organizing a perfected society, but he has deliberately not disclosed it. He hasn't taken "the highest moral ground" because "such a position" is "a mere abstraction": his readers are not ready for it.[22]

It could be argued that the article is abstract enough in any case. But Lane was aware that the rarefied arguments of his *Liberator* pieces would soon be supplemented by something concrete, a public experiment at leading the good life. As their letters had already established, he and Alcott regarded Concordia itself as a utopian experiment, but it was a kind of surreptitious one, a simple adaptation of the status quo. It provided no opportunity for drum rolling, for the announcement of a new start. Over in England the first number of the *New Age and Concordium Gazette* gave its address as the Concordium, Alcott House.[23] Lane felt himself diminished by his enmeshment in the domesticity of the Alcotts and he must by now have been yearning for a Concordium that wasn't simply grafted on to an Alcott house.

He may have been given further motivation by the reappearance of Henry Wright, who returned from his sojourn at Lynn with Mary Gove on May 7th. Arriving with him was a young man in his early twenties, one Samuel Larned, son of a merchant in Providence, Rhode Island and part of the reforming circle associated with Christopher Greene and the *Plain Speaker*. He was what the world calls "genteel," Lane commented approvingly.[24]

Larned had spent some months at Brook Farm, but by temperament and principle was clearly more at home in the Concordia ethos. Allegedly he had passed an entire year living wholly on crackers, only to follow it with another surviving on apples. While at Brook Farm he had refused to drink milk and wore nonleather shoes.[25] According to Concordia dietetics he must have already been well on the way to building up the "human body divinely."

In 1842 he and two friends, wearing Byronic collars (like Wright when Mary Gove met him), beards, broad brimmed hats, and sack coats, had gone off on a pioneering journey through New England, without making use of money. Or nearly: just as they set out they discovered they had to pay a toll of two cents to cross the bridge over the Charles River. So that they wouldn't be tempted again after this unfortunate start, they threw all the money left in their pockets into the water below. From then on they relied on the generosity of people they encountered on their way for lodging and food, though given their severe dietary restrictions, that wasn't asking much.[26]

Some of their hosts might have been taken aback by Larned's bad language, however. He believed that swearing elevated the spirit in some way (perhaps he had a premonition of Freud's theory of repression), and according to Louisa May Alcott's later testimony, would greet people by saying, "Good morning, damn you."[27] (It may be that he suffered from Tourette's syndrome.) The picaresque journey perfectly captures the radicalism of the period, looking backward toward the medieval tradition of pilgrimage, and forward toward the late nineteenth- and twentieth-century mythology of the open road.

The journey was described in an after-dinner speech given much later by one of Larned's acquaintances, and published many years after that, so the account is not wholly reliable, and was claimed to be an exaggeration by one of the friends, George Burleigh, with whom Larned traveled.[28] But such anecdotes provided an entrée to Concordia, qualifying Larned for membership on both nutritional and economic grounds, if not on linguistic ones. Indeed Larned may well have influenced the two older utopians to take more extreme measures than they were taking already.

During his time at Brook Farm, Larned had enthusiastically espoused the dress code that was developing there. Hawthorne had been a member of the community for some months during 1841, its first year of operation. On the face of it this is surprising, given his reclusive habits and his skeptical attitude towards Transcendentalism, but one of his motives was to save up enough money to marry his fiancée, Sophia Peabody. He was also interested in the effects of manual labor on his sedentary occupation as a writer. During his stay there Sophia sent him "a thin frock" which met with such general admiration he was confident that it would become the accepted uniform of the community—which indeed happened. The following year, Larned, along with several other Brook Farmers, called on the writer Thomas Wentworth Higginson. Sure enough Larned was "peculiarly costumed" in a kind of smock, belted at the waist. Such blouses, Higginson adds, were made of brown Holland (like those at Alcott House) or even "gay-colored chintz" (he does not say which color scheme Larned went for, but perhaps the adverb "peculiarly" tells its own story).[29] Certainly at the time of Larned's arrival at Concordia, Alcott moved on to a new stage of his self-sufficiency project, dressing the children "in costume of my fashioning and cutting."[30] Sophia Dobson had thought this sort of home dressmaking unfeasible and a great waste of time and labor, but she had been under the impression that there was, or should be, a heart to society: she had missed the point about establishing one's independence from it.

This was an issue Lane tackled in his next letter on "A Voluntary Political Government," penned on May 4th. Commitment to a larger identity than one's own inevitably caused diminishment. "The price one must pay for the most honorable participation in public affairs is to sink one's manhood into the narrow dimensions of a three hundredth or a four hundredth part of a man."[31] This argument suggests he has now found a way to reconcile himself to the loss of his original ambition on arrival in America to take only a fractional part in a large upheaval.

A few years previously Emerson had explored the same issue in his "American Scholar" address. "Man is not a farmer, or a professor, or an engineer, but he is all." However, in "the divided or social state, these functions are parcelled out to individuals, each of whom aims to do his stint of the joint work, whilst each other performs his." It should be possible to go back to base from time to time, to make contact with the human totality—"to embrace all the other laborers." But unfortunately "this original unit, this fountain of power, has been so distributed to multitudes, has been so minutely subdivided and peddled out," that rather like Humpty-Dumpty, it can't be put together again. "The state of society," Emerson claimed, "is one in which the members have suffered amputation from the trunk, and strut about so many walking monsters,—a good finger, a neck, a stomach, but never a man."[32]

According to Lane, society attempts to reassemble a whole man for itself by botching together these scattered parts, rather like Frankenstein building his monster, though that is not the comparison Lane himself makes. "The country, not possessing a real man, attempts to make one, somewhat as the bees their queen: with this remarkable difference, that the bees succeed, and the men fail."

Lane devotes much of this essay to inspecting the constitution of the state of Massachusetts, finding himself in the awkward position of using it as a precedent, and dismissing its relevance, in quick succession. The precedent is that in its preamble the document declares that "*The body politic is formed by a voluntary association of individuals.*" But this sound preliminary is immediately betrayed by the first clause, which establishes that the "end of this renowned institution is to maintain and protect itself!" It has become a self-perpetuating entity in its own right, rather than a free alliance of individuals.

What Lane pits against this collectivization is the "old geometrical principle of inverse ratio." Everyone agrees that smaller states operate more efficiently than bigger ones; the American union itself is a reflection of that belief. "Why not, then, carry out this principle a little further?" Let the county make its own decisions, as far as it can, rather than have the state legislate on its behalf. And in turn let the county's decisions, where possible, be abridged in favor of the town's. Why not go one stage further than that?, he asks, his Realometer detecting an even firmer "*point d'appui*"—"let it be thrown upon every family to legislate wisely and virtuously in and for itself."

Lane has found a mathematical formula to vindicate his American experience and reconcile him to the small scale in which he finds himself working.

"Public opinion rules at last; and why not rule at first?"[33] (Though Lane's writing is usually far more abstract than Thoreau's, at moments like this one senses the younger man may have derived a little of his rhetorical muscle from the older one, along with a good portion of his political theory.) But Lane was undoubtedly also telling himself that when this process was accomplished, the formula could go into reverse, and perfection spread outward toward the totality.

Meanwhile, in Concordia reconciliation with Wright did not last long. He soon began to row with Alcott and Lane—with Lane in particular, as he felt he had not been reimbursed for his share of Greaves's library—and it is probable that he left the cottage quite soon for New York.[34] But there were many other visitors at this time, and clearly a buzz of expectation that the next stage of the experiment in living was about to get under way. Lane and Alcott began to search in earnest for a new dwelling for their community.

They scoured the state, in fact, looking at properties in Milton, Roxbury, Brookline, Watertown, Southborough Bridge, Stowe. They inspected a place called the Halloween Farm, which might have confirmed Emerson's fears about the miasmic glow given off by Greaves's writings. Towards the middle of the month Alcott made a trip to Oriskany in New York State to visit his mother and brother Junius.[35] According to Lane he was also checking the potential for establishing their community in that neighborhood. They had heard that the land was fruitful there, though the inhabitants were deficient in spiritual-mindedness—more soil than soul, as Lane understood.[36] Of course he and Alcott saw their mission as reconciling the two. Alcott met with no success however. On the way back he stopped off at Braintree, Vermont, and spent some days with Benjamin Dyer, whom he had visited previously and who had expressed an interest in joining their community.[37] That came to nothing too.

Back at Concordia Abigail was once more fed up with Lane. He must have said something that suggested admiration of his home country, because she complained to her brother Charles that he "is vain of his country for the excellent reason that *it produced him.*" That was the problem with the English, she concluded (perhaps with Wright in mind as well): she liked them well enough but hated their "haughty conceit."[38]

Meanwhile on May 17th Lane dashed off yet another piece in his series of articles. This one opened with a powerful passage in which he evoked the persistence of the monster of aristocracy, now taking a new form. "No longer duke, or count, or baron, he can become president, merchant, banker . . . As the baronial hall crumbles to dust, the huge, grim factory rises to a greater height." Despite being a successful commodities journalist himself, Lane professed none of Emerson's admiration for the tradesman or merchant who survives on his wits and thrives despite the "antagonism of the tough world." On the contrary: he feels that such a discipline is likely to reflect or create a blinkered outlook. "A man who has worked his way up from poverty to riches against a contending world," he claims, "fancies it is in the power of every one else to do the same, not knowing that the processes which to him were agreeable enough are utterly repugnant to conscientious souls."[39] Appropriate sentiments from a friend and colleague of Alcott's.

Having returned from his unsuccessful trip to New York State and Vermont, Alcott went with Lane to look at some land for sale on the Concord Cliffs, under which Junius, Abigail, and the girls had bobbed in their little boat the *Undine* the previous summer, while he was in England. That trip had meant a lot to his family. Years later Abigail sent a message to Junius to tell him that the boat was still "floating sweetly" on the Concord River, but that the girls were so grown they would no longer all be able to fit into it.[40] Sixteen acres of young orchard were available at the Cliffs, along with some woodland. Lane, feeling tired, went home, leaving Alcott to fantasize about clearing a space there and setting up a community, thereby staying in touch with the "classic town" of Concord.

When Lane arrived back at Concordia, a young man was waiting for him. He had heard that Lane and Alcott were looking for a property. It so happened he had one for sale. And his carriage was just outside; they could go and view it at once. But Lane was still tired, so he suggested Samuel Larned should go instead. Larned gave a favorable report because the following morning Lane and Alcott walked the fourteen miles to the place (no waiting vehicle this time) to see it for themselves.

They didn't even know the name of the vendor, but it turned out to be Maverick Wyman. His "slice of the planet" was situated in a commanding and beautiful position on a hillside overlooking the Nashua Valley. The elevation was actually called Prospect Hill. Wyman, Prospect—the very names must have suggested an earthly *Pilgrim's Progress* to the two men on a mission. "It is very remotely placed," Lane told Thoreau, "nearly three miles beyond the village, without a road, surrounded by a beautiful green land-scape of fields and woods, with the distance filled up by some of the loftiest mountains in the State."[41]

The village in question was called Harvard—not to be confused with the university some thirty miles to the east, though named in its honor by some graduates in 1732. There was a Shaker community in the town already (indeed Mother Ann Lee herself had once lived there), and another in the nearby village of Shirley. Their simple way of life, their use of music and dancing in religious observances, and above all their abstention from sex, would each strike a chord with Lane. He looked at the beautiful, empty land-scape and decided it offered far more "facilities" than could be provided by the Cliffs of Concord; emptiness obviously being a facility in itself.[42] All that local celibacy gave moral sharpness and clarity to the expanse of view, providing a whole new dimension to the notion of a virgin landscape.

Actually it was not quite as empty as he claimed. There was another property just a quarter of a mile to the south, lived in by a family called Lovejoy, and connected to the Wyman place by a country lane which ran all the way to Madigan Lane in Harvard village itself.[43] Lane, dubious about the advantages of transportation, found it convenient to overlook this little road.

Alcott was perhaps less impressed. Later he claimed to have disliked the place from the start, but this might have been a case of wisdom after the event. It was, of course, a moment of truth. Up until now he had been leading the charge. The community-cum-school of the English Transcendentalists had been named in his honor. Lane and Wright had come over to America on his say-so, and they had been his guests in Concordia Cottage. Now it was time for the pendulum to swing, because if they were to take over the Wyman property, it would be Lane who had to pay for it.

The property, Alcott noted, consisted of about ninety acres of land, comprising seventy-four arable and fourteen woodland (he doesn't account for the missing two, bookkeeping not being his strong point).[44] No orchard, he observed. Lane told Thoreau that there were in fact a few apple trees, and plenty of nuts and berries. Both he and Alcott agreed that the house and barn were in poor condition. They had been jerry-built twenty or more years

1 The young Bronson Alcott. A copy of an unfinished drawing now lost. This picture gives an idea of how Alcott must have looked as he sat beneath a picture of Jesus at his desk in the Temple School.

2 Alcott in middle age. "A majestical man," his friend Emerson called him.

3 Charles Lane. The only photograph, taken long after the Fruitlands period. His face looked as if "the washwomen had rubbed it on a washboard," claimed Lydia Maria Child, adding that his appearance would "make me slow to put myself in his powers."

ALCOTT HOUSE, HAM COMMON, NEAR RICHMOND.

An Association founded for the purpose of securing, by co-operation, those results which are impracticable by private enterprise.

Having not for result the realization of pecuniary advantage, it seeks to enter into such arrangements with parents as shall furnish it with all means and facilities to accomplish its mission, which is, to develope manhood to the highest possible extent consistent with the admissions of present society, or the more favourably conditions which the immediate future promises.

In the EDUCATIVE DEPARTMENT, it asks support upon the grounds—

1st, That it acknowledges the highest and purest worth in humanity, and accepts it as the standard of culture, proposing, to the utmost of its ability, to render its pupils personations of Clearness, Goodness, and Beauty.

2nd, That it is Cosmopolitan in character, commanding connexions in foreign parts, in some of which it proposes eventually to establish schools, while it attracts from them classes of scholars, securing thus for its inmates the advantages of Germany, France, &c., without the necessity of emigration.

3rd, That it is universal in sentiment, being free without infidelity, and religious without sectarism or superstition.

4th, That its disciplinary superintendence is uninterrupted, contemplating always the promotion of sound health in body, intellect, and affections.

At this Institution, Children are Boarded, Clothed, Educated, and in every respect entire attended to and parentally treated.

The Course of Instruction includes five Languages; namely, ENGLISH, GERMAN, FRENCH, LATIN, and GREEK, as desired: WRITING, DRAWING, MUSIC, SINGING, PHYSIOLOGY, ANATOMY, GYMNASTICS, GEOGRAPHY, DANCING, MATHEMATICS, including Mental Arithmetic, HISTORY, NATURAL HISTORY, CHEMISTRY, DOMESTIC ECONOMY, GARDENING, &c.

Pupils of either sex are received at a stipulated sum per annum, payable quarterly in advance, which includes protection through the whole, there being no vacations, unless desired by the parents. The treatment being based on strict attention in cleanliness, diet, exercise, and on medical knowledge on the part of the conductors, there is never any charge for medical treatment, nor for any other extras.

Children are not required to bring other things than a simple outfit of clothing; no notice of leaving is necessary; and, as the Institution is carried on entirely by moral means, no punishments whatever are introduced.

Parents who send several children, may benefit by the common funds, with which the Society is provided, as well as Parents who, having a child of favourable pre-organization, may be unable to meet the whole charge.

Excursions are made—

1st, Daily, for health and instruction in Natural History.

2nd, Occasionally for the foregoing purposes, combined with initiation into social intercourse and customs.

3rd, Annually to the Continent, for a participation in which a special arrangement is made with the parents in each case, so as to meet the peculiar expenditure.

Applications, either personally or by post, may be made to the Society, at Alcott House, Ham Common, near Richmond, Surrey.

4 Alcott House, Ham, England. Named in honor of Bronson Alcott, it provided a blueprint for Fruitlands. "The inmates practised abstinence from marriage and most things else," reported a visitor. "Their cardinal doctrine was that happiness was wrong."

5 James Pierrepont Greaves, leader of the English Transcendentalists. "There he sat with an eye—'twas unfathomable!" one of his disciples exclaimed. "Oh! The wonders of that eye!"

6 Henry Gardiner Wright, Fruitlands apostate. His admirer Mrs. Gove quoted him as saying that he wore his hair long because "though its waves and rings are entirely natural, its appearance is improved by art."

7 Portrait of Abigail May Alcott in late middle age, many years after the Fruitlands experiment.

8 Anna Alcott, taken when she was grown up. She was only thirteen when she lived at Fruitlands.

9 Louisa May Alcott, also as an adult. She had her eleventh birthday at Fruitlands.

Concord June 21st 1840.

Dear Mother,

I write from my little cottage in Concord, (18 miles from Boston) into which we moved on the first of April last, and find much happiness by this change from the city to the country. I cultivate a garden and a field, in all about an acre and three quarters, and find constant occupation on this my frail farm: my vegetables look finely at this time. I shall raise more than a supply for my family. Abba does all her work and the children all go to school in the village close by, and we are free to do all

10 Concordia Cottage, also known as Dove Cottage, where the experiment known as Fruitlands actually began. Bronson Alcott's sketch, in a letter to his mother.

11 The central part of Concord as depicted by John Warner Barber in 1839, shortly before the Alcotts moved there. Bronson Alcott pasted this picture into his scrapbook.

12 Joseph Palmer, complete with the notorious beard that brought about his imprisonment.

13 Ralph Waldo Emerson, who funded Alcott's English trip but later regretted it.

14 Margaret Fuller. She laughed at the contrast between the Fruitlanders' idealism and life on the frontier, "where strong instincts and imperative necessities come upon you like the swoop of a hawk."

15 Henry David Thoreau. "He is as ugly as sin," Hawthorne wrote, "long-nosed, queer-mouthed and with uncouth and rustic, though courteous manners."

16 Fruitlands in the late nineteenth century, when it had once again become as tatty as it was when the utopians lived there.

previously, and had obviously been neglected ever since.[45] Wyman offered them the whole package for $2,700.

This was more than Lane possessed, particularly as he had come to realize that if they were to move from Concord, he would have to settle Alcott's local debts there ("I need not tell you on whom that falls," he told Oldham resentfully). So Wyman modified his offer. They could have the land for $1,800 and borrow the buildings gratis for a year.[46] Even this was slightly more than Lane could manage on his English savings. After paying what Alcott owed the Concord tradesmen (Lane claimed it amounted to $300), he could manage $1,500. Wyman told him that if he could find a guarantor for the amount outstanding, it could be paid at six-monthly intervals in installments of $75. The sums might seem trivial, but in terms of modern purchasing power, $1,800 was worth over $54,000, and the installments of $75 amounted to $2,250.[47] Lane was obviously expecting that surplus crops would enable him to pay off the remainder of this debt, despite his hostility to trade and belief in subsistence living.

Presumably Alcott sat patiently through these transactions. Their hard-headedness would have undermined his own evasions and wishful thinking, the airy talk to Parker Pilsbury and others about "obtaining the free use of a piece of land," the high hopes that the project would need "no costly appa-ratus, no expensive outlays" because "its apparatus and resources are the gifts and graces of its subjects." Let us not say no and take it, Emerson had irritably advised. By this point Alcott was saying nothing, and taking it.

Back in Concordia, events moved quickly. Lane contacted Abigail's brother Samuel May and asked him to guarantee the loan from Wyman, as well as to act as his agent in the transaction as a whole, which he agreed to do, probably relieved that Alcott's affairs were being sorted out at last, at least for the time being. A gift of £10—that sum again!—arrived opportunely from William Oldham, and went toward the settlement. On May 25th Lane purchased the property.[48]

However much Lane repudiated the hardnosed values of business, he had spent a great deal of his life evaluating commodities and he couldn't quite stop now. Some of the land was worth $100 dollars an acre, he told Oldham proudly, though he'd only paid twenty. "Everyone says we have made a good bargain." Perhaps fearing that this sounded too materialistic, he piously wished "some of the English half-starved were on it!" He was in fact a little nervous because he calculated that he had actually left himself $500 in the red altogether—the Wyman mortgage plus another $200. Presumably the months he had already spent with the Alcotts had been a drain on his savings. Only a couple of weeks before he had castigated the state of Massachusetts for its profligacy in choosing a Speaker; now he had done much the same thing on a smaller scale by backing a Conversationalist. Successful businessman that he had been, with money in his pocket, he had caught the debt contagion from hapless Alcott.

He still believed his own hardheadedness could have an impact. This enterprise would be "an attempt at something which will entitle transcendentalism to some respect for its practicality." Unfortunately for this hope, the experiment was being founded on a basis of ambiguity, the same one that had been dogging Concordia ever since his arrival from England. It was all very well to announce in the *Liberator* that society should be built on the foundations of family, but was that the right word to describe the set-up that was about to be established on the slopes of Prospect Hill? If not, what was? "I seriously hope we are forming the basis for something really progressive," he told Oldham, "call it family or community, or what you will."[49] It was an issue that would never be resolved.

After the deal had gone through, Lane camped out in the house, rehearsing for life there. His son William was with him, along with Larned and another man who had arrived at Concordia in the last month and who was to become a member of the community, a shadowy figure originally called Abraham Everett. He was forty-two, a cooper by trade, and had once been confined to a lunatic asylum, a "rather deep experience," according to Lane, one brought about because he owned a little property (Lane being sensitive on that topic at present). Abraham had reforming principles and had rechristened himself in order to face a new world with a new identity, changing Everett to Wood. That gesture didn't strike him as sufficient, however, so he then reversed the sequence, becoming Wood Abraham or Abram, perhaps to give himself an environmental emphasis.[50]

One cannot help feeling sympathy for eleven-year-old William Lane, perched in that dilapidated creaking house with a compulsive swearer, a mentally unstable man of shifting identity, and a difficult austere father who was anxious and evangelical by turns. There was also a hired hand to help the utopians as they settled into a farming life.

Lane returned to Concord late in May to help out with the move, leaving William behind with his odd companions. All the others would move house from Concord on June 1st.[51] Emerson was taken aback by these high-speed arrangements. The imminent parting made him wonder if he had let the Concordians down in some way. "My friends are leaving the town," he told his diary, "and I am sad at heart that they cannot have that love & service from me to which they seem by their aims & the complexion of their minds & by their unpopularity, to have rich claims." For his part Lane felt that Emerson could indeed have done more to encourage them all to stay in Concord. "Mr Emerson is not so well pleased with our departure as he would be with our company," he told Oldham bitterly, "but as he did nothing to keep us we must go."

Emerson's reference to their unpopularity suggests that the eccentrics of Concordia had not gone down well with Concord at large. He himself, he admitted, had never really taken to Lane. "Especially C. L. I seem to myself to have treated with the worst inhospitality inasmuch as I have never received that man to me—not for so much as one moment."

What Emerson realized, as he thought about it, was that there were two aspects to Lane. On the one hand he was a "pure superior mystical, intellectual & gentle soul, free & youthful too in character, & treating me ever with marked forbearance." On the other he was formidable, "a fighter in the ring." Emerson suspected that this might reflect a gulf between the English in general and New Englanders. There was something definite and adversarial about the products of the old country. "They strike twelve, the first time."[52] Perhaps Abigail Alcott had been getting at this when she used the word "haughty" of them. Certainly Lane would have fueled such a suspicion in a conversation he had had with Emerson the previous December. He was talking about Christopher Greene, the Providence radical who had edited the *Plain Speaker* and published Alcott—on the face of it, a kindred spirit. "The true place of the reformer is on the land," Greene had proclaimed, and he took a thoroughly Greavesian line in an article on "Marriage," claiming that women should take the lead in relationships because they were more adept than men at identifying true, chaste love. But Lane had transatlantic reservations about him. "C. Greene may be a trader, or a priest, or a soldier as probably as a progressive reformer," he asserted. The cause of this dubious flexibility (the listed career possibilities were all ones Lane himself would reject in his *Liberator* series) was that, as an American, Greene had more opportunities to diversify his identity, while "the English and Europeans are girded as with an iron belt of condition."[53]

Emerson, who recorded this claim in his journal, would have taken much the same view of Lane's arrogance as Abigail. He himself was fascinated by the phenomenon of metamorphosis, and in a poem written in 1840 pictured life's riddle, the Sphinx, as speaking through a thousand voices.[54] He celebrated the variety of existence at the same time as he proclaimed its underlying unity, and his reference to an "iron belt" was undoubtedly his disapproving summary of Lane's claim for English integrity and consistency. As he thought about him now, Emerson decided that Lane was "born a warrior, the most expert swordsman we have ever seen." He went on, in that lethal, delicate fashion of his, to point up the ultimate irony: the man was "metallic in his nature, not vegetable enough" (despite all those years of veganism!). And Lane was insensitive to nature. Also, despite his hopes of bringing out Transcendentalism's practical possibilities, he was qualified to do no such thing: his hands were "as far from his head as Alcott's own." All in all, Emerson decided, he was alien, and had a freezing effect on him.

But as usual Emerson wondered whether the ultimate fault lay with himself. The utopians had a mystical faith, after all, and he respected that. They could "trust the Universe to give the hospitality of the Omnipresent to the good." He, meanwhile, had to commit to the imperatives of daily life, "to do the honours with offices, money, and clatter of plates."[55]

It was a moment of truth, the parting of the ways.

10

Diffusive Illimitable Benevolence

THEY CALLED THE NEW property Fruitlands. The land below the farm-house, stretching down toward the Nashua River, had been known as the Plum Tree Meadows since early colonial times, so that name provided a sort of precedent.[1] The connection would one day be honored in Louisa May Alcott's *Little Men*, when Jo calls her school Plumfield.[2] But in June 1843 the name Fruitlands was hardly a description, more a statement of intent, since apart from the few apple trees mentioned by Lane (years later Louisa remembered just ten in all, old ones at that), there was no orchard. It takes fifteen years for an orchard to come (in the most literal sense) to fruition. Given the importance of fruit in the Fruitlanders' diet and indeed in their plan to reinstate the Garden of Eden, this seems a serious oversight.

In her short memoir *Transcendental Wild Oats*, written many years after the event, Louisa claimed that the Fruitlanders possessed "the firm belief that plenteous orchards were soon to be evoked from their inner consciousness."[3] This was (ironically) less ironic and more literally true than she intended, since their commitment to what the Greavesians called the Antecedent, the world before the Fall, encouraged a notion that perfection could be instantly rediscovered, a fascination with the "flash" of germination rather than with the slow, earthly process of developing and ripening. In his mocking letter a couple of months previously, Ellery Channing had described Lane's article on Alcott as reminding him of "some retired gentleman who is making cucumbers of moonshine," as if, with a flick of the wrist, one could produce vegetable matter instantaneously out of one's sleeve or hat.[4] In a sense that was just what Alcott and Lane tried to do by giving their unfruitful property its name.

Fruitlands was destined to be unfruitful in another sense too. One of the reasons for the austere diet to which the members subscribed was to purify the body so that a new generation could be born with their pristine spirit uncontaminated by physical evils. But the Alcotts had their family already, and Lane certainly had no interest in producing more offspring. No mention of this possibility had been made during their time at Concordia. The task of reproducing perfect men, as Alcott had put it, seems to have been overlooked in planning the community, along with the intention to buy "a good orchard."

June 1, 1843 was a cold sharp day for the time of year. Abigail had scrubbed Concordia Cottage till it was "clean as a new book"—even Lane praised her "great energy." They hired a couple of carts to take their possessions. It was fourteen miles from Concord to Fruitlands, done at walking speed—indeed, twelve-year-old Anna went on foot for part of the way—and they arrived at the property in the late afternoon.[5] William Lane was no doubt pleased and relieved to see his father and the others again.

That first night they camped indoors. They didn't have time to put the beds together, so slept on the floor. The girls were in the attic, except for little Abby May, who stayed with her parents, while William shared with his father and the other men took up quarters in the barn.[6] The house consisted of two small front rooms and one long room on each of the two floors. The three older Alcott girls had the low-ceilinged attic as their bedroom during their time at Fruitlands. It was windowless and hot in the summer, cold in the winter. Indeed, it is likely that the second floor of the house was also unheated.[7]

Before she went to bed Abigail made an entry in her journal. She thought about all that had happened in the three years at Concord—the birth of little Abby May, the death of her father, her husband's visit to England, and his return with Lane and Wright. She imagined gathering like-minded men and women into the community, so they could all lead "quiet exemplary lives."

She knew it would be difficult, but their motives were innocent and true, and for the good of others. If they failed "it will be some consolation that we have ventured what none others have dared."[8] For her, as undoubtedly for the other participants, the community was a unique experiment for humanity.

Next day, work started. The men washed themselves in a nearby brook. The woman and children used a shower of Alcott's devising. He built a frame of clothes horses and wrapped sheets around it. They stood inside while he climbed a stepladder and poured water down on them through a sieve.[9] The diet was much the same as in Concordia. According to Louisa it consisted of unleavened bread, porridge, and water for breakfast; bread, vegetables, and water for (midday) dinner; bread, fruit, and water for supper.[10]

The Fruitlanders did their best to sort out the furniture and put the house in order.[11] Their library of a thousand books arrived during the course of the day and had to be piled up somewhere, giving off its phosphorescent glow until they could find a local carpenter to build them the hundred feet of shelving it required.[12] Alcott was a good woodworker himself, but had other tasks to occupy him. Outside, the challenge must have seemed almost overwhelming. Wyman had left them a few crops and some livestock which was sold off within a couple of weeks. Though the Fruitlanders could reassure themselves that they would soon be rid of the animals, the ominous significance of their presence in the first place does not seem to have struck home. Perhaps this was the wrong type of farm altogether? But at least for the time being they could use a yoke of oxen for plowing. They had to begin planting as soon as possible, since it was already late in the farming year. Lane was fascinated to see how good Alcott was at keeping a straight furrow. He was a farmboy from Spindle Hill, Connecticut, after all, and the hired hand looked slovenly by comparison. The challenge of this new place triggered an initial burst of energy from him. "His hand is everywhere," Lane noted, "like his mind."[13]

Lane's mind was also active. He had started the final letter in his series for the *Liberator*, and finished it on June 3rd, just two days after his arrival at Fruitlands. The question he confronted was, given that the world is out of kilter with the "principles we know and acknowledge to be true . . . what are we to do?" There he was, scribbling in the chaos of the move, with the challenge of a rickety house around him, and frenzied catch-up planting waiting for him outside, with thousands of earnest and indignant words already committed to paper, and the advice he now gives, the punchline of his story, is so anti-climactic that its impact is a bombshell: "I reply 'do nothing.' "[14]

Negativity, though, can have its own layers of meaning, its own ambiguities. Lane explains that there is no point in taking action against the state (that would, after all, be opposing force with force). Just occasionally there "may be some obnoxious result of human activity in the way, which human activity may remove," but on the whole the Greavesian panacea of passivity, negativity's twin, was the answer.

Again there are levels of interpretation here. Passivity means refusing to fight back against the oppression of the government. The image of a hippy sliding a flower down a National Guardsman's rifle comes to mind, a hundred and twenty years in the future—that gesture obviously owes something to the nonresistance advocated by Garrison and amplified by Samuel May and Bronson Alcott himself, among others, but perhaps it also derives from a line of transmission that passed from Greaves to Lane to Thoreau. At the same time, passivity also means choosing not to implicate oneself in the state's oppression, as Alcott did by refusing to pay his poll tax. Just before leaving Concord, Lane had been approached by the tax assessor "for an inventory of the contents of my pocket," and he too had refused to comply. He was now awaiting the outcome.[15] (The liability was backdated, so his move to Harvard did not affect it.)

Then there was the most elevated form of Greavesian or Transcendental passivity: accessing one's own indwelling moral nature and relying on that to shape one's actions and indeed one's life as a whole. If a person falls into the river, we run to help him out: we do not need to make a "public and congregative noise" to come to that decision. Morality, in effect, operates like an instinct; following its dictates enables one to "effect domestic and family order." If everyone did so, the state would cease to have a function and would wither away. Lane presents this process as a natural outcome of American history (perhaps he is still explaining to himself the logic of that journey from old to New England). There used to be a notion that the governors and the governed were two different races, just as the whites and the slaves were still regarded now. The American Revolution, sixty years before, had proved that the two groups could be one. Less than a lifetime later, the time had come to internalize that development. "We have to show that one hat can at one moment cover both these characters."[16]

Lane signs off the series by announcing the move to Fruitlands. "My sojourn in this country has had reference throughout to a connection with the land as the outward basis of all the holy and wholesome existence." Now, with Alcott and other friends, he is about to try to achieve a state of things "some steps in advance of the present," a journey into the future (though at the same time of course it is a rediscovery of the distant past). He adds a note of caution, reflecting that disappointment he expressed months earlier to Abigail: the experiment will possibly not comprehend "all that is ideally living in the mind."

Still, he told his readers, there were nearly a hundred acres available for the community, "if not totally free from all relation to property; yet approaching as nearly as circumstances will permit." This is another example of the sort of finessing of financial reality that so angered Emerson. The Fruitlands transaction had nothing in common with Greaves's capacity to enjoy a beautiful landscape without owning it. On the contrary, the farm had been bought in exactly the same way as farms usually are. Money and deeds had exchanged hands. An amount was still owing, payable over two years. Abigail's brother was having to stand as guarantor of payment. Lane had already announced—and would do so again—that he had made a profitable investment. He seems in his *Liberator* piece to be exhibiting the same mindset as the one that brought about the community's name. Say the word "fruit" in the expectation fruit will follow; assert the suspension of ownership in hopes that it will fracture the economic continuum.

Perhaps to restore his good faith, he goes on to explain that the house itself is merely lent, and only for a short time at that. Since his capital has been exhausted in "obtaining the freedom of restoring, subduing and using a piece of God's earth," this means that there is a lot of work ahead. The very incompleteness of the deal provides its moral integrity: the Fruitlanders cannot claim ownership of the tatty farmhouse and its barn.[17]

The motive underlying his public admission that he does not own the house can be understood better by reference to the nearest thing we have to a mission statement for the Fruitlands community. Three years previously, while on a visit to his disciple Alexander Campbell in Stockport, Greaves drew up a table illustrating the relationship between inner spiritual health and the external environment: the circumstantial law. Lane revised it for publication in the *Healthian* in 1842, and copies of this version were glued into both Alcott's Autobiographical Collections and Abigail's journal.[18]

The preamble to the table represents the usual Greavesian unease about the role of circumstances. They can't be seen as generating the "Creative Power," because the very etymology of the word means that they "stand around" something that already exists, the Antecedent. Nevertheless circumstances can produce results. The table itself can be seen as a graph, with the vertical axis going from bad to best. Greaves's original version was the other way around, with the bad on top, reflecting his serene independence of the temporal process. Lane's reversal gives a sense of aspiration, or development, the possibility of rising through circumstances—reflected by his assertion in the *Liberator* piece that Fruitlands as a community does not reflect all that is "ideally living in the mind."

THE CIRCUMSTANTIAL LAW.

The True Practical Socialist, being aware that Man is not a simple, but a compound, or, rather, a complex Being, whose threefold Character is formed by the threefold Law in the sympathetic, intellectual, and physical Circumstances, or Conditions, by which he is constantly surrounded, is desirous of presenting to such Law, in its several spheres, the circumstances most conducive to Man's harmonious development.

Though it be true that the CREATIVE POWER cannot properly be attributed to the CIRCUMSTANCES, because the latter term is used to designate the things which STAND ROUND something already created, yet, for as much as RESULTS can never be attained without circumstances, or conditions, or secondary causes, and it is only over these that Men individually, or socially, have any interfering power, the furnishing of suitable conditions, is a subject demanding the deepest consideration. While neither etymology, nor logic, nor truth, permits the assertion, that Circumstances form the Character; we may safely affirm that the END, or the CAUSE in CIRCUMSTANCES produces RESULTS.

The following Table is submitted as a Scheme, attempting to show the sort of conditions which should be offered in the Physical Sphere, according to the intention or desire for developing the higher or the highest natures. As a consequence it serves as a key to the interior state of any individual. Each one becomes in this manner a condition to others, for the evolution of the like nature, to that of which such conduct is an exhibition.

For the better understanding of the pure conditions, there is subjoined a hint of the present prevailing errors in each department.

Table No. 1. PHYSICAL CIRCUMSTANCES.

	AIR.	FOOD.	CLOTHING.	HABITATION.	EMPLOYMENT	EDUCATION.	RELIGION.	MARRIAGE.
Best, for the Spirit Nature. Love Conditions.	Pure Balmy Atmosphere.	Ripe uncooked Saccharine Fruits.	Linen Robes	The Tent. An unfixed Locality.	The Orchard.	Progressive Gymnastic Exercises. Growth of Nerve.	Active Benevolence. Love for the unlovely.	Union of Spiritc selected pairs in sympathetic harmony.
Better, for the Soul, or Human Nature. Light Conditions	Pure Temperate Atmosphere.	Green, or Succulent Vegetables.	Pervious and Flowing Cotton Garments; undyed.	The House: Social and scientific conveniences.	The Garden.	Progressive Gymnastic Exercises. Growth of Muscle.	Thoughtful Thought for the thoughtless	Co-education, or betrothment of Spirit-selected pairs.
Good, for the Body. Life Conditions.	Pure Bracing Atmosphere.	Farinaceous Grain & Pulse.	Cotton or HempenDress, undyed.	The Public Hall. Accomodation, Rest and Amusement.	The Field.	Progressive Gymnastic Exercises. Growth of Bone.	Practical benevolence. Bread for the hungry.	Social intercourse of Families, Races and Nations.
Bad, for all Nature. Prevailing erroneous Conditions	Ill ventilated apartments; atmosphere corrupted in coal-dust, smoke, tobacco, &c.	Fermented and Cooked Fruits. Vegetables and Roots. Flesh of Animals. FermentedLiquors	Woollen fabrics, tight and impervious to perspiration; Animal skins; Metal decorations, &c.	Towns and Cities; dirty, dense & dark. Luxurious Mansions and dilapidated Cottages.	Exchange of Commodities, useful & useless. Factory & other Slave-Labour.	Treatment of the Being as a passive blank. Routine of discipline.	Physical representations and deadening Ceremonies.	Legal Bonds. Animal Lust.

Charles Lane

Greaves's Table of the Circumstantial Law, as revised by Charles Lane

It is quite important to stress that though one rises *through* circumstances, one never rises above them entirely. The top level may look austere and minimal to those of us trapped in legal bonds and eating (as well as drinking) fermented fruits, but the elevated soul derives enormous joy and gratification from the few circumstances still available—still standing around—at his or her level, as various Fruitlanders would in due course bear witness. What we have is a double process: release from the entanglement of adverse circumstances, and gratification from the carefully selected few that are life-enhancing and therefore allowed to remain. The Fruitlands program didn't involve rejecting the world but transforming it into its ultimate state.

Not long after arriving in America, Lane had decided that the receptivity to the "universe law" which, in his early enthusiasm, he detected all around, had to do with the country's Puritan legacy. "Their life-blood," he declared, "still flows in the veins of New Englanders."[19] Clearly much of the Fruitlands ethos can be related to that inheritance, in particular their circuitous way of treating circumstances and dealing with cause and effect. The Puritans who had inhabited the New England landscape two centuries previously had believed redemption could not be earned but was the result of God's grace, freely given. At the same time, they held on to the doctrine of justification, which meant that a good life could provide evidence of that predetermined salvation. In the same way, the Fruitlanders held that perfection came at birth but was nevertheless intrinsically bound up with a life lived according to certain austere principles. But they differed from their predecessors in one all-important respect. Their community was posited on a belief in the perfectibility of life on Earth, rather than targeted at establishing one's worthiness for heaven.

The circumstantial table can be used to determine the current utopian status of the Fruitlanders at the time of their move to the site. Their ultimate destination seems to be a return to what we would now call a hunter-gatherer way of life, with the hunting part omitted. But without our current knowledge of the history of prehistory, their romantic yearning for the noble savage's existence folds naturally into a literal interpretation of the story of the Garden of Eden. However, they were some distance away from re-entering that sacred territory. In most respects they were only at the "Good" level, in fact, but they teetered on the brink of something better. In leaving Alcott House behind, Alcott and Lane had moved on from the Public Hall, though given the state of the Fruitlands building it could be argued that this had turned out to be a regressive step—to a dilapidated cottage, in fact, as described in "Bad, for all Nature." But from another point of view, the fact that their occupation of this shoddy building was provisional and temporary must have given them a sense of leapfrogging over the next stage—"The House"—altogether, and arriving not far short of the one above it, "The Tent. An Unfixed Locality."

At that ultimate level of the graph, all the problems facing the Greavesians will have been resolved. Family life is a feature simply of the "good" phase, along with the "social intercourse" of races and nations. Above that the "better" level allows for the input of education until, when we reach the "best," that vexed issue has been resolved, and we are left with "Spirit-selected pairs in sympathetic harmony." At the same time, industrialization gives way to the agricultural way of life which in turn transmogrifies into gardening and lastly becomes simply a matter of picking fruit in an orchard and eating it raw—consuming the life force itself. Climate modulates from pollution to bracing conditions, then to temperate ones, and finally to a "Pure Balmy Atmosphere." Mary Lyndon, in Mary Gove's memoir, is already attuned to this possibility when she goes off to the picnic where she will meet Mr. Mooney and his English friends, and fall for the charms of Wright/Lynde, her spirit-selected other half. She hopes that "with a better life and culture for the earth," the world's climate might be ameliorated. Just like those at the top of the circumstantial scale, who have taken to living in tents in unfixed localities, Lyndon believes "you may as well bottle sunshine, as transfer to any hall or house the electric joy that is the especial property of out-door life." She too feels the need "to drink in the subtile life of nature."[20]

Lane concludes his final article on "A Voluntary Political Government" by explaining that his writing will have to give way to other forms of work, directed at the heart rather than the mind. He expresses the faith that his Fruitlands labors will prove to be that "real deed," the one which "must move mankind in a deeper manner than to a change of opinion, or to a scientific knowledge."[21] Fruitlands would be the "*point d'appui*" that would change the world.

Three days after the move, Abigail took the children on a walk to survey their new grounds. It was only a "little territory," but it had "one of the most expansive prospects in the country." As she looked at the view she noted how one "is transported from his littleness and the soul expands in such a region of sights and sounds." This led her to play with the juxtaposition of large and small, microcosm and macrocosm, the static and the dynamic. The household could, if it chose, resist the centrifugal pull of the vast expanse all around, and instead become "an isolated being occupying but a foot of earth and living but for ourselves." Alternatively, "we may look again, and a feeling of diffusive illimitable benevolence possesses us as we take in this vast region of hill and plain." That phrase, "diffusive illimitable benevolence," captures better than anything written by her husband, or indeed by Lane, the way in which the individually redeemed unit can transmit its perfection to the totality. Abigail is describing the mechanism by which Fruitlands could have a redemptive effect on the world as a whole.

She goes on to say that on the walk she gathered "an apron of chips" (small pieces of wood for kindling) while the children picked flowers. For her these different responses to the environment provide an allegorical tableau. "Like provident Mother Earth I gathered for use, they for beauty." Every action, however small, is given its due utopian weight. The functional and the decorative both provide pleasure (she has none of her husband's and Lane's reservations about love of nature). They both reveal something about the actors involved. "It was very characteristic in me, and most natural in them."[22] Her attention to detail, her impulse to test what might seem from the outside to be routine behavior for its ultimate significance, brings to mind the particularity with which Lane drew the seating arrangements around the fire at Concordia for the benefit of William Oldham.

However, the demands of Fruitlands meant that the children had to learn to be functional as well as natural. On June 6th Anna described clearing the breakfast table, washing the dishes, and preparing the midday dinner with her mother. In the evening she did the dishes again before going to bed. The following morning she began her school—in other words, as the oldest child (just twelve) she took charge of the others. She started them off by giving them a song to sing, then her pupils worked on their books while she wrote up her journal. After that, there was an arithmetic lesson. "I then gave them a recess," she explains proudly. When they came back in, she carried on with more lessons, making them spell and read, and getting Louisa to recite some geography. Anna dismissed her little school at eleven o'clock.

That afternoon, however, she was able to switch back from functional mode to the natural one again. She went off to the woods where she made oak leaf wreaths for her mother and father, decorating them with flowers. After supper she sang with Samuel Larned (she always calls him Christy)[23], her mother, William, and her sisters. The following day she took charge of her morning school again, but in the afternoon she herself was on the receiving end, with Christy teaching her arithmetic and composition. Her first writing assignment, perhaps inevitably, was to describe "our plan of life," and she began this ambitious project (on which her parents and Charles Lane were also engaged, each in his or her own fashion) with an essay on "flesh-eating," indignantly putting forward the orthodox Fruitlands position. "O how many happy lives have been destroyed and how many loving families have been separated," she exclaimed anthropomorphically, "to please an unclean appetite of men!"[24]

The following day, June 9th, Lane expressed parallel disgust in a long letter to Thoreau. "Generally it seems to be thought that the setting aside of all impure diet, dirty habits, idle thoughts and selfish feelings, is a course of self-denial scarcely to be encountered or even thought of," he exclaims, despairing at the pervasiveness of depravity. By contrast—and demonstrating his belief that rarefied circumstances mean not a lessening but an intensification of pleasure—Lane finds his mode of life "luxurious in the highest degree." His letter is clearly intended to convince Thoreau to join the community. Like Abigail in her journal entry, he plays with the notion of being anchored in a specific place while at the same time having access to what lies beyond, telling Thoreau that in the Fruitlands fields, "you may at once be at home and out," getting a sense of how life would be for those elevated beings who have reached the final stage, the unfixed locality, of the circumstantial law. As a sympathetic soul, Thoreau would find "enough to love and revel in," though Lane explains that the actual accommodation is poor and that the manual labor is so strenuous it has affected his handwriting. Interestingly, he remarks that Mrs. Alcott is the most hardpressed of all of them and asks Thoreau to let him know of any women who are likely to want to join the community and reduce her load.

He also explains that he and Alcott dream of going beyond farming—taking their experiment to the next level of the circumstantial table in fact, that of "Light Conditions," where gardening will be the mode of cultivation.

They have worked out where they will build cottages for new members. "Fountains can be made to descend from their granite sources on the hill-slope to every apartment, if required," he explains enthusiastically, and in this version of the pastoral idyll, herds of people rather than animals will wander picturesquely over the landscape. "Gardens are to displace the warm grazing glades on the south, and numerous human beings, instead of cattle, shall here enjoy existence." If gardening was the ultimate objective, it seems odd that they had committed themselves to a farm. It would on the face of it have been much more logical to buy a smallholding of say, ten or fifteen acres, complete with established orchard, and cultivate that instead. Such an enterprise would have fitted in with their endorsement of the small scale. Lane concludes with one more effort to bring Thoreau into the fold, claiming that their woodland "offers to the naturalist and poet an exhaustless haunt."[25]

The following day, June 10th, Emerson also wrote to Thoreau, worrying that he hadn't yet heard from Lane and Alcott. He perceptively diagnosed that they had got things the wrong way around. "They have near a hundred acres of land, which they do not want, & no house, which they want first of all." Nevertheless he expressed his respect for, as well as his concern about, projects that "so often seem without feet or hands."[26] That very day, though, Alcott and Lane were putting their calloused hands to paper and writing a letter to the *Dial* to explain their experiment to a waiting world. In point of fact the letter was primarily written by Lane—as indeed was most of the material published during the lead-up to Fruitlands and during the course of its existence.[27] Alcott was of course all the time recording his own thoughts and feelings in his journal. It's a fair guess that he was primarily concerned with the inner processes of utopia, while Lane concentrated on what he would have termed its "exoteric" manifestation. Partly this was a matter of horses for courses—Alcott had been told often enough, by friends and opponents alike, that he couldn't express himself comprehensibly in print. It also suggests that Lane, having put up the money, felt himself to be the leader of the enterprise. But when a document is signed by both men, it is reasonable to assume that it represents an agreed position, no matter who put pen to paper.

Once again the prose flies high over the tawdry details of an actual business transaction. "We have made an arrangement with the proprietor of an estate of about a hundred acres," they explain (inflating their property by more than 10 per cent), "which liberates this tract from human ownership." They go on to celebrate the lovely position of their liberated territory. "For picturesque beauty both in the near and the distant landscape, the spot has few rivals." Beauty rather than function obviously takes priority here, despite their fear of aestheticizing nature, and indeed they go on to describe the land in ornate prose more suited to the park of some aristocratic mansion in old England than to a New England smallholding—to a "hard, cold farm," as Mary Gove described it. "The vale, through which flows a tributary of the Nashua, is esteemed for its fertility and ease of cultivation, is adorned with groves of nut-trees, maples, and pines, and [is] watered by small streams."[28]

Ironically on the very day the Fruitlanders were penning this account, Emerson was describing a radically different prospect in Concord, as the town found itself being connected to the world at large by the construction of the railroad. "The town is full of Irish," he told Thoreau, "& the woods of engineers with theodolite & red flag singing out their feet & inches to each other from station to station." Concordia Cottage was in the thick of things. "Near Mr. Alcott's the road is already begun."[29]

A few months later Emerson told Margaret Fuller that people were saying "the railroad has made Massachusetts Boston."[30] In their July 10th article for the *Dial*, Alcott and Lane pointed out that Fruitlands was only thirty miles from Boston but was nevertheless isolated from it, in a "serene and sequestered dell." Once again geography develops an allegorical significance. "No public thoroughfare invades it, but it is entered by a private road." They are prepared to admit the road's existence this time around, but the fact that it terminates at the Fruitlands property enables them to see it as a way of leaving the big wide world rather than as providing a route toward it. The hamlet of Still River is a "field's walk of twenty minutes" (perhaps its name, like Fruitlands and Prospect Hill, had its own reverberations, suggesting as it does both stasis and movement); and Harvard village is "reached by a circuitous and hilly road of nearly three miles." The relationship between the "foot of earth" and the "vast expanse," to use Abigail's terms, is constantly being reassessed, like a telescope being looked through from each end in turn.

The task is to "initiate a Family in harmony with the primitive instincts in man." Family isn't defined apart from being capitalized, leaving it open as to whether it is fundamentally a biological unit or a closely knit society. At present it numbers ten, "five being children of the founders"—which leaves the whole matter delicately poised, as usual. Alcott and Lane mention their plan to replace the unsatisfactory accommodation with "suitable and tasteful buildings," along with the ambition to transcend traditional agriculture—"Ordinary secular farming is not our object." Instead, it "is intended to adorn the pastures with orchards, and to supersede ultimately the labor of the plough and cattle, by the spade and the pruning-knife." They list the crops they are planting: fruit, grain, pulse, garden plants, herbs, and flax. (According to Louisa, they accidentally superimposed three of them by sowing different grains on the same field in succession.[31]) The point was that they were not going to specialize but to establish subsistence cultivation, catering for all their own needs, including, of course, spiritual ones.

This was a two-way process. An "ever bounteous Providence" would provide succor because of the "union with uncorrupted [i.e. unmanured] fields and unworldly persons." At the same time "the cares and injuries of a life of gain are avoided" (though of course there was still the matter of the outstanding debt to be serviced). The land will yield goodness because of the virtue of those cultivating it; they in turn will be protected from the corrupting effects of the world because of the goodness of the land. Alcott and Lane conclude by emphasizing the importance of internal husbandry, a "constant leaning on the living spirit within the soul." This process will be aided by a "choice library" and the outcome will be spiritual eclecticism or synthesis. "Our plan contemplates all such disciplines, cultures, and habits, as evidently conduce to the purifying and edifying of the inmates." Transcendentalism can be maddeningly vague at times, particularly in the hands of Alcott and Lane. No specific Christian framework is evoked; that adverb "evidently" has to do all the work, establishing a sort of subjective pragmatism, by means of which the Fruitlanders trust their sense of what is right for them, and can pick out from the wisdom of the ages the axioms they need to live by.

Despite the delights of the way of life they have described, they conclude by admitting that they do not expect many to join them in the near future. They revert to their old image of "the gates of self-denial," though now it is oddly substantiated by the physical description they have already provided of their "sequestered dell," invaded by no thoroughfare but "entered by a private road." A psycho-geography, like that of *Pilgrim's Progress*, is being imposed on the external landscape. Just as different grains have been sown in the same field, so inner and outer experience are superimposed on the same location. Their concluding point catches their double attitude to abstention, the way in which rarefied circumstances are both a deprivation and a luxury. "Felicity," they claim, "is the test and the reward of obedience to the unswerving law of love." In other words, if you don't recognize their way of life as a happy one, you have failed the challenge it offers you.[32]

Margaret Fuller read this letter while visiting Chicago. Its earnest idealism made her laugh until she cried since it "contrasted so whimsically" with all she was experiencing on the raw frontier, "where strong instincts and imperative necessities come upon you like the swoop of a hawk."[33]

After writing their letter, Lane and Alcott set off to visit the Shaker community in Harvard, about an hour's walk away. It was a hot Saturday morning, and back at Fruitlands Anna was cleaning the bedrooms, making bread, and getting things ready for the midday meal. The absence of the two leaders of the community when there was work to be done would soon become a major cause of stress at Fruitlands, but on this occasion they had a mission, a double one in fact. They needed to buy seeds for their belated planting, and the Shakers were already famous for the quality of theirs; they also wanted to check up on another community that made its members pass through the "gates of self-denial." They were impressed with what they found.

By this time Shakerism had been established in New England and New York for about seventy years, and had spread as far as the midwest. In Ann Lee's day it had been an ecstatic sect, addicted to whirling and frenzied dancing. Ann herself was regarded as the female messiah. The veto on sexual intercourse and reproduction reflected a belief that the millennium was about to take place and that the ordinary course of nature would not continue. After her death, when it became clear the end was not nigh after all, Shakers settled down to a more orderly way of life, with choreographed dancing, singing of devotional songs or hymns, and a simple daily routine involving mainly agriculture and furniture-making. The cult of Mother Ann herself diminished though there was still an emphasis on gender equality. The prohibition of sex was maintained, which meant that the communities could only continue by taking in children, mainly from impoverished parents who surrendered their offspring because they would be well fed and learn a trade. For ten years from the late 1830s a revival took place, involving a reversion to Ann Lee's cult—it was known as "Mother Ann's Work"—though the local community at Harvard was calm and sedate when Lane and Alcott made contact with it.[34]

They found the Shakers much more intellectually alive than they had expected. A couple of years later Emerson visited them too, and received a very different impression, watching in horror as the believers performed their "dunce-dance," holding their hands in front of them and shaking them like the paws of dogs. From his point of view their sexual abstinence was an unhealthy obsession. "You find such exaggeration of the virtue of celibacy," he noted in his journal, "that you might think you had come into a hospital-ward of invalids afflicted with priapism."[35] Lane too noted that "upon their peculiar point of abstinence from marriage they are as zealous as recent converts," but he saw this as part and parcel of an atmosphere of "order, cleanliness and quiet" that deeply appealed to him. There were only thirty-six children in a community of over 200, he reported back to his friends in Ham in a letter he wrote a week later, "none being younger than 4." Perhaps thinking of the 50 per cent ratio of children in the cramped quarters of Fruitlands, and before that, of Concordia (including two-year-old Abby May, whom he regarded with disapproval), he decided that the Shaker arrangement, whereby they only took children from the outside world to convert and train, held the secret of "domestic serenity." In other words, what he admired about the "United Society of Believers"—their proper name, as he explained in his letter—was the extent to which they were *different* from a family.[36]

Lane explored this issue in more detail in an article about this visit, "A Day with the Shakers," which he wrote for the *Dial* (so much for relinquishing his pen in favor of manual work).[37] Once again he noted the proportion of children in the community and the fact that because the Shakers didn't produce any of their own, they were spared the presence of babies. "Not one is younger than four," he reiterated. He admired the way in which they attracted recruits not through proselytizing but by showing anyone interested that they were "fully realizing" their principles by the way they lived their lives.[38] Obviously he believed Fruitlands should do the same, though he was rather contradicting that plan by being so quick on the draw with his pen (Alcott's reluctance to write for publication during this period might suggest a firmer commitment to the force of example).

The two men bought some books during their visit, and Lane was delighted to find that the Shaker take on the Garden of Eden corresponded to Greavesian orthodoxy. Though in practice they were strictly celibate, they believed that sexual intercourse was hypothetically permissible. If only "that libidinous and lawless passion which was infused by the serpent . . . could be *entirely purged out of the natural man* . . . he would feel a very different sensation in this act, and would be in no danger of violating the true order of nature by it." On the face of it, Lane (and the Shakers) would seem to be advocating feeling no sensation at all in the said act, but of course you have to remember the compensatory element: as circumstances diminish, what remains becomes more acute.

In other respects, Lane was less impressed. The Shakers still ate meat, drank milk, and, he added darkly, the old ones consumed "tea, coffee, and the like." This led to "extensive interchanges of money" and "frequent intercourse with the world," preventing the true independence that a subsistence economy would give. In spite of these failings the Shakers shared Lane's and Alcott's belief that the true Christian would not have his or her sins forgiven, but would live without sinning at all. And perhaps Lane took comfort from the fact that when a Shaker joined the community, "as soon as rationally convinced of the stability of the associates, [he or she] does not wait to count coins."[39] That was something to remember when he felt troubled about the investment he had made in Fruitlands, though there might have been an edge to his mention of "stability."

Lane claimed to be particularly struck by the fact that the Shakers were following in the footsteps of a woman. This corresponded with his own belief that "Woman must ere long give the ruling tone to society"—the moral tone, that is to say. This was orthodox Greavesianism, of course, but one can't help wondering if Lane's enthusiasm about female leadership was strategic, particularly in the light of his remark to Thoreau that Abigail Alcott was doing too much of the community's work. If he was worried about keeping her on side, then it made perfect sense to celebrate the fact that this "most successful experiment of associate life, and community of property, was founded by A WOMAN," in an article Abigail Alcott would be certain to read. But at the same time as he makes known that he appreciates her, or at least her gender's, contribution, Lane takes the opportunity to steer her in the direction he wishes her to go, reminding her that the "union of the two sexes in government, in influence, in chaste celibacy, is an achievement worthier of greater renown than many works of greater fame," the key phrase being "chaste celibacy." Ann Lee, he goes on to point out, "seems to have had in her mind the true idea of the holy family; that of representing through the simplest domestic labours the most exalted spiritual sentiments."[40] Remember that a family should be holy rather than biological, he could be telling Abigail; and be content with hard work, because it brings spiritual exaltation in its wake.

Abigail, meanwhile, was more preoccupied with her biological family. The day after her husband and Lane visited the Shakers, daughter Anna conducted her little school as usual (no day of rest at Fruitlands) and then in the afternoon was on the receiving end of her own lessons from Christy. In the evening, when the domestic post office was opened, Anna had a surprise. Her mother had sent her a little present of notepaper, along with some of those improving wafers about the virtues of temperance and the harmfulness of flesh-eating so beloved of the Fruitlanders. It was a hint, of course: she wanted Anna to write to her more often. But it was also an acknowledgement of the responsibility her twelve-year-old child was shouldering. "You have so much to do lately," she wrote, "that I cannot expect you to write often to me." She goes on to transcribe a poem comparing happiness to a bird enfolding its young under its wings, adding "I am sure I feel as if I could fold my arms around you all, and say from my heart, 'Here is my world within my embrace.' "

The context makes it perfectly clear that the world to which she refers is that of her children. It is within the enclosed environment of her embrace that she sees the possibility of achieving goodness and beauty. No mention of "diffusive illimitable benevolence" here; at this point she is not thinking at all of the addition of like-minded men and women to the community. The letter is in fact an expression of passionate motherhood, and seems to belong to a different world from that evoked by Lane's praise of Shaker serenity, of their celibacy, and of their six to one ratio of adults to children. Abigail concludes with a little poem:

> Be the dove of our ark,
> Dear Anna remark
> You're my eldest and best
> Now you know all the rest.[41]

Fruitlands was only eleven days old, but its fault lines were beginning to be apparent.

11

The New Waves Curl

TAKING ADVANTAGE OF A WET morning, the indefatigable Lane put pen to paper on June 16th to send another progress report to William Oldham back at Ham. Once again he stressed the bargain he had got. "It seems to be agreed on all hands . . . that we have not made a bad exchange, even in the commercial sense, of our cash for land." He expatiates on his theme, grabbing his old colleague by the lapels: "Only think, brother Oldham"—land four pounds an acre, one large area of peat, "black as ink,—valued at 200 to 300 dollars per acre!" He might have liberated the property from ownership but still felt the need to convince himself he had got a bargain in doing so. The habit of establishing the price of commodities was deeply ingrained.

He describes the work they are doing, the progress they have made. The fields are mainly set to meadow and pasture, but they are plowing them up in order to sow clover and buckwheat which they can then turn under, "so as to redeem the land without animal manures, which in practice I find to be as filthy as in idea." Just as a Greavesian would prefer to eat raw food in order to incorporate its life force, uncurtailed by cooking, so soil should be fertilized by living vegetation turned back into the ground, so that life can spring from life, not death. Ironically they are using animals to accomplish this very task, but it has been a trial. "We have been much plagued, and a little cheated, with the cattle, but our stock is now reduced to one yoke of oxen." Butchers are likely to be dishonest precisely because they are butchers; by the same token you are sure to get your fingers burned when you sell farm animals.

Meanwhile, though, Alcott has turned out to be "as persevering in practice as last year we found him in idea. To do better and better, to *be* better and better is the constant theme." Even as Alcott rises to the challenge of the farm, Lane is determined to detect a bedrock of *being* underneath his busy surface, that Iamity proclaimed by Coleridge, endorsed by Greaves.

The Fruitlanders are awaiting a new arrival—Samuel Bower, friend and historian of the Ham Concordium, is due the following day. If he likes what he sees, he will stay. If not, he will give Brook Farm a try. Meanwhile, a carpenter has produced shelving for all their books.[1]

Two days later, Alcott too was writing a letter, telling his brother Junius that they had just completed the planting and pruning. As so often with him, hope triumphs over experience. Three acres of corn were ready for the hoe; there were two acres of potatoes; one of beans—but, he goes on to admit, they were preparing "an acre or two more" for "barley, carrots, turnips, beans" and were about to plow for winter wheat and rye. For a man accustomed to speaking in the prophetic mode it was perhaps inevitable that he would conflate intention and deed. Some fruit was already on the site; but there was scope for planting orchards, those hostages to a far-off fortune. Meanwhile there was sufficient timber already available for building with, and for fuel. (Years later Alcott dug out his copy of this letter and gloomily indulged what by then had become a compulsion for editing his own experience, adding the prefix "in" to "sufficient" in his mention of fuel—the memory of another savagely cold winter making him rescind his premature verdict.)

Alcott uses the ever-handy passive voice to skirt the issue of expenditure— "For the land $1800 was paid." Later in the letter he asserts that "My friend Lane . . . blessed of the like influence" to his own, will be a "not unapt coadjutator in the humane work." He somehow manages to make the man who forked out the money (and who was of course known to Junius already through his own correspondence) sound like some new follower who is showing a certain amount of promise. Given Lane's acute awareness of the level of his own investment, we can see another fault line beginning to develop, as the two men, almost unawares, start to jostle for priority.

Alcott reiterates his satisfaction at the way the property, that "sequestered dell" reached only by "private lanes," was disconnected from the "busy haunts and thoroughfares of trade." The location provided a "dignified independence," protected "from the invasion of the ruder secular world." Nevertheless the neighbors seemed well disposed (Mrs. Lovejoy and Mrs. Willard had in fact visited Abigail the previous week, and Mrs. Willard had returned the following day to help with the washing).[2] As before, Alcott tries to persuade his brother to join them. He produces the modest roll call of the community's members, now eleven in total since Bower had turned up as promised the previous day. However, Christopher Greene, the radical ex-newspaper editor from Providence, has not yet joined, and Mr. Dyer is still on his native mountains but will visit in the autumn and may commit to Fruitlands then.

Meanwhile all his hard work is giving Alcott "the truest delight." "This dell is the canvas on which I will paint a picture . . . a worthy picture for mankind."[3] The detachment and aestheticism of the phrasing here is curiously at odds with all the hard work he has just laid claim to, and contrasts with his hostility to love of nature. It also suggests (though there is an inevitable danger of overinterpretation with someone who writes as impulsively and abstractly as Alcott) that he is seeing the Fruitlands venture as a gesture toward what may ultimately be possible rather than as the actual inauguration of paradise on earth.

A picture of an ornate and ceremonious kind was certainly painted at Fruitlands on June 24th, little Elizabeth's eighth birthday. Before five o'clock that morning, her mother sneaked out of the house and stole off into the woods, taking Anna, Louisa, and William with her. They hung Elizabeth's presents on a little pine tree, and Anna made an oak wreath as decoration. Then they crept back. After breakfast, the Fruitlanders marched as a body to the glade (except Wood Abraham, busy elsewhere). Lane had his fiddle with him and everyone sang to the birthday girl. Then Alcott recited a long ode he had written for her in which he evokes a pastoral scene that could belong to Merry England (or classical Greece) as much as to central Massachusetts:

Here in the Grove
With those we love
In the cool shade

Near mead & glade
With clover tints overlaid . . .[4]

(Samuel Bower, their new arrival, succumbed to a similar *trompe d'oeil*,
writing back to his friend Oldham with his first impressions of Fruitlands and
superimposing the gentle English countryside upon the larger, more austere
sweep of the New England landscape. The highest hill in sight, he reported,
is "famous for having been the resort of an Indian sachem," but nevertheless
"the scene reminded me strongly of the Vale of Evesham, in Worcestershire,
where seen when one approaches it from Oxford."[5])

Alcott goes on to celebrate the dual nature of the ideal territory he
has evoked: "A haunt that God—ourselves—have made." Both parties are
responsible for creating this beautiful place, because it represents an inter-
section between the divine and the earthly.

Given the occasion, it is perhaps not significant that family gets priority
over community:

Father's here
And Mother dear,
And sisters all
The short & tall;
And father's friends
Whom Britian [sic] lends
To noblest human ends . . .

Having included Lane and Bower he adds in the youthful Larned, "With
younger arm/ From 'Brooklet Farm.' "

Alcott concludes his affectionate poem with the assertion that at
Fruitlands, Elizabeth will be "secluded from all sin" and therefore continue
to bloom like a never-fading flower:

A plant matured in Gods device
An Amaranth in Paradise.

Each member of the party then had to say which flower would be appropriate for Lizzie, with roses, the lily of the valley, a forget-me-not, the trailing

arbutus, the wake-robin (a pure white trillium native to North America—
Anna complained in her diary that she didn't know what the word meant) all
being chosen. Lane, characteristically, nominated a piece of moss (for
humility). Then Lizzie took her presents from the tree. They were modest
enough, in keeping with the values of the community. Abigail gave her a silk
thread balloon, Anna a fan, Louisa a pin-cushion, William a book, and baby
Abby a little pitcher. "Lizzie looked at her presents and seemed pleased,"
Anna recorded. Even Lane rose to the occasion, reciting a graceful little
poem he had written for Elizabeth:

> May your whole life
> Exempt from strife
> Shine forth as calm and bright.[6]

The formality of this ceremony, its poetry, its classical frame of reference,
and its natural setting combine to give it something of the quality of a
masquerade. Over at "Brooklet Farm" such festivities had become a part of
the fabric of the community. Two years previously in fact, a party in the
woods had been held to celebrate the sixth birthday of one of the children
there. Hawthorne was a member of the community at the time and recorded
the event in his *American Note-Books*, later using the material to portray an
elaborate masquerade in *The Blithedale Romance*, his novel based on the
experience of Brook Farm. He depicts a crowd of people drawn from
different communities, cultures, and mythologies: an Indian chief, the
goddess Diana, a Bavarian broom girl, foresters from the Middle Ages, a
Shaker elder, shepherds of Arcadia, and so on. All these costumes contribute
to an atmosphere of "dream-work and enchantment," a sense that identities
can be transformed and reality itself become equivocal. "I saw a concourse of
strange figures beneath the overshadowing branches," reports Hawthorne's
narrator, Miles Coverdale; "they appeared, and vanished, and came again,
confusedly, with the streaks of sunlight glimmering down upon them."[7] Now
you see them; now you don't.

Nothing so elaborate took place in the cool shade of the Fruitlands grove,
of course, and the members would have disapproved of such baroque
frivolity in any case. But their own tableau had something of the stylization

and transforming power, the suspension of daily reality, that characterized the Brook Farm celebrations, as though art was imposing itself over life—as though Alcott had already succeeding in painting his picture in that sequestered dell.

And in fact the Fruitlanders did dress up in their own fashion, in a way that rather corresponded to the Brook Farmers' "uniform" of rustic smocks. A few days after Elizabeth's birthday celebrations, Lane wrote to Oldham describing hard work on hot midsummer days. "We are all dressed in our linen tunics," he told him, "Abraham is ploughing, Larned bringing some turf about the house, Alcott doing a thousand things, Bower and I have well dug a sandy spot for carrots, the children and Lady are busy in their respective ways, and some hirelings are assisting."[8] The clothing consisted of loose trousers (for both males and females, pre-dating bloomers by a decade), tunics, and broad-brimmed hats; linen was the material of choice because it was not an animal product and unlike cotton did not involve the use of slave labor (which makes his hauteur about the poor "hirelings" somewhat ironic).[9] Sympathetic as he professed to be about Mrs. Alcott's workload, Lane once again seems conde-scendingly vague about what it actually involves; and he depicts Alcott, perhaps appropriately, in a whirl of indefinite activity.

We only have glimpses of the Fruitlanders going about their business. One of them, in anticipation of the era of the transistor radio and the iPod, developed the habit of putting a musical box on the wall while he hoed, and singing sentimental songs to the children as they worked.[10] Wood Abraham was apparently dark and melancholy. He cultivated a fine head of hair and worked like a beaver, proving particularly supportive of Abigail. To the great delight of the children he had a tendency to crow like a cockerel from time to time, and one visitor commented that he would have been put in a lunatic asylum if he hadn't already served his time in one.[11]

Of course Larned was capable of adding his own strange sound effects, given his alleged predeliction for swearwords, but he was nevertheless entrusted with teaching Anna as well as doing heavy work on the land. He was the youngest and therefore most recently schooled of the adults on the farm, so perhaps had a more vivid recollection of being on the receiving end than the others; on the same principle Anna taught her sisters, and on at least one occasion, when Anna was unwell, ten-year-old Louisa taught eight-year-old

Elizabeth (their father, the most famous American educator of his day, presumably being too busy doing his thousand things).[12] William does not seem to have been at the lessons, at least in these early days—he continues to be a shadowy figure during most of the lifespan of the community, but perhaps he was needed to contribute to the manual work, though the little girls did their share too.

The English newcomer, Samuel Bower, was the most hardline member of them all. It was he who gave the community the reputation of refusing to eat potatoes because instead of aspiring toward the sky they grew downward in the earth. He wouldn't eat them himself because he believed in eating only raw food, in order to participate in the life force without being guilty of causing vegetable death. According to Louisa's later memoir, he lived on dried beans and uncooked grain, sorrel, mint, green fruit (presumably fruit that was still ripening), and new vegetables.

He was also a dedicated nudist, another way in which to be at one, rather than at odds, with the environment, of participating in the totality of things instead of being insulated from it.[13] This belief was apparently shared over in Alcott House by a German member of that community who was discovered in the garden digging "mit nodings on," just as in those days when Adam delved and Eve span, and had to be taken into the protection of Thomas Carlyle, well known for his understanding of the German mind.[14] Like Alcott House, Fruitlands was an essentially decorous community, as the tableau we have of Alcott standing on a stepladder and pouring water down a canvas chute on to his womenfolk makes clear, and Lane would have kept a sharp eye on any tendency to hanky-panky. *"Lust abounds and love is deserted,"* he told Oldham in his letter of June 28th, underlining his grim verdict. *"Lust of money, of food, of sexuality, of books, of music, of art."*[15] Bower had to confine his nudity to the night time and even then was compelled to wear a white shift for decency's sake, which apparently caused rumors of a ghost seen clambering about the Fruitlands slopes.[16]

The short night would have been dark, however. The community would not use whale oil lamps and had bought bayberry wax to make candles with, though unfortunately none of them knew how to do it. In an emergency they had to make do with pine knots, the resinous branches of pine trees. Only Abigail rebelled against this regime, insisting that she needed a light to sew by.[17] The Massachusetts evenings were of course light in June, yet it still seems extraordinary that after the hard day's grind Lane was able to take up his pen in the shadowy house and turn out the letters and articles that mediated the utopian experience of Fruitlands to the world beyond its sequestered dell.

In fact his most substantial piece yet, an article titled "Social Tendencies," would appear in the July issue of the *Dial*, though like his essay on Alcott it was so lengthy that the second half had to be held back to the next number of the magazine. Margaret Fuller for one regretted that the essay had to be cut in half. She felt that Lane's arguments were more effective in large doses. "He needs to fall his whole length to show his weight."[18]

"Social Tendencies" begins with a poetic image of the sea, as Lane imagines the waters of society rising without obvious cause. "In irregular intervals, the new waves curl, crisp and yeasty, over the shell-strewn beach, with an unusual surge, although no fresh breeze is sensible above the surface of the waters." Lane is referring to the rise of "a number, almost deserving the appellation, 'a multitude,' who, being moved from a greater depth than ordinary, manifest a purpose which may . . . be designated *human*." As in the *Liberator* articles, Lane finds it easier to say what this new perspective is not, rather than what it involves. At the moment people are valued according to their ownership of property. "The State-doctors, like those who study medicine, judge of humanity by its excrements, or wait until itself is excrement."[19]

Interestingly Hawthorne had developed a similar perspective during his time at Brook Farm a couple of years previously. Soon after he joined the community, he was given a pitchfork by George Ripley, the leader, and found himself making "a gallant attack on a heap of manure." A couple of months later the novelty had worn off, and he was complaining of the "abominable gold mine." "Thank God," he told his fiancée, "my soul is not entirely buried under a dung-heap."[20] Essentially his chain of connection is parallel to the one Lane is making here: manure = materiality = threat to spirit. Perhaps it is not surprising, after all, that Ellery Channing would worry that Hawthorne might become one of the austere philosophers.

Lane reiterates the point Emerson made in "The American Scholar" that in a presocial dispensation human beings were units rather than fractions:

In a state of barbarism, the individual man gives up but a very small portion of himself; he looks little to others for support; he is self-reliant. He runs not to the baker for bread, to the butcher for flesh, to the teacher for grammar; but hunts and cooks and speaks for himself.

By contrast, in modern society, "Everything, every person is vicarious. No one lives out his own life, but lives for all."[21] Lane wants to find the Garden of Eden once more because he yearns for a lost holism; modern society has made us all into specialists.

The ramifications of this tendency are found in every department of civilization. The first example Lane gives is predictable. The farmer pollutes the soil in order to provide excess crops so that other people do not need to produce any for themselves. "The farmer applies fresh quantities of foul animal manure to force heavier crops from his exhausted fields; which, when consumed, generate a host of diseases as foul as the manures to which they are responsible." He goes on to give other examples of vicariousness: "The legislator represents the conscience, the judge the gravity, the priest the piety, the doctor the learning, the mechanic the skill of the community, and no one person needs to be conscientious, grave, pious, learned, and skilful." One begins to understand the underlying logic of the circumstantial law. Circumstances should not be concentrated: they should be thin and evenly spread. Then they will affect everyone to the same degree. What we have at present are a "few intense spots of wealth, learning or heroism, amongst an endless range of poverty, ignorance and degradation."[22] It is an extraordinary and in its way a profound analysis that can equate manure with the intelligentsia, but both are inappropriate concentrations of a particular substance; both imply a consequent lack or diminishment elsewhere.

Lane goes on to consider how change will come. Sometimes the disturbances in the metaphorical sea turn out to be delusive, causing mere bubbles. One example involves faith in modern communications. True, in "the days of slow travelling, the mercantile community still entertained hope that rapid communication would aid their prosperity"; now steam packets and railways "almost bring the ends of the earth together," but instead of proving the point, they have brought that delusion to an end. Uncannily anticipating and dismissing the "global village" envisioned in the 1960s (not to mention the

Internet), he claims "the merchant no longer thinks he should be relieved, if communications were electrically instant."[23] In *The Blithedale Romance*, Hawthorne would parody all such hopes of abrupt utopian transformation, of the dawning of an era that "would link soul to soul." A charlatan by the name of Professor Westervelt stands in a village lyceum and explains "as if it were a matter of chemical discovery" how this linkage is supposed to happen. Hawthorne's narrator says he wouldn't have been surprised had Westervelt "pretended to hold up a portion of his universally pervasive fluid, as he affirmed it to be, in a glass phial." Despite a "delusive show of spirituality" this unifying substance amounted to "cold and dead materialism"—Lane's point exactly.[24]

Lane gives brief consideration to two relatively large-scale communities that have been set up. The first of these was a phalanstery in Citeaux, France, established according to the theories of the French thinker Charles Fourier. Fourier was born in 1772, and began elaborating his vast utopian scheme in the early years of the nineteenth century. He had in fact died in 1837, but his theories were just now attracting considerable interest in both Europe and America. The second was an Owenite experiment at East Tytherley in Hampshire. Robert Owen was an almost exact contemporary of Fourier, but was still very much alive. He was internationally famous for his reforming work at the mills of New Lanark, and for utopian communities in America and Great Britain. But for Lane, both the Fourierist and Owenite communities he was examining were "wanting in respect of the inmost life-germ" because "the scheme rather than man is placed first in importance."[25] While it is true that a "sufficient arc is known to prove the fact of a concentric orbit," that calculation cannot be put "beforehand into books, and systems, but must be realised, day by day, from the centre itself, as are the planetary motions." In short, there has to be "a gradual outworking of society." We have to glide in an "almost unobservant manner, as the growth of animate bodies proceeds." If there is a "strained effort at a preordained result," we will end up with a "dead granite building" rather than "the perfection of a living being."[26]

This organic metaphor leads Lane into difficult territory, the vexed problem of Greavesian generation. He has dismissed the notion that civilization is reparable. He has rejected large-scale utopian planning. He has asserted that the hope of a more unified world through improved communications is nothing but a delusion. Nevertheless it is still necessary to accomplish humanity's great work, "to open a place, to clear an arena." The arena he is left with turns out to be that of the family.

Every human being enters into the world, he points out, as a member of a family. Simple mathematics: two people are necessary to produce a third. It is an obvious enough point, but it comes out from between gritted teeth, as always when an English Transcendentalist bumps into the facts of life. "The family may now be an example of anything rather than of amity; yet exist it must," he concedes, "and from this relationship all action must be dated." It is easy to picture him glaring round at the children swarming over the little Fruitlands farmhouse while he wrote that sentence. And Abigail Alcott glaring back at his disapproval, because he goes on to claim that society is making a great mistake in not permitting as much female influence as male. "Society is male, not family, not humane."[27]

He may have been influenced by another of New England's formidable women too. The July issue of the *Dial* began with Margaret Fuller's essay on "The Great Lawsuit: Man *versus* Men. Woman *versus* Women." It was an eloquent account of the way in which "femality" was undervalued in modern civilization, and contained an immensely learned survey of woman in history and myth through the ages. When it was republished a year later as *Woman in the Nineteenth Century*, Lane, who had a somewhat rocky relationship with Fuller, gave it an enthusiastic (and much appreciated) review. In fact Fuller's view of gender roles did nothing to contradict the Greavesian position. "The especial genius of woman," she believed, was "electrical in movement, intuitive in function, spiritual in tendency." As a result she "is great not so easily in classification, or re-creation, as in an instinctive seizure of causes, and a simple breathing out of what she receives that has the singleness of life, rather than the selecting or energizing of art."[28]

In his article, Lane goes on to picture the way social transformation will be accomplished. "More and more recruits will daily be enlisted from the old crowd, and swell the orderly of the new phalanx" (phalanx and phalanstery were used interchangeably for the communities proposed by Fourier).[29] He is imagining an accretion of individuals to compose a new entity, like tiny organisms making up a coral reef. In orthodox Fourierism a phalanx was a community of nearly 2,000 people—Emerson somewhat sarcastically defined it as a mechanism for rebuilding a complete human out of the fractured sort produced by the current society. "It takes 1680 men to make one Man, complete in all the faculties," Emerson wrote, "that is, to be sure we have got a good joiner, a good cook, a barber, a poet, a judge, an umbrella-maker, a mayor and alderman, and so on."[30]

The "one Man" of the phalansterian structure is in truth a composite figure rather than a reintegrated one; and Lane himself uses the term loosely—he too disapproved of schematic Fourieristic enterprises. It is a considerably larger structure than any family, as he reminds himself in the second half of his sentence: "But let it not be forgotten that the family relations cannot be lightly or irreverently treated." Then he builds up a small surge of enthusiasm: "Not in public halls, but around the hearthstone"—that hearthstone he drew for Oldham when he was living in Concordia—"it has ever happened that improvement has been first discussed." Here, he asserts, is the key. "In the family, the last, the noblest, the redeeming secret lies hid." But no sooner has he made this claim than he starts to blow cold again, reminding himself that "in this circle man's fall originated, and in it is perpetuated."

It is almost painful to watch him zigzag from one perspective to its opposite. The fact that the family, as represented by Adam and Eve, was the cause of all the troubles of the world might mean that it will be the scene of its redemption. Perhaps. "Logically and retributively that fact [the Fall] should at least not preclude, if it does not confirm the prognostic, that in the family are to be sown the permanent seeds of new life."[31] Hardly a ringing endorsement.

The long, two-part article began with a vision of the mighty ocean, and ended with testimony to the "Sacred precinct" of the family. That transition represented Lane's own shift, from a new arrival in America—like so many new arrivals through its history—believing that large-scale social upheaval was possible here, to a man whose horizons shrank as he found himself embedded in the world-as-it-is rather than as he hoped it would be, the world in this case being the tight domestic one of the Alcotts.

12

Utter Subjection of the Body

WHILE LANE CONTINUED TO try to accommodate Alcott's commitment to the family, Alcott was doing his best to move in the other direction. On July 2nd he gave a lecture to his fellow members of the Fruitlands community, back in a familiar role, teacher's chalk in hand. "Mr Alcott most beautifully and forcibly illustrated on the black board the sacrifices and utter subjection of the body to the Soul," Abigail wrote in her journal, "showing the + on which the lusts of the flesh are to be sacrificed."

"Most beautifully"—she does her best to approve, the loyal wife even as marital relations are being proscribed; "forcibly"—maybe she has no choice.

She goes on to quote her husband's words—maybe they were written on the board too, given that he liked complicated diagrams with detailed explanations. "Renunciation is the law, devotion to Gods [sic] will the Gospel," he explained. "The latter makes the former easy, sometimes delightful."[1] (That could be Lane himself, telling Thoreau that his way of life was "luxurious in the highest degree".) Next, he covered the inverse logic of the circumstantial law: "Pure resignation elevates and illuminates life." The less you have, the more acutely you can see and experience what is left. Most important of all, he reiterated the connection between inner and outer worlds, claiming "Sweet heaven already fans the air near my crops."[2] Sacrifice the flesh and immediately it is made easier to tend the fields of cereal. Perfect your way of life, and bingo, the weather—indeed, the climate—improves. The logic is exactly that described in the letter he and Lane had sent to the *Dial*. Providence would provide succor to uncorrupted fields and unworldly persons.

It was high summer and that renunciatory breeze was a blessing. But the sun itself was a blessing too, one that at some point Alcott experienced in a much more elemental way. At the back of the MS of the doomed *Psyche* he had written five years previously, he scribbled a poem which he dated "Fruitlands 1842" (Alcott at least knew *where* he was, though confused about when):

> . . . As Phoebus joys the oblivious world to fly
> And feed her blindness from his blazing eye
> As nascent babe in helplessness of years
> Instinctive seeks maternal hemispheres
> Quick with obsequious proferring [sic] turns
> To drink sweet succour from her liberal urns
> So Providence benignly all her children feeds
> And yields her swelling paps to every needs.[3]

Suddenly, albeit crudely, we have a classical and sensual evocation of nature's bounty. Juggling circumstances and living an austere life seem to have nothing to do with it. Providence is not assessing the uncorruptedness of fields or the unworldliness of persons but is benignly feeding "all her children."

Over at Alcott House, a poetic member of that community by the name of James Elmslie Duncan was taken aback, while walking in the garden, to come upon the statue of a flimsily draped Venus, and felt moved to put pen to paper: "Judge, ye gods, of my surprise/ A lady naked in her chemise!"[4] Alcott's poem, just as unintentionally comic, seems to register a similar incongruity, a pagan perspective and joy in nature abruptly surfacing through layers of inhibition and prohibition. Two years previously he had insisted one-year-old Abby should drink nothing but water, and had to be persuaded by Abigail's aunt, Hannah Robie, to let her have milk. Now in his poem he rejoices in maternal hemispheres, in liberal urns, and swelling paps.

The apostate Henry Gardiner Wright would have been surprised to discover breasts being celebrated at Fruitlands. According to Lane he left

Concordia because of the coldness of the potatoes and the absence of milk; Mary Gove claimed that all he wanted was to pour a little cream on his mush. Now Wright had parted from her in turn, and after a brief attempt in early May to take up residence once more at Concordia, he was on the high seas returning to his wife and child in England. Mary Lyndon, in Gove's account, waved Lynde off having had the most wonderful experience of her life and having earned, as a consequence, the condemnation of the community. It may be that the unconventional relationship between Wright and Gove had simply become unsustainable. According to Bower, Wright was by now ailing and out of heart in any case, suffering in fact from a tumor of the chest that would kill him within three years.[5]

On July 4th the captain of the ship on which he had taken passage ordered guns to be fired in celebration of the American Declaration of Independence, to be followed by a fireworks display that evening. Wright listened glumly to the noisy festivities. "Is American liberty like this," he asked himself, "all fire, and smoke, and whiz?" He reflected bitterly on the social deprivation he had encountered in America, the plight of the factory workers, for example, in the industries that had sprung up there just as they had in England. "Rejoice, toil-crushed lads and maidens! Ye are in the land of 'Declarations,' and your institutions are free!" he proclaimed sarcastically.[6] Lane would have regarded this as missing the point, demonstrating a desire to right wrongs rather than transcend them altogether. The *New Age* recorded Wright's return and explained his disillusion with the United States: "His sympathies are not at all in harmony with their democratical government; neither do the tone and character of the Americans generally so far please his taste as to induce him to remain in that country."[7]

Still, if one sadder and wiser utopian had left, another was eager to join. Over at Brook Farm a young man by the name of Isaac Hecker was preparing to make a switch to the more extreme and "ultra" set-up (as a contemporary called it) at Fruitlands.[8] Hecker was the son of Prussian immigrants who were running a successful bakery business in New York. He got involved with Orestes Brownson's Working Men's Party in 1834, when he was fourteen. He was an intense, neurotic young man. In 1842 he had been troubled by dreams and seems to have begun a period of spiritual crisis.

As with the English Transcendentalists, part of the problem involved sex. On December 26, 1842 he wrote to his brothers John and George: "To keep company with females—you know what I mean—I have no desire. I have no thought of marrying, and I feel an aversion to company for such an end. In my whole life I have never felt less inclined to it." In fact Hecker hated being touched by anyone. He was aware that this recoil set him apart from the mainstream of existence: "If my disposition ran that way, marrying might lead me back to my old life, but oh! that is impossible."[9]

That being the case it made some sense to be part of a larger community that was not based on the family structure, and he joined Brook Farm in January 1843. He was troubled from the start of his time there. One of the members of the community, Georgianna Kirby, noted that on his first night he "had been nearly crazed by the direct rays of the moon, which made the circuit of the three exposed windows of his room."[10] At first he paid $4 a week towards his board and worked as the community's baker, but after a while he recoiled, as Hawthorne had done before him, from the nullity of physical labor. "In the World one cannot live a spiritual life," he wrote on June 1st, the very day that the Alcotts moved to Fruitlands, "because it requires so much labor to supply one in food & clothing that he looses [sic] his inward eternal life for the material and life in time." He began paying full board so as not to be distracted from the inward and eternal, but other problems remained.[11]

He may well have been toying with the possibility of a more extreme regime from early in the year. On February 15th Alcott had written to another member of Brook Farm, describing the regime at Concordia, and that letter found its way into Hecker's possession. It is the one in which Alcott affirms that he has "no belief in associations of human beings for the purpose of making themselves happy by means of improved cultural arrangements alone, as the fountains of happiness are within, and are opened to us as we are pre-harmonized or consociated with the Universal Spirit."[12] Hecker was a perfect candidate, austere in his diet and personal habits and recoiling from physical contact; by the same token, he was ill-adapted to the jollification and intimacy of life at Brook Farm.

The situation was complicated by the fact that despite his distaste for sex he seems to have fallen for the charms of a fellow member of the community,

"one who is too much to me to speak of, one who would leave all for me."
Matters reached crisis point on June 27th, when a friend reiterated his
doctor's advice that marriage was the solution to his problems. After
agonizing overnight, he made his mind up: "Rather than follow this advice I
would die."[13]

The day after Henry Wright gloomily observed Fourth of July celebrations in the middle of the Atlantic, Hecker decided to visit Fruitlands, and by
July 7th he had made up his mind to move there. It would, of course, mean
leaving his beloved. "Alas!" he wrote in his journal, "him I must leave to go."
Given the aversion he had expressed about keeping company with females,
and the nature of the medical advice he had received (not to mention his
extreme reaction to it), it seems obvious that this relationship was homo-
sexual. But in fact he originally wrote "her" in this entry, subsequently
altering the word to "him." And indeed a woman called Almira Barlow, much
feted as Brook Farm's beauty, had come into his room and declared her love
for him. She was twelve years his senior, a widow with three children, and he
had felt himself "influenced to keep her at a certain distance." It could be that
he was susceptible to her charms, and changing her gender was a way of
maintaining that "certain distance." Or possibly the original attribution of
gender was a fudge, and subsequently he decided to be honest about his
attraction to a man.[14]

Interestingly he was equally concerned about the dress code in the more
extreme regime he was now about to enter. As we have seen, the Brook
Farmers liked to assume farmers' dress, but Hecker obviously decided that
the Fruitlanders' linen tunics were considerably more provocative. He
agonised over the prospect like someone going to a costume party and
wondering if he can really get away with his giant rabbit outfit. "I will gradually simplify my dress without making any sudden difference," he decided,
"altho it would be much easier to mak a radicel and thourough change of all
than it is peice by peice [sic]."[15] He seems to have decided on a sort of slow-
motion stripping—perhaps he had heard about Bower's nudism.

While Hecker was recoiling from sex and worrying about dressing up (or
down), Emerson was celebrating life's motley, in preparation for his own
first visit to the austere community. "Life," he wrote as a heading in his
journal—perhaps he needed to remind himself of what it was before

venturing forth. "Fools & clowns & sots make the fringes of every one's tapestry of life, & give a certain reality to the picture." Emerson insists on being inclusive rather than renunciatory. What he loves about his hometown is that, unlike Fruitlands, it allows for cakes and ale. "What could we do in Concord without Bigelow's and Wesson's bar-rooms & their dependencies? What without such fixtures as Uncle Sol and old Moore who sleeps in Doctor Hurd's barn? And the red charity-house over the brook?" Even deprivation and dystopia are part of the tapestry. "Tragedy & comedy always go hand in hand."[16]

On July 8th, a day or two after this entry, Emerson traveled to Fruitlands along with Ellery Channing.

What struck Emerson most was how peaceful the place seemed. "The sun & the evening sky do not look calmer than Alcott & his family at Fruitlands," he wrote in his journal, ignoring Lane for the moment. Perhaps this calmness meant they had achieved the spiritual harmony they were seeking. "They seemed to have arrived at the fact, to have got rid of the show, & so to be serene." As so often with Emerson, it becomes apparent that despite his generous wish to take the achievement of the idealists at their own valuation, an imp of skepticism niggles away just below the surface. "Their manners & behaviour in the house & in the field were those of superiour men, of men at rest," he continues. "What had they to conceal? What had they to exhibit?" Calmness, serenity, men at rest—Emerson had some respect for these quiet qualities. "So hot, my little Sir?" he asks in one of his essays.[17] But the adjectives accumulate somewhat soporifically here, and contrast with all the hard work the Fruitlanders are laying claim to. They are "superiour" men perhaps—but only a day or so previously Emerson had been pointing out that life needed its reprobates.

He reverts to an earlier notion, that it would be worth keeping Lane and Alcott like animals in some Transcendental zoo for the delectation of the public at large. "I thought, as often before, so now more, because they had a fit home or the picture was fitly framed, that these men ought to be maintained in their place by the country for its culture. Young men & young maidens, old men & women should visit them & be inspired." In terms of the distinction Abigail had made between beauty and function, he is in no doubt which side the community's two leaders are on. "I think there is as much merit in beautiful manners as in hard work," he writes supportively, but is well aware of the practical danger of endorsing being over doing, whatever Greaves may have claimed. "I will not prejudge them successful," he decides, adding prophetically, "They look well in July. We will see them in December."

Emerson picked up on the tension that was developing between the two men. "I know they are better for themselves, than as partners. One can easily see that they have yet to settle several things. Their saying that things are clear & they sane, does not make them so." The harshness of that reference to sanity undercuts the apparent praise he has bestowed, and he goes on to revise his notion that the Fruitlanders' role could simply be force of example, invoking the necessity of service. "If they will in very deed be lovers & not selfish; if they will serve the town of Harvard, & make their neighbors feel them as benefactors, wherever they touch them; they are as safe as the sun." The tone is still positive, probably because he is summarizing what he actually told Lane and Alcott, but there is a sting in the tail, because he obviously thinks being superior and at rest should be supplemented by active engagement with the community.

This leads him to ponder on the fact that money is simply an inconvenience if it is not used to help others. While both Lane and Alcott, for different reasons, choose to think of the community as somehow above or beyond a sordid financial transaction, Emerson is always aware that genteel manners, stylized posturing, are being underpinned by Lane's capital investment. It is "the dowdy farmer's wife who meets you at her door, broom in hand, or pauses at her washtub to answer your question," whose house is really serene and majestic. "Ours is not, let our ideas be what they may," he explains, sugaring the pill by using the first person plural to implicate himself in the fallacy, "whilst we may not appear except in costume, & our immunity at the same time is bought by money & not by love & nature."[18]

In effect, having tried to praise the Fruitlanders for the pose they have taken up, he ends by accusing them of playacting in the pejorative sense, merely pretending to be farmers. Perhaps, in his fear of donning the Fruitlands costume, Hecker intuited the same deception.

Nevertheless he arrived at the community on the afternoon of July 11th. After tea (as they called it, despite the commitment to water), he went out with the others to rake hay.[19] He might have been a little taken aback by that particular task, given he had just entered a vegan establishment. But despite their unhappy experience with animals at the commencement of the experiment, the Fruitlanders were still using what they had been given to understand was a team of oxen. The animals had been provided by Joseph Palmer, the man who had gone to jail as a result of having a beard.[20] Palmer had taken an active interest in Fruitlands from the start, lending some of his furniture and as the summer wore on becoming increasingly involved in its day to day running—as an experienced farmer, his input was vital.

In her later memoir, *Transcendental Wild Oats*, Louisa recalled the conversation Palmer had with her father on the subject of the animals, delighting in the memory of his country accent.

"Haou do you cattle'ate to treat the ten-acre lot?" Palmer asked.

(Louisa based the character of Silas, Mr. Bhaer's farm manager in *Little Men*, on Joseph Palmer and has him use exactly the same odd version of "calculate."[21])

"We shall spade it," Alcott answered.

Palmer shook his head and produced the team anyhow. But when the animals arrived, one of the oxen turned out to be a cow, so to the problems of animal exploitation and manure production was added the pairing up of the sexes. Asked to explain himself, Palmer replied that he "must be let down easy, for he couldn't live on garden sarse entirely." In fact he would go off to the barn and drink the milk from his cow, which made the Alcott children, peering at him round the door, imagine he was doomed. Many years later Louisa still recalled the odd match between the bridal white of Palmer's linen tunic (the other Fruitlanders wore brown linen) and the snowiness of his beard.[22]

The incongruity of the presence of these animals, and the consequent need to provide hay for them, had struck Ellery Channing forcibly during his visit with Emerson a few days before. Going one better than the Fruitlanders themselves, he told Emerson he hoped there would be no cows in heaven (a crushing remark given that the community was itself trying to plant paradise). He had discovered what cows were for, he added, "namely, to give farmers something to do in summer time." Here they were, at mid-summer, in the lull between planting and harvest. "All hands would be idle," Channing claimed, "but for this ox & cow, which must be fed & mowed for." He wickedly parodied Lane's self-righteous tone, pretending to dig a moral bonus out of this apparent backsliding. "Thus Intemperance & the progress of crime is prevented!"[23]

When Hecker and the others had finished their haymaking, they stood in the barn and asked for a blessing on their labors. "I take off my hat," one of them said, "not that I reverence the barn more than other places, but because this is the first fruit of our labor."[24] Perhaps this gesture sanctified not just the barn but the task of providing animal fodder; perhaps it helped give manual work the spiritual value which Hecker himself was seeking.

Then they all returned to the house, where they had a Conversation on the subject of clothing, no doubt at Hecker's request. Very fine things were said, and he was relieved to find he agreed with most of them. Maybe he established that nudity was not the community's official policy. Alcott, possibly remembering the bracing discussion of three days previously, told him that "to Emerson the world was a lecture-room."

At breakfast the next day the Conversationalists took on another topic close to Hecker's uneasy heart: the nature of friendship, "its laws and conditions." Alcott said "innocence" was its most important pre-requisite, Larned "thoughtfulness"; for Hecker himself, it was "seriousness" (after all he had just left Brook Farm in search of a tougher regime); Lane, possibly worrying about the tension between himself and Alcott that Emerson had remarked on, plumped for fidelity.

Conversations were as important to the health of the community as raking hay—at least the members thought so. The following morning at breakfast there was yet another, this time on the Highest Aim. Each of the men (no mention of a contribution from Abigail or the children) had to identify his guiding light in life. For Alcott it was integrity. Hecker, already *au fait* with Greavesian terminology, chose harmonic being. Lane trumped him with progressive being, while Larned advocated the annihilation of the self, and Bower went for repulsing the evil in ourselves.

The Fruitlanders wanted to be as transparent as the water they were drinking with their meager breakfast of porridge and unleavened bread, eradicating every detail of individuality and misbehavior in order to surrender to the order of the universe at large. But there were obstacles standing between them and the "highest air," that "pure balmy atmosphere" which the circumstantial table associates with linen robes, a tent, fruits, gymnastic exercises, love for the unlovely and—at the furthest extreme from yoking together an ox and a cow—the union of spirit-selected pairs in sympathetic harmony (this last perhaps particularly appealing to Hecker, given the emotional complications he had been suffering). His problem, he explained to the others, wasn't lack of willpower nor of sight to see his way. What he feared was pursuing a chimera, "the doubt whether light *is* light."[25]

One can imagine long looks over the table. Here was a hint of apostasy within a couple of days of Hecker's arrival at the community.

Over the next few days, Hecker's turmoil became acute. Part of the problem was that Larned, echoing the doctor Hecker had consulted at Brook Farm, told him he would eventually solve his problems through marriage. This made Hecker feel he ought to pin his hopes on Alcott and Lane, and their message of renunciation, after all. But as soon as he expressed that possibility to himself, more doubts set in. "Here I cannot end," he wrote in his journal for July 13th, having hardly begun. A week previously Emerson had asserted that the Fruitlanders were superior men; after a week's actual exposure to them, Hecker reached the opposite conclusion. "They do not awaken in me the sense of their high superiority," he wrote, "which would keep me here to be bettered, to be elevated." True, they have some distinguished qualities. Hecker admired Alcott's capacity for self-denial, and Lane's unselfishness over money matters. The thought of those virtues gave him pause. Perhaps he should sit at their feet after all, and learn to be like them. But the process would not be reciprocal, because for all he appreciated them, they did not understand him in turn. Maybe he should be patient anyway, and wait for mutual comprehension. There is, after all, a certain "something" in the community that he has never encountered elsewhere, a something which hints at the possibility of helping him achieve his "highest life."

Hecker twists and turns in his anguish. Does the community offer him enough to keep him there? "If I can prophesy, I must say no." It will not answer to all his needs. He asks God to strengthen his resolution, but of course the real problem is that he doesn't know what it is he is resolving. He concludes by excoriating himself for his sins—"Lord, could I only blot them out of my memory."[26] He sounds at this moment more like a guilt-ridden Puritan in a Hawthorne romance than a Fruitlander.

Five days later his struggle has become more focused. Now he is able to see it boils down to a choice between family and spirit. He would love to go back to his kin, but it would mean abandoning his spiritual development. If only he could reconcile the two! It is the classic Fruitlands dilemma, the one that is slowly creating tension between the Alcotts, husband and wife, as well as between Alcott and Lane. If only Hecker could have both at once, "I could not hesitate a moment, for it would not compare; there would not be room for a choice." But sadly it is a question of one or the other. Returning to his family would mean re-entering their world of business, and indulging himself with their sort of food and "garmenture"—obviously, despite his initial fears, he is now committed to the Fruitlands dress code. Such a relapse would be unacceptable. He must follow the dictates of the spirit. The problem with that alternative—and here he recoils from one of the basic Transcendentalist assumptions—is that the spirit is abstract and colorless. "What it leads me to do," Hecker writes, "will be the only evidence of its character. I feel as impersonal as a stranger to it."[27]

Matters came to a head a couple of days later, on July 20th. In the morning Lane taught Anna fractions, with great success. "I think I have learned more lately than I ever did before," she cheerfully claimed, obviously appreciating his efforts. Mrs. Lovejoy from the property next door came over in the afternoon with her baby, along with a couple of children from the locality.[28] That evening, after supper, Alcott and Lane asked Hecker where he stood. They wanted to know what his plans were in relation to his own family and whether he was going to stay or go. They also wanted him to tell them of the problems he had encountered since arriving at Fruitlands.

Hecker had prepared himself for these questions. In his journal, in fact, he numbers his replies, rather like a miniature version of the theses Martin Luther nailed to the church door at Wittenburg. The first four of Hecker's points are directed specifically at Alcott, whom he obviously saw as the source of his difficulties. The first was Alcott's lack of frankness. The second, his failure to confide in or consult the other members of the community. The third was Alcott's commitment to his own family. Abigail's brother Samuel had visited Fruitlands a couple of days before, with his wife and children in tow, and that may have enforced Hecker's sense that the community revolved too much around Alcott's domestic loyalties, particularly as for

Hecker membership of the community represented a repudiation of his own family.

The next item on Hecker's checklist concerned Fruitlands itself. It betrays its name by having "very little fruit on it which it was and is their desire should and ought to be the principle [sic] part of their diet." The final problem was that he believed Alcott and Lane were interested in literature and writing at the expense of "the success & immediate prosperity of their object."[29]

Two things are clear. One is that Hecker felt that Alcott was a dominating and selfish influence. He detected "an insinuating and persuasive way with him." He also suspected that knowing of the material prosperity of Hecker's family's business, Alcott was hoping he would bring some money into the community with him. Lane, on the other hand, "was entirely unselfish."[30]

The final two complaints in Hecker's list were closely interrelated. One thing Hecker thoroughly approved of was the dietary code at Fruitlands. A week or two after he had left he recorded with satisfaction that as a result of his experiments at community living he could live on a diet of grain, fruit, nuts, and water. In fact he planned to go one step further than eating unleavened bread—he would try baking it without grinding the wheat first. His recoil from the bodily functions of sex and digestion was fully Greavesian, which was perhaps why he felt sympathetic towards Lane. "I wish I could dispense with the whole digestive apparatus," he wrote a year later, an understandable sentiment if he had been exposing his digestive apparatus to unground wheat.[31] For him, the paucity of fruit was a betrayal of Fruitlands' very identity; coupled with its leaders' tendency to talk rather than do, it suggested the experiment was hypothetical and abstract rather than a deliberate attempt to change the world: a mission statement, not a mission.

The conversation with Alcott and Lane obviously marked a point of no return. A couple of days later Hecker had made up his mind to go back to his own family. He later claimed that when he announced his decision, Alcott said, "Hecker has flunked out. He hadn't the courage to persevere. He's a coward." Lane apparently replied, "No; you're mistaken. Hecker is right. He wanted more than we had to give him."

Many years later Hecker recalled the discussion leading up to Lane's endorsement. "I said to them: If you had the Eternal here, all right, I would be with you." Their self-denial was admirable in its own way, but not enough. "I agree with you fully. I admire your asceticism; it is nothing new to me; I have practiced it a long time myself. If you can get the Everlasting out of my mind, I'm yours. But I know that I'm going to live forever."[32]

Hecker has identified a feature of the Fruitlands community that perhaps made it unique—or at least, in conjunction with Alcott House, made it half of a unique pairing. Establishments for the purpose of living the good life are usually either spiritual, like the monasteries and the Shaker communities, or secular, like the Owenite experiments, or Brook Farm. But Fruitlands was posited on the idea of spiritual perfectibility and the re-establishment of the Garden of Eden, while embodying little sense of an after-life, or of preparation for heaven. The deferment of spiritual reward is a consistent feature of the Christian narrative, but one which had no place on the Fruitlands agenda. The aspiration there was for a perfected here and now. Lane may have sympathized with Hecker, but his and Alcott's asceticism was of a different sort, testifying not to a repudiation of earthly things but to a belief that the material and the spiritual realms could be unified. Oddly, from our later perspective, where we have a sense of the interrelatedness of living things and of the imminent possibility of environmental catastrophe, it is easier to understand the Fruitlanders' passionate engagement with the world around them than it can have been for someone like Hecker on his anguished but ultimately more conventional journey.

On July 22nd, Hecker wrote definitively: "This is not the place for my soul." Anna noted in her journal the next day that Lane was unwell.[33]

Hecker left Fruitlands on July 26th, after being there for just over two weeks. There was no formal announcement—he, Alcott, and Lane simply set off on a journey to Boston. Anna reported the fact in her journal without making anything of it. Two days earlier she had recorded the departure of Larned, a presence closer to her heart, obviously fearing that he might not return, though he was back at Fruitlands a few days later.[34] Her mother might even have been relieved to see the last of Hecker. On July 24th Abigail wrote a list of all the visitors Fruitlands had already had—twenty-three altogether, plus various Shakers and children. She made no distinction in her list between people like Wood Abraham who actually joined Fruitlands, Joseph Palmer who was a part-time member, a woman called Ann Page who was checking it out with a view to joining, and simple observers like Emerson and Ellery Channing. They were all visitors from her point of view, probably because they were not Alcotts. "I did not think so much curiosity could have existed among our friends to see our new home," she wrote, sounding jaded.[35] This was Fruitlands as example, as zoo—as rhetorical gesture. That was what Hecker himself had implied in his fifth thesis: that the experiment was a gesture suggesting utopian possibility to interested onlookers instead of enacting it.

July 26th was baby Abby's birthday. Because of her age (three) there was none of the ceremony that had marked Elizabeth's, but she did have a stocking with presents in it.[36] This little manifestation of Alcott solidarity was Hecker's last glimpse of the community.

The three men called briefly at Emerson's on their way to Boston, but said nothing of the parting of the ways.[37] Lane in fact does not seem to have known for sure that Hecker was going for good. On July 30th he wrote to Oldham that Hecker had gone to New York to sort things out with his family, though he clearly suspected the new recruit would not return. "They appear to be so loving and united a family with such strong humane attachments that though he has done much towards breaking away, I fear that in his desire to bring his brothers further into the inner world he will himself be detained."[38] Actually Hecker had gone back to Brook Farm, but he did in fact return to his family a couple of weeks later, so Lane's fear was justified.[39] From Lane's perspective, love, unity, and humane attachments were obstacles rather than virtues. His skepticism in this respect makes additionally ironic Hecker's point that Fruitlands revolved too much round the concerns of Alcott's biological family.

13

The Consociate Family Life

ALCOTT AND LANE MADE SOME purchases in Boston and visited Brook Farm at West Roxbury (though they were obviously unaware of Hecker's intention to return there for the time being). "There are 80 or 90 persons playing away their youth and day time in a miserably joyous frivolous manner," Lane reported to Oldham. Most of the adults were there to "pass 'a good time,'" he concluded grumpily (this is the same letter in which he worried about the love, unity, and humanity of Hecker's family). He was horrified at the "prominent position" of animals in the community, totting up sixteen cows, four oxen, a herd of pigs, several horses, all the result of what he darkly called "Mr Ripley's tendency." Not content with their own animal products, the Brook Farmers bought in butter to the tune of $500 per year.

Competitiveness was inevitable among rival utopians. Lane quickly went on to assess the rest of the local opposition. There was the Northampton Association of Education and Industry which had been set up the year before, advocating abolition and temperance. That establishment, he concluded, was all about industry (they produced and spun their own silk to avoid participating in the slavery-dependent cotton trade). Then there was the Hopedale Community, also inaugurated in 1842. It was led by the Universalist Adin Ballou, and it too advocated abolition and temperance, along with women's rights. Its primary objective was "practical theology," Lane decided. He concluded that Brook Farm was the best of the bunch, its mission being "taste."

Despite his dismissal of its hedonism, Lane was taken aback by the scale and vitality of the place. Perhaps, he told Oldham, Brook Farm is not just the best but actually "the best which can exist." He thought of the tiny size of Fruitlands, even tinier now Hecker had gone. "At all events," he went on, "we can go no further than to keep open fields, and as far as we have it, open house to *all* comers." He clearly still longed to make a big impact. How maddening that Brook Farm could assemble such a multitude in the name of frivolity! But if Fruitlands tried to pack in recruits, many would recoil at the severity of its regime. "We know very well that if they come not in the right name and nature they will not long remain." It was almost as if their community had inadvertently set up an entrance requirement: "Our dietetic system is a test quite sufficient for many."[1]

Diet hadn't been Hecker's problem, of course. Nor was it Samuel Bower's, given his insistence on eating only raw food. But *he* might be about to depart also. "He is not so happy in body or mind as he ought to be," Lane told Oldham. "He thinks Mr Alcott is arbitrary or despotic, as some others do," he added, thinking back to Hecker's list of complaints. As a result of his disaffection, Bower "confesses to the possession of a little Nomadic blood in his veins," though he, Lane, would encourage him to stay and "cheerfully amend what is amiss."[2]

Lane is beginning to sense danger. Not surprisingly, given the competition from Brook Farm, the fewness and dissatisfaction of the Fruitlanders, he asks Oldham to advertise the Fruitlands community to young men and women on his side of the Atlantic. He switches abruptly to enthusiastic mode as he does so, and we once more glimpse the businessman in him. Fruitlands could offer all the opportunity of the American west at a mere day's walk from the east coast. And something important could be just about to happen (despite those signs of impending disaster). "There is now a certain opportunity for planting a love colony the influence of which may be felt for many generations, and more than felt; it may be the beginning for a state of things which shall far transcend itself."[3] For Lane, as for the seventeenth-century Puritans with whom he had so much in common, the notion of a plantation meant growing produce and community at the same time.

Still, however much he cranked up his optimism, he had to concede that at present not many people were seeking out the potential love colony. He was clearly thoroughly disheartened by Hecker's apostasy, though in fact another new recruit had arrived some time in July, a woman called Ann Page.[4] It may be, though, that while he had believed Hecker to be a fellow spirit, he did not have quite such high hopes of her. Miss Page probably joined at the suggestion of Samuel Larned, since she came from Providence, Rhode Island, like he did—like Christopher Greene too, the newspaper editor who had published Alcott and who (Alcott believed) was continually on the verge of himself joining the community. She seems to have been a progressive of the soft-centered, well-meaning and mystical type, far removed from the steely commitment that characterized Lane. Years later Louisa recalled her as "a stout lady of mature years, sentimental, amiable, and lazy." She "wrote verses copiously, and had vague yearnings and graspings after the unknown."[5]

Despite his wish for female support for Abigail, and his acknowledgement of the female principle behind Shakerism, Lane makes no mention of Ann Page's arrival and instead tries to convince Oldham—and himself—that the lack of numbers at Fruitlands is not important, that what matters is not the size but the quality of membership. What the community needed most was an authentic response to the spirit, a conversion of its internal energies ("the intuitions which are gifted to us") into outward life and relationships. In this respect individuals can do great work, even "in the absence of what are usually called facilities."

Even as he tries to look on the bright side, Lane's disappointment is clear. Just seven weeks before, he had assured Thoreau that Fruitlands offered an abundance of facilities, though remoteness, absence of roads, and the view of the landscape were the main ones itemized. He had obviously become less convinced that such qualities had a practical value. Nevertheless, he could, if he wanted, tell Oldham all about "mowing, hoeing, reaping, ploughing"— but he won't, because what matters is the way these external activities are driven by "the grand principle to which they are obedient."

At this point in his letter Lane the mystic is supplemented once more by Lane the canny entrepreneur. It would be a bad idea to divulge the "external revelations of success" because people would only try to make money out of them. "We will therefore say little concerning the sources of external wealth until man is himself procured to the End which rightly uses these means."[6] The man who invested his savings in Fruitlands and who went into partnership with Bronson Alcott manages to worry about being so successful that he might corrupt the uninitiated. One has a sense of him clutching at straws.

Lane and Alcott returned to Fruitlands on July 29th, a Saturday. Alcott was ill when they arrived, seriously enough to alarm Abigail. In fact by the next day she actually thought he was dying and wrote a panicky letter to her brother Samuel. Her husband was in fact suffering from savage diarrhea, perhaps dysentery. Ellery Channing arrived to spend the day and was appalled at his sepulchral voice and languid bearing. He also concluded Alcott was in a distressed state of mind.[7] Like Lane, he was succumbing to a fear that the community would disband. Channing went back to Concord and reported to Emerson that "Mr A already anticipates the time when he shall be forsaken of all, & left alone, inasmuch as none will probably stand by him in the rigidness of his asceticism." His report made Emerson even more doubtful than he already was about the future of Fruitlands. "I infer that no stability can be safely promised to the society," he told Margaret Fuller.[8]

It was on the same Sunday as Channing's visit that Lane put pen to paper to tell Oldham all about Brook Farm and Alcott's despotism, making no mention of his prostration. It is odd how a drama afflicting some members of a small household could pass others by.

By Tuesday the acute phase of Alcott's illness had passed, but Abigail didn't believe he was essentially any better. When she asked what could be done to help him, he replied, "Thy faith shall heal thee." One can imagine how ominous that would have sounded in a sepulchral voice. But it was the only dignified response possible in the circumstances. Here he was, a diet revolutionary, in the grip of an appalling stomach upheaval. For Abigail commonsense overruled her faith in such a regimen, she told Samuel in another letter, obviously disapproving of her husband's resigned attitude. Actually the regime she fixed on was perfectly in accordance with Alcottian principles— "Blackberries, Spearmint tea, shower bath twice a day."[9] By Friday August 4th Alcott was well enough to begin a long letter to his brother—not Junius this time, but the other surviving one, forty-one-year-old Chatfield, with whom, long ago, he had gone on peddling trips to the Deep South.

Like Lane a few days previously, he lays claim to agricultural success. "Our early harvest is all stored; and the ploughing for winter and spring grain and roots is in a state of forwardness." They had plowed clover into the fields as "sweet manure." Alcott tells his brother that the community has numbered fifteen or sixteen members (though there is no evidence for more than thirteen members at its peak) but is smaller by three or four now "we have less need of assistance"—rather letting the cat out of the bag: they have dispensed with hired hands.

He then goes on to make an extraordinary claim. "The care and burden of the work," he says, "falls on Abba and myself." He makes no mention of Lane's contribution, either here or at any other point in his letter. Instead he makes the familiar complaint that Abigail needs assistance with household responsibilities (clearly Ann Page was not pulling her weight at this point). He then goes on to ask Chatfield and his family to join them. It's a perfect moment for entering the community: the members have a chance of realizing their hopes sooner than could ever have been expected by moving to a "most desirable Estate" at Leominster, only a couple of miles away.[10]

Sooner indeed: Fruitlands has been in operation for just two months; but of course it represents a way of life, not a fixed habitation.

It is hardly surprising, given his past career, that from time to time Lane comes across like a tough-minded businessman but slightly unnerving to find Alcott doing the same, in fact sounding exactly like a glib realtor. There are 150 acres on offer at Leominster, fifty of which "are as valuable as any lands in the county of Worcester," he boasts. The property has water privileges and was improved twenty years previously by "an opulent gentleman who invested large sums" in it. The house is the "richest and most desirable residence in the vicinity." The same went for the land. The "arable fields are enriched," he tells Chatfield—with animal manure, presumably.

"We obtain the whole for about $5,000," Alcott explains, making subtle use of the first person plural. Two thousand of that will come from the sale of their present property. The same again from Joseph Palmer (who was in point of fact the instigator of this plan, coming from the Leominster area himself, and having a practicing farmer's eye for a good opportunity). The remaining thousand, Alcott says airily, will be contributed by Abigail's family (did Samuel May know about that?). But it would be better, Alcott thought, if Chatfield contributed that portion instead. In short what he was offering his brother was the chance to spend a thousand dollars.

True, Lane wanted to free Fruitlands from ownership. But surely if he read this letter, he would have been put out to find Alcott, who had contributed nothing but his own previous debts to the enterprise, spending his partner's investment and other people's money in this blasé fashion. Alcott concludes by expressing his hope and belief that Junius will join them too.[11] True again, Lane himself had tried to proselytize Junius some months before, but with both brothers on board, the new Leominster Fruitlands would be transformed into pretty much an Alcott family enterprise.

Hecker's complaint number three had identified Alcott's family as one of the stumbling blocks. If we put Lane's letter to Oldham and Alcott's to Chatfield side by side, noting that Lane accused Alcott of authoritarianism while failing to mention his illness, and that Alcott failed to mention Lane at all, while laying claim to all the work, appropriating ongoing financial transactions, and trying to get other Alcotts to join, one can begin to suspect that the fault lines at Fruitlands were becoming a visible crack, somewhat like the one in Edgar Allan Poe's "Fall of the House of Usher" (written four years previously, and concerning siblings morbidly turned in upon themselves).

The day he wrote this letter, Alcott set off with Lane to visit the Harvard Shakers once more. They were accompanied this time by James Kay, a wealthy businessman from Philadelphia who would become an important supporter of Brook Farm and act as George Ripley's adviser.[12] He was presumably shopping for a community to sponsor. This time the Shakers themselves took note of the visit. The society's journal for that day records clear and pleasant weather; they got hay in from "the Haskell and White Meddows" and then "two men by the names of Alcott & Lane (Transcendentalest) and a man from Philadelphia came here took dinner and stayed till towards night[.] They seem to be inquiring into our principles."[13]

The visitors' affiliation, inserted in the writer's rural drawl, has an official solidity, as if you can be a Transcendentalist in the same way as you can a teacher or surveyor—or, indeed, a Shaker.

It was a fruitful meeting in one sense. The Shakers would let them have 200 trees at a special discount because of their temperance habits and because of the importance of fruit in their diet, even offering to come over and help them plant.[14] Presumably Lane and Alcott convinced their hosts, and themselves, that they were in for the long haul, prepared to think in terms of planting an orchard for fifteen years ahead, lighting that long green fuse; while all the time Alcott, at least, was pondering an upheaval that might take place within days. Back at home, ten-year-old Louisa was reading *Oliver Twist*, that tale of undernourishment and youthful resilience, then thinking about it a little, before going to bed.[15]

When he got back, Alcott was feverish again. He had been too feeble to cope with the trip, Abigail realized. As people do when they have an immediate worry, she tried to escape it by visualizing the long, slow passage of time (perhaps news of the Shakers' offer to provide an orchard encouraged her to). While James Kay was taking his leave she told him he would have to come back in ten years to get her verdict on Fruitlands. "Dear Lady," he replied, "you will not be here to answer me." He had obviously seen enough to come to his own conclusion. Perhaps he was right, she reflected.

In any case, whether the place ended up as "a barren wilderness or a fruitful Paradise," it would have to be without her help. She felt defiant and rebellious again. "My genius is too rigidly set in the old mould to make great progress," she decided, in a mixture of pessimism and self-assertion. She hated society, of course she did, with all its "its fallacies and shams," but for her own part she remained irreducibly "real." Her neighbors would just have to put up with how she was, her husband included. "I cannot live his principle," she told Samuel. It's an interesting distinction: her own reality versus his "principle," the contrast between being a person on one hand, and a colorless instrument of the spirit on the other. In short, the Shakers would not be able to write "Transcendentalest" after *her* name. It was another nail in the coffin.

Over the next days Alcott's condition got worse again. On Sunday August 6th there were more visitors, "Beard Palmer and Son," and no doubt as a result further discussion of the Leominster opportunity. Too much company, was Abigail's verdict. It was making her husband's brain "morbidly active." What she had wanted was for them both to get away in a chaise for a while, leaving the children in the care of Lane and Wood Abraham.[16] By now Bower had finally succumbed to his nomadic blood, and left the community altogether. Palmer had offered him some land in No Town, a very isolated spot where it would be easier for him to practice nudity. Larned was also away at this time—Emerson came across him at Plymouth, down toward Cape Cod, where Larned assured him he intended to return to Fruitlands in due course.[17]

No, Alcott replied in response to his wife's suggestion. All he wanted was rest, and perfect quiet. When he next went on a journey, he told her chillingly, it would "be a long one—and *alone*."

Abigail was terrified. "I do not allow myself to despair of his recovery," she told her brother, her choice of words suggesting she was within a hair's breadth of doing just that. But she was troubled by an even more horrific prospect than her husband's death. "Oh Sam," she exclaimed, "that piercing thought flashes through my mind of insanity."

Alcott must have been on the point of mental collapse; maybe he was delirious, talking gibberish. Anything rather than that—she would rather he *were* dead. "A grave yawning to receive his precious body would be to me a consolation compared to that condition of life."

Samuel May offered to come and support her. She thanked him, but he could do no "particular good." And they couldn't cope with him at present. Instead "I shall shut up Mr A from all care and company," hardly a utopian solution. If that did not work, she would "unbeknown to him send for Emerson." Of all people (including Samuel May, presumably), he was the one who would know just what to do. "He has good sense enough not to be afraid of human aids for human ends," good sense being exactly what Alcott so conspicuously lacked, with his commitment to "principle."[18] As Abigail is "real," so Emerson is "human"; these are the very qualities missing from the Fruitlands agenda, and without them her husband is in danger of descending into madness.

But in fact life carried on in the community. Lane and Ann Page took charge of teaching the children, with Alcott helping out when he was well enough.[19] And two days after Abigail confided her terrors to her brother, little Louisa went berrying all morning with William and Anna, perhaps picking the blackberries that her father was being fed on (along with spearmint tea). That same afternoon Louisa made clothes for her doll. On Thursday August 10th Alcott was well enough to go to Leominster to have another look at the property there. Abigail, Lane, and baby Abby went with him. Meanwhile Louisa did some ironing and went off berrying again with William and Lizzy. The weather was bad but she felt "happy within."[20] Everything was back to normal.

But the acuteness of Alcott's physical illness, the sharpness of his misery, the extent of his wife's terror, all testify to the stress and claustrophobia of life at Fruitlands.

Sometime in August, Lane and Alcott wrote an open letter attempting to explain what their community stood for. It was entitled "The Consociate Family Life" and was published in the *New York Evening Tribune* on September 1st, the *Herald of Freedom* the following week, and finally in the *New Age and Concordium Gazette* on November 1st. The document was addressed to A. Brooke, of Ohio, himself a prolific writer of letters to the press, who had asked for further information about the experiment—though perhaps its real purpose was for Lane and Alcott to clarify their objectives for themselves. Alcott cut out a copy of the letter and glued it into his scrapbook.[21]

Certainly Brooke was a sympathetic recipient. He had been a contributor to the *Plain Speaker* during its short life, cheek by jowl with Alcott himself, and his ideas about inherited traits, ingeniously related to the influence of circumstances, would have rung a bell with both Alcott and Lane. Past generations, Brooke claimed, had been mentally and morally blinded by "defective civil, religious and social arrangements." This blindness had then been transmitted "by the laws of hereditary descent to their offspring," resulting in their own "defective mental and moral manifestations."[22] In short, evil institutions affect biology; biology in turn creates damaged individuals who perpetuate evil institutions. Seven years before, while still teaching at his Temple School, Alcott had caught a similar process of action and reaction in a journal entry: "That men form and modify institutions is true; but it is equally true that these institutions, by a reflex influence, form men—shape individual and national character."[23]

The Fruitlanders' letter takes up this vexed issue again, claiming that "it appears not so much that improved circumstances are to meliorate mankind, as that improved men will originate the superior conditions for themselves and others." It does not go into how these improved men are to be improved in the first place, but talks at great length about the virtue of the Fruitlands diet and farming practices, clearly implying that amelioration is indeed dependent on getting these circumstances correctly calibrated, on establishing a regime of "simplicity in diet, plain garments, pure bathing, unsullied dwellings," and so on. Property will be redeemed from ownership—and while on that subject the letter talks of "removal to a place of less inconvenience," obviously the farm at Leominster. So much for the "sequestered dell." Trade must be replaced by subsistence farming (and barter where necessary). Farm animals must be dispensed with.

By this time, a summer lull had meant that the Fruitlanders were able to return Joseph Palmer's ox and cow (though he continued to bring the team with him from time to time when he came).[24] The letter almost seems to recapitulate Ellery Channing's satirical remarks on the evils of livestock. Cattle require people to wait on them as "cook and chambermaid"; they necessitate the "excessive labor of mowing, curing, and housing hay"; they take up large tracts of countryside—and without them the human population could be four times as dense as it currently is, without creating the malignant concentration in cities that Lane described in "Social Tendencies." Above all the pollution and "debauchery" of manure would be eliminated—as noticed before in this ideology, there is a crossover from purity of soil to sexual innocence; and conversely from pollution to sexual excess. In Hawthorne's novel based on Brook Farm, Zenobia, the sexual temptress of the Blithedale community, is identified with fruit and flowers grown "where the soil had doubtless been enriched to a more than natural fertility."[25] "No hope is there for Humanity," Alcott and Lane claim melodramatically, "while Woman is withdrawn from the tender assiduities which adorn her and her household, to the servitudes of the dairy and the flesh pots." The pun on "flesh pots" is obviously intentional.

Their letter's title, "The Consociate Family Life," takes us straight to the nub of the current problems at Fruitlands. It begins in Lane's first-person singular; then Alcott comes on board and the text modulates into the first-person plural. Near the end, the writers say somewhat archly that the "narrative . . . has undergone some changes in its personal expression which might offend the hypercritical."

The opening is very much in Lane's voice. He describes the impact of Alcott's visit to England, and uses the mythology of going west to explain both the promise and disappointment of his own journey to America. "It would be well to cross the ocean of Life from the narrow island of selfishness to the broad continent of universal Love at one dash," he says wistfully, "but the winds are not always propitious, and steam is only a recent invention." Lane goes on to make a familiar complaint, as well as produce a familiar consolation. "Instead of forming items in a large enterprise, we are left to be the principal actors in promoting an idea less in extent, but greater in intent, than any yet presented to our observation."

What does the phrase "consociate family" mean, or imply? A transitional structure, there to be outgrown? Or a small-sized community mirroring—to an extent based on—the biological unit? By the time this issue is tackled head on, Alcott is clearly co-authoring. "Let it be admitted as the most vital and creative of all human acts, and we are convinced of the absorbing importance of family life." Here is an echo of Alcott's previous celebration of mettle, "Behold the creative jet!"

There is nothing essentially unGreavesian about this sentiment, of course, except for its optimism about the consequences of sexual intercourse. If parents in this generation conform to the divine will, they will influence the character and happiness of their offspring—the flip side of Mr. Brooke's own downbeat analysis in the *Plain Speaker*.

The passage continues with a significant comparison. "As birds migrate to our latitude in the warm season, build and use their nests, sing a song or two, and as the cold approaches depart to a warmer zone, so man is sent from balmier climes to breed upon the earth." When they first moved into the Fruitlands farmhouse, Abigail had compared herself to a mother bird sheltering its young under its wings, and the nesting image here carries with it some of that notion of cozy bonding even though, as it goes on, the sentence takes a sterner stance, as if Lane has elbowed Alcott away from the sheet of paper, and taken up the pen again himself, "and all other activities should be but preparative to this of securing an off-spring unprofaned by any self-will, untinctured by lust."

Lane continues to hold sway at the desk. The Holy Family "disdains all animal sensualities." The Shakers are an example. "We witness in this people the bringing together of the two sexes in a new relation." The suggestion now is that "consociate family" means nothing more than a group sharing a house and a point of view. At the end of the letter there is a list of questions to which the right-minded individual will answer no, covering the obvious Fruitlands taboos: "Shall I sip tea or coffee?"; "Shall I stimulate with milk?"; "Shall I warm my bathing water?" One of the questions is "Shall I become a parent?" So much for those birds in their nests. Back in the issue of the *Plain Speaker* in which he shared newsprint with Mr. Brooke of Ohio, Alcott had replied to a reader asking "Is it right to marry?" with a paean in praise of the institution: "As the fellowship and charities of the family are alike the germ and fruit of all excellence; so is every soul not planted in this Eden of its Being, defrauded of its needful culture."[26]

In short, this letter by Alcott and Lane provides an accurate picture of Fruitlands family philosophy because of its very evasiveness and muddle. By the time it was republished in the *New Age* in November, Lane had sorted out the confusion. The nesting passage had been omitted, and he had become the sole signatory. But that was for his home territory, back in England. It was more of a challenge to get the issue sorted out in central Massachusetts, where he had Abigail Alcott to deal with.

14

Penniless Pilgrimages

ON AUGUST 26TH ABIGAIL ALCOTT visited the Shakers to see their way of life for herself. For Lane they exemplified a successful and well-ordered community founded on sexual abstinence, female leadership, and a new balance between the sexes. Abigail reached precisely the opposite verdict. "I gain but little from their domestic or internal arrangements," she confided to her diary. "There is servitude somewhere, I have no doubt." Far from finding evidence of sexual equality, she detected signs of exploitation. "There is a fat sleek comfortable look about the men," she observed, "and among the women . . . a stiff awkward reserve that belongs to neither sublime resignation nor divine hope."

In fact the visit led her to ponder on the woman's yoke, which she saw wherever she turned. Some take what is meted out because "they are but beasts of burden"; others remain silent through pride. Another group, however (and Abigail is obviously one of this number), find that "it galls and chafes." Such women "feel assured by every instinct of their nature that they were designed for a higher, nobler calling than to 'drag life's lengthening chain along.' "

It's surprising, perhaps, to see this bitter response come out of an encounter with the Shakers, after a summer spent at Fruitlands, both communities ostensibly dedicated to "a higher, nobler calling." But she is adamant that it is only men who get the credit for, and gain the advantages of, such experiments. And Miss Page agreed.

Ann Page had obviously begun to make her presence felt. August had been a "busy toilsome month," but made easier by her presence and help. Abigail decided she was "an amiable active woman whose kind word and gentle care-taking deed is very grateful to me." She had made "a good remark, and true as good, that a woman may live a whole life of sacrifice, and at her death meekly says 'I die a woman.' " A man, on the other hand, "passes a few years in experiments in self-denial and simple life, and he says, 'Behold a God.' "

Ann Page's sharp analysis got Abigail thinking again about the distinction she had made between being real (or human) on the one hand, and principled on the other. "Woman lives her thought," she decided, while "man speculates about it." This leads her to her own take on love and marriage, one that deflates all the high-toned talk about a union of spirit-selected pairs in sympathetic harmony. "Woman's love is enduring, changeless," she asserts, while man "is fitful in his attachments." Her verdict sheds light on her relationship with her husband, particularly coming as it does only a couple of weeks after she feared he was dying or losing his mind. "Man's love is convenient," she goes on, "not of necessity."

On the face of it, this is the last charge one might expect her to make. Her husband might be hapless, disaster-prone, self-centered, but it seems strange to think of him as pragmatic. Yet in his letter to Chatfield he blithely proposed spending money belonging to Lane, the May family, Joseph Palmer, and indeed Chatfield himself, without showing the slightest awareness that some investment might be owing from himself. Hecker certainly nourished a suspicion that Alcott was interested in him because his family was wealthy; Lane too had shown signs of resentment that he had had to repay Alcott's debts as well as take on the burden of the community—which would never have come into existence in the first place if Emerson had not given Alcott the wherewithal to go to England and meet him. The fact that he was able and willing to tap all these sources of unearned income does come to seem a little "convenient." And of course Lane, Hecker, and Samuel Bower had all recently become restive at Alcott's authoritarianism. "Woman is happy in her plain lawn," Abigail concluded. Man, meanwhile, "is better content in the royal purple."[1]

Abigail's feminism had been reinforced by some female bonding. She had become friendly with her neighbors, Mrs. Lovejoy and Mrs. Willard, and her beloved aunt by marriage, Hannah Robie, had taken lodgings in the neighborhood to be near her. "It's a great comfort to see her occasionally and have a good talk," Abigail told her brother Charles.[2] And finally Ann Page was proving to be an ally.

She was living in the barn "like another man," at least according to Mary Gove, and despite having to conform to Fruitlands mores by wearing linen bloomers, she might well have used seclusion from the house to undertake a modest dietary rebellion. She "hankered after the flesh-pots," Louisa claimed (surely quoting Lane's loaded term), and took "private sips" of milk, like fellow reprobate Joseph Palmer, going one further by nibbling on crackers and cheese.[3] Indeed, Abigail's cousin, Samuel Greely, spent a couple of days at Fruitlands and concluded that Miss Page possessed an "appetite for the products of the cow and the hen"—so perhaps she surreptitiously boiled herself the occasional egg too.[4]

On August 28th there was a Conversation on the subject of faults. Louisa wished to get rid of impatience; Lane, of self-will. Years later Louisa would make Mr. Bhaer conduct a similar Conversation with Jo's boys.[5] That evening they had bread and water for supper.[6] One can imagine the ample form of Miss Page brooding about her tidbits in the barn. Greely described such a session. "The little girls served parched corn with salt, or slices of bread and cold water," he explained, while "high thinking . . . was kept aflame by original remarks or citations by the leaders."[7] Perhaps he envied Ann Page her private stores. On August 30th there was a female outing to check out the property at Leominster, comprising two little women, Louisa and Anna (presumably Ann Page was looking after the other children), along with Abigail, Hannah Robie, and someone called Harriet. Louisa decided she liked the place "pretty well."[8]

The following day Abigail sat down to write a letter to her brother Charles, taking the opportunity to look back over recent weeks. "Mr Alcott and I have too much to do," she complained, "and we have had a constant succession of company—unprofitable enough." Just as in the case of her husband's letter to *his* brother, she makes no mention at all of Charles Lane. She either regarded his contribution as negligible, or wanted to emphasize that Fruitlands was an Alcott family project—Larned and Wood Abraham get no credit either. She took a dim view of the visitors, on the whole. Some come out of curiosity, some to scoff, some for prayers, she said. "Some remain long enough to enjoy the joke, others long enough to taste the discipline," but "few to join the aspiration for a better life." Despite this failure to make converts, the Fruitlanders give what they have, and this is a source of satisfaction, even if their efforts are not appreciated. "Our hospitality is for service, not for show," she assured Charles, "and there is the dignity of the host satisfied."

All in all their hard work has been lengthy and profitless. She tries to console herself. "I cannot think that so much energy as mine will be lost in the great account of human activity." And perhaps deprivation has its own value, though she makes no attempt to follow Lane's lead in finding a bonus in doing without. "It is a great experiment, this of renunciation," she told her brother. "I am stronger than I thought."[9] He must have sensed that she was speaking through clenched teeth.

Hannah Robie returned to Boston on September 1st. That day Louisa provides us with a child's eye-view of life at Fruitlands. She got up at five, and had a bath. "I love cold water!" she exclaimed, true child of her parents. Then after breakfast she washed the dishes. After that she ran on the hill. School that day consisted of writing, spelling, and doing sums, followed by listening to Mr. Lane read a story sternly entitled "The Judicious Father." It concerned a rich girl who persecuted a poor one, and was made to change clothes with her to learn the error of her ways. "After that," Louisa explained, "she was good to shabby girls." Given the inevitable shabbiness of the Alcott children it's interesting that she identifies with the rich girl, deciding, "I shall be kind to poor people."

They had a dinner of bread and fruit, and an inevitable Conversation. Alcott asked what was God's noblest work. Anna said that men were, but Louisa countered with babies, on the grounds that "men are often bad; babies never are." Their neighbor Mrs. Lovejoy brought her baby around on her visits, and of course sister Abby was only just three. Given Lane's own hostility to Abby, he might have tried to qualify Louisa's general approval. In any case they had a long talk. Louisa felt better after it, she said, "and *cleared up*" (the italics signifying that she means her thoughts had been cleared up, not that she had dealt with the dishes this time). Then she read, walked, and played until supper. Afterwards they all sang. She noticed the moon looking down on her as she went to bed, and thought back to how she had been bad-tempered that day, and had defied her mother. She cried, then felt better, saying to herself, "I must not tease my mother." Then she recited poetry to herself until she went to sleep—she had learned, she said, a great deal by heart.[10] It was an intellectually bracing regime, as well as a rigorously moral one for a ten-year-old.

Despite—or because of—her makeshift accommodation, Ann Page decided she needed to have her own furniture around her, and toward the end of August she persuaded Lane and the still feeble Alcott to hire a vehicle and go to Providence with her to collect it.[11] When they arrived, they found the town in a bustle because of university Commencement Day. Alcott and Lane visited an abolitionist couple, George and Frances Clarke, in hopes of gaining recruits for their community. But the Clarkes had just lost a child, so the visit became another stand-off between the claims of family and consociation. "We made little progress in gathering any of them into our circle, as we somewhat expected for two of the young women," Lane complained irritably, "for they had found enough employment in comforting each other."

From the grieving Clarkes they went on to visit Mrs. Newcomb, the mother of an intense young man called Charles King Newcomb, a member of Brook Farm who had deeply impressed Emerson ("a true genius," he told Margaret Fuller) and other members of the Concord set with a story he had published in the *Dial* the year before.[12] It was called "The Two Dolons. From the MS. Symphony of Dolon. The First Dolon," and as its title implies was an obscure, desperately overwritten piece depicting a young man obsessed with nature and roaming about over "gurgle-reserved silent meadows." As it turned out, Newcomb's perceived promise came to nothing—the "result is zero," Emerson concluded sadly some years later.[13]

In conversation at the prodigy's mother's house, Alcott enthused over the way competition had generated excellent transportation facilities (perhaps the journey to Providence had given him new energy—Abigail had thought a change of scene would do him good, after all). He suddenly suggested that he

and Lane should make use of them to go to New York. Lane, despite his skepticism about recent developments in travel, drily replied that "there was no
other objection than the want of means." One could add: apart from running
a farm, and taking responsibility for a community that included five children.

Maybe what was happening in this Conversation was another example of
what Abigail Alcott had called "convenience." The rest of the company in
Mrs. Newcomb's house, having heard that the two men were prevented from
going to New York by want of funds, instantly coughed up the necessary
amount for the journey.[14]

On the face of it, the decision to go to New York at that moment in time
seems completely incomprehensible—and indeed it was certainly the
strangest and most quixotic decision made during the lifetime of this strange
and quixotic utopia. True, the farm had been going through a quiet period,
but harvest time had now arrived. The decision seems to bear out Abigail's
claim about men being fitful in their attachments. We do not have an explanation of the motives of either man. "Some call of the Oversoul," Louisa later
suggested.[15]

Lane and Alcott were, however, committed to the notion that the impact
of Fruitlands could and should be transmitted outward to the world at large.
They also had a mystical faith in the transforming power of properly
conducted Conversations. Moreover they were searching for recruits, and
clearly were disappointed at the response in Providence. Alcott had on a
previous occasion simply stepped away from the cares of his normal life, and
taken passage to England. As a result of that journey he had met Charles
Lane and obtained the support and wherewithal to start the enterprise.
Perhaps he thought another journey now would have a similar effect. But like
so much of what happened during the course of the Fruitlands experiment,
this apparently whimsical decision seems to have allegorical reverberations.
They were abandoning the farm in order to go off after new members; in
searching for one kind of harvest they were sacrificing another. They were
breaking the vital utopian link between microcosm and macrocosm.

Back at Fruitlands, Abigail had no idea the two men were about to disappear over the horizon for a couple of weeks. The barley had been cut but was
still in the fields, and Joseph Palmer was away too, back at No Town
checking up on his livestock.[16] A couple of days after the departure for

Providence a late summer storm began to threaten. Abigail assembled Anna, Louisa, Elizabeth, and William, harnessed them (and herself) to clothes-baskets and linen sheets, and off they went, gathering in the grain before it was drenched. Looking back on this scene, Louisa saw Abigail as Abigail saw herself, "a mother-bird with a brood of hungry nestlings to feed."[17]

Alcott and Lane, now subsidized, made the most of the facilities of modern travel. They took the railroad and then caught a ferry through Long Island Sound to New York, "one of the magnificent Steamboats furnished with nearly 400 beds," Lane told Oldham, suddenly discovering an enthusiasm for innovation (meanwhile Ann Page was presumably left to make her own way back to Fruitlands with her furniture). The travelers arrived in New York at six in the morning and went off to the Graham House to have breakfast, where they found, according to Lane, "some people half if not quite alive," an impressive score by his standards. The graph soon flattened out. "The number of living persons in the 300,000 inhabitants of N.Y. is very small," he subsequently decided.

Nevertheless they promptly found themselves in a vortex of the most living ones available, reformers like the Fourierists Parke Godwin and Albert Brisbane, as well as the political economist Henry Vetheck, whom Lane described as the "Greaves of New York," though adding cautiously, "if there be one." They had high hopes of Edward Palmer, a reformer who visited Concord from time to time, and stayed with the Emersons. He was no relation of Joseph, but he too had radical beliefs, having lived for three years without using money. He was now engaged in manufacturing herbal pills with a colleague, Dr. Wooster Beach, "a progressive man in medicine." "Edward Palmer is a man of extreme gentleness," Lane decided, "but pretty firm." Palmer was becoming disillusioned however, having been led into pessimism by the influence of William Chace, former editor (along with Christopher Greene) of the Providence *Plain Dealer*, but himself sadder and wiser since the paper's collapse. "Lately he [Palmer] has been somewhat hopeless of seeing anything better than the present order upon earth," Lane said, though he and Alcott hoped to change all that by taking him back to Fruitlands. They also visited Mrs. Rebecca Black and her mother, "both mystic characters," as well as the abolitionist author Lydia Maria Child, a close friend of Margaret Fuller.[18]

When Lane and Alcott called round, Mrs. Child asked them, "What brings you to New York?"

"I don't know," Alcott replied, "it seems a miracle that we are here."

Child found Lane distinctly unprepossessing. She confided in a friend, Augusta King, that his face looked as if "the washwomen had . . . rubbed it on a wash-board," a very different effect, obviously, from that translucent scrofula on the face of Henry Gardiner Wright so admired by Mary Gove. Child didn't like the expression on Lane's rough face either. It would "make me slow to put myself in his powers," she told Miss King.[19]

At this time a member of the Channing family, the Reverend William Henry Channing, was conducting a series of meetings in Brooklyn on Christianity. In a year or two Channing would become associated with Brook Farm in its Fourierist phase, and without formally joining the community would in effect act as its chaplain.[20] Now he took the chance to let Alcott and Lane expound their utopian principles at one of his sessions.

These meetings were normally "moderately attended," Lane explained to Oldham, but numbers swelled for the appearance of the two Fruitlanders. The room was "crowded and attentive," and they "discoursed on the deepest topics." As it happened, Lydia Maria Child's husband David, himself a radical lawyer, was in the audience, along with a friend called John Hopper. The atmosphere was stifling, and both men came back to the Childs' home with a headache. David Child arrived first and his wife asked him what had been discussed.

"I don't know," he replied.

"But can't you tell anything they said?"

For some time he couldn't, but she pressed him "unmercifully" and finally he explained, "L[ane] divided man into three states; the disconscious, the conscious, and the unconscious. The disconscious is the state of a pig; the conscious is the baptism by water; and the unconscious is the baptism by fire."

She laughed and asked, "Well, how did the whole discussion affect your mind?"

"Why, after I had heard them talk a few minutes," he told her, "I'll be cursed if I knew whether I had any mind at all."

Hopper had more staying power, but even he left while the meeting was still in full swing. "Have you been pleased?" Mrs. Child asked him.

"They've put my mind and body in the devil of a muss," he replied, "and I wish they had stayed at home."

"What did they talk about?"

"They didn't know themselves—how then should I?"

Again, she forced the issue. "What did they say?"

"Why, W[illiam] H[enry] C[hanning] seemed to think there was some connection between mind and body; but those Boston folks, so far as I could understand 'em, seemed to think the body was all a d—d sham."[21]

The peripatetic philosophers visited their "friend and sometime inmate," Isaac Hecker, and Lane admired the extensive baking and corn-grinding business he ran with his brothers. Hecker had discovered how to pearl wheat, a breakthrough that was much admired. Lane had his doubts, however. "I think it is too intense for frequent use," he told Oldham.[22] Pearling is the removal of the outer layer of bran from the grain of wheat, usually by abrasion, ensuring that the nutrients are no longer "diluted" by its presence. As in the case of the use of manure, or the clustering of the intelligentsia in cities, Lane was automatically suspicious of any attempt to create a kind of hot spot of concentrated material, believing that the qualities of a substance should be spread evenly.

Despite all their efforts, the trip to New York yielded no new recruits. Nevertheless they didn't return straight home. Instead, Alcott wanted to show Lane his birthplace in Connecticut, so they took a steamer to New Haven.

They boarded it without any money in their pockets—they were on a penniless pilgrimage, after all. In a sense this whole excursion was an affirmation of utopian possibility. The two men were living in a new world where it was not necessary to have money, a world that was somehow being superimposed over the old one. They were sitting on the deck in their linen tunics and straw hats, enjoying the breeze, when the ticket collector came along.

Alcott explained that they had no money or scrip to pay for the journey, but they would happily contribute an improving Conversation for the benefit of the passengers instead. It was a simple matter of barter.

The collector was not pleased, but since the boat was well under way, there was no option. They held forth, according to Louisa's later account, "in their most eloquent style," and the listeners were "moved to take up a collection for these inspired lunatics." In fact there was more than necessary for the price of the tickets, but Alcott and Lane apparently turned down the surplus, telling their audience, "You see how well we get on without money." Perhaps they did accept a small amount, however, because they afterward took a coach from New Haven to Waterbury, the nearest town to Wolcott, where Alcott was born.

Lane was not impressed. "This is the most wretched agricultural place I have seen," he told Oldham. Alcott's sister Phoebe and her husband, William Norton, were farming the old place on Spindle Hill where Alcott had spent his childhood. Lane clearly thought Norton—"the puniest fellow in the place"—wasn't up to the job, and regretted the passing of the old days when the farm was "once so well managed." He only had his partner's word for that of course, and the visit might have sowed some doubts in his mind about Alcott's farming background.[23]

Over in Fruitlands, the abolitionist Parker Pillsbury was paying a visit, and Louisa recorded in her diary that they all "talked about the poor slaves." That day, September 14th, she had a music lesson with Ann Page, now back at the community with her furniture. Louisa decided she hated her because she was so fussy. After school, Louisa "ran in the wind and played be a horse," then pretended to be fairies with Anna and Lizzie, wearing gowns and paper wings they had made themselves. "I 'flied' highest of all," she wrote. There is a natural transcendentalism of childhood, however hard-won the adult variety might be. In the evening, because of the absence of the men-folk, their Conversation centered around the subject of traveling. Louisa remembered how she had felt when her father went off to England. That reminded her (precocious as she was) of a verse of Byron's about leaving the shores of Naxos:

Not a sigh or faltered accent
Told my bosom's struggling swell.

When she went up to her bed in the attic, the atmosphere of lyrical melancholy persisted. It was raining, but the drops "made a pretty noise on the roof."[24]

The wanderers returned to their little Naxos three days later, September 17th. Abigail had hoped that on their travels they would at least have come to a decision about the future, but they hadn't. "Still undecided about the Lexington place," she wrote sadly in her journal, muddling her brother Sam's town with Leominster.[25] The two men eagerly checked out the list of visitors who had come during their absence. In addition to Pillsbury, their former colleague Samuel Bower had called in. He had been writing articles for the *Liberator*, predicting the full regeneration of the human race "if we can rid the kitchen of its horrors and keep our tables free of the mangled corse"—staying on-message even while off the premises.[26] But he had become tired of his solitary regime in No Town and was on his way to Lowell, a very different environment—the Manchester of New England, as Lane called it. Perhaps, like Wright before him, he wanted to check out the conditions of the factory workers. Lane tried to look on the bright side. "If his aims are high and his head clear he will not wander far from us," he decided, "but a wanderer it is certain he must [be] allowed to be."

The problem was that Wood Abraham was also showing signs of succumbing to his inner nomad. He "comes and goes with some regard to the law within him," Lane noted, but for the time being was "busy with our latter hay, the maize, buck wheat, &c." Remarkably Lane was able to make these remarks without showing any awareness that he and Alcott had been wanderers too, and that Abraham might be tempted to slip away precisely because he had found himself so busy with the harvesting.

A certain Mr. Hammond from New Hampshire had also shown up during their absence. Lane and Alcott decided he might be a promising candidate for the community, and almost as soon as they had come through the door they were off again, walking a distance of about twenty-five miles.[27] When they arrived, they decided Hammond would indeed be worth recruiting. For one thing, he had "an exoteric wife of some good household qualities." This was Greavesian terminology for the fact that she was a practical person, and might therefore be helpful to Abigail. Moreover, Hammond himself was "an expert workman" who had built a cottage with his own hands. He also had a "respectable talent" for painting portraits, "which he estimates humbly without a consciousness of humility," Lane told Oldham. All in all, a perfect catch for Fruitlands, second only in desirability to Edward Palmer.

Hammond introduced them to four women who, along with himself, "constitute the whole of the town, vitally considered" (Mrs. Hammond obviously did not count as her attributes were merely exoteric). Lane, perhaps trying to justify their second abandonment of Fruitlands in quick succession, decided that these ladies would have found it helpful to see him in the flesh. They had read his articles on "A Voluntary Political Government," "yet the presence of the living person is much more real a thing." His arrival did indeed strengthen their resolve, indeed too much so in the case of the oldest member of the group, who insisted that she would never eat meat again. Unbelievably, Lane tried to dissuade her, "on account of her years."[28] It's the only moment when his faith in the physical as well as the moral and spiritual benefit of a vegan diet ever seems to have wavered.

But despite having the privilege of a personal encounter, none of the five living inhabitants of New Ipswich, nor indeed the exoteric Mrs. Hammond, followed Lane and Alcott back to Fruitlands.

Almost immediately, on Saturday September 24th, Lane left it again, this time in company with Anna Alcott, for a visit to the Emersons in Concord (there is no mention of her father going with them). The young girl "most magnanimously walked her little legs fourteen miles in about five hours down to old Concord," Lane said, deeply impressed by her stamina. He was not so impressed by what he found when they arrived, however. Unlike the energetic child, their friends in Concord appeared "to have been pretty somnolent since our departure." Touché, given that when Emerson visited Fruitlands in July he had described Alcott and Lane as "men at rest." "Mr Emerson is I think quite stationary," Lane concluded. "He is off the Railroad of progress, and merely an elegant, kindly observer of all who pass onwards, and notes down their aspect while they remain in sight; of course when they arrive at a new station they are gone from and for him."

It is an interesting verdict, given Lane's own adherence to the doctrine of "being" over "doing." Only a year previously Emerson had congratulated him on his commitment to "ceasing from doing," and of course Lane himself tended to attack the pointlessness of high-speed, steam-driven travel, at least when he was not taking advantage of it. But however much he proclaimed the virtues of stasis and passivity, he had a strong urge to make things happen, to be part of a large-scale process of social transformation. He was an impatient, proactive man, out of gear with the sedentary aspect of Greavesianism, that weakness of the lower limbs Emerson had pointed to, as well as with Alcott's familial frame of reference. He was temperamentally ill-suited to his closest allies.

Lane believed (quite rightly) that Emerson had an essentially literary take on life. He noted that the playwright John Sterling had just dedicated his new tragedy, *Strafford*, to him—"no very alarming honor!" in Lane's opinion. This led him to a bitter reflection on the ineffectualness of Emerson's friend Carlyle (no doubt Lane had some awareness that Carlyle regarded *him* as a bottomless imbecile). "I suppose Thos. Carlyle with all his famous talking does not yet *actually* lead the people out of their troubles," he told Oldham. "These worthy and enlightened scribblers will do little to save the nations." Of course he was a famous talker and enlightened scribbler himself, but that was a different matter, since his words circled round the vortex of a practical experiment. "Some there are of more real solid metal," he continued, clearly using the word "real" in a different sense from Abigail—indeed, in the opposite sense, signifying commitment to utopian principles.[29]

Abigail was in fact doing her best to conform to those principles. On the day Lane and her daughter left for Concord, she made preparations to counter the oncoming cold. "Tried the experiment to-day of 2 shower-baths," she wrote in her journal, "to fortify against the severe weather of winter." Her theory was that two showers in succession might have an effect analogous to that of wearing two layers of clothes. "I wish it might subserve the purpose of more clothing particularly the use of flannel[,] a thing much to be desired." She was obviously alarmed at the difficulty of surviving in her linen tunic and "bloomers." "Being unable to change the elements we inhabit, we should harden our bodies[,] familiarize ourselves with the intemperance of the seasons and turn them to the benefit of our health."[30] It is a splendid example of that strange environment in the higher reaches of the circumstantial law: wearing cold showers as protection from the weather.

Back in Concord, Emerson was coming to a conclusion about his visitor that seemed strangely to echo Lane's own verdict on talkers and scribblers. He felt Lane and Alcott were trying too hard to spread their word. No doubt he was shocked to hear about all their gallivanting over the country, and sensed the way in which the penniless pilgrimages betrayed the whole point of Fruitlands. "The appeal to the public indicates infirm faith," he thought, "like people whose heads are not clear & must see a house built before they can comprehend the plan of it." Lane was indeed skeptical of using plans to visualize a finished product. As he had said in "Social Tendencies," a calculation cannot be put beforehand into books, but must "be realised, day by day." For him, the proselytizing was an example of such daily making real, except, sadly, that it had borne no fruit whatsoever. As usual when he criticized the utopians, Emerson tried to draw the sting by reverting to the positive. "Yet this must be said in defence of Alcott & Lane," he continued, "that their appeal to the public is a recognition of mankind, a proof of abiding interest in other men, of whom they wish to be saviours."[31]

Lane and Anna Alcott left Concord on the Monday.[32] Emerson watched them go and, aware of the lateness of the season, marveled that Lane was "dressed in linen altogether, with the exception of his shoes, which were lined with linen, & he wore no stockings."[33] (No doubt Anna was in similar attire.) That very day Lydia Maria Child, over in New York, was also thinking about Lane's dress code. He would cast off his linen for a "primitive fig-leaf" if his "scruples" demanded it, she wrote to a friend. Her husband, clearly still reeling from the Conversation he had attended, believed he would go one step further, and had been expecting him to strip off completely before he left New York. "Even this [the fig-leaf] might be cast aside before his visit was concluded should it happen to occur to him that it was used for purposes of hiding, and that hiding, being all a sham, would have no place in the diviner unconscious state." (This was Bower's position after all, so the Childs' intuition was not far off.) There was "no prank so mad," Lydia Maria Child concluded, that would surprise her from Lane and Alcott, "these insane, well-meaning egotists."[34]

Emerson certainly felt that Lane had lost none of his radicalism. "He was full of methods of an improved life," he noted, and believed that there was still room for tightening up the regime at Fruitlands. Lane seemed particularly preoccupied with animal exploitation. It brought into sharp focus the problem of living vicariously, an issue on which Emerson would have felt some sympathy, at least in the abstract. "It was no use to put off upon a second or third person the act of serving or killing cattle, as in cities, for example," Lane had told his host. If you did, "it would be sure to come back on the offending party in some shape, as in the brutality of the person or persons you have brutalized."[35]

Lane was still thinking about the matter as he and Anna took the long walk back. By now she was the apple of his eye. "We returned on foot," he told Oldham, "and accomplished something towards the liberation of the animals by a heroine of 13." He was much less impressed by her father, whom he blamed for the defections of Hecker and Bower and the community's failure to persuade visitors to become members. "Mr Alcott makes such high requirements of all persons," he pointed out three days after arriving back from Concord, "that few are likely to stay, even of his own family, unless he can become more tolerant of defect." The reference to the Alcott family seems ominous. Perhaps he suspected that Abigail too was becoming nomadic.

Just as he criticized Emerson for being overliterary, Lane accused Alcott of being too artistic—and not in the humble fashion exemplified by Mr. Hammond of New Ipswich. "He is an artist in human character requiring every painter to be a Michael Angelo," he wrote. Oddly this verdict corresponds with Emerson's positive comment that Fruitlands was "a picture fitly framed," but by now Lane was becoming impatient with such posing.[36] Perhaps it reminded him of the attitude of nature lovers. As it happened, Lane's little heroine, Anna, was taking much the same stance as her father. "I like to hear beautiful words and thoughts," she wrote in her diary a couple of weeks previously. "Beautiful is my favourite word." As a thirteen-year-old she was perhaps in transition from the unconscious transcendentalism of childhood to the fully fledged variety, because she goes on to note that she cannot tell the color of the word "beautiful." She and Louisa went for a walk, and when they returned, "I wrote down all the beautiful names we could think of, and in the evening wrote the colors of them."[37] Beyond the specifics of color lies that colorlessness of the absolute. She is beginning to perceive the world through a transparent eyeball.

It is the last entry we have. The rest of the pages of Anna Alcott's Fruitlands diary have been torn out, almost certainly by her father. It may be that she kept a closer record of the decline of the community than was convenient in retrospect. Louisa suffered a similar fate, and it was not for over a century that a number of torn-out pages from her journal were discovered in a house in Walpole, New Hampshire, where the Alcott family moved in 1855.[38] As was clear in relation to the children's contributions at Temple School, truth to the spirit overrode keeping an accurate record of what took place in the fallen world.

Lane complained that Alcott "does not wish to keep a hospital, nor even a school," perhaps thinking of the fact that he, Larned, and Ann Page had been entrusted with teaching the great teacher's children. But only seven months previously Lane himself had been assuring Oldham that "we are not going to open a hospital" because "we wish to begin with the sound rather than to heal the sick." Now, though, he saw this aspiration as overweening. Alcott wanted "to be surrounded by Masters—Masters of Arts, of the one grand Art of human life." Nobody could put up with that—not even the members of Alcott House. "Such a standard would soon empty your Concordium," he told Oldham, "as well as every other house."

Lane was pointing to the restlessness and dissatisfaction of others as a way of establishing a context for his own, because he was now beginning to think about abandoning his American experiment and returning to England. Not immediately, however. If he was losing hope of attracting converts and thereby transforming the world, he still had curiosity to keep him going. "I purpose to pass at least another winter in New England to know more averagingly what they are, as the last was particularly severe." He clearly thought there was something heroic about pitting himself against the elements. "I have gone about these several journies [sic] in the simple tunic and linen garments," he boasted to Oldham, "and mean to keep them on as long as I can." The weather was already beginning to provide a test. "Sharp frost this morning yet we took our bath as usual out of doors in the gray of the morn at ½ past 5."[39]

If his dietary theories and dress code were not about to return humankind to the Garden of Eden, at least they provided Lane himself with a sense of well-being. "Health, the grand external condition, still attends me, every stranger rating me 10 or 12 years younger than I am; so that if such are the effects of climate I may indeed be happy, for my youthfulness is not all appearance—I *feel* as buoyant and as boyish as I look, which I find a capital endorsement to my assertions about diet, &c." Suddenly he seems less like a pioneering radical and more like a smug faddist. His appearance, he believes, "staggers the sceptical and sets their selfish thoughts to work."[40]

He would have been mortified to know that ten days previously one of the skeptical, Lydia Maria Child, had decided his face looked as though it had been rubbed on a washboard.

15

Softly Doth the Sun Descend

WHEN LOUISA MAY ALCOTT woke up on October 8th, her first thought was "It's Mother's birthday: I must be very good." She ran down to give her a kiss and wish her happy birthday. After breakfast the Fruitlanders gave Abigail their presents. Louisa's was a cross made of moss, and a piece of poetry. To celebrate, school was canceled for the day and instead the children played in the woods and collected autumn leaves. Louisa and Anna had a row. "O she is so very very cross I cannot love her," Louisa told her mother in a letter she put in the household mailbox at the end of the morning. "It seems as though she did every thing to trouble me," she complained, "but I will try to love her better." She enclosed another present—"Please axcept [sic] this book mark from your affectionate daughter," adding with her usual frankness, "It is not very pretty but it is all I had to give." Things had calmed down by evening and everyone danced and sang. Bookworm that she was, Louisa also found time to read a story called "Contentment."

The tale's theme caught her on the raw, serving to highlight the tensions and anxieties that had beset the community. The mood had changed so much since the rural idyll that marked Elizabeth's birthday in June. "I wish I was rich, I was good, and we were all a happy family this day," Louisa wrote in her journal, clearly feeling guilty about her altercation with Anna. She concluded the day's entry by giving the words of one of the songs they had sung, "Hail, all hail, thou merry month of May." "I think this is a very pretty song," she wrote, "and we sing it a good deal." But it was October now, and the year was closing in.[1]

There were some good moments still. Four days later the community was in harvest festival mood. Louisa reports that after school (and after she had done the ironing, in addition to reading a little Plutarch), she went to the barn along with the others, including the educator William Russell, who had encouraged her father since his earliest days as a teacher, and they all husked the corn. "It was good fun," she said. She marked the setting of the sun with a little poem:

Softly doth the sun descend
To his couch behind the hill . . .

Her sister Anna was impressed, though Louisa, perhaps aware even at her age of the derivative imagery, didn't like it much herself. As the darkness fell they were allowed oil lamps for once, a great treat, so that they could continue the work until eight o'clock.[2]

The next day Abigail took Elizabeth off on a trip to Boston. After their return, Alcott and Lane followed in their footsteps, making yet another penniless pilgrimage.[3] They called in on the Emersons on their way. Lidian Emerson shook her head in disbelief and amusement at the self-inflicted austerity of Fruitlands life. "Queenie thinks the Fruitlands people far too gross in their way of living," her husband reported in his journal. "She prefers to live on snow."

Lane and Alcott explained their Leominster plans. Emerson understood for the first time that the Palmer they hoped to go into partnership with was not Edward, who was currently making herbal pills with his friend Dr. Wooster Beach, but "bearded snaith-making Palmer" (snaiths being the shafts of scythes).[4] Emerson was not impressed by the proposal, however. For him it was obviously just one crack-brained scheme after another. Lane and Alcott simply failed to think things through properly. "They have no repose, no self-satisfaction," he told his brother William, "but as quick as they have conceived a thing they are wretched until it is also published."[5]

Lane in fact was eager to publish in the more conventional sense of the word. The comments he had made about Brook Farm in a letter to Oldham the previous July—"80 or 90 persons playing away their youth and day time in a miserably joyous frivolous manner"—had found their way into the *New Age* for September 1st, and he was uneasy about how the inhabitants would feel should a copy of that journal fall into their hands, likely enough given the intense interaction between communitarians.[6] He wanted to take advantage of their trip to Boston to visit the community again and write a more balanced piece for the *Dial* to set the record straight.

The opening of the ensuing article is almost ingratiating, at least by his standards: "Wherever we recognize the principle of progress, our sympathies and affections are engaged." Life at Brook Farm had a pure moral atmosphere—"so far," at least. There was no talk about playing away youth and daytime on this occasion; instead what he found was "a strong desire to walk ever on the mountain tops of life." But Lane had the same reservation about that kind of aspirational walking as he did about Alcott's behavior at Fruitlands—he suspected that it involved a kind of puritanical dandyism. "Taste, rather than piety, is the aspect presented to the eye," he decided.[7]

Still, he was "gratified by observing several external improvements during the past year; such as a larger and a more convenient dining room, a labor-saving cooking apparatus, a purer diet, a more orderly and quiet attendance at the refections, superior arrangements for industry, and generally an increased seriousness to the value of the example, which those who are there assembled, may constitute to their fellow beings."[8] Perhaps the reference to "example" reflects what he was now finding unsatisfactory about Alcott's regime, that it was too concerned with achieving an exactitude of spiritual discipline rather than with inspiring others.

Lane was particularly impressed with the Brook Farm school, which was one of the community's major attractions and most profitable enterprises. "The tuition being more heart-rendered, is in its effects more heart-stirring." Alcott House, after all, had understood that education could and should be at the heart of a utopian experiment. (Odd, then, that Alcott had taken no interest in that possibility—the damage done by the failure of the Temple School obviously went too deep.) In this field, as in their manufacturing, Lane foresaw Brook Farm contributing social improvement, though he went on to make a distinction that pulls the rug from under his praise of progress in the opening sentence of the article: "We say *improvement,* as distinct from *progress.*"[9]

The reason for making this distinction is that Brook Farm is not truly a community, and therefore even though the members walk on mountaintops, it does not "stand so high above the present world, as to conduct its affairs on principles entirely different from those which now influence men in general." Progress, in the sense Lane is using it here, means a total abandonment of the current social ordering, and its replacement by a different one, like the metamorphosis of an enormous insect.

Brook Farm in fact was nothing but an aggregation of individuals, about seventy in all—fewer than before, Lane thought, though what a number that must have seemed to him and Alcott, who apart from their own families had only succeeded in attracting Wood Abraham, Samuel Larned, Samuel Bower, and Ann Page, with Hecker joining for a mere two weeks, and Palmer coming and going.[10] Of these seventy, thirty were children at the school, and some of the adults were also there primarily to pursue their own education. So, however admirable, the school encouraged a certain short-termism. Lane then goes on to make what at first glance seems (for him) a surprising complaint: "In the society there are only four married couples." As a result "it is almost certain that the sensitive and vital points of communication cannot be well tested."

What Lane was hoping for—either in practice at Brook Farm, or in his own intellectual response to the place—was a way of dealing with the issue that was breaking Fruitlands apart. It was time to confront the "great question, whether the existence of the material family is compatible with that of the universal family, which the term 'Community' signifies." He wishes there were more families resident at Brook Farm so he could see for himself whether this reconciliation is possible. Since there are not, he can at least make an attempt to sort out the issue in his own head—and he devotes the second half of his article to doing so, with hardly a mention of Brook Farm itself.

Unfortunately, his argument perpetuates ambiguity instead of resolving it. "The maternal instinct," he says, "as hitherto educated, has declared itself so strongly in favor of the separate fireside" that association has been made impossible. "Instinct?," "educated?"—it is the perennial problem.

It becomes perfectly obvious at this point that Lane is wrestling with Fruitlands, not with Brook Farm. Though fathers feel the family bond less strongly, he says, "there is an indefinable tie, a sort of magnetic *rapport*, an invisible, inseverable, umbilical chord [sic] between the mother and child, which in most cases circumscribes her desires and ambition to her own immediate family." It is this maternal instinct that provides the cornerstone of present society, as acknowledged by reformers like Pestalozzi and his followers (among whom Greaves and Alcott can of course be numbered). But if "the separate family is in the true order of Providence, then the associative life is a false effort." If, on the other hand, "the associative life is true, then is the separate family a false arrangement." Monasteries and convents throughout history have existed by eradicating familial affections. The Shakers, though they allow both sexes as members, "yet only maintain their union by forbidding . . . the growth of personal affection" on which the separate family is based.

However, Lane now believes there may be, so to speak, a third way. You might not have to choose between family and association, after all. "Social science ventures to assert their harmony," he claims. Maybe the two definitions of family, the organic and the consociate, don't "really neutralize each other," after all. This is the "grand problem now remaining to be solved." Perhaps it is a fallacy that "the human heart cannot be set in two places; that man cannot worship at two altars?"

Frustratingly he leaves his discussion there, simply raising the possibility of a grand reconciliation of the perennial conflict. As things stand, parents just want "the best for themselves and their families": this causes the world to be overpopulated, and "a wilderness of selfhood." And the associationists want universal love, which "forecloses all possibility of an individual family." He concludes by saying that the problem haunts all attempts at association, not just Brook Farm—and perhaps it dogs the Fourierist communities in particular.[11]

As it happened, Brook Farm was being drawn towards Fourierism and would formally convert to the French utopian philosopher's scheme the following year. If the circumstantial law seems to reduce human behavior to a grid, it has nothing on the Fourierist model. As far as industry was concerned, for example, Fourier broke down its structure into groups and series of groups. A group would be formed of at least seven people, and would be organized with two wings and a center. A series would take the same form, only composed of groups rather than individuals. Each section of the structure would be concerned with a particular aspect of the work being undertaken. The ascending wing will be occupied with the heaviest or bulkiest aspect of the task, the center with the intermediate requirements, and the descending wing with the lightest and smallest. In short, work was to be broken up into small, precisely defined units. So were the individual's predilections, his or her "attractions" as Fourier put it; so indeed was time itself, in Fourier's proposed communities, the phalanxes.

In practical terms this meant that an individual would, for a specific period of time, feel attracted toward doing one specific segment of an industrial task. He would slot into the exact, appropriate spot in the group to accomplish this—and be fitted by his abilities for exactly that task. He would then be attracted to something equally specific somewhere else. If the phalanx were correctly organized, everyone's attractions would mesh together, every minute of the day, like the cogs of a watch, and all the necessary tasks would get done.[12]

But this structure applied to everything, including sex. Lane disingenuously claims that Fourierists are "acute and eloquent in deploring Woman's oppressed and degraded position in past and present times, but are almost silent as to the future." That simply is not true of Fourierist theory, which envisaged total gratification and promiscuity on the part of both sexes (it was Fourier who coined the word *féminisme* just before his death in 1837). The erotic life was organized on the same basis as the industrial one, with individuals following their attractions, and sexual possibilities arranged in groups and series of groups. It is not surprising that Lane chose to pretend that this aspect of Fourierism did not exist. Tantalizingly, it offered a fully fledged alternative to the traditional family structure, that holy grail which he had been seeking for years, never more desperately than now. But at the same time it acknowledged the power of the sex drive and the authority of the passions.

Lane's own hostility to sex and all the other lusts of the flesh (within the phalanx people could also give full rein to their culinary whims), his aspiration toward some kind of virtually bodiless harmony between spirit-selected pairs, must have made him recoil from Fourier's program in confusion. Far easier to pretend that the French prophet had been silent on the topic. In any case, the Brook Farmers never had any intention of following this particular part of the blueprint, any more than the other Fourieristic experimenters did—they, too, were happy to draw a veil of silence over it. But the public's awareness of its existence would damage their community, causing gossip and loss of faith among parents of children who had been enrolled in the school.[13]

Fourierism was absolutely incompatible with the conventional family unit, and Brook Farm, while not following its orgiastic implications, would show no more support for marriage and family life in its phalansterian phase than it had in its less doctrinaire period. One of its leaders, Charles Anderson Dana, had to slip away from the community for a secret wedding with a fellow-member, Eunice Macdaniel, exactly as Henry Gardiner Wright had slipped away from Alcott House to wed Elizabeth Hardwick. Only one wedding ever took place in the community itself, and that happened late in 1846, when Brook Farm was in terminal decline.[14]

In short, at no point in its history could Brook Farm offer itself as a useful example of the compatibility of family and association; instead, its set-up supported Lane's original position, that family life had to be superseded—a position that had brought him into permanent conflict with Abigail Alcott. Lacking a conclusion, his article fades away as blandly as it began, with a vague prophecy that "Brook Farm is likely to become comparatively eminent in . . . the attempts, to render labor of the hands more dignified and noble, and mental education more free and loveful."[15]

After visiting Brook Farm, Lane and Alcott decided to check out a possible property in the town of Hingham, about fifteen miles below Boston on the South Shore. They caught the ferry without any money in their pockets, dressed in their linen garments—"a jaunt," Alcott called it. On their return they priced a set of communion plate in one of Boston's most upmarket shops, Long, Lowe, and Balls. Hitching ferry rides was one thing, but obtaining goods from a shop without the use of money can only be classified as robbery, so it is hard to imagine what they had in mind. The motivation must have been that because their frugal meals represented for them a perfected relationship with the earth, they regarded eating as essentially sacramental, and wished their meals to be served in a way that celebrated that fact. The shop window-gazing, which fortunately came to nothing, was significant enough for Alcott to record it in his autobiographical index.[16]

Late October was a gloomy time. Larned, Bower, Hecker, even Abraham, had by now all gone for good. "All the persons who have joined us during the summer . . . have quitted," Lane told Oldham. In point of fact Ann Page was still at Fruitlands. Lane had not noticed her arrival at the community, and he seems not to have noticed that she still remained after all the others had left. The fact that he was oblivious of her existence suggests that despite his public admiration of Woman, he rated women rather less than he might have.

As far as Lane was concerned, the (near-) exodus was because Alcott was so despotic. From Alcott's point of view it was because the members had not been "equal to the Spirit's demands." Back at the Temple School an image of Jesus had hung directly over his head. Clearly a danger intrinsic to Transcendental identification of the individual with the Absolute is the possibility of confusing personal whims with instructions from on high.

Just to compound matters, William had gone down with a bilious attack, the second to afflict the community in less than two months. Given the centrality of diet to the whole enterprise, and Lane's recently expressed joy at the rejuvenating effects of his personal regime, that too must have been a blow to morale.

There was worse. The Leominster farm, which the Fruitlanders had inspected so often and discussed at such length, had been sold to someone else. Still, Joseph Palmer was willing to search out another property for them. Lane told Oldham that Palmer was doing their farm work for love, as he had over the whole summer, but "still remains in the same relation he ever did as he never proposed to dwell with us." Palmer was willing to invest $2,000 of his own money in land and a house for them (this was the figure Alcott had quoted to Chatfield in his letter the previous month), preferably in the Leominster area, his own stamping ground.[17]

Alcott, though, had decided he would rather be near Boston. He was worried about being stranded in the deep countryside during the winter, and also had the urge to resume public Conversations. He was back in Boston at that moment, in point of fact, visiting acquaintances like Margaret Fuller and William Lloyd Garrison, reminding himself of the possibilities of the big city.[18] His idea was that Lane should sell Fruitlands and use the money to set up near the city, where they had more chance of attracting recruits. This time around, Lane was deeply skeptical about following Alcott's lead. "I am not inclined to this dissipation," he told Oldham, "or if it is to be done I think I could do it myself."

A further complication was that Palmer had taken Lane's assertions about freeing Fruitlands from ownership very literally (perhaps more so than Lane himself ever had). "Having once declared this land free we should never go back," he had told Lane, "at least until the world has been fairly tested." How this determination squared with the proposal of buying afresh near Leominster is not clear. In any case, Lane had now realized that their crops were not sufficient to pay the installments on his loan, and he was absolutely determined not to slide further into debt. Also their tenure of the Fruitlands farmhouse would expire on May 1, 1844 (a mistake on Lane's part, as the twelve months would be up a month later).

Above all there was the problem that had beset the community ever since the earliest days, a year ago now, in Concordia. "Mrs Alcott has no spontaneous inclination towards a larger family than her own natural one." In order to keep the latter together "she does and would go through a good deal of exterior and interior toil," but "of spiritual ties she knows nothing."

All in all, Lane had "a small peck of troubles." They were "not quite heavy enough to drive me to a junction with our friends, the Shakers, but sufficiently so to put the thought into one's head."[19] After all that flailing about in his Brook Farm article, he had now lost hope of reconciling family and consociation.

So had Alcott. On his way to Boston he visited Emerson, superficially with his ideas and ideals intact. "A[lcott] came, the magnificent dreamer, brooding as ever on the renewal or reedification of the social fabric after ideal law, heedless that he had been uniformly rejected by every class to whom he has addressed himself, and just as sanguine & vast as ever." The problem, Emerson felt, was that whereas normal men were content with trying to redeem the dullness of life with "the occasional fine action or hope," Alcott "would weave the whole [into] a new texture of truth and beauty." In other words, it was all or nothing: he had no concept of an intermediate position. And in the conflict between all and nothing, nothing was what he tended to get.

Just as Lane had made his mind up on the family issue, so had Alcott. "He spoke of marriage & the fury that would assail him who should lay his hand on that institution, for reform," Emerson noted in his journal. No doubt Abigail had recently given him a sample of that fury. While thinking about his article, Lane had obviously discussed Fourier's sexual proposals, because Alcott raised the topic with Emerson. "He spoke of the secret doctrines of Fourier," Emerson wrote. "I replied, as usual,—that I thought no man could be trusted with it." Presumably he means that no man could be trusted with the task of replacing the institution of marriage with a sexual free-for-all.

Emerson is obviously aware that this issue represented a parting of the ways for the two men, because he doesn't perceive Alcott as a Fruitlander now but as he always was, or at least as he had been since the collapse of his school, a man on the road, looking for followers. "Very pathetic it is to see this wandering emperor from year to year making his round of visits from house to house of such as do not exclude him, seeking a companion, tired of pupils." Emerson, like Lane, believes Alcott to be a sort of spiritual aesthete. Just before this entry he quoted a French maxim: "Spirit is a sort of luxury that destroys one's commonsense, just as luxury destroys one's fortune." And just after the entry he added a maxim of his own: "Wish not a man from England."[20]

A few days later, Emerson thought of the Fruitlanders again, perhaps trying to explain to himself the reasons for their failure to attract members to their community. "The reformers wrote very ill," he decided. Possibly Alcott had delivered Lane's muddled submission on Brook Farm when he called in, and Emerson, as current *Dial* editor, had already tried to make sense of it. And of course he had never admired Alcott's own writings. "They made it a rule not to bolt their flour," Emerson went on, "& unfortunately neglected also to sift their thoughts." A month previously Lane had judged that Emerson was stationary; now Emerson returns the compliment (again) by deciding that he and Alcott "lack feet." If, in Lane's words, the Brook Farmers walk the moral mountaintops, the Fruitlanders go one better (or higher). "They are always feeling of their shoulders to find if their wings descend for the benevolent purpose of leading back apostate souls to right principles."[21]

In a literal sense, however, Alcott's feet were more than serviceable. He arrived back from Boston on November 2nd, having walked the whole distance in a day. It had put him into a good mood, and Abigail noticed how his cheerfulness contrasted with Lane's gloom, so much so that she almost felt sorry for her adversary. Her reaction suggests that she was beginning to feel the magnanimity of victory. "I only wanted to see Mr Lane in a better mood," she wrote. "It is sad to see greatness so subject and pitiable." Then her magnanimity faded somewhat, as she remembered how he had treated her. "But no man is great to his valet said Sterne, or Somebody else. Neither is he always sublime to his housemaid."[22]

That day, Louisa wrote that she and Anna did the housework. Then, in the evening, "Mr. Lane asked us, 'What is man?' These were our answers: A human being; an animal with a mind; a creature; a body; a soul and a mind. After a long talk we went to bed very tired." The grown-up Louisa May Alcott was indignant when she came across this message from her former self. "No wonder," she wrote against this entry, "after doing the work and worrying their little wits with such lessons."[23]

Even now the animals with minds were juggling possibilities, as if they could still sort out their differences and repair their community. One idea they had, Abigail told her brother Sam, was to sell Maverick Wyman back thirty acres of his land, the section on which the house and barn stood, and use the money to build themselves a cottage in the valley where they could plant an orchard and cultivate a garden. "How this will be done the deferment saith not," she added skeptically.[24] Two days after she had recorded this thought she sat down and wrote her other brother Charles a long letter summing up the current state of things, and her own feelings about it.

"I am not dead yet," she begins, "either to life or love." This is a rhetorical device she uses a number of times, accentuating the positive in a way that only serves to emphasize despair. She claims that Lane and William are thinking of searching out a warmer climate or returning to England (contradicting Lane's own previously expressed intention of seeing how he could cope with the oncoming winter). Her husband, too, sometimes feels discouraged, and with more reason. "The right people, with right motives, and holy purpose, do not come, and we are both wearing ourselves out in the service of the transient visitors and ungrateful participants." As before there is no mention of Lane wearing himself out, but she reiterates that "Mr Alcott has labored excessively hard." "This is a Hotel," she tells her brother, "where man and beast are entertained without pay, and at great expense." She sounds at the end of her tether. "I keep saying 'Oh when will rest come.' "

When Alcott met Margaret Fuller in Boston it had struck him that she would make an excellent helpmate for Abigail. Only he could have come up with such a bizarre idea, teaming the brilliant, edgy—somewhat neuras-thenic—intellectual with his sharp-tongued practical wife. But Abigail was having none of it anyway. "I am too generous to tackle anybody into this harrow," she told Charles, "for drag as you will you cannot get the ground smooth: the asperities are too sharp. The sinuosities too deep." (There is an energy and attack in her writing at its best that her husband could never achieve; a summer and fall of farming at Fruitlands lies behind her metaphors.) She no longer believed it was possible or even desirable to attract new members. "It is absurd to suppose that all move in the same circle."

What she now wanted was charity to all and acceptance of difference, a tolerant approach that would "permit each to be good in his own way." She was perfectly well aware that this kind of individualism ran directly counter to the Transcendentalism espoused by her husband. "I do not wish to tran-scend humanity: I wish to transcend nothing but evil and sin." The word "transcend" beats through this passage, as she makes it clear she has taken her leave of the movement. Almost as if she had read Emerson's remarks about Alcott and Lane feeling for their angel's wings, she asserts her own desire to remain in the earthly world. "I hope not to transcend my senses: they are the sentinels to guard the citadel of my soul."

It is likely she was a party to the discussion between Alcott and Lane on Fourier's "secret doctrines," which would explain why Alcott had been on the receiving end of her fury. But while Abigail could never have any time for the great promiscuity machine of the phalanx, she also vehemently disap-proved of a blanket rejection of the "passional life." She had tried to follow that path in early July, when her husband had most "beautifully and forcibly illustrated on the black board the sacrifices and utter subjection of the body to the Soul, showing the + on which the lusts of the flesh are to be sacrificed." Now, four months later, she rejected that stance. "Even our passions are heralds announcing a deep nature," she assured her brother Charles. She thought back to the Conversation on "What is Man?" of four days earlier. Man, she decided, is more than an animal with a mind, or (probably Lane's definition) a soul and a mind. "A passionless person is to me a tame, half-whole animal."

Ironically, the passions themselves, "if rightly governed," keep us on the straight and narrow, "render us invulnerable to All the heresy of Sin."[25] This is a specific repudiation of Greavesianism; indeed, in its way, it is a vindication of Fourier's doctrines to the extent that they involve allowing each aspect of the personality to seek fulfillment. It is not by transcending the passions, Abigail asserts, but by accepting them as a part of your make-up, that you can live a good life. She has, after all, by now had a year's practical experience of the consequences of repression.

In effect, Abigail Alcott has rejected what Fruitlands stands for. Over the months Lane had betrayed an uneasy awareness that she would make a dangerous opponent. Now the time had come for her to show her hand.

16

Nectar in a Sieve

IT HAPPENED OFF-STAGE, so it is impossible to tell if Abigail Alcott herself took the initiative, or her brother Sam. When the Fruitlands deal went through, Lane had paid only $1,500 of the required amount of $1,800. The missing $300 had gone to settling Alcott's debts, and was due to be paid to Maverick Wyman in installments at six-monthly intervals over two years. The sum of $75 had therefore now become due. Because he had needed a mortgage on the property, he had been forced to farm for profit, rather than live self-sufficiently, which had been the intention. Emerson had told Thoreau that the utopians had bought themselves a farm without a house when what they needed was a house without a farm. What they had needed in particular was to pay outright for a house with a large garden or small-holding, where they could have grown the fruit and vegetables they needed for domestic consumption. Farming required the use of animals in order to turn the soil; it was posited on the notion of over-production in order to sell surplus crops. Neither of these necessities conformed to Fruitlands princi-ples; perhaps as a result, they had lost interest in the crops just when the hard work of harvesting had to be done, and now they were left unable to service the debt the farm had brought with it. Lane admitted in his letter to Oldham of October 30th that the crops had failed to yield a profit, and that he was not prepared to follow the example of his partner and slide into debt.[1] Samuel May was the guarantor of the loan, so the responsibility devolved to him.

Given her current mood, it is quite possible that Abigail told Sam not to settle. She had just made a visit to him at Lexington.[2] Or, having heard what she had to say, he may have taken that decision himself, for her protection. He probably felt indignant that Lane had washed his hands of the liability, but one thing is certain: he was a loyal and loving brother who would always have put the interests of his sister first. And he gave the community a killer blow by refusing to settle the debt. It was a decision that marked the triumph of the biological family over the consociate one.

Abigail was delighted. "Dear S," she wrote on November 11th, "Your letter was already received and pleased me better than it did the other proprietors of the Estate—I do not wish you to put a cent *here*." She certainly felt the time had come for her to take matters into her own hands. "I am sifting everything to its bottom—for I will know the foundation, centre and circumference—."

Clearly word had already gone around that the community was open to offers. A farmer in Boxboro had offered $25 an acre for thirty acres of the land, presumably the prime ones (those that Lane had proudly boasted were worth $100 an acre). Joseph Palmer's son (a dentist living in the area) had offered $1,400 for the whole, representing a loss of $400 (given the support his father had provided for nothing all summer long, there is no reason to doubt this was a fair, perhaps generous, valuation at the time). "Mr Lane thought of accepting it and letting us go out naked," Abigail told her brother bitterly. She seems to have been under the impression that Lane had some sort of obligation to give them ongoing support, though on the face of it there is no reason why he should have. It was obviously this sort of assumption that made Lane so determined not to go further in debt on behalf of the Alcott family. "I am ready for it," Abigail assured Sam, "and should feel it a clean transaction to go with my skin." She could not stand the current juggling with finance. "I do not like the concern—this is a griping propensity somewhere—."

Her husband needless to say had ideas of his own. "Mr Alcott talks of buying the frame of Mr Wyman's small barn—hauling it to the woods—and building a house, selling part of the land etc etc." As usual he was blissfully oblivious of the fact that the property was not his to sell, and that he had no money of his own to buy. Abigail, however, understood that his scheme would necessitate continued reliance on Lane's goodwill. "I see no clean healthy safe course here in connection with Mr L—It is not clear to me."

This summer had been worse than the one before, she told her brother. Given that no one complained of the weather until November set in, she was presumably referring to agricultural productivity as a way of explaining the loss in value of the land. So much for the farming procedures of the new Eden. Once again she blamed the problem on the stream of visitors. "People have been and devoured our substance and turned round to scoff at our efforts." But despite her anger and unhappiness, she did not at this stage foresee an immediate dispersal. "We'll work out something before Spring," she tells Sam.[3]

The next three pages of her correspondence have been torn out of the manuscript letter book. The destruction, though obviously intended to conceal the conflicts and bad feelings that occurred, has the accidental effect of acting like a metaphor for the fate that was overtaking the "Holy Family" of Fruitlands.

The same day, Lane wrote to Hecker, the only wealthy ex-member of Fruitlands. Hecker had sent a barrel of "superfine wholesome wheatmeal" to the community (he sent a sample of his pearled wheat to Brook Farm, though it had arrived there in less than perfect condition—and Lane had already expressed his reservations about that particular product, in any case). Lane professed himself grateful for the "healthful bequest." He needed to unburden himself, he goes on, "candidly to the generous." It is the sort of opening that could send a warning shiver down the spine of any recipient. He explains that Samuel May has declined paying the first installment of the amount owed, and points out that he has exhausted his own funds in "buying and keeping up the affair." In short he had been "left in a precarious position, out of which I do not see the way with out some loveful aid."

He proposes that Hecker could forward the $75 against the security either of crops (despite his admission to Oldham that they had failed to yield a profit), or land, or books from the library, the one that he and Alcott had brought over from England, and about which they had had bitter arguments with Wright. "You shall select such books as will suit your own reading," he suggested. They "would cover your advance in cash any day you choose to put them up to auction, if I should fail to redeem them."

Lane went on to talk of his current woes. William had still not recovered from his illness and had not sat up for three weeks. Lane's diagnosis was "excessive work." The Alcotts felt they did everything; Lane returned the compliment. Certainly his own hands were chapped from being outside in inclement weather. He had lost his former enthusiasm for facing the challenge of winter, as Abigail had already implied in her letter to her brother Charles. Indeed, he told Hecker, "if I could find employment in a more southern position that would support me and the boy, and leave a little to be applied to the common good, I would undertake it."[4]

Three weeks later Lane still had hopes of Hecker. On December 3rd he told Thoreau about the approach he had made. "As well as wounded hands permit I have scribbled something for friend Hecker which if agreeable may be the opportunity for entering into closer relations with him." As with Alcott, he cherished the hope that this proposed alliance could be the basis of large-scale change. The course would be "mutually encouraging, as well as beneficial to all men."[5] Hecker did not take advantage of the opportunity.

Apart from the Lanes and Alcotts, only Ann Page was left at Fruitlands, and she was gone by November 20th. In *Transcendental Wild Oats*, the adult Louisa gives her version of what happened. While visiting a neighbor, Miss Page ("Jane Gage") had given into temptation and eaten a portion of fish. News got back to Lane and when he confronted her with it, she burst into tears.

"I only took a little bit of the tail," she explained, finally having to admit she allowed herself some latitude with the vegan regime.

Lane replied, "Yes, but the whole fish had to be tortured and killed . . . Know ye not, consumers of flesh meat, that ye are nourishing the wolf and tiger in your bosoms."

Miss Page was so upset that she promptly packed her trunk and returned to Providence.[6] She had "lapsed from Parnassus to Philistia," as Abigail's cousin, Samuel Greely, put it. He quoted Abigail's rueful comment: " 'They spare the cattle,' she said, 'but they forget the women and children.' "[7]

Lane's own version was quite different. As far as he was concerned Ann Page's fate was an example of Abigail Alcott's hostility to everyone who was not a member of her own family. "Every person who has tried to join us," he told Oldham, "has been so treated that junction was impossible; the last instance, that of Anne Page appearing to me a little short of a kicking out of doors chiefly on the part of Mrs A. who vows that her own family is all she lives for or wishes to live for."[8] At least Miss Page had finally come to Lane's notice.

Whatever the truth of the matter, the case of Ann Page demonstrates that by now the different factions at Fruitlands were at daggers drawn.

On November 20th Louisa got up as usual at five in the morning. She washed the breakfast dishes and helped her mother with the other house-work. She was obviously sensing that the community had reached its last days, because she records in her diary that her sister Anna was off in Boston staying with relatives, and that Ann Page had left. In the afternoon she looked after little Abby, and as evening came on made some clothes for her doll. Then there was a crisis meeting. "Father and Mr L. had a talk, and father asked us if *we* saw any reason to separate." It was the moment of truth. "Mother wanted to," Louisa wrote, "she is so tired." The tension and suspi-cion that had been undermining Fruitlands for so long came to a head at this moment: Abigail Alcott made her wishes clear.

Louisa's loyalties were split. "I like it," she wrote, but then went on to exclude the non-Alcottian element: "but not the school part or Mr L."[9] It's not likely, though, that the ten-year-old would have dared to say as much to Lane's face.

A few days later Alcott wrote to his daughter Anna in Boston in his usual affectionate and moralizing style. He seems both maddeningly obtuse and admirably consistent at the same time—a magnificent dreamer, as Emerson said. He tells his daughter he misses her presence in their "Family Circle," whatever that now means. "Our household thoughts and ways" are simple, he explains to her, and he goes into exactly the same raptures as he had a year previously, before the Fruitlands drama had begun to unfold. "Beautiful indeed, and as comely to Heaven's eye, as to the sight of man, is a pure and Holy Family, whose inmates are united in a serene and lively love, and whose hands and hearts are alike servants of a gentle and all-[illegible] affection."

He is obviously trying to reassure a homesick twelve-year-old, but he hadn't concealed the crisis from his ten-year-old, six days previously, and in any case the sugar coating need hardly have extended to the use of words like "serene" and "gentle." He is still able to depict the pastoral never-never land he has consistently superimposed over the Fruitlands landscape. "Only the rustic beauties of field and dell, of woods and fountains[,] of gardens and orchards, are fit ornaments and worthy accompaniments of such simple persons [i.e. the members of the Holy Family previously mentioned]." He writes out a little poem composed for the occasion, which concludes:

> To me came meek content,
> My constant habitant,
> In humblest cot,
> Midst orchard plot,
> Where, with familiar friends
> I dwelt to holiest ends,
> And tenures free are given
> By love divine and heaven.

That reference to free tenures, given by love divine, must have taken Lane aback if he saw the poem. Alcott's capacity for not being ironic seems almost infinite.

The letter goes on, "All things remain as when you left us." At that point, however, he finally admits that matters are in a state of flux. "All manner of plans are drawn for our residence and way of living in the future," he tells Anna. He doesn't specify what these might be, but goes on to say, "whether we stay *Here*, or go *There*, matters little." Somehow he manages to give philosophical weight to vagueness itself, in effect replacing the very concept of place with his private environment and internalized fireside. He goes on to tell his daughter that though winter is coming, nature smiles on them— rearranging even the weather.[10] It is another example of Transcendentalism as *trompe d'oeil*.

That same day Lane was telling Oldham a very different story. William was ill for a whole month in all, "so that he could not sit up in bed for one minute." Lane "had to nurse him with hands so chapped and sore that I was little more capable than the patient." He goes on to explain about Samuel May's refusal to honor his guarantee and the consequent "endless discussions, doubts, and anticipations concerning our destiny" (meanwhile, Alcott was telling Anna that "Providence will overrule [i.e. rule over] all our schemes for good"). Then Lane comes to the bombshell Abigail had dropped at the meeting of November 20th. "Mrs Alcott gives notice that she concedes to the wishes of her friends and shall withdraw to a house which they will provide for her and her four children."

Sam had found suitable rooms for them near him in Lexington. What is striking about this announcement is that it excludes Alcott himself. The only explanation is that he had not risen to the occasion when his wife made her announcement six days previously. He must have failed, there and then, to agree to go with her. That would explain why Louisa made her own heavily qualified assertion that she liked Fruitlands—she was trying to occupy the middle ground between her parents.

The previous December, after Abigail had made her fleeting escape to Boston over Christmas, Alcott had written to his brother Junius explaining how happy he was, and describing a cozy scene with himself and Lane each side of the fireplace. It seems likely that the intense and in many ways destructive relationship between the two men had some degree of homo-erotic underpinning.[11] That would explain Abigail's anguish and resentment at being overlooked. Certainly Lane himself was fully aware that he was involved in a triangle. "Of course Mr A. and I could not remain together without her," he told Oldham. "To be 'that devil come from Old England to separate husband and wife', I will not be, though it might gratify New England to be able to *say* it."

Lane mournfully anticipates being left entirely destitute. "As she will take all the furniture with her, this proceeding necessarily leaves me alone and naked in the new world." It is a very different new world now from that land of opportunity he had previously celebrated, where property was cheap and minds were open to new possibilities. Now the horizons had dwindled to the dimensions of the biological family unit. "I do not desire to live for so narrow a purpose and if there was on the part of any one the design to bend me and my appurtenances to that end, upon the cunning ones let the consequences fall."

An appalling idea has crossed Lane's mind: he has been made use of merely to provide support for the impoverished Alcotts. He had thought back to the past and found there another possible narrative, completely different from the one he had thought he was living through at the time.

Amazingly, even Alcott was aware such a reinterpretation was on the cards. Lane quotes a remark his partner had made a day or two before. "You think that before the outlay of money began I expressed certain high moral principles, that during the expenditure these principles were for lower and selfish ends suppressed; and that now the money is all expended I recur to the higher moral principles formerly avowed." Lane was taken aback at the way this analysis chimed with his own fear. "I trust it was mere speculation and not consciousness which suggested this thought to him," he told Oldham. "His conduct is certainly liable to such interpretation."

But as Lane thought about it, his original understanding of his relationship with Alcott seemed to take hold once more. "I deem him rather wayward and notional than wicked or acquisitive, and more borne down by his wife and family than wishful to abandon any affirmation he may make." He thought back to a plaintive question Alcott had recently asked him. "Can a man act continually for the universal end while he co-habits with a wife?" In a single sentence, Alcott had finally penetrated the problem that dogged Greavesianism in general, and the experiment in living he had undertaken with Lane in particular.

Lane's commentary on the question Alcott posed is revealing. "How different a state of mind must this thought have issued from to that which caused him to shed tears on the same subject eighteen months ago at Ham!! Hopeful prospect!" He seems to be suggesting that during his English trip Alcott had been willing to put aside loyalty to wife and family in favor of allegiance to the "universal end." Moreover he is recalling this alleged commitment to Oldham, who had been there at the time—who was a witness, in fact. Yet during that whole period Alcott had written passionate letters to his wife, even to the point of proposing a re-enactment of their marriage vows when he returned. This contradiction caused the structural weakness that made the failure of the Fruitlands experiment completely inevitable.

Clearly Alcott had been gratified by the admiration of the Alcott House contingent, and of course he had a proven capacity for ignoring life's intractable problems. Perhaps he had convinced himself that this circle would be squared somehow, some day. Perhaps he even believed that his second wedding to Abigail (which of course never took place) would in some way redefine the marital relationship to make it compatible with the universal end. After all, the Greavesians did allow for very occasional and pleasureless sexual intercourse as well as some kind of spirit-selected pairing-off, and it seems that Alcott made an attempt to preach this gospel at Fruitlands during that session in which he drew a cross upon the blackboard. Indeed, for a brief interval, even Abigail was taken by the idea of renunciation. But it is hard to avoid the suspicion that, consciously or not, Alcott must have misled Lane. Certainly Alcott had put himself in the position where it was inevitable that he would betray *some*one.

"Poor fellow," Lane continues, "between his cherished idiosyncrasies and his secular or social difficulties, his high moral principles have a sad time of it." He hoped that he would retain enough influence to "help the latter to a larger expansion, and to contract the two former as much as I can." Alcott would find parting a wrench—Lane was obviously confident of his sincerity in that respect. "The mere thought of separation is painful to him," he assured Oldham. "Personally he will feel, as I shall, a great loss of hopeful friendship." But even this assertion has to be qualified by the limitations of Alcott's character. "Pecuniarily I expect he will feel somewhat, for I do not wholly excuse him from the parasite nature."

Alcott's main problem, though, is that he will feel humiliated by the failure of his great experiment. "How to explain it to the public is his greatest puzzle, for after all his defiance of orthodox opinions I have felt justified in telling him many times that he regards too much the question 'what will Mrs Grundy say?' " Despite the seclusion of the dell in which Fruitlands nestled, for Alcott it was essentially a public stage; despite his celebration of individualism and his belief in surrendering himself to the spirit, he had (according to his partner at least) a fear of being humiliated.

Having made it clear to Oldham that Alcott was at the bottom of Fruitlands' failure, Lane goes on to see it as an enterprise that had played itself out anyway. "I believe I have followed out this experiment to the ultimate," he explained. "The future will be merely repetitions of the past." He felt more sorrow than anger, and more hope than either. "Everything about me, both within doors and without, convinces me more and more that the individual family life must soon cease." The phrase "within doors" is telling:

it implies that the Alcott family itself is proof that the family as an institution is no longer viable. This little revenge enables him to end on an upnote. "Common sense, economy and good feeling must put an end to the separation of man from man which only the grossest selfishness and ignorance could tolerate for one hour, especially in a country where human action is so free as here it is." He has even managed to reclaim some of his confidence in America.[12]

Lane finished his letter on November 29th, Alcott's forty-fourth birthday and Louisa's eleventh. "We had some nice presents," Louisa told her diary. It was not warm enough, in more ways than one, for pastoral festivities. Instead, the children played in the snow before school. Afterward Abigail read to them. In the evening her father had one of his improving Conversations. What fault troubled each of them the most? For Louisa it was bad temper. Her mother wrote in her book: "Remember, dear girl, that a diary should be an epitome of your life." The moralizing was relentless; no private space was permitted, no latitude in thought or emotion allowed. "May it be a record of pure thought and good actions, then you will indeed be the precious child of your loving mother."[13] Above all, the family bond was paramount. There was no mention in that day's entry, as father and daughter celebrated their birthdays, of Mr. Lane.

On December 10th Louisa set pen to paper once more. She did her lessons, she recorded, then went for a walk. After that her father read from their beloved *Pilgrim's Progress*. "Mr. L. was in Boston, and we were glad," she explains. "In the eve father and mother and Anna and I had a long talk. I was very unhappy, and we all cried." They were crying because of the stress and bad feeling, the failure of the community, the loss of their home. But that was not all. "Anna and I cried in bed," she continues, "and I prayed God to keep us all together."[14] Louisa is not convinced that the imminent break-up will leave the Alcott family intact. It is possible that her father had suggested he might leave with Charles Lane.[15]

Lane took the Harvard stage back from Boston. It broke the journey at Concord, and while it was there Lane finally managed to get himself arrested for not paying his poll tax, all those months previously. He refused to bring any friend to answer for him, and was put in jail.

It must have been a brief moment of happiness and accomplishment at a miserable time in his life. He had failed to establish an alternative community, but at least he had rejected, and been rejected by, society as it now stood. It could be considered as a first step toward creating a new world in the new world.

Sadly, Rockwell Hoar, son of Alcott's bête noir and like the squire a liberal and abolitionist, heard what had happened, and came to Lane's rescue. Like Alcott before him, and Thoreau three years later, Lane found himself promptly, and unwillingly, a free man once more.

On his release Lane went to Emerson's house, only to find he wasn't there, another anticlimax. He chose to wait, glumly. When Emerson returned—he too had been in Boston, visiting Margaret Fuller—he found Lane "sad and indisposed." Emerson recounted the disappointing jail experience in a letter to Fuller, and gave her the latest version of Fruitlands orthodoxy. "He [Lane] and Mr Alcott think they have been wrong in all these years with Pestalozzi in lauding the Maternal instinct & the Family, etc.," Emerson reported. "These they now think are the very mischief."[16] The plural is significant. Lane could have been disingenuous in trying to implicate Alcott in this hostility to the maternal instinct and the family, though he would have been just as likely to vent his spleen at his partner's backsliding. But given Louisa's fearful comment in her diary, it is more likely that Alcott had not yet made an explicit commitment to his biological family.

Even if Alcott was still blowing hot and cold, Lane knew Fruitlands was finished. After he got home he wrote to Emerson and asked him to act as his agent in the remaining transactions over the property. When good-natured Emerson agreed (perhaps happy that this implied that the Alcotts would stay together after all), Lane wrote to Samuel May asking him to execute a deed transferring responsibility.[17]

Severe weather set in, with a succession of snowstorms. The path to the sequestered dell became blocked and had to be cleared twice by neighbor Lovejoy, so that the Fruitlanders could get their mail.[18] Alcott leafed through his journal for 1839 and found that on March 16th that year he had transcribed a couple of lines from Coleridge's "Work without Hope." His school by that stage had dwindled to a tiny class held in his own house, and he had been on the brink of closing it altogether. Now he was in a similar situation, as the second great experiment of his life entered its death throes. The couplet in question went:

Work without hope draws nectar in a sieve
And hope without an object cannot live.

Beside this entry he wrote: "Dec: 1843/ Harvard/ Even so now!"[19]

Abigail was longing to leave. "Our situation here quite uncomfortable," she wrote. "Mr. Lane moody and enigmatical." The problem, though, was "where and how to go." Her eyes were playing her up so she could not sew or read in the evenings in the dimly lit house.[20] Louisa, having played with the Lovejoys' baby, announced that she wanted a brother of her own. Abigail persuaded her that three sisters were sufficient, and when she went to bed that night Louisa, so often prone to guilt, was able to congratulate herself for having been "obedient and kind to Father and Mother and gentle to my sisters." Never complacent, she added, "I wish I could be gentle always."[21]

As Christmas approached, her father announced he was going off to Boston to attend a convention on "property," of all topics.[22] One can imagine Lane becoming even more moody and enigmatical on hearing that news.

The convention was in fact to be devoted primarily to an exposition of the doctrines of Fourier and was being held to mark Brook Farm's transition to a phalanx, which would formally take place on January 18, 1844. Though Alcott seems, as so often, tactless and guilty of bad timing, he was presumably going in order to decide if the community in its new form would be an appropriate haven for his family. Perhaps he also hoped light would be shed on that matter of Fourier's "secret doctrines" on the sexual relation. Despite the appalling weather he left for Boston after breakfast on December 24th. For the second year running, the Alcotts failed to be together when Christmas came around.

After her father had gone, studious Louisa spent the morning reading and writing. She washed the dishes after midday dinner and then made some Christmas presents. In the evening Joseph Palmer and his son came around. Louisa did not go to bed until ten o'clock. On Christmas morning she "rose early and sat some looking at the Bon-bons in my stocking," obviously trying to extract every drop of magic from the humble present, storing up the sweetness like a bee for later use when she will describe the March girls' Christmas at the beginning of *Little Women*. The father is absent there too, and the girls' only presents are a Bible each; moreover they have to give away their breakfast to the impoverished Hummels. At Fruitlands the candy was supplemented by a poem from Abigail, which Louisa diligently transcribes:

> Christmass is here
> Louisa my dear
> Then happy we'll be
> Gladsome and free . . .[23]

It was a difficult day for Abigail. The weather was severe. She organized a little merrymaking in the evening with the neighboring children. There is no mention of a contribution from Lane, even though everyone sang, trying "to cheer the scene within to render the cheerlessness without more tolerable."[24]

17

Cain and Abel

ALCOTT'S OLD COLLEAGUE, Elizabeth Palmer Peabody, also attended the convention in Boston over Christmas and New Year, and reported its proceedings in the *Dial*. She arrived already aware of Fourier's secret doctrines. "We confess to some remembrances of vague horror, connected with this name," she said, but these doubts were immediately dispelled by the contribution of William Ellery Channing, the Christian Fourierist who had chaired the Conversation Alcott and Lane held during their penniless pilgrimage to New York. Channing put her mind at rest by showing how Fourier's scheme could be reconciled with religious morality.[1]

It must have been galling for Alcott, with Fruitlands on its last legs, to hear the very principles on which it had been founded being rehearsed at the conference. "Geologists and geographers," Peabody reported, "have intimated to us heretofore, that the earth needs to be dressed and kept by men, in order not to become in several ways desert, and that the climates, which depend much more upon the state of the surface of the earth, than upon its relations with the sun, should be ameliorated." It is one of those moments when one blinks in amazement, as the perspective of 1843 becomes indistinguishable from that of today. Another shock of recognition for Alcott would have come with understanding how Fourierism merged with the circumstantial law. "Fourier would demonstrate that *the cursing of the ground for man's sake . . .* is no metaphor," Peabody reported, "but that, literally, man's falling below his destiny, has, as its natural consequence, the return of the earth to a state of chaos." The solution to this problem corresponded with the one adopted at Fruitlands, correct treatment of the soil. "The human race must cultivate the whole vegetable creation, if not the animal, to a perfection which would involve an agricultural science, absolutely sublime in its extent." This will enable "the earth to be restored to the state of Paradise, through the labours of man."[2]

Peabody was not completely won over herself. "The question is," she concluded, "whether the Phalanx acknowledges its own limitations of nature, in being an organization, or opens up any avenue into the source of life that shall keep it sweet, enabling it to assimilate to itself contrary elements, and consume its own waste; so that, Phoenix-like, it may renew itself forever in great and finer forms."[3] It was the old issue of waste, as embodied in history, in manure, in conflict.

The issues raised by the convention must have made Alcott more distressed than ever that his own experiment was disintegrating. He described his Boston experience in his autobiographical index: "Attend 'A property Convention' in Boston. Meet J.A. Collins, Garrison, Brisbane, W.H. Channing, G. Ripley, Brownson, Bower etc." Immediately after the mention of Samuel Bower, one of the apostate Fruitlanders, three pages are torn out. Significantly the document resumes: "and advise conciliation. I speak to G. Ripley about going to Brook Farm with my family."[4] Once again the censorship is eloquent. In the missing pages Alcott must have described the conflict and argument at Fruitlands, culminating with someone's advice to mend fences with Lane. In destroying the account he acknowledges, indeed he demonstrates, that waste has indeed overtaken the economy of his utopia. Coming after the torn pages, the proposal to join Brook Farm reads like a confession of failure. In his journal, Emerson wrote: "At the Convention of Socialists in Boston last week, Alcott was present, & was solicited to speak, but had no disposition, he said, to do so." The great Conversationalist had been too sick at heart to make a contribution.

Ever loyal, Emerson added: "Although none of the representatives of the 'Communities' present would probably admit it, yet he is more the cause of their movements than any other man."[5]

Alcott left the convention early, arriving back at Fruitlands on January 1st. But at least he had made up his mind. "Concluded to go to Mr. Lovejoy's until Spring," Abigail wrote that day in her diary, "having dissolved all connection with Fruitlands." The Lovejoys (another resonant name) had become good friends, and had offered the Alcotts three rooms for the nominal sum of fifty cents a week.

Lane meanwhile had decided to join the Harvard Shakers. They at least could offer a stable community, along with watertight celibacy. There would be no wives or mothers, no troublesome families to deal with, no children under four cluttering up the place. It was an inevitable decision at this time, but still a difficult one. He was an energetic, practical man who had embarked on the biggest adventure of his life, traveling to another country, and trying through his own investment and his own efforts to bring about a new world. Now he had to admit that the experiment had failed, and become a member of someone else's utopia.

He left Fruitlands with William on January 6th.[6] When she heard of it, Margaret Fuller was unsympathetic. "I trust he will thus try out his total abstinence experiment so completely as to give it up."[7] Samuel Bower, whose abstinence experiment was even more total than Lane's, also joined the Shakers.[8]

The day Lane left, Abigail Alcott sent a load of goods to the Lovejoy place, which of course was only a matter of yards from the Fruitlands property, and on January 7th she catalogued and packed their books, at least the ones Lane had left behind. "He takes most of the Greaves library with him," her husband reported bitterly.[9] It is ironic how that collection, intended to inaugurate a spiritual dispensation, provoked so much squabbling and ill-feeling.

"The arrangements here have never suited me," Abigail reflected. Her husband subsequently tried to draw the sting out of the remark by inserting "wholly" immediately before "suited." "My duties have been arduous," she continued, "but my satisfaction small." She resented all the care she had expended on Lane and his son. "My children have been too much bereft of their mother, and she has murmured at a lot which should deprive her of their society."[10]

As preparation for their new life, Abigail did what she could to raise a little money. She sold her cloak to a neighbor, Mrs. Whiting, for the sum of $12, a difficult sacrifice in the middle of a savage winter. Even worse was parting with a silver slice to a relative for another $10. Her beloved Hannah Robie had given it to her. There was no choice, however, as she tried to settle their debts. "I am sure she would not think hardly of me for it," Abigail wrote. It was the old problem. "I have been driven to many of these straights during these last few years . . . Mr. Alcott cannot bring himself to work for gain; but we have not yet learned to live without money or means." Her brother Sam sent her $10 too.[11]

It is not possible to be sure which day the Alcott family left Fruitlands. There is a letter from Abigail to Sam dated January 11th, in which she claims that their move was the day before, but it has been transcribed by her husband and it is likely that he misread the number 17, since January 16th accords more closely with the evidence. "Fruitlands, ah me! is broken up," Emerson told his brother William on the 17th.[12]

On their final day the Alcotts ate their last morsel of food and burned their last stick of wood, before calling Mr. Lovejoy over "to come and get us out, which he did." Abigail's wording suggests they were being rescued rather than removed.[13] Later on, Alcott came across a picture of a sled drawn by a team of oxen taking people away from a snowbound house. It reminded him of his own family's departure, so he cut it out and stuck it into his scrapbook.[14] Perhaps Lovejoy too had brought animals to the aid of the Fruitlanders, as Joseph Palmer had done before him, the final twist of the knife for a failed vegan endeavor.

"Mr Lane's movements have been so equivocal that it was thought best to be as independent as possible," Abigail told Sam. "Besides we found that he did not intend to provide at all for the family." She was indignant that Lane did not see his way to keeping the Alcotts afloat with his own money, an example of the implacable nature of her family loyalty. Given her husband's refusal to work for a living it is hard to see why Lane should have felt obliged to do any more than the considerable amount he had done already. For the benefit of her brother, Abigail contrives to make it seem as if their move was motivated by a sound grasp of financial reality. "We thought it therefore good economy to get into winter quarters, and Mr Alcott and myself are heartily glad to get rid of the whole concern." It is as if the Alcotts themselves had made the initial investment, and had just succeeded in unloading it on someone else. In fact she even manages a note of triumph. "I feel it is no small boon to have come out of the Fruitlands concern. For all Mr Lane's efforts have been to disunite us. But Mr Alcott's conjugal and fraternal instincts were too strong for him."

Abigail tells Sam that they are thinking of joining one of the other communities, and when spring comes around she might spend some time at Hopedale and Northampton to try them out. Intriguingly, in their discussion at the Boston Convention George Ripley had told her husband that he wished Abigail would come and "superintend the Brook Farm concern."

Given Ripley was a fine manager himself, with able colleagues, and ultimately kept his community functioning for six years, it is hard to take this suggestion at face value. The most likely explanation is that Alcott had offered his own services in this role, and Ripley had side-stepped his proposal by acknowledging instead the organizational prowess of his wife, who had after all kept her family afloat without support for years and who would in the future prove to be hardworking and efficient as a sort of social worker and prototype employment agent for the Boston poor. In any case, she had no illusions. "I had rather be a subordinate," she told Sam, "and Mr Alcott does not do well in power."[15] It was the nearest she ever got to admitting that her husband could be oppressively authoritarian, as Lane and other Fruitlanders so often complained.

Abigail wrote to Hannah Robie on January 21st, reporting, "there is an inexpressible comfort in being alone" (no mention of having to sell the silver slice). From the perspective of their three rooms at the Lovejoys, Fruitlands seemed to her to have been a "public tavern sort of life . . . tedious beyond bearing." Once again, Charles Lane was the villain of the piece. "He kept much back and expected more of others than he was willing to give himself."[16] It was the same charge that Lane had leveled at Alcott.

It is possible she thought Lane had not pulled his weight in practical terms. Alcott was born to farming and as time went on proved surprisingly handy at woodwork too, so it is likely that he achieved more in those departments than his colleague. Lane, however, ends a number of his letters by mentioning that he was about to go off and labor in the fields—and of course his "wounded hands" suggest he had made an effort at manual work.[17] Moreover, the penniless pilgrimages had meant that both men had neglected the farm at the crucial period, harvest time. And there are several references to Lane teaching the children—none to Alcott doing the same, except for a brief period in August while he recovered from his illness.[18]

Above all, through his articles in the newspapers Lane had done everything that he could to keep the community in the public gaze. Fruitlands was a structure of words as well as a geographical location, and in that respect Lane was its architect. True, Alcott must have devoted a great deal of diary space to his inner experiences there, but they were not transmitted to the public at large at the time, and as circumstances turned out never would be. In this respect his relationship with Lane oddly parallels the experience with Elizabeth Palmer Peabody. In the case of the Temple School too, he had relied on his partner to bring the experiment to the attention of the general public. Peabody had lived with the Alcotts just as Lane would do. And husband and wife joined together to reject her just as they eventually did Lane. When Alcott sat down in February and March 1844 to produce "some Account of the Fruitlands Enterprise," he was presumably putting pen to paper to write the community's obituary and give his side of the story. It was only at that point that he seems to have resumed some responsibility for teaching his children.[19]

As usual, Lane receives no credit from Abigail for settling the Alcotts' Concord debts and putting up the money that made Fruitlands possible. "He has left us poor as he found us, yet takes all and asks us to be *grateful*," Abigail complained to Hannah Robie. Gratitude was indeed in short supply. In fact, Abigail blames him for being unduly mercenary. "I am more jealous of the power of money over the human mind than I ever was before," she concludes darkly.[20]

Thirty years later Louisa May Alcott would build on her mother's verdict to create an allegory out of the conflict between the two men in her sketch *Transcendental Wild Oats*. Her account pokes gentle fun at the unwordliness of the whole enterprise, but she makes it perfectly clear where her allegiances lie. Her father is presented as the serene and saintly Abel Lamb, while Lane becomes Timon Lion, intent on founding "a colony of Latter Day Saints, who, under his patriarchal sway, should regenerate the world and glorify his name for ever."[21] Clearly her own childhood memory of her family under threat would have given a basis to these melodramatic stereotypes. Other adults at the time, Mary Gove and Emerson among them, found Lane cold and grim. But Gove's perspective was colored by her allegiance to Wright, and Emerson, ever fair-minded, also took pains to acknowledge Lane's energy and idealism.

Louisa's determination to see her father as an innocent victim led her to portray him as almost literally broken-hearted when the community collapsed. "Silently he lay down upon his bed, turned his face to the wall, and waited with pathetic patience for death to cut the knot which he could not untie."[22] But within days of the break-up, her mother was telling Hannah Robie that "my satisfaction is great that Mr. Alcott comes away cheerfully and is convinced that Mr. Lane and he were never truly united."[23] Though Alcott would experience manic and depressive episodes over the next months, it is likely Louisa is remembering his illness in the previous August, when her mother did indeed fear for his life.[24] And to a degree there is an appropriateness in that substitution, because one cause of Alcott's symptoms then had almost certainly been his realization, after just a couple of months, that Fruitlands was riven by an unresolvable conflict.

Instead of waiting for spring, Abigail almost immediately carried out her plan of giving other communities a trial. She went with her friends the Lovejoys so Alcott presumably stayed behind to babysit—he would make a similar trip a couple of months later. She decided that at Northampton "life is quite elementary and aimless," its only purpose being (here's the sting) to pay off debt. At Hopedale she could find "nothing higher than living quiet inoffensive lives." There was some "sackcloth and ashes there," she suspected. Brook Farm was the best of the bunch, with "more neatness, order, beauty and life," but ultimately showed "no advance on the old world" except in its educational program. Membership of any of these communities, as far as she was concerned, would involve an old problem, "unwarrantable alienation from our children."[25] "I am not ready for community life, or is it not ready for me," she told Hannah Robie. "I intend to look out for a little cave and take my cubs and retreat."[26]

Another old problem was her husband's refusal to take on regular paid work. "Should like to see my husband a little more interested in this matter of support," she wrote on her return from her travels. His mood at that time was resigned and even hopeful. "I love his faith and quiet reliance on Divine Providence," she went on, "but a little more activity and industry would place us beyond most of these disagreeable dependencies on friends." She does her best to give her husband the benefit of the doubt, but her tone becomes rather plaintive. "Mr Alcott is right in not working for hire, if thereby he violates his conscience; but working for bread does not necessarily imply unworthy gain."[27]

Meanwhile her husband had other concerns.

During the deep midwinter Bronson Alcott finally put the circumstantial law to its fullest test. He described what happened in a remarkable diary passage written eight years later, the only sustained record we have of his inmost thoughts during this period.

He claims that the experiences occurred during the extreme cold of the winter of 1844, when he was at Fruitlands, and lasted until the spring. Clearly, either the date or the place is incorrect. While it would be characteristic of him to get the year wrong (elsewhere he gives 1842 as a date for the community), it seems unlikely that he misremembered a whole season, and he certainly never passed a spring at Fruitlands. In any case in his autobiographical index he claims that he had a clairvoyant experience during the months of February and March 1844.[28] So the location was in fact his new dwelling, which was only a matter of a few hundred yards from Fruitlands anyway. Given that Concordia acted as the first phase of the experiment, it is perfectly symmetrical to see the Lovejoys' house as its final one, at least as far as Alcott himself was concerned.

The circumstantial law was not ultimately about self-denial but intensification; it was a matter of sloughing off harmful or irrelevant experiences in order to experience more elevated and blissful ones. One had to cleanse one's connections to the world in order to participate fully in its harmony. In this passage Alcott describes both the discipline and the reward of such a program.

He stayed indoors and kept writing from dawn until midnight, day after day. Sometimes he carried on until the following dawn, leaving his room only to get fuel and water for bathing twice a day, at sunrise and sunset. He lived on fruits and biscuits (as usual) and drank only water, "exclusively and often"—another reminder that the regime was based not simply on abstention but on consumption as well. He could not have made much use of the fuel because he describes the bathing process in considerable and unheated detail. He stood in a large tub of cold water and poured pails of it over his body, ducking down several times in succession to put his head and shoulders under the water. Afterward he dried himself briskly with linen towels, and "practiced friction with the flesh brush."

The result of these energetic and chilly ablutions could be dramatic. "In the coldest mornings there was a crackling and lambent flash following the passage of my hand over the pile of the skin, and I shook flames from my finger ends, which seemed erect and blazing with phosphoric light."

Like Emerson's account of turning into a transparent eyeball, this is a moment when Transcendentalism becomes an experience, rather than just a philosophical position. It teeters on the edge of the absurd simply because it takes us beyond our normal apprehension of the world, transcends it, in fact. Despite all the words expended by Greaves and Lane, neither of them conveyed a phenomenon like this; they concentrated instead on the conditions that would be necessary to bring it about. Here, though, the life force invades the body and then passes beyond its boundaries back into the world. The trajectory is inward and outward in quick succession. "The eyes, too, were lustrous, and shot sparkles whenever I closed them."

All the senses were engaged. "On raising my head from the flood there was heard a melody in the ear, as of the sound of many waters; and rubbing the eyes gave out an iris of the primitive colors, beautiful to behold, but as evanescent as a twinkling . . . I tasted mannas, and all the aromas of field and orchard scented the fountains, and the brain was haunted with the rhythm of many voiced melodies." Here is the landscape Alcott had imagined for Fruitlands, the fields and orchards, the fountains; here the conversion of hunger into manna; here, in the cold white winter, a rainbow of colors, primitive ones: a vision of the original lost world.

Perhaps it is not surprising that he was vague about when and where this ecstasy occurred, since its location was free of the normal constraints of time and place. He tried to put the experience down on paper, his old problem. "It was not easy to write prose while thus exalted and transfigured."

The exaltation continued for some considerable time but took its toll eventually. "I enjoyed this state for a couple of months or more, but was left somewhat debilitated when spring came, and unfit for common concerns."[29]

Lane, over in the Harvard Shaker community, was also putting pen to paper. Alcott rediscovered the Garden of Eden in his own head, a place of fountains and trees and brilliant colors. Lane meanwhile, in his more measured fashion, was locating it in its mythic and possibly historical past. Man in his "pristine condition" contravened his Creator's will, and in the very first generation quarreled with and murdered his brother. The story, he suggested, was a "signature of operations in the human soul," and might indeed be literally true. If so, its significance must be that the first human dwelling was built not to protect people from the weather but "from the assaults of man against his brother" (even in the depths of a severe winter Lane was determined not to regard the weather as a problem).[30]

In short, houses are unnatural. A person living in the open has a sharper and more direct apprehension of his surroundings than one living in a wigwam behind a stockade (which was how he visualized the earliest dwellings). While Alcott is regularly experiencing sudden overwhelming sensual acuity, Lane has to settle for describing it: "The eye, the nose, the palate, the touch, and every sense is an inlet of the book of nature."[31] Electricity sparks from Alcott's skin, and flames sprout from his finger tips; Lane meanwhile contents himself with quoting David Brainerd's account of a Native American's mystical experiences in New Jersey a hundred years previously, when a man appeared clothed in the day, and "everything that was beautiful and lovely in the earth was upon him." As a result of this apparition, the Indian who had witnessed the visitation was himself transfigured. "He was all light, and not only light himself, but it was light all around him."[32]

At secondhand—or rather thirdhand—and over the chasm of time, Lane has to imagine what that might be like.

Lane's piece is called "Life in the Woods," a phrase that would in due course be borrowed by Thoreau for the subtitle of *Walden*. Indeed at times Lane seems to anticipate the experiment in living Thoreau would undertake the following year, and (perhaps surprisingly) tries to steer him away from it. "By the time the hut is built," he warns, "the rudest furniture constructed, the wood chopped, the fire burning, the bread grown and prepared, the whole time will be exhausted, and no interval remain for comfortably clothing the body, for expansion in art, or for recreation by the book or pen."[33] Perhaps Thoreau's careful itemizing in *Walden* of the expenditure of money and labor involved in building his hut (not much of either) was his rebuttal of this claim.[34]

Lane's point is that a true life in nature is not isolated or reclusive. On the contrary, "the tribe is a better type of universal family than the city." The natural man "lives not alone; he merely occupies a large space" (just the sort of remark Thoreau himself might make, whatever his differences with Lane about the building of huts).[35] But in point of fact neither civilization nor the "sylvan life" can provide the means of achieving the good, the perfect life for us now. At this point Lane seems disillusioned with the circumstantial law— perhaps the experience of Fruitlands had seemed to give it the lie. "If there be any conditioning required, it is not to be sought in persons, events or things without and about man, so much as in himself." Indeed, far from making inexorable progress towards the higher state, it is when things seem at their worst, he now thinks, that bleak time when "every door of human sympathy is closed against us . . . It is in this sad hour . . . that the holy flame descends." And when that happens, "the outward conditions of life . . . become a matter of light importance."

He ends on an odd note, explaining that the human mind has the habit of viewing all things as male and female. The forest is regarded as the former; the city the latter; their marriage might be expected to produce "offspring more conducive to human bliss" than either of their parents could achieve on his or her own. But Lane returns to the old Greavesian argument at this point: "It is difficult to conceive how corrupt parents shall have pure progeny." Instead, he suggests that the forest and the city are both males.

"And, as in the olden history, the tiller of the ground is again destined to destroy the keeper of sheep, the hunter of deer."[36] The farmer murders his brother, the nomadic herder and hunter. That story is often interpreted nowadays as a myth demonstrating how a hunter-gatherer way of life gave way to an agricultural one. But for Lane, Fruitlands was intended to be a step on the way from farming back toward a nomadic existence; and that plan had been thwarted by Alcott, the farmer's son. Lane undoubtedly saw himself as the wronged Abel; inevitably, Louisa May Alcott would in due course assign that name to her father.

The story could also be seen as a warning against the corruption of parent-hood. After their exile from the Garden of Eden Adam and Eve had children, one of whom was killed by another. Here is the source of Greavesian pessimism about family life: sinful parenthood leading to fratricide. Because of Alcott's uxoriousness, he and his brother in utopia have had a fatal quarrel. It is all predicted in the Book of Genesis. Lane wrote another piece at the same time as "Life in the Woods," a short article praising the Shakers with whom he was now living. His main concern is to defend their doctrine of celibacy. God's will should be done on earth as it is in heaven; in heaven "they are neither married nor given in marriage"; QED.

The possibility of salvation now seems to him to be a matter for the indi-vidual soul, and the outcome could go either way. "The consciousness of this latent germ of grace within him, and the conviction that in some degree its birth depends upon himself" combines "to worry, anger, and vex the soul until it either boils over in fiery prejudice, or turns inwardly to HEAVENLY LOVE."[37] Birth is an inward matter, the generation of grace. But that too can be subject to conflict and distortion. It is a vague, equivocal restatement of the philosophical struggle that has preoccupied him for so long, the reasoning of a tired and defeated man.

Over in England Henry Gardiner Wright, the community's first apostate, had become tired and defeated too. He was now suffering badly from his tumor. After arriving back he had stayed at Alcott House for a time, and resumed his relationship with his wife on at least one level, because they had another child. Early in 1844 he started teaching at the school in Chipping Ongar where he had been an usher before becoming involved with the English and then the American Transcendentalists. It was as if none of his intellectual and geographical voyages had even happened. "What have I ever done?" he asked Oldham, and answered the question for himself. "Nothing, absolutely nothing. I have dreamed only of great deeds. Let me never attempt again what is beyond my being's power."[38]

Alcott was also feeling exhausted: the repeated exaltation had taken its toll. At this time he followed in Abigail's footsteps to visit possible communities and during the trip stayed with Emerson for a few days; by then he was in a distraught and manic state. "Very sad, indeed, it was to see this halfgod driven to the wall, reproaching men, & hesitating whether he should not reproach the gods," Emerson wrote. Alcott had given the world a trial and found he could not live in it. As "a lover of law he had tried whether law could be kept in this world, & all things answered, NO." He even threatened suicide. "If he should be found to-morrow at the roadside, it would be the act of the world."

It was a moment when Emerson felt the need to evaluate and sum up his old friend. On the downside he was "tedious & prosing & egotistical & narrow." Emerson was fully aware that Alcott exaggerated, had a one-sided picture, saw his conflicts in terms of personalities, lacked a sense of humor. On the other hand: "a profound insight, a Power, a majestical man." Alcott did not belong in this moment of time—he had "a painful sense of being an orphan & a hermit here"—but he somehow had access to a changeless world that was above and beyond history, "looking easily along the centuries to explore *his contemporaries.*" He did not attract the allegiance of women, Emerson decided, presumably thinking of the male culture of Alcott House, and the fratricidal battle with Lane (and overlooking the relationship Alcott had initially had with Elizabeth Palmer Peabody during the Temple School period, as well as his marriage to Abigail). Alcott had told him that he had been writing poetry all winter, but Emerson had no expectations of it. "His overpowering personality destroys all poetic faculty."[39]

Alcott arrived back at the Lovejoys' having decided, like Abigail before him, that none of the communities he had sampled on his trip was suitable. "We must then take up the family cross," Abigail wrote on his return, "and work on, isolated and poor, a while longer."[40] A few months previously the lusts of the flesh (including the marital relationship in its physical sense) were to be sacrificed on the cross; now they were carrying the cross of their family along: a full reversal from the cross as termination to the cross as journey, from repudiation of the organic family to a commitment to it.

In April, the Alcotts left the Lovejoys' house and moved to a small property in nearby Still River village. If the forest represented Lane's take on Eden, a cottage garden seems to have become Alcott's, and he immediately set to work. "What a few days previously was stone and stubble, a rude rough chaos, is now squared into neat regular beds and borders, verdure presenting itself and food promising for us," Abigail wrote admiringly. "What a holy calling is the husbandman's!"[41]

Over in England a sick Henry Gardiner Wright was wondering rather forlornly what had happened to his old colleagues. "I have been told that Mr Lane says Alcott is an impractical dreamer," he wrote to an unknown correspondent (most likely Mary Gove). "Alas! How far shall we have to go to find those who will deliver the same opinion of C.L., of W.[illiam] O.[ldham], and of others whom I could mention." He included himself in the "others." "Sometimes I almost suspect that of myself the world has decided pretty truly," he concluded sadly. "I begin to respect its decision and to suspect my own."[42]

The Alcotts had their fourteenth wedding anniversary on May 23rd, and Abigail wrote a tiny verse expressing the strains that their relationship had undergone, and hoping for the best:

I thought that you loved me!
At least I believed!
Sure—I am not decieved [sic][43]

That day brought her news from her late father's executors that her legacy had been settled at last, and was rather larger than expected. The Temple School creditors had accepted $2,000 as settlement for outstanding debts of $6,000 and there was $1,375 left over for Abigail (more than $40,000 in terms of modern purchasing power), plus an annual stipend of $225 settled on her by her relatives. To prevent the money from disappearing into her husband's bottomless pit, the amount went into a trust administered by her brother Samuel and her cousin Samuel Sewall.[44]

Nevertheless Alcott's first thought was to use it for another attempt at the good life. It was his old custom of spending other people's money. "She will bind her interests with mine, I trust," he wrote to Junius, "and rely on something more sure and worthy than Boston Gold." In other words, instead of hanging on to her legacy she would be persuaded to spend it on "adherence to the law of Justice, and the labours of self-support."[45] He was still sighing for paradise, as he put it in the title of a poem at this time that defies Emerson's fears by being heartfelt and direct, even though it clunkily incorporates a five-syllable word:

Lonely my dwelling here
Lonely the Sphere
Weary the present, dark the future
Nor home have I, nor any coadjutator;
O, when to me will come
The long sought home
The friendly bosom
The tenement I covet,
Earth underneath & firmament above it,
And tenures clear to prove it.[46]

What he hoped was to use Abigail's inheritance to obtain that coveted tenure somewhere (perhaps out west) and establish a "True Family settlement." His coadjutators were to be his real brothers Junius and Chatfield rather than his mythic brother Charles Lane.[47]

With this in mind he went on a trip to visit them both in July, taking Anna with him. He also took all his writings of the last few years, volumes of it, in a wooden trunk: his diaries for 1842, 1843, and for 1844 to date, his account of Fruitlands, a book called *Prometheus* that contained his philosophical musings about the experiment, copies of his letters from 1838 to the present, and an autobiographical poem.[48] This archive might seem excessively bulky for a trip of just three weeks or so, but it constituted Alcott's utopian aspirations in dehydrated form. He had left the community behind, but in a sense could still take it along with him. And the whole purpose of his journey was to gain adherents from his own family. He could, in effect, show them the experience he had gone through, and the beliefs he had put to the test. The sheer weight of paper was an index of his commitment.

On August 4th, on their way back, he and Anna stopped in Albany, New York, while waiting for the Boston train. When it was due, they took the omnibus down to the ferry (the railroad station was on the other side of the river). The trunk of manuscripts was heaved up on to the roof of the vehicle. The trunk had a broken lock and was held shut with a strap. Alcott's name and address were marked out in tacks on the lid.

At the dock, he left the carriage and stowed Anna on the boat. Then he returned to fetch down his trunk, but the omnibus had gone. He told himself that the driver must have placed the trunk on board before departing. But when the ferry got to the other side of the river and they disembarked, it was nowhere to be seen.[49]

Alcott made enquiries for years, but his papers were never found.[50] Perhaps this marks the moment when the Fruitlands experiment can truly be said to have ended.

18

Tumbledown Hall

On October 1, 1844 the Alcotts moved back to Concord, renting rooms in a house belonging to a cousin of their old landlord Edmund Hosmer.[1] Emerson, on impulse, had just bought fourteen acres of land by the shores of Walden Pond, a mile or so from the center of the village, one of his favorite haunts. Now he could grow his own blackberries, he told his brother William. He was not surprised to find Alcott immediately on the prowl. "The dreaming Alcott is here with Indian dreams that I helped him to some house & farm in the Spirit Land!"[2]

Alcott wrote to Junius about those dreams. "Emerson has offered to buy me a few acres and build me a plain house, and Mr. May and others desire to aid in placing us on the soil, free of rents and landlords," he announced. As always, this dependence on others was transformed into a posture of generosity on his own part. "I hope to obtain space and dwellings for several families by these means," he told Junius, and then warmed to his theme so much he sounded just like his erstwhile "coadjutator," Charles Lane. "I cannot consent to live solely for one family; I would stand in neighborly relations to several, and interpose a check to all selfish and narrow interests; institute a union and communion of families, instead of *drawing aside within the precincts of one's own acres and kindred by blood* [Alcott's emphasis]."[3]

While Alcott was making expansive gestures, Lane was pulling his horns in. Over in the Shaker community at Harvard he reasserted his hostility to transportation. Far from being penniless, pilgrimages were disastrously expensive. No doubt brooding about those unfruitful trips to New York, to Providence and Hingham, to Mr. Hammond and his exoteric wife in New Hampshire, he decided that proselytizing cost more than it brought in. "I stage the distance by a hired vehicle, at the expense of the poor horses, who are urged to their speed by a drunken driver; I sojourn at a tavern, advertise in the papers, hire a hall, and amuse the people for an hour or two; possibly affect one or two beneficially," he explained to the readers of the *New Age and Concordium Gazette* in the summer of 1844. "And then I have to come back again with my whole being disturbed, and set to work to earn this cash expenditure which I have thrown into so many corrupt channels." He remembered the disappointing yield of the Fruitlands' fields. "Several bushels of corn must be grown to make up this sum," he complained.[4] His analysis resembles an early attempt at determining a carbon footprint. He fell back on the Greavesian solution: being rather than doing.

It would be Thoreau, not Alcott, who took advantage of the Walden purchase. He moved on to Emerson's land in 1845, built his hut, and took being to its ultimate limits, living there for two years (with frequent visits to relatives and friends in Concord). Ten years before, one of the observers of Greaves's tavern meetings had expressed puzzlement at the philosopher's attendance: "Why he came to the meetings and seemed to like them, was a problem, his theme always being, that people should *not* meet together." Thoreau perhaps was more consistent, establishing a community of one, and fulfilling Greaves's dream of "a most intimate union with the Infinite."[5]

Nevertheless, the loyal Emerson came to the aid of the Alcotts once again, helping them with the purchase of a house with eight acres of land not far from his own in January 1845. Abigail's executors provided $850 toward the cost, with a further $500 given by Emerson himself. Generous as he was, he felt a touch of resentment too, complaining in familiar fashion to his journal: "The whole human race spend their lives in hard work from simple & necessary motives, and feel the approbation of their conscience; and meet with this talker at their gate, who, as far as they see, does not labour himself, & takes up this grating tone of authority & accusation against them." Clearly the Concord community objected to the Alcotts' failure to pay their way. "His unpopularity is not at all wonderful," Emerson added.[6]

Unaware of such considerations, Alcott's first thought was to invite Junius to join them in the new property. "There is land not quite sufficient for the support of several families," he claimed, inviting disaster along with his brother.[7] Junius obviously did not rise to this somewhat equivocal bait because in February 1845 Abigail (amazingly) wrote to Lane with the same offer. Her husband must have persuaded her to put pen to paper, knowing that Lane would assume that any suggestions from himself could be sabotaged by her. It was a remarkable turnaround after just a year. Perhaps the knowledge that part of the investment was her own made her feel more able to cope with the prospect of trying to reinstate Fruitlands.

But of course, in Greavesian terms the past was manure, or as Lane put it in his reply: "Even to look backward, to think backward is to be changed into a pillar of salt—to be petrified into a piece of dead and contemptible history." He also suspected Emerson's motive in contributing toward the cost of the property—it smacked of kindness. He "does not act, nor profess to act, wholly on universal grounds," he explained to her. "Unless I am wrong, it is an act of the purest individual friendship." This motive would "entirely neutralize the good moral result that could not fail to arise in a building founded on the true rock."

Perhaps he was aware of sounding rather fierce, because he went on to modify his dogmatic tone, conceding "there is work for individuals, there is work for association; and, in the natural order, for the private family." The family's contribution would be a physiological one (breeding perfect children, obviously), but this was not a task to which he personally was suited. She was better equipped for the role, he told her gracefully. "I believe that you have been faithful to every ray of light as it shone upon your path." But his letter had a sting in the tail. He concluded by giving her a list of Shaker precepts, the first being, "Pay all your just debts."[8]

The Alcotts moved into their new dwelling on April 1, 1845. They did have one extra member of the new household, a woman called Sophia Foord who was going to help with teaching the girls and ultimately, it was hoped, run a school with Alcott for the children of Concord.[9] In the meantime Alcott set to work on the property. He rechristened it Hillside, a descriptive name rather than an allegorical one like Concordia, or a mission statement like Fruitlands. Perhaps this marked a more focused and practical approach because he began to work on the house and grounds with sustained energy, remodeling the building, terracing the eponymous hillside, and planting the field on the other side of the road.[10]

Visitors came to see what was going on, triggering Abigail's standard reaction. "It makes up my days unprofitably but the rites of hospitality are sacred," she complained to her brother Sam on June 8th.[11] Those rites were put to the test in August, when Charles Lane made an appearance after all, having decided that despite his hopes the Shakers were not the answer. Abigail suspected that the true cause was that the time had come when the Shakers required him to contribute his assets, "which is too deep a one for him yet to solve, he cannot give up *all* to follow *Christ*."

He was quiet and gentle, she noted, and apparently sad. Certainly the abrasiveness was absent.[12] Alcott's garden was "the best piece of preaching he has for a long time preached," he assured them, and indeed the way of life Alcott had taken up, cultivating the soil and the minds of his children, was "as happy for him as could be found, in his mixed and inevitable relations." Lane was not intending to stay long, in any event, hoping to get back to England before the cold weather set in (his experiment of coping with a second cold Massachusetts winter had not been a success). The problem was that he could not release William from the Shakers' clutches.[13]

The Shakers, as a celibate sect, were dependent on indenturing children in order to keep their communities going. Lane's dilemma was deeply ironic. He had always believed family bonds were an obstacle in the way of achieving a perfected life. The Shakers had taken him at his word. He told Abigail that he hoped to use "love argument" to get William away from them.[14] Normally such a phrase from his lips would indicate a universal abstraction, such as the one he had pitted against Emerson's act of friendship a few months previously. But of course the Shakers would be able to argue that their claim on William conformed precisely to that principle, which left Lane having to make a case for the primacy of paternal love.

In the meantime he joined in enthusiastically with the Hillside chores. He worked out a timetable accounting for every hour of the day, just as he had at Concordia. He had no plans to revisit history and set up the old regime, however. This was simply a "Table of Indoor Duties for Children," a schedule for the education of the Alcott girls, with contributions from himself, the Alcotts, and Miss Foord.[15] Louisa was despondent at seeing her mother's erstwhile enemy back in harness. "I wish we could be together and no one else," she wrote in her diary. "I don't see who is to feed and clothe us all, when we are so poor now."[16] By late September Lane was despairing of getting William released, and a month or so after that he was in New York to spend the winter.[17] Sophia Foord left too. So much for Alcott's planned school. She had fallen in love with Thoreau to such an extent that she proposed to him. Loyal to his intimate relations with the infinite, he replied, he told Emerson, with "as distinct a no as I have learned to pronounce."[18]

In January 1846, Alcott wrote to Lane that the "Comforter enters only through the doors of the Private Heart into the Private House to gladden the Family Circle."[19] The little wicket gate opened inward, after all, not outward toward the world as a whole. In his diary at about this time he put the issue in fraught and embattled terms: "The Family is a Colony of emparadised Souls, planted in Time, and charged with subduing it, as the sole condition of returning to Heaven. Wide the wilderness lying around, and fierce the savages that prowl abroad, glaring at and invading this Human Retreat."[20] Perhaps he saw Lane as one of those glaring savages. Nearly four years previously, over at Alcott House, he had thought back to colonial times in an optimistic spirit, establishing a parallel between the Puritans' plantations and his own utopian plans. Now he saw those early days of settlement in a darker, more threatening—more threatened—light.

Lane had come to accept, over the course of his American experience, that the wicket gate was indeed very little. In New York he attended a crowded soirée and fondly recalled the unpopularity of Greaves's events. "The meetings do not of course compare to those which Mr Greaves held," he told Alcott. "If they did few persons would attend them." True fellowship could only originate in small groups. Nevertheless for him the wicket gate still opened outward. "Let but the true thing be done—let but the true being be—& tho' the doing and being pertain to the veriest recluse in New England, I am satisfied that the results will inevitably follow. What is revealed in the secret chamber shall be proclaimed on the housetop." No significant change is yet apparent in the world's institutions—the fundamental shift cannot happen until "a new vital principle is inseminated in the human constitution." But until people are generated anew, education is the most rewarding activity since it will "conserve the best results" we can at present achieve. Nevertheless meeting just a few kindred spirits ensures that "one catches anew the heaven born conviction that ere long the new day will appear. Let us not forget that this conviction *is* the new day."[21]

Meanwhile, over in England, Henry Gardiner Wright died from his tumor, in conjunction with lung disease, on March 15, 1846, at the age of thirty-two. His wife died the following October. One of their two children died young too, though their daughter lived until 1905, when she perished in a cycling accident.[22]

In March 1845 Joseph Palmer bought the Fruitlands farmhouse from Maverick Wyman. The following summer he and Lane drew up a prospectus, proposing an association for a school and a home for the aged and destitute to be established on land in Harvard and Leominster the following year. The amount necessary would be $5,000, to be raised by selling shares at $100 each. This was of course piecemeal philanthropy, not a structural change, and Lane had no plan to take a direct part. In fact he sold the Fruitlands fields to Palmer as part of the arrangement, for the price of $1,700. Despite all his hopes his investment had in the end made a small loss of $100. Palmer made a down payment of $400, agreeing to pay the same amount the following year and the final installment of $900 in 1849. In return Lane paid Palmer $100, the price of his share in the new association.[23]

William was still trapped by his indenture. "I cannot think the melancholy principles of the Shakers will last long," Lane wrote to Emerson, "but they may continue long enough to kill him."[24] Lane visited Concord for the final time in June 1846 and spent a few days at Hillside. He was back to his waspish self. Alcott kept his garden clear of weeds, he reported, and Mrs. Alcott kept the house "clear of all intruders."[25] Then in September he returned (without William) to Alcott House.

Years later Oldham told Alcott that on arrival Lane looked "so altered and destitute that we did not recognize him."[26] It was not until the summer of 1848 that Emerson was able to use his influence to extract William from the clutches of the Shakers. Now sixteen, he stayed with the Alcotts for six weeks before departing for England. They sent him off, Alcott told Lane, "with profound memories of adventures in which father as well as son, played with us in the same game with Destiny—the parts still inexpli[c]able, but necessary (and victorious) we may believe to all parties enga[g]ed."[27]

At Alcott House the deceased Elizabeth Wright's responsibilities had been taken over by a "managing sister" called Hannah Bond. At some time in the late 1840s Lane began an affair with her. Oldham was not able to endure the "consciousness of evil" and closed the school down in 1849, when Lane returned to editing the *Mercantile Price-Current*. He and Hannah had three sons and a daughter together. Their first boy was christened Pierrepont, a tribute that might have made Greaves uneasy.[28]

Though this irregular arrangement preyed on Oldham's mind for a number of years, he too had an unmarried liaison with a woman called Eliza Sutton. Strangely, all three of Greaves's closest disciples eventually defied not just the master's austere rules but the basic sexual propriety of their time. "It was a work too high and pure and good for such imperfect persons to carry out," Oldham reflected. "From one cause and another we every one of us broke down, one was not good enough another not wise enough and another not strong enough so it all fell to pieces."[29] When Lane died in 1870, a wealthy man, Oldham communicated with him beyond the grave. He had not gone straight to heaven, Oldham discovered, because "he cannot forget his money affairs and his family."[30]

On January 1, 1847, Joseph Palmer reopened Fruitlands as a refuge for the destitute. He rechristened it Freelands and kept it going for several years, with a pot of beans and one of potatoes always on the fire.[31] In 1849 he tried to persuade Samuel Bower (who like Lane had left the Shakers) to return, but after due consideration Bower decided that there was nobody in either England or America "Realist enough" to bulk out the community. As for himself, he was still determined to take the nudist path. "I shall most assuredly, if the Infinite Spirit wills, make my home in the open heavens and resume the right so long in abeyance of being naturally and therefore well and sufficiently clothed."[32] If Greaves, Lane, and Alcott regarded the story of the Garden of Eden primarily as a fable about correct eating, Bower saw it above all as a warning against the oppressiveness of fig leaves.

Despite not recruiting his old colleagues or selling his shares, Palmer seems to have made ends meet on his altruistic farm, though he closed Freelands in the early 1850s.[33]

Samuel Larned married a slave-holding woman from Alabama a few years after leaving Fruitlands. He took to dressing well, and renounced his previous principles, which he had come to regard as "vagaries."[34] He died of consumption in New York in about 1850, just twenty-eight years old.[35] Wood Abraham and Ann Page disappear from view after leaving the community. Isaac Hecker became a Catholic, and eventually founded the Paulist Fathers in New York, a different kind of community altogether, one unthreatened by sexual conflicts.

Back in Concord, Alcott busied himself cultivating his garden. In 1846 he constructed a bower at the back of his house, an elaborate piece of design involving gothic columns, willow lattices, "animated seats woven of hazel rods on a warp of locust," along with gables and a "serpentine rustic fence." No sooner had he finished realizing this flight of fancy than his head buzzed with another project. "I am sleeplessly busy on a Garden House," he told Samuel May.[36] Seeing his delight in such projects Emerson commissioned a summer house for his own use. He watched in amusement as Alcott and Thoreau got to work on it. "I think to call it Tumbledown Hall," he told Margaret Fuller.[37] A few years later the sages of Concord—Emerson, Hawthorne, Thoreau, Alcott—got into the habit of meeting on Monday evenings in Emerson's library, and these sessions were the subject of a published piece which Alcott pasted into his scrapbook. He is described as "Plato Skimpole, then sublimely meditating impossible summer houses in a little house upon the Boston road." Alcott underlined "Skimpole" and wrote "lie!!" in the margin.[38]

Certainly there are resemblances to the character in *Bleak House* (1853) who made free with other people's money and avoided all responsibilities by claiming "I am but a mere child!" But perhaps those impossible summer houses anticipate another Dickens character too, the clerk Wemmick in *Great Expectations* (1861) who fortified his home with cannon in order to defend it against encroachment from the grim workaday world, and in so doing helped to establish the concept of suburbia. Alcott didn't go out to work, of course, at least on any sort of regular basis, and was a pacifist, but nevertheless his channeling of the utopian impulse into the creation of charming effects seems to represent a similar desire to create a domestic space protected by its serpentine rustic fence from the outside world. He had become an advocate and architect of leisure—so much so that his enthusiasm and commitment kept him awake at nights. He had believed that the Garden of Eden could be re-established and the human race perfected; now he was interested in gardening as an "ocular dividend of opulence and Beauty," as he told Samuel May.[39]

He was aware that this represented the failure of his ambitions, and put the problem to Thoreau (who was content with isolation). "I asked Thoreau if it were a proof positive of our insufficiency that we had not attracted by our bearing and opinions some fine youth—it were sufficient were it but one—some maid from the farmer's hearth, some stripling from farmhouse or workshop to our house and thoughts and thus evidenced unmistakably our position and real existence here in the world, in this 19th century, during this winter of '48 and in this Concord town where we dwell."[40]

He continued to hold Conversations when he could, and as the years rolled on he undertook a number of tours to the west, where he held forth on his favorite topics. But it was a matter of family on one hand, the world on the other. In a sense it was left to his daughter Louisa to bridge that gap when she wrote her celebration of family life, *Little Women* (1868), and sold it to the public at large in huge quantities. Her book provided vindication of a sort (as well as solving the Alcotts' financial problems at last), but it also perpetuated the paradoxes and ironies of the Fruitlands experiment. The father figure in that ostensibly tightly knit group is off-stage for almost the whole book, at work on his larger mission.

Conclusion

The Fruitlands fiasco was the product of misunderstandings and mistakes on every level, practical, personal, philosophical.

It is quite obvious that Lane and Alcott should not have acquired a farm in the first place. By its very nature a farm involves overproduction and the trading of surplus produce, while the Fruitlanders wished to be self-sufficient and avoid vicarious living. Their way of life required a large garden-cum-orchard, or a smallholding. The excess acreage represented the afterglow of Lane's original ambition to be part of a large project. The fact that in walking the land Mrs. Alcott felt the pull of "diffusive illimitable benevolence" shows how the Alcotts too could be seduced by sheer space, by the prospect of Prospect Hill.

At the heart of this mistake about land lay a misunderstanding about family. For Lane it was a transitory social unit, which would give way to larger structures. But for Alcott it was a mystical entity, a paradigm to be imitated. Lane did what he could to accommodate himself to Alcott's perspective when the contradiction dawned on him. At the same time, Alcott (buoyed up by his reception in England) fell under the spell of Lane's version of utopia. Ultimately a triangle developed, with Lane arguing for large associations, Abigail Alcott endorsing the nuclear family, and Bronson Alcott oscillating uneasily in the middle.

This dilemma was compounded by a confusion about the roles of education and reproduction. Alcott in his Temple School days enthusiastically proclaimed the role of the teacher, yet at the same time put forward the view that the redemption of humankind would come about by breeding "perfect men." Exactly the same contradiction manifested itself among the English Transcendentalists, as Greaves's original enthusiasm for Pestalozzian methods gave way to faith in a purified form of generation. As a result the Fruitlanders were torn about whether they should cultivate their land (though none of them had breeding in mind in any case) or go off and try to teach their principles to the public at large.

One of Emerson's most consistent complaints concerned the way the Fruitlanders simultaneously repudiated money and desired it. They wanted to step out of the world in which they found themselves into another one, but there had to be a point of connection between the two. That little wicker gate required a toll before they could pass through it. Like all the other paradoxes, this one involved a conflict between movement and stillness, doing and being, between the historical realm where money was earned and spent, and the eternal domain, as they saw it, of nature—the Garden of Eden, where ownership and the workaday life that made it possible had been transcended.

It seems strange that the Fruitlanders should have been so committed to a biblical mythology and yet so uninterested in all the paraphernalia of Christianity. In Alcott's case this perspective was influenced by the iconoclasm of the New England Transcendentalists, their emphasis on the human nature of Christ, and their belief, derived from the Puritans, in a direct interaction between an individual and the divinity. Such attitudes were largely shared by the English Transcendentalists who sat at the feet of James Pierrepont Greaves. Both Alcott and Lane are embodiments of the tendency, during the last years of the eighteenth century and the early part of the nineteenth, for Christianity to lose definition and modulate into a romantic pantheism. They manage to come across as believers in the universal spirit and biblical fundamentalists at one and the same time.

For all these reasons the utopians seem in certain respects quite comic and confused figures, blundering in the dark. At the time of their experiment, which relied on an optimistic and stable view of nature, Darwin was already brooding on the evolutionary battle for survival. Just fifteen years after Fruitlands, America became convulsed in a bloody conflict that made the assumption that it could provide the locale for paradise-planting seem naive (tellingly, Louisa May Alcott set her exploration of domestic life, *Little Women*, against the backdrop of the Civil War). For people who were so worried about the wrongs of society, the Fruitlanders' disdain for piecemeal reform cuts them off from the mainstream concerns of the time, from the radical agitation of New England Transcendentalists like Theodore Parker and Orestes Brownson, from the Chartists in England, even to an extent from the abolitionists, since what they took from that movement was a belief in anarchism that caused them to reject the totality of current society rather than to devote their energies to righting a specific injustice. And given they were so concerned with interpersonal relations, their prescriptiveness and naivety about sex and indeed their hostility towards it, their lack of awareness about what makes people—about what made themselves and fellow members of the group—actually tick, seem bizarre to us now, more than a century after the disciplines of psychology and psychiatry came to the fore.

Ironically, their most eccentric obsession of all, the belief that diet holds the key to human perfection and the inauguration of a redeemed world, is the aspect of their creed which most ensures their relevance today, enabling them to leapfrog over the intervening span of political and social thinking and establish a connection with our current priorities. Spirit is dependent on the perfectibility of the body; the properly organized body is dependent on the ingredients it obtains from the world: the effect is to anchor human beings firmly in their surroundings, to create the possibility of what we now call "environmentalism." They did not understand how nature had evolved through time, but they did believe an individual had to be part of the web of life, nourished by it and feeding back into it in turn. They anticipated the science of ecology in their intuition that life is a single phenomenon and the world an organism needing delicate handling—an egg, Alcott called it. Pollution causes environmental and therefore human damage.

Despite their austerity, the Fruitlanders advocated happiness and enjoyment of life. They used Puritan self-abnegation to undermine the Puritan legacy. This achievement anticipates Beat and hippy culture, the suburban ideal, the lifestyle preoccupations of the present. The most cursory Googling

of keywords like "utopia" or "commune" shows at once how their ideas anticipated those of the modern counterculture. "Hippie Communes—Past,
Present, and Future" tells us, "By rejecting violence, the hippies preach
harmony between human beings and the environment . . . They do not kill
animals, and may become vegetarians. Also traditional marriage is replaced by
love."[1] "Sweet Earth: Experimental Utopias in America" gives brief accounts of
a number of past and present-day communities: Cordes Junction, Arizona
("To avoid wasting materials, gardens, solar heating, and natural cooking
move the community towards self-sufficiency"); The Farm, Summertown,
Tennessee ("All members agreed to a vegan diet, non-violence, a shared purse,
and voluntary poverty"); Heathcote Community, Freeland, Maryland ("The
School of Living was founded to teach . . . small-scale subsistence farming and
living, such as carpentry, organic gardening, and food storage").[2] And so on,
almost indefinitely.

But it is not simply a matter of alternative communities. Any broadsheet
newspaper will have daily articles on such topics as climate change, the threat
to the landscape, the damage done by industrialized farming, urban sprawl,
the methane emissions of cattle, the consequences of bad nutrition, the harm
caused by unnecessary travel, the relationship between environmental
neglect and behavior, the Gaia hypothesis.

Alcott was fond of the image of Janus, and we can see the Fruitlanders
taking up a Janus stance, one face toward the lost world of the Book of
Genesis, and the possibility of a return to Eden; the other toward our own
concern with our surroundings, with the interconnectedness of things, with
the "planet," with leisure—with living a good life, in the several senses of that
phrase.

Finally, there is meaning for us in the very failure of the Fruitlands experiment, the extreme brevity of its lifespan. Both Lane and Alcott were acutely
aware of the fleeting nature of experience. Lane wished for a "white type"
that might capture its evanescent nature; Alcott regretted that its original
freshness and beauty eluded the printed word. At Alcott House he had
suggested that America was the place where paradise could be planted; by

1856 he had come to the conclusion that his country's characteristic contribution to culture involved addressing the momentum of the passing day. He
made a list of "purely American organs and institutions":

> Garrison made the Convention,
> Greeley made the Newspaper,
> Emerson made the Lecture,
>   and
> Alcott is making the Conversation.[3]

These are structures to accommodate the moment as it comes; it is typical
of Alcott that he saw his particular contribution to the architecture of the
ephemeral as unfinished, ongoing. What happened at Fruitlands was ultimately a Conversation, sometimes affectionate, often bad-tempered, occasionally enlightening, frequently plagued by misunderstandings. Moreover,
as happens with conversations, those of us at a distance only overhear
intriguing snatches.

One day in January 1846, Alcott happened upon a newspaper report of a
lecture to the Royal Society by Michael Faraday. His subject was the relation
of electricity and magnetism to light. "I venture to conjecture," Alcott told
his diary, "that the three are states of One Substance, and that this, by whatsoever name it is designated, is the *immediate* Breath of Life, the nexus of
Spirit and matter." Pondering on this topic brought back his experience at
the Lovejoy house a couple of years previously. "The hair on the human head
is an electric pile, and in lesser measure the skin itself." Life is experienced at
the speed of light itself. The "magnetic current circulates through the pores
and rushes from the atoms of all bodies . . . From the chaos of matter
creation springs at the incoming of the organic light."

When the utopian hopefuls grouped together at Concordia Cottage
and then at the Fruitlands farmhouse, they believed they could achieve
heaven on earth. In that respect the project was doomed and ultimately irrelevant. Eternity might dial itself on time, as Alcott had claimed in his first
"Orphic Saying," but if eternity prevails there can be no more dialing, no
movement, no life at all. As the poet Wallace Stevens asks in "Sunday
Morning":

Is there no change of death in paradise?
Does ripe fruit never fall? Or do the boughs
Hang always heavy in that perfect sky,
Unchanging . . .?[4]

Two years after the collapse of Fruitlands, Thoreau built his hut by
Walden Pond. He stayed there for two years and two months; the book he
wrote about it covered just one year, and was organized around the progres-
sion of the seasons. He left, he said, because he had other lives to lead.[5]
Perhaps he had learned from his friends the Fruitlanders how to adapt his
life, or his lives, to the temporal process. A hut is by its nature a temporary
shelter, as is the tent that represents the most desirable form of habitation in
the circumstantial table; as was Fruitlands itself, the borrowed farmhouse in
its mortgaged fields.

The men, women, and children who lived and worked in it for that short
interval were attempting to seize the day and fully inhabit their own Now.
They wanted to feel the relationship between their inner spirit and the materiality all around, to celebrate an intimate engagement with their environment. True, they aspired to transform the world as a whole; even Abigail
Alcott, the most skeptical of the participants, felt the urge to achieve "diffusive illimitable benevolence." But aspiration is part of the very process of
breathing, and in the end Fruitlands was an endeavor to experience "the
immediate Breath of Life."

Notes

Manuscript materials are prefixed by [MS]. If they are from the Fruitlands Museums collection this is specified. If not, they are from the Houghton Library holdings of Harvard University, and readers should consult the Houghton cross-references at the end of the endnotes to determine the location and its call number.

Chapter 1: To Reproduce Perfect Men

1. Accounts of Alcott's life can be found in: Odell Shepard, *Pedlar's Progress*; Frederick Dahlstrand, *Amos Bronson Alcott*; Madelon Bedell, *The Alcotts*; and John Matteson, *Eden's Outcasts*.
2. F.B. Sanborn, *Bronson Alcott at Alcott House, England, and Fruitlands*, p. 77.
3. For Sewall, see Richard Francis, *Judge Sewall's Apology*; for Abigail Alcott see Bedell, *The Alcotts*, pp. 22–33.
4. Megan Marshall, *The Peabody Sisters*, pp. 294–5.
5. Ralph Waldo Emerson, "Divinity School Address," in *Nature, Addresses, and Lectures*, p. 81.
6. Amos Bronson Alcott, "Journal for 1836," p. 39, entry for March 1, 1836.
7. Elizabeth Palmer Peabody, *Record of Mr. Alcott's School*, pp. 146–9.
8. Bronson Alcott, *The Journals of Bronson Alcott*, p. 73, entry for December 21, 1835.
9. Peabody, *Record*, p. 112.
10. Marshall, *The Peabody Sisters*, p. 318.
11. Marshall, *The Peabody Sisters*, p. 298.
12. Dorothy McCuskey, *Bronson Alcott, Teacher*, p. 91.
13. Bronson Alcott, "Journal for 1836," p. 30.
14. Peabody, *Letters*, p. 152.
15. Marshall, *The Peabody Sisters*, p. 322.
16. Helen Graham Carpenter, *Reverend John Graham*, pp. 183–4, 188–9.

17. Bronson Alcott, "Journal for 1836," pp. 39, 41.
18. Sylvester Graham, *New Experiments*, p. 62.
19. Bronson Alcott, *Conversations with Children on the Gospels*, vol. 2, p. 247, vol. 1, pp. 137, 134.
20. Peabody, *Letters*, p. 157, fn 2.
21. Bronson Alcott, *Conversations*, vol. 1, p. xxxiii.
22. Bronson Alcott, *Conversations*, vol. 1, p. 68, fn.
23. Peabody, *Letters*, p. 181.
24. Peabody, *Letters*, pp. 157–63. For correction of date see Marshall, *The Peabody Sisters*, p. 542, endnote for p. 324.
25. Peabody, *Record*, pp. 85–6.
26. Emerson, *Nature*, in *Nature, Addresses and Lectures*, p. 10.
27. Christopher Pearse Cranch, [MS] "Illustrations of the New Philosophy."
28. Emerson, "The Over-Soul," in *Essays: First Series*, p. 164.
29. Quoted in Shepard, *Pedlar's Progress*, p. 185.
30. Peabody, *Record*, pp. 85–6.
31. Marshall, *The Peabody Sisters*, p. 325.
32. Pasted in Bronson Alcott, [MS] autobiographical collections, 1834–9.
33. Bronson Alcott, [MS] autobiographical index.
34. Bronson Alcott, [MS] letterbook, 1836–50; [MS] autobiographical index.
35. Reproduced in Charles Lane, "A. Bronson Alcott's Works," p. 422.
36. Bronson Alcott, *Journals* (entry for December 21, 1835), p. 73.
37. Quoted in Bedell, *The Alcotts*, p. 139.
38. Harriet Martineau, *Society in America*, vol. 3, pp. 176–7.
39. Lane, "A. Bronson Alcott's Works," p. 423.
40. Bronson Alcott, *Letters*, ed. Richard L. Herrnstadt, pp. 36–7.
41. Bronson Alcott, [MS] journals (entry for October 1837), pp. 468–84.
42. Quoted in Roger William Cummins, *The Second Eden*, p. 69.

Chapter 2: Now I Know What Thought Is

1. George Henry Lewes, "Spinoza," pp. 385–6.
2. There is one book-length biography of Greaves: J.E.M. Latham, *Search for a New Eden: James Pierrepont Greaves (1777–1842)*.
3. Samuel Taylor Coleridge, *Biographia Literaria*, p. 363.
4. James Pierrepont Greaves, *Letters and Extracts*, vol. 1, p. 196.
5. Lane, "James Pierrepont Greaves," pt 2, p. 289.
6. Latham, *Search*, p. 57.
7. Greaves, *Letters*, vol. 1, p. xix.
8. William Harry Harland, "Bronson Alcott's English Friends," p. 32.
9. Harland, "Bronson Alcott's English Friends," pp. 39–60.
10. Samuel Bower, *The Peopling of Utopia*, p. 12.
11. Harland, "Bronson Alcott's English Friends," pp. 34–9.
12. Henry Gardiner Wright, "My first Interview with James Pierrepont Greaves," p. 136.
13. Lane, "James Pierrepont Greaves," pt 2, pp. 285–6.
14. Wright, "My First Interview," p. 138.
15. Greaves, *Letters*, vol. 1, p. 206.
16. Greaves, *The New Nature in the Soul*, p. 9.
17. Greaves, *New Theosophic Revelations*, p. 265.
18. Greaves, *Letters*, vol. 1, pp. 136–7; *New Nature*, p. 56.
19. Greaves, *New Nature*, pp. 10–11.

20. Greaves, *Letters*, vol. 2, p. 180, vol. 1, p. 35.

21. Lane, "James Pierrepont Greaves," p. 286.

22. Quoted in Latham, *Search*, p. 127.

23. Lane, "James Pierrepont Greaves," p. 282.

24. Greaves, *Triune-Life Divine and Human*, p. 95.

25. Greaves, *Letters*, vol. 1, p. 32.

26. Greaves, *Letters*, vol. 1, pp. 33–4.

27. Quoted in Latham, *Search*, p. 170.

28. Wright, *Marriage and its Sanctions*, pp. 7, 5.

29. Greaves, *Letters*, vol. 1, p. 32.

30. Greaves, *Revelations*, p. 119.

31. Greaves, *Letters*, vol. 2, p. 230.

32. Greaves, *Revelations*, p. 119.

33. Greaves, *Revelations*, pp. 97, 83.

34. Greaves, *Revelations*, p. 97.

35. Wright, *Marriage*, pp. 8, 3–4.

36. Greaves, *Three Hundred Maxims*, pp. 7, 30.

37. Greaves, *Letters*, p. xiv.

38. Quoted in "On Association," *New Age, Concordium Gazette and Temperance Advocate*, vol. 1, xvi (April 1, 1844) p. 95.

39. Greaves, *Letters*, vol. 2, p. 195.

40. Wright, *Retrospective Sketch of an Educative Attempt*, p. 3. A copy is glued into Bronson Alcott, [MS] autobiographical collections,1840–4.

41. Wright, *Educational Establishment, Alcott House*, pp. 3–4.

Chapter 3: A Joy in a Winding Sheet

1. Bronson Alcott, [MS] journal excerpts, Fruitlands.

2. Bronson Alcott, [MS] *Psyche, An Evangele*.

3. Bedell, *The Alcotts*, p. 144, fn; Bronson Alcott, *Journals*, p. 112.

4. Bronson Alcott, [MS] autobiography 1843.

5. Bronson Alcott, *Journals*, pp. 114–15.

6. *Healthian*, vol. 1, viii (Aug. 1842), p. 66.

7. Bronson Alcott, *Journals*, p. 115.

8. Bronson Alcott, *Letters*, pp. 41–2.

9. Abigail Alcott, [MS] fragment of an autobiography.

10. Bronson Alcott, *Journals*, p. 119; *Letters*, p. 41.

11. Bronson Alcott, *Journals*, p. 121.

12. Bronson Alcott, [MS] journals (entry for April 1839), p. 661.

13. Quoted in Bedell, *The Alcotts*, p. 43.

14. Quoted in Bedell, *The Alcotts*, p. 74.

15. Bronson Alcott, [MS] journals (entry for April 1839), p. 614.

16. Sanborn, *Bronson Alcott at Alcott House*, p. 28; Bronson Alcott, *Journals*, p. 125.

17. Bronson Alcott, *Journals*, pp. 125–6.

18. Bronson Alcott, [MS] *Journals* (entry for May 1, 1839).

19. Emerson, *Poems*, p. 139.

20. John A. Heraud, *The Educator*, p. 218.

21. Emerson, *Journals and Miscellaneous Notebooks*, vol. 2, p. 231 (entry for November 4, 1839).

22. Philip Gura, *American Transcendentalism*, p. 5.

23. Margaret Fuller, *The Letters of Margaret Fuller*, vol. 2, p. 95; Joel Myerson, *The New England Transcendentalists and the* Dial, p. 30.

24. Quoted in McCuskey, *Bronson Alcott, Teacher*, p. 118.

25. Sanborn, *Bronson Alcott at Alcott House*, p. 9.

26. Marshall, *The Peabody Sisters*, p. 397.

27. *New Moral World* (June 1840), pp. 284–5; see also Latham, *The Search*, p. 184.

28. McCuskey, *Bronson Alcott, Teacher*, p. 109.

29. Bronson Alcott, *Letters*, p. 51.

30. Emerson, *The Letters of Ralph Waldo Emerson*, vol. 2, p. 281.

31. Myerson, *The New England Transcendentalists*, p. 47; Bronson Alcott, "Orphic Sayings."

32. Emerson, "Self-Reliance," in *Essays: First Series*, p. 28.

33. Bronson Alcott, "Orphic Sayings," nos 31 (p. 93), 43 (p. 96), 17 (p. 89), 24 (p. 91), 12 (p. 88).

34. Bronson Alcott, *Journals*, p. 162.

35. Emerson, *Journals*, vol. 7, p. 211.

36. Bronson Alcott, *Journals*, p. 138.

37. Sanborn, *Bronson Alcott at Alcott House*, p. 9; Fuller to William H. Channing in Fuller, *Letters* vol. 2, p. 194.

38. *Prelude*, Book 11, lines 258–60.

39. *Dial*, vol. 1, iv (April 1841), pp. 524, 527, 528, 536.

40. Myerson, *The New England Transcendentalists*, pp. 26, 53.

41. *Plain Speaker*, vol. 1, ii (March 1841), p. 6.

42. See Emerson, *Letters*, vol. 2, pp. 371, 382, 389; Bronson Alcott, *Letters*, p. 57; Fuller, *Letters*, vol. 2, p. 208.

43. Bronson Alcott, "Days from a Diary," p. 427.

44. Dahlstrand, *Bronson Alcott*, p. 187; *Plain Speaker*, vol. 1, v (June 1841), p. 18.

45. Bronson Alcott, "Days," p. 426.

46. Sylvester Graham, *Lectures on the Science of Human Life*, vol. 2, p. 419.

47. Bronson Alcott, [MS] autobiographical collections 1840–44; William Ellery Channing, letter to Peabody, in W.H. Channing, *The Life of William Ellery Channing*, p. 54.

48. *A Prospectus for the Establishment of a Concordium*, p. 3.

49. pp. 6, 8. I have modified the punctuation and added italics to make the sentence less obscure.

50. *A Prospectus*, pp. 5, 4; George Jacob Holyoake, *The History of Cooperation*, vol. 1, p. 153.

51. Harland, "Bronson Alcott's English Friends," p. 36.

52. Abigail Alcott, [MS] diary, in memoir, 1878.

53. Sanborn, *Bronson Alcott at Alcott House*, p. 21.

54. Wright, *Retrospective*, p. 5.

55. Latham, *The Search*, p. 173.

56. *Liberator*, vol. 8, xxxix (September 28, 1838), p. 156; vol. 8, xliv (October 26, 1838), pp. 171–2; report in *Boston Morning Post* reprinted in *Liberator*, vol. 11, xl (October 1, 1841), p. 158.

57. Bedell, *The Alcotts*, pp. 161–2.

58. Louisa May Alcott, *Little Women*, pp. 27–8; Abigail Alcott, [MS] memoir, 1878; Sanborn, *Bronson Alcott at Alcott House*, p. 28.

59. *Dial*, vol. 2, iv (April 1842), p. 410.

60. Bronson Alcott, "Days," pp. 423–5.

61. Bronson Alcott, *Letters*, p. 62.

62. Fuller, *Letters*, vol. 3, p. 34.

63. Abigail Alcott to Samuel May (April 1842), in [MS] family letters.

64. Emerson, *Letters*, vol. 3, pp. 7, 8, 11; *Selected Letters*, p. 263.

65. Abigail Alcott, [MS] diary, 1841–4.

66. Bronson Alcott, *Letters*, pp. 61–2.

67. Abigail Alcott in Bronson Alcott, *Journals*, p. 141. Shepard has included extracts from Abigail Alcott's journals from 1842 to 1844 in his edition of her husband's journals to make up for missing material by Alcott himself.

68. Abigail Alcott, [MS] diary 1841–4.

69. Fuller, *Letters*, vol. 3, pp. 49–50.

70. Bronson Alcott, *Letters*, p. 61.

71. Quoted in Kenneth Walter Cameron, "Junius S. Alcott," p. 57.

72. Abigail Alcott in Bronson Alcott, *Journals*, p. 142.

73. Bronson Alcott, *Letters*, p. 64.

74. Emerson, *Journals*, vol. 8, p. 181.

Chapter 4: Fabling of Worlds

1. Abigail Alcott, [MS] diary 1841–4. Advertisement for ships inserted.

2. Bronson Alcott, *Letters*, p. 66.

3. Bronson Alcott, *Letters*, pp. 65, 67.

4. Bronson Alcott, *Letters*, pp. 69, 70.

5. *Healthian*, vol. 5, i (April 1842), pp. 37–8

6. Bronson Alcott, *Letters*, p. 69.

7. Bronson Alcott, *Letters*, pp. 69–71.

8. Bronson Alcott, *Letters*, pp. 80, 91.

9. Bronson Alcott, *Letters*, p. 70.

10. "The Third Dispensation," pasted in Bronson Alcott, [MS] autobiographical collections 1840–4, pp. 171–4. However, future references will be to the more accessible version in the *Present*, November 15, 1843, pp. 110–21.

11. Lane, "The Third Dispensation," pp. 110–11, 117–18.

12. Bronson Alcott, "Bronson Alcott's Journal for 1836" (entry for May 22, 1836), p. 59.

13. Bronson Alcott, *Letters*, p. 72.

14. Austin Feverel, "The Concordists of Alcott House," pt 4, p. 7.

15. Samuel Bower, *A Brief Account of the First Concordium*, p. 5.

16. Feverel, "The Concordists," pt 4, p. 7.

17. Feverel, "The Concordists," pt 4, p. 7.

18. Bronson Alcott, *Letters*, pp. 72, 75.

19. Samuel Bower, *A Sequel to the Peopling of Utopia*, p. 17.

20. Bronson Alcott, *Letters*, pp. 73, 72.

21. Bronson Alcott, *Letters*, pp. 75–6.

22. Bronson Alcott, *Letters*, p. 74.

23. *The Correspondence of Emerson and Carlyle*, pp. 320, 323.

24. *The Correspondence of Emerson and Carlyle*, pp. 338, 326. Bronson Alcott, *Letters*, p. 78.

25. Shepard, *Pedlar's Progress*, pp. 316–17.

26. Bronson Alcott, *Letters*, p. 78; *The Correspondence of Emerson and Carlyle*, p. 333.

27. Emerson, "English Reformers," p. 241.

28. Quoted in Feverel, "The Concordists," pt 2, p. 7.

29. Lane, "Transatlantic Transcendentalism," p. 168.

30. Bronson Alcott, "Days," p. 231.

31. Pasted into Bronson Alcott, [MS] autobiographical collections 1840–4, p. 164.

32. Emerson, "English Reformers," pp. 242–5.
33. Emerson, "English Reformers," pp. 245–7.
34. Quoted in Francis, *Judge Sewall's Apology*, pp. 191–2.
35. Bronson Alcott, *Letters*, p. 84.

Chapter 5: Rembrandt's Pot
1. *Dial*, vol. 3, i (July 1842), p. 11.
2. Now lost, but described in Emerson, *Journals*, vol. 9, p. 397. See also Emerson, *Letters*, vol. 3, p. 76.
3. Abigail Alcott, in Bronson Alcott, *Journals*, p. 146.
4. Abigail Alcott, in Bronson Alcott, *Journals*, p. 145.
5. Bronson Alcott, *Letters*, p. 87.
6. Abigail Alcott, in Bronson Alcott, *Journals*, pp. 145–6.
7. Bronson Alcott, *Letters*, p. 87.
8. Lane, "Transatlantic Transcendentalism," p. 166.
9. In Bronson Alcott, [MS] autobiographical collections 1840–4, p. 150.
10. Bronson Alcott, [MS] autobiographical collections 1840–4, pasted on p. 25.
11. Bronson Alcott, *Letters*, p. 88.
12. Abigail Alcott, [MS] diary, 1841–4.
13. Bronson Alcott, [MS] autobiographical collections, 1840–4, p. 150.
14. Bronson Alcott, *Letters*, pp. 89–90; Abigail Alcott, in Bronson Alcott, *Journals*, pp. 146–7.
15. Inserted in Bronson Alcott, [MS] letterbook, 1836–50.
16. Lawrence H. Officer, "Purchasing Power of British Pounds."
17. in Bronson Alcott, [MS] letterbook, 1836–50.
18. Abigail Alcott in Bronson Alcott, *Journals*, p. 147; Abigail Alcott, diary (June 18, 1842), in [MS] memoir, 1878.
19. Abigail Alcott, in Bronson Alcott, *Journals*, p. 147.
20. Report of Meeting of Health Association, pasted into Bronson Alcott, [MS] letterbook, 1836–50.
21. Quoted in Matteson, *Eden's Outcasts*, p. 92.
22. Bronson Alcott, "Autobiographical Index," p. 710.
23. Quoted in J.E.M. Latham, "Fruitlands: A Postscript," p. 64.
24. Emerson, "English Reformers," p. 227.
25. Emerson, "English Reformers," p. 229.
26. Lane, "James Pierrepont Greaves," pt 1, p. 255.
27. Emerson, "English Reformers," p. 236.
28. Emerson, "History," in *Essays, First Series*, p. 22.
29. Bronson Alcott, "Orphic Sayings," p. 85.
30. Emerson, "English Reformers," pp. 236–7.
31. Letter to William Emerson in Emerson, *Letters*, vol. 3, p. 88.
32. Abigail Alcott, letter 49, [MS] Family Letters.
33. Quoted in Latham, "Fruitlands," p. 64.
34. Bronson Alcott, [MS] autobiographical index (entry for October 22, 1842).
35. Cameron, "Junius Alcott," p. 58.
36. Abigail Alcott, in Bronson Alcott, *Journals*, p. 148; Emerson, "English Reformers," p. 237.
37. Bronson Alcott, *Letters*, p. 91.

Chapter 6: Hesitations at the Plunge

1. Emerson, *Letters*, vol. 3, pp. 93, 96.
2. Lane, "Dial," p. 357.
3. Emerson, *Journals*, vol. 8, pp. 305–6.
4. Emerson, *Journals*, vol. 8, p. 299.
5. Emerson, *Journals*, vol. 8, pp. 305–6
6. Emerson, *Letters*, vol. 3, p. 96.
7. Emerson, *Letters*, vol. 3, p. 96; Harland, "Bronson Alcott's English Friends," p. 41.
8. Emerson, *Journals*, vol. 8, p. 301.
9. Emerson, *Journals*, vol. 8, p. 304.
10. Emerson, *The Journals*, ed. Edward Emerson, vol. 6, p. 294.
11. Emerson, "*Over-Soul*," p. 160.
12. Emerson, *Journals*, vol. 8, pp. 254–5; Bronson Alcott, "Days," p. 427.
13. Emerson, *Letters*, vol. 3, p. 95.
14. Quoted in Emerson, *Letters*, vol. 3, pp. 95–6.
15. Lane, "James Pierrepont Greaves," pt 2, p. 286.
16. Emerson, "The Over-Soul," p. 165.
17. Mary S. Gove [Nichols], *Mary Lyndon*, pp. 179, 187–8.
18. *Mary Lyndon*, pp. 181–2. Lane's musical analogy is in *Spirit of the Age*, November 17, 1849, p. 30.
19. Quoted in Harland, "Bronson Alcott's English Friends," p. 50, fn 65.
20. Bronson Alcott, "Autobiographical Index," p. 710.
21. Emerson, *Journals*, vol. 8, pp. 310–12.
22. *Mary Lyndon*, p. 203.
23. Greaves, [MS] "Notes and Sentiments," Fruitlands; Thoreau, *Walden*, p. 82.
24. Emerson, *Journals*, vol. 8, pp. 310–12.
25. *Mary Lyndon*, p. 203.
26. Emerson, *Letters*, vol. 3, p. 98.

Chapter 7: The Mind Yields, Falters, and Fails

1. Emerson, *Journals*, vol. 8, p. 307.
2. *Little Women*, pp. 194, 200.
3. Bronson Alcott, *Letters*, p. 92.
4. Bronson Alcott, *Letters*, p. 93.
5. Abigail Alcott, in Bronson Alcott, *Journals*, pp. 148–9, and fn p. 149.
6. Harland, "Bronson Alcott's English Friends," p. 41.
7. *Walden*, p. 90.
8. Harland, "Bronson Alcott's English Friends," p. 41.
9. Sanborn, *Memorabilia of Hawthorne, Alcott and Concord*, p. 32.
10. Emerson, *Journals*, vol. 8, pp. 305–6.
11. Emerson, *Journals*, vol. 6, p. 319.
12. Bronson Alcott, "Autobiographical Index," p. 711.
13. Abigail Alcott, diary, 1841–4.
14. Bronson Alcott, "Autobiographical Index," p. 711; Fuller, *Letters*, vol. 3, p. 108.
15. Bedell, *The Alcotts*, p. 200.
16. Abigail Alcott, in Bronson Alcott, *Journals*, p. 149.
17. Bronson Alcott, *Letters*, pp. 94–5.
18. Sanborn, *Bronson Alcott at Alcott House*, pp. 33–4.
19. Harland, "Bronson Alcott's English Friends," p. 36.

20. Harland, "Bronson Alcott's English Friends," p. 42.

21. Harland, "Bronson Alcott's English Friends," pp. 36–7.

22. Wright, *What, When, Where, and How*, p. 24.

23. Sanborn, *Bronson Alcott at Alcott House*, p. 36; Emerson, *Journals*, vol. 8, p. 329.

24. *Mary Lyndon*, pp. 204, 207; Sanborn, *Bronson Alcott at Alcott House*, opposite p. 28.

25. Harland, "Bronson Alcott's English Friends," p. 37.

26. *Mary Lyndon*, pp. 218–25.

27. *New Moral World*, vol. I, xxii (November 26, 1840), p. 346; *Boston Quarterly Review*, vol. 18, iii (April 1842), p. 255.

28. Latham, *Search*, p. 207; Bedell, *The Alcotts*, p. 197.

29. Abigail Alcott, in Bronson Alcott, *Journals*, pp. 149–150.

30. Abigail Alcott, in Bronson Alcott, *Journals*, p. 150.

Chapter 8: The Little Wicket Gate

1. Lane gives this date. Alcott (not reliable on dates) gives the following day.

2. Michael Volmar, *Freelands*, pp. 1–2.

3. This, and Lane's subsequent letters to the *Liberator* on issues arising from Alcott's arrest, have been published as *A Voluntary Political Government*, ed. Carl Watner, and all references will be to this source, pp. 46–9.

4. Lane, *A Voluntary Political Government*, pp. 47–8.

5. Hawthorne, *The American Notebooks* (entry for September 1, 1842), pp. 353–4.

6. Lane, *A Voluntary Political Government*, p. 48.

7. Emerson, "Samuel Hoar," pp. 405–18.

8. Lane, *A Voluntary Political Government*, pp. 48–9.

9. Thoreau, *Correspondence*, pp. 77–8.

10. Lane, *A Voluntary Political Government*, p. 48.

11. Emerson, "Hoar," p. 410.

12. See Broderick, "Thoreau, Alcott and the Poll Tax," p. 624.

13. Broderick, "Thoreau," p. 623.

14. Lane, *A Voluntary Political Government*, pp. 47–8.

15. Lane, *A Voluntary Political Government*, p. 46.

16. Lane, *A Voluntary Political Government*, pp. 47–8.

17. Abigail Alcott, in Bronson Alcott, *Journals*, p. 150.

18. *Little Women*, pp. 154–7.

19. Abigail Alcott, in Bronson Alcott, *Journals*, pp. 151–3.

20. Lane, *A Voluntary Political Government*, p. 50.

21. Lane, *A Voluntary Political Government*, pp. 50–1.

22. Thoreau, "Resistance to Civil Government," in *Reform Papers*, pp. 69, 89–90.

23. Lane, letter in Abigail Alcott, [MS] diary 1841–4.

24. Lane, letter in Abigail Alcott, [MS] diary 1841–4.

25. Louisa May Alcott, *Journals*, p. 47.

26. Bronson Alcott, *Letters*, pp. 96–7.

27. Anna Alcott, [MS] journals (entry for November 1839); Matteson, *Eden's Outcasts*, p. 92.

28. Bronson Alcott, *Letters*, p. 97.

29. Bronson Alcott, *Letters*, pp. 97–8.

30. Bronson Alcott, *Letters*, p. 98.

31. Bronson Alcott, *Letters*, pp. 99–100.

32. Richard Francis, *Transcendental Utopias*, p. 38, fn 8.

33. Francis, *Transcendental Utopias*, pp. 39, 47, 57.

34. Bronson Alcott, *Letters*, pp. 99–100.

35. In Thoreau, *Correspondence*, pp. 91–2.

36. Lane, *A Voluntary Political Government*, p. 53.

37. Lane, *A Voluntary Political Government*, pp. 54–5.

38. Harland, "Bronson Alcott's English Friends," pp. 42–4.

39. Louisa May Alcott, *Little Men*, p. 42.

40. Harland, "Bronson Alcott's English Friends," pp. 42–4.

41. Emerson, *Journals*, vol. 6, p. 374.

42. Harland, "Bronson Alcott's English Friends," p. 44.

43. Feverel, "Concordists," pt 4, p. 7.

44. Abigail Alcott, in Bronson Alcott, *Journals*, p. 152.

45. Letter of March 7th, in Bronson Alcott, [MS] autobiographical collections, 1840–4, p. 267.

46. Lane, *A Voluntary Political Government*, pp. 62–3.

Chapter 9: The Principle of Inverse Ratio

1. *The Correspondence of Emerson and Carlyle*, p. 338.

2. Emerson, *Journals*, vol. 8, p. 374.

3. Emerson, *Journals*, vol. 6, p. 371.

4. Abigail Alcott, letter to Louisa May Alcott (March 12, 1843), in [MS] Alcott Family Additional Papers.

5. Lane, *A Voluntary Political Government*, p. 66.

6. *Walden*, p. 98.

7. Lane, *A Voluntary Political Government*, pp. 68–72.

8. Emerson, *Journals*, vol. 8, p. 397.

9. *New Age*, vol. 1, ii (May 13, 1843), p. 13.

10. Lane, "A. Bronson Alcott's Works," p. 420.

11. "A. Bronson Alcott's Works," pp. 425, 423.

12. "A. Bronson Alcott's Works," p. 442.

13. Bronson Alcott, [MS] journals (entry for January 4, 1839), pp. 29–30; Lane, "Transcendentalism," *New Age*, vol. 1, ii (29 May), p. 12.

14. "A. Bronson Alcott's Works," pp. 421–2; Herman Melville, *Moby-Dick*, p. 4.

15. Inserted in Abigail Alcott, [MS] diary, 1841–4. This reference to Bronson Alcott was deleted by Nathaniel Hawthorne when the skit was published in book form in *Mosses from an Old Manse* (1846).

16. "A. Bronson Alcott's Works," p. 452.

17. Sanborn, *Bronson Alcott at Alcott House*, pp. 35–7.

18. Quoted in Myerson, *The Transcendentalists*, p. 171.

19. Lane, *A Voluntary Political Government*, pp. 75–7.

20. *Walden*, p. 52.

21. Lane, *A Voluntary Political Government*, p. 75.

22. Lane, *A Voluntary Political Government*, p. 81.

23. *New Age*, vol. 1, i (May 6, 1843), p. 16.

24. Harland, "Bronson Alcott's English Friends," pp. 37, 48.

25. Clara Endicott Sears, *Bronson Alcott's Fruitlands*, p. 40.

26. Robert Carter, *The Newness*, p. 129.

27. Louisa May Alcott, "Transcendental Wild Oats," reprinted in Sears, *Bronson Alcott's Fruitlands*, pp. 145–74, 160.

28. *Century Magazine*, vol. 39, iv (February 1890), p. 637.
29. Hawthorne, *Letters, 1813–43*, p. 540; Thomas Wentworth Higginson, *Cheerful Yesterdays*, p. 84.
30. "Autobiographical Index," p. 712.
31. Lane, *A Voluntary Political Government*, p. 83.
32. Emerson, "The American Scholar," in *Nature, Addresses, and Lectures*, p. 53.
33. Lane, *A Voluntary Political Government*, pp. 83–8.
34. Harland, "Bronson Alcott's English Friends," p. 38.
35. "Autobiographical Index," pp. 711–12.
36. Lane, letter to Junius Alcott (March 7, 1843), in Bronson Alcott, [MS] autobiographical collections 1840–4.
37. Harland, "Bronson Alcott's English Friends," p. 40, fn 42.
38. Quoted in Cummins, *The Second Eden*, p. 101.
39. Lane, *A Voluntary Political Government*, pp. 90–1.
40. Postscript, Bronson Alcott, letter (June 13, 1847), in Bronson Alcott, [MS] letterbook, 1836–50.
41. Harland, "Bronson Alcott's English Friends," p. 45; Lane, [MS] letter to Thoreau (June 9, 1843), Fruitlands.
42. Lane, [MS] letter to Thoreau (June 9, 1843), Fruitlands.
43. Michael Volmar, *Archaeological Excavations at the Willard-Atherton Site*, p. 16.
44. Bronson Alcott, "Autobiographical Index," p. 712.
45. Michael Volmar and Mary Fuhrer, *Archaeological Site Reconnaissance*, p. 50.
46. Harland, "Bronson Alcott's English Friends," pp. 45–6. Harland has misread the price of the land as $1,000 instead of $1,800.
47. Lawrence H. Officer, "Purchasing Power."
48. Harland, "Bronson Alcott's English Friends," pp. 45, fn 56, 46.
49. Harland, "Bronson Alcott's English Friends," p. 46.
50. Most commentators, including Bedell, Matteson, and Harriet Reisen in her book *Louisa May Alcott*, treat Abraham Everett and Abraham Wood/Wood Abraham as two different people. I follow Dahlstrand, *Amos Bronson Alcott*, p. 195, in believing that they are one person whose name was changed twice. Actually the name might have only changed once: Abraham Everett could have decided to call himself "Wood" Abraham as a sort of nickname, and later Clara Endicott Sears in her book *Bronson Alcott's Fruitlands* may simply have assumed that name was Abraham Wood in reverse (p. 21). Everett and Abraham Wood/Wood Abraham are never listed together in any contemporary records I have found; reference is usually to "Abraham." Apart from the Alcotts and Lane, Louisa May Alcott only gives names to four Fruitlanders in her sketch "Transcendental Wild Oats." Moses White is clearly Joseph Palmer, John Pease is the Englishman Bower, and Jane Gage is Ann Page. This leaves Forest Absalom, clearly intended to stand for Wood Abraham, a melancholy and silent individual according to Louisa May Alcott. There is then no equivalent of a separate Abraham Everett (though it has to be admitted that Larned is not given a name either). Negative evidence is provided by both Bronson Alcott and Abigail. Alcott's list of the "Fruitlands Fraternity" in [MS] autobiographical collections, 1840–4, p. 296, includes "Abram Everett" but omits Wood Abraham. On July 24, 1843, Abigail Alcott gives a list of people who have come to Fruitlands, making no distinction between residents and visitors. She includes "Wood Abraham" but does not mention Abraham Everett (Abigail Alcott, in Bronson Alcott, *Journals*, p. 154). On July 25th Isaac Hecker listed the members of the community as Alcott, Lane, Abraham, Bower, Mrs. Alcott, and the children (Isaac T. Hecker, *Diary*, p. 121). The likelihood therefore, as I see it, is that Everett and Abraham Wood/Wood Abraham are one and the same.
51. Harland, "Bronson Alcott's English Friends," pp. 45–8.

52. Emerson, *Journals*, vol. 8, pp. 403–4; Harland, "Bronson Alcott's English Friends," p. 46.

53. Christopher Greene, "Marriage," *Plain Speaker*, vol. 1, vii (December 1841), p. 27; Emerson, *Journals*, vol. 8, p. 321.

54. Emerson, *Poems*, pp. 9–13.

55. Emerson, *Journals*, vol. 8, pp. 403–4.

Chapter 10: Diffusive Illimitable Benevolence

1. Volmar, *Archaeological Site Reconnaissance*, p. 27.

2. Louisa May Alcott, [MS] letter to Mr. Wiley (May 13, 1873), Fruitlands.

3. Louisa May Alcott, "Transcendental Wild Oats," pp. 149–50.

4. Sanborn, *Bronson Alcott in Alcott House*, p. 36.

5. Harland, "Bronson Alcott's English Friends," p. 46; Anna Alcott, "Diary," p. 86.

6. Matteson, *Eden's Outcasts*, p. 123.

7. Information emailed to author by Michael Volmar of Fruitlands Museums, August 13, 2009.

8. Abigail Alcott, in Bronson Alcott, *Journals*, pp. 152–3.

9. Sears, *Bronson Alcott's Fruitlands*, p. 71.

10. Louisa May Alcott, "Transcendental Wild Oats," p. 157.

11. Anna Alcott, "Diary," p. 87.

12. "Literary Intelligence," in *Dial*, vol. 3, iv (April 1843), pp. 545–8; Harland, "Bronson Alcott's English Friends," p. 48.

13. Harland, "Bronson Alcott's English Friends," pp. 45–8.

14. Lane, *A Voluntary Political Government*, p. 98.

15. Lane, *A Voluntary Political Government*, p. 102.

16. Lane, *A Voluntary Political Government*, pp. 99–100.

17. Lane, *A Voluntary Political Government*, p. 102.

18. For the original table, see Greaves, *Letters*, vol. 2, pp. 80–1. For the 1842 version, Bronson Alcott, [MS] autobiographical collections 1840–4, p. 139; Abigail Alcott, [MS] diary 1841–4 (entry for October 8, 1842).

19. Lane, "Dial," *Union*, vol. 1, viii (November 1842), p. 257.

20. *Mary Lyndon*, p. 178.

21. Lane, *A Voluntary Political Government*, pp. 102–3.

22. Abigail Alcott, in Bronson Alcott, *Journals*, p. 153.

23. It is my belief that by "Christy" Anna Alcott is referring to Larned, not to Christopher Greene as claimed by Sears (*Bronson Alcott's Fruitlands*, p. 21). In her Fruitlands diary, Anna Alcott mentions "Christy" as being already at the farm (along with Wood Abraham and William Lane) when the Alcott family arrived (entry June 6th, p. 88), and she records him teaching her from June 8th; however, ten days later, on June 18th, her father writes to Junius that Christopher Greene and his wife have "not yet come" (Bronson Alcott, *Letters*, p. 103). He often wrote carelessly, but it would be strange for him to say Greene hadn't yet come if the man had greeted him when he arrived at Fruitlands. None of the principals ever mentions Greene as a member. However, many years later Anna Alcott told F.B. Sanborn that she remembered Christopher Greene at Fruitlands with affection (Anna [Alcott] Pratt, [MS] letter to F. B. Sanborn {September 21st}, Fruitlands). My conclusion is that Anna called Larned Christy and subsequently confused his name with Greene's. Her father calls Larned "Christopher" in his list of the "Fruitlands Fraternity" (Bronson Alcott, [MS] autobiographical collections, 1840–4). It is known that Christopher Greene started a school in Tyngsboro, Massachusetts, about ten miles from Harvard, in 1843, so Harriet Reisen in *Louisa May Alcott*, p. 71, assumes he came over to Fruitlands to help out with the teaching. However

Abigail Alcott does not name him in the list of members and visitors she made on July 24th (in Bronson Alcott, *Journals*, p. 154) and she would have been unlikely to omit a man who had taught her children.

24. Anna Alcott, "Diary," pp. 88, 90.

25. Lane, [MS] letter to Thoreau (June 9, 1843), Fruitlands.

26. Emerson, *Selected Letters*, p. 290.

27. Myerson, *The New England Transcendentalists*, p. 173.

28. Lane, Bronson Alcott, "Fruitlands," *Dial*, vol. 4, i (July 1843), p. 173; *Mary Lyndon*, p. 222.

29. Emerson, *Selected Letters*, p. 289.

30. Emerson, *Letters*, vol. 3, p. 215.

31. Louisa May Alcott, "Transcendental Wild Oats," p. 159.

32. Lane, "Fruitlands," p. 173.

33. Fuller, *Letters*, vol. 3, p. 137.

34. Ann Lee's ministry at Harvard is described in Richard Francis, *Ann the Word*, pp.157–267 and the phenomenon of "Mother Ann's Work" pp. 332–5.

35. Emerson, *Journals*, vol. 9, p. 114.

36. Lane, "Shakers," *New Age*, vol. 1, viii (August 1, 1843), p. 75.

37. Matteson mistakenly identifies this article as the product of a later visit on August 4th, though Lane dates it as June 1843. See Matteson, *Eden's Outcasts*, pp. 150–2.

38. Lane, "A Day with the Shakers," *Dial*, vol. 4, ii (October 1843), pp. 165–6.

39. Lane, "A Day with the Shakers," pp. 167, 169, 173.

40. Lane, "A Day with the Shakers," pp. 171–2.

41. Anna Alcott, "Diary," pp. 90–1.

Chapter 11: The New Waves Curl

1. Harland, "Bronson Alcott's English Friends," pp. 46–8.

2. Anna Alcott, "Diary," pp. 91–2.

3. Bronson Alcott, *Letters*, pp. 102–3.

4. Anna Alcott, "Diary," pp. 93–7; ode quoted from Bronson Alcott, *Letters*, pp. 104–6.

5. Harland, "Bronson Alcott's English Friends," pp. 44–5.

6. Anna Alcott, "Diary," pp. 93–7; Bronson Alcott, *Letters*, pp. 104–6.

7. Hawthorne, *American Notebooks*, pp. 201–3; Hawthorne, *Blithedale Romance*, pp. 209–10. For masquerade at Brook Farm see Francis, *Transcendental Utopias*, pp. 35–66.

8. Harland, "Bronson Alcott's English Friends," p. 49.

9. Sears, *Bronson Alcott's Fruitlands*, p. 68.

10. Louisa May Alcott, "Transcendental Wild Oats," p. 160.

11. Louisa May Alcott, "Transcendental Wild Oats," pp. 152, 160.

12. Anna Alcott, "Diary," pp. 92–3.

13. Louisa May Alcott, "Transcendental Wild Oats," p. 152; Sears, *Bronson Alcott's Fruitlands*, p. 119.

14. Feverel, "Concordists," pt 2, p. 7.

15. Harland, "Bronson Alcott's English Friends," p. 49.

16. Sears, *Bronson Alcott's Fruitlands*, p. 119.

17. Louisa May Alcott, "Transcendental Wild Oats," p. 157.

18. Fuller, *Letters*, vol. 3, p. 137.

19. Lane, "Social Tendencies," pt 1, pp. 65, 68.

20. Hawthorne, *Letters*, pp. 528, 545, 558.

21. Lane, "Social Tendencies," pt 1, p. 71.

22. Lane, "Social Tendencies," pt 1, p. 72.
23. Lane, "Social Tendencies," pt 1, p. 76.
24. Hawthorne, *Blithedale Romance*, p. 200.
25. Lane, "Social Tendencies," pt 1, pp. 85, 86.
26. Lane, "Social Tendencies," pt 1, p. 86; pt 2, p. 193.
27. Lane, "Social Tendencies," pt 2, pp. 199, 201.
28. Fuller, "The Great Lawsuit"; Lane's review is in *The Reasoner*, vol. 1, p. 29.
29. Lane, "Social Tendencies," pt 2, p. 203.
30. Emerson, "Fourierism and the Socialists," p. 87.
31. Lane, "Tendencies," pt 2, p. 203.

Chapter 12: Utter Subjection of the Body

1. Abigail Alcott, in Bronson Alcott, *Journals*, p. 153.
2. Abigail Alcott, diary, in [MS] memoir, 1878 (entry for July 2, 1843).
3. See inside back cover of Bronson Alcott, [MS] "Psyche".
4. Holyoake, *The History of Cooperation*, vol. 1, p. 265.
5. Latham, *The Search*, pp. 206–7; Harland, "Bronson Alcott's English Friends," p. 38.
6. Wright, "Diary," *New Age*, vol. 1, xiii (January 1, 1844), p. 152.
7. Editorial announcement, *New Age*, vol. 1, viii (August 1, 1843), p. 75.
8. Carter, "Newness," p. 128.
9. See Walter Elliott, *Life of Father Hecker*, pp. 21–30, letter quoted pp. 36–7; Lindsay Swift, *Brook Farm*, p. 95.
10. Swift, *Brook Farm*, p. 98.
11. Isaac T. Hecker, *The Diary*, p. 106; Elliott, *Life*, p. 71.
12. Elliott, *Life*, p. 78.
13. Elliott, *Life*, pp. 73–4; Hecker, *The Diary*, p. 113; see also p. 114.
14. Hecker, *The Diary*, pp. 95, 116; Elliott, *Life*, p. 82.
15. Hecker, *The Diary*, p. 115.
16. Emerson, *Journals*, vol. 8, p. 432.
17. "Spiritual Laws," in *Essays: First Series*, p. 79.
18. Emerson, *Journals*, vol. 8, pp. 433–4.
19. Elliott, *Life*, p. 83.
20. See Anna (Alcott) Pratt, [MS] letter to F.B. Sanborn (September 21st), Fruitlands.
21. Louisa May Alcott, *Little Men*, p. 40.
22. Louisa May Alcott, "Transcendental Wild Oats," pp. 151, 164.
23. Emerson, *Journals*, vol. 8, pp. 345–6.
24. Sears, *Bronson Alcott's Fruitlands*, p. 76.
25. Hecker, *The Diary*, p. 116.
26. Hecker, *The Diary*, pp. 116–17.
27. Hecker, *The Diary*, p. 117.
28. Anna Alcott, "Diary," pp. 100–1.
29. Hecker, *The Diary*, p. 118.
30. Hecker, *The Diary*, p. 119.
31. Quoted by Swift, *Brook Farm*, p. 104.
32. Elliott, *Life*, p. 81.
33. Elliott, *Life*, p. 88, Anna Alcott, "Diary," p. 101.
34. Anna Alcott, "Diary," pp. 102, 101.
35. Abigail Alcott, in Bronson Alcott, *Journals*, pp. 153–4.
36. Anna Alcott, "Diary," p. 102.

37. Emerson, *Letters*, vol. 3, p. 191.
38. Harland, "Bronson Alcott's English Friends," p. 50.
39. Hecker, *The Diary*, pp.121, 132–3.

Chapter 13: The Consociate Family
1. Harland, "Bronson Alcott's English Friends," p. 50.
2. Harland, "Bronson Alcott's English Friends," p. 52.
3. Harland, "Bronson Alcott's English Friends," p. 51.
4. See Bronson Alcott, journal (entry for July 18th), in [MS] autobiographical collections, 1840–4. Her first name is also given as Anne and Anna. I follow Alcott in calling her Ann (in his list of the "Fruitlands Fraternity"), partly to distinguish her from Anna Alcott.
5. Louisa May Alcott, "Transcendental Wild Oats," p. 162, where she is called Miss Jane Gage.
6. Harland, "Bronson Alcott's English Friends," p. 51; an abbreviated version of this letter was published in *New Age*, vol. 1, ix (September 1, 1843), p. 90.
7. Abigail Alcott to Samuel May, letter 53, [MS] family letters. Only dated "Sunday noon," but internal evidence shows it was written on August 6th.
8. Emerson, letter (August 7, 1843), *Letters*, vol. 3, p. 196.
9. Letter 53, in [MS] family letters.
10. Bronson Alcott, *Letters*, p. 107.
11. Bronson Alcott, *Letters*, p. 108.
12. See Francis, *Transcendental Utopias*, p. 95.
13. See William Henry Harrison's edition of Louisa May Alcott, *Transcendental Wild Oats and Excerpts from the Fruitlands Diary*, p. 31, fn.
14. letter 53, in [MS] family letters.
15. This entry is in the diary pages discovered in Walpole, N.H., many years after Cheney's edition of Louisa May Alcott's journals. See Louisa May Alcott, *Journals*, p. 43.
16. Letter 53, in [MS] family letters.
17. Harland, "Bronson Alcott's English Friends," p. 55; Sears, *Bronson Alcott's Fruitlands*, p. 119; Emerson, *Letters*, vol. 3, p. 196.
18. Letter 53, in [MS] family letters.
19. Abigail Alcott, in Bronson Alcott, *Journals*, p. 154.
20. Louisa May Alcott, *Journals* p. 43.
21. Bronson Alcott, [MS] autobiographical collections, 1840–4, pp. 293–5.
22. *Plain Speaker*, vol. 1, vi (May 1841), p. 24.
23. Bronson Alcott, [MS] journals (entry for April 23, 1834), p. 151.
24. See for example, Harland, "Bronson Alcott's English Friends," p. 56, postscript.
25. Hawthorne, *Blithedale Romance*, p. 148.
26. *Plain Speaker*, vol. 1, vi (May 6, 1841), p. 21.

Chapter 14: Penniless Pilgrimages
1. Abigail Alcott, in Bronson Alcott, *Journals*, pp. 154–5.
2. Abigail Alcott, letter to Charles May (August 31, 1843), in [MS] memoir, 1878.
3. *Mary Lyndon*, p. 222; Sears, *Bronson Alcott's Fruitlands*, p. 68; Louisa May Alcott, "Transcendental Wild Oats," p. 163.
4. Samuel Sewall Greely, [MS] letter, Fruitlands.
5. Louisa May Alcott, *Little Men*, p. 46.
6. Louisa May Alcott, *Journals*, p. 44.
7. Greely, [MS] letter, Fruitlands.
8. Louisa May Alcott, *Journals*, p. 44.

9. Abigail Alcott, letter to Charles May (August 31st) in [MS] memoir, 1878.

10. Louisa May Alcott, *Journals*, p. 45.

11. Abigail Alcott, [MS] diary, 1841–4.

12. Harland, "Bronson Alcott's English Friends," pp. 52–3.

13. Charles King Newcomb, "Dolon," p. 112; Emerson, *Letters*, vol. 5, p. 87.

14. Harland, "Bronson Alcott's English Friends," p. 53.

15. Louisa May Alcott, "Transcendental Wild Oats," p. 166.

16. Sears, *Bronson Alcott's Fruitlands*, p. 115.

17. Louisa May Alcott, "Transcendental Wild Oats," p. 167.

18. Harland, "Bronson Alcott's English Friends," pp. 53–4.

19. Lydia Maria Child, *Letters*, pp. 52–3.

20. See Francis, *Transcendental Utopias*, pp. 115–40.

21. Child, *Letters*, p. 52.

22. Harland, "Bronson Alcott's English Friends," p. 54.

23. Sears, *Bronson Alcott's Fruitlands*, p. 114; Louisa May Alcott, "Transcendental Wild Oats," p. 165; Harland, "Bronson Alcott's English Friends," p. 54.

24. Louisa May Alcott, *Journals*, p. 45.

25. Abigail Alcott [MS] diary, 1841–4.

26. Sears, *Bronson Alcott's Fruitlands*, p. 119.

27. Harland, "Bronson Alcott's English Friends," pp. 54–5. Louisa May Alcott, *Journals*, p. 45, says they went to New Hampshire on September 24th, but it must have been before that because Lane went to Concord with Anna Alcott on September 23rd, and stayed there until September 26th (Harland, "Bronson Alcott's English Friends," p. 55). The original of this part of Louisa's journal is now lost, and her first editor, Ednah Cheney, frequently mistranscribed dates.

28. Harland, "Bronson Alcott's English Friends," pp. 54–5.

29. Harland, "Bronson Alcott's English Friends," p. 55.

30. Abigail Alcott, [MS] diary, 1841–4.

31. Emerson, *Journals*, vol. 9, p. 23.

32. Harland, "Bronson Alcott's English Friends," p. 55 says Tuesday, but Emerson dates his diary entry as Monday, so he is probably correct. Emerson, *Journals*, vol. 9, p. 29.

33. Emerson, *Journals*, vol. 9, p. 29.

34. Lydia Maria Child, *Selected Letters*, p. 204.

35. Emerson, *Journals*, vol. 9, p. 29.

36. Harland, "Bronson Alcott's English Friends," p. 55.

37. Anna Alcott, "Diary," pp. 103–4.

38. See Louisa May Alcott, *Transcendental Wild Oats,* ed. Harrison, pp. 34–7.

39. Harland, "Bronson Alcott's English Friends," pp. 55–6, 44.

40. Harland, "Bronson Alcott's English Friends," p. 56.

Chapter 15: Softly Doth the Sun Descend

1. Louisa May Alcott, *Journals*, p. 46; *Selected Letters*, p. 3.

2. Louisa May Alcott, *Journals*, p. 46.

3. The exact date of the trip is not given except in the "Autobiographical Index," p. 713, where it is recorded for October, but this is the most likely sequence.

4. Emerson, *Journals*, vol. 9, p. 35.

5. Emerson, *Letters*, vol. 3, p. 214.

6. Harland, "Bronson Alcott's English Friends," p. 57.

7. Lane, "Brook Farm," pp. 351–2.

8. "Brook Farm," pp. 354–5.
9. "Brook Farm," pp. 352–3, 354.
10. "Brook Farm," p. 355; Harland, "Bronson Alcott's English Friends," p. 57.
11. "Brook Farm," pp. 355–6.
12. See Francis, *Transcendental Utopias*, pp. 60–1.
13. Francis, *Transcendental Utopias*, pp. 94, 126, 133; Roland Barthes, *Sade/Fourier/Loyola*, pp. 114, 77–8.
14. Francis, *Transcendental Utopias*, p. 94.
15. "Brook Farm," p. 357.
16. "Autobiographical Index," p. 713.
17. Harland, "Bronson Alcott's English Friends," pp. 56–7.
18. Abigail Alcott, letter to Samuel May (November 4, 1843), in [MS] memoir, 1878.
19. Harland, "Bronson Alcott's English Friends," p. 57.
20. Emerson, *Journals*, vol. 9, pp. 50–1.
21. Emerson, *Journals*, vol. 9, pp. 53–4.
22. Abigail Alcott, letter (November 4th) in [MS] memoir, 1878.
23. Louisa May Alcott, *Journals*, pp. 46–7.
24. Abigail Alcott, letter (November 4th) in [MS] memoir, 1878.
25. Abigail Alcott, letter to Charles May (November 6, 1843), in [MS] memoir, 1878.

Chapter 16: Nectar in a Sieve
1. Harland, "Bronson Alcott's English Friends," p. 57.
2. Bedell, *The Alcotts*, p. 227.
3. Abigail Alcott, letter to Samuel May (November 11, 1843) in [MS] family letters.
4. In Elliott, *Life*, p. 92.
5. Lane, [MS] letter to Thoreau (December 3, 1843), Fruitlands.
6. Louisa May Alcott, "Transcendental Wild Oats," pp. 163–4.
7. Greely, [MS] letter, Fruitlands.
8. Harland, "Bronson Alcott's English Friends," p. 58.
9. Louisa May Alcott, *Journals*, p. 47.
10. Bronson Alcott, *Letters*, pp. 109–10.
11. Suggested in Bedell, *The Alcotts*, p. 228.
12. Harland, "Bronson Alcott's English Friends," pp. 58–9; for the reference to rooms in Lexington, "Autobiographical Index," p. 713.
13. Louisa May Alcott, *Journals*, p. 47.
14. Louisa May Alcott, *Journals*, p. 47.
15. Larry Carlson makes this suggestion in "The Inner Life of Fruitlands," p. 106.
16. Emerson, *Letters*, vol. 3, p. 230.
17. Emerson, *Letters*, vol. 3, p. 231.
18. Abigail Alcott, in Bronson Alcott, *Journals*, p. 155.
19. Quoted in Cummins, *The Second Eden*, p. 157.
20. Abigail Alcott, in Bronson Alcott, *Journals*, p. 155.
21. Louisa May Alcott, *Journals*, p. 48.
22. "Autobiographical Index," p. 713.
23. Louisa May Alcott, *Journals*, p. 48.
24. Abigail Alcott, in Bronson Alcott, *Journals*, pp. 155–6.

Chapter 17: Cain and Abel

1. Peabody, "Fourierism," pp. 473–4.
2. "Fourierism," p. 477.
3. "Fourierism," pp. 481–2.
4. "Autobiographical Index," p. 713. Missing pages evident in Bronson Alcott, [MS] autobiographical index.
5. Emerson, *Journals*, vol. 9, pp. 60–1.
6. Abigail Alcott, in Bronson Alcott, *Journals*, p. 156.
7. Fuller, *Letters*, vol. 3, p. 170.
8. See Abigail Alcott, letter to Samuel May (April 9, 1844), in [MS] family letters.
9. "Autobiographical Index," p. 714.
10. Abigail Alcott, diary (entry January 7, 1844), in [MS] memoir, 1878.
11. Abigail Alcott, in Bronson Alcott, *Journals*, pp. 156–7.
12. See Abigail Alcott, letter to Samuel May (January 11, 1844) in [MS] memoir, 1978; Emerson, *Letters*, vol. 3, p. 235.
13. Abigail Alcott, letter to Samuel May (January 11, 1844) in [MS] memoir, 1978.
14. Bronson Alcott, [MS] autobiographical collections 1840–44.
15. Abigail Alcott, letter to Samuel May (January 11, 1844), in [MS] memoir, 1878
16. Abigail Alcott, letter to Hannah Robie (January 21, 1844), in [MS] memoir, 1878.
17. Harland, "Bronson Alcott's English Friends," pp. 46, 56.
18. See for example, Anna Alcott, "Diary," pp. 100, 101; Louisa May Alcott, *Journals*, p. 45.
19. "Autobiographical Index," p. 714.
20. Abigail Alcott, letter to Hannah Robie (January 21, 1844) in [MS] memoir, 1878.
21. Louisa May Alcott, "Transcendental Wild Oats," p. 150.
22. Louisa May Alcott, "Transcendental Wild Oats," p. 170.
23. Abigail Alcott, letter to Hannah Robie (January 21, 1844), in [MS] memoir, 1878.
24. William Henry Harrison, in the introduction to his edition of Louisa May Alcott, *Transcendental Wild Oats*, p. 2, suggests that the description of Alcott taking to his bed in despair was "probably fabricated for a reading public with an insatiable appetite for the sentimental and melodramatic," since there is no supporting evidence for the incident.
25. Abigail Alcott, in Bronson Alcott, *Journals*, p. 157.
26. Abigail Alcott, letter to Hannah Robie (March 12, 1844), in [MS] memoir, 1878.
27. Abigail Alcott, in Bronson Alcott, *Journals*, p. 157.
28. "Autobiographical Index," p. 714.
29. Bronson Alcott, *Journals* (February 9, 1851), pp. 240–1.
30. Lane, "Life in the Woods," pp. 415–16.
31. "Life in the Woods," p. 418.
32. "Life in the Woods," pp. 419–21.
33. "Life in the Woods," p. 422.
34. *Walden*, p. 49.
35. "Life in the Woods," p. 423.
36. "Life in the Woods," pp. 424–5.
37. Lane, "Millennial Church," pp. 539–40.
38. Harland, "Bronson Alcott's English Friends," p. 39.
39. Emerson, *Journals*, vol. 9, p. 86.
40. Abigail Alcott, in Bronson Alcott, *Journals*, p. 158.
41. Abigail Alcott, in Bronson Alcott, *Journals*, p. 158.
42. Harland, "Bronson Alcott's English Friends," p. 39.
43. Abigail Alcott, [MS] diary, 1841–4 (May 23, 1843).

44. See Bedell, *The Alcotts*, endnote for p. 234 on p. 377, though in her main text she wrongly gives the date of the settlement as 1845.
45. Bronson Alcott, *Letters*, p. 111.
46. Bronson Alcott, "Sighs for Paradise," [MS] Still River, 1844, Fruitlands.
47. Bronson Alcott, *Letters*, p. 111.
48. Bronson Alcott, list of lost MSS, in [MS] letterbook, 1836–50.
49. Bronson Alcott, letter to keeper of Rail House (August 11, 1844), in [MS] autobiographical collections 1840–44.
50. See Bronson Alcott, letter to keeper of Rail House (December 7, 1850), in "Eighty-Six Letters," pt 2, p. 199.

Chapter 18: Tumbledown Hall

1. Cynthia H. Barton, *Transcendental Wife*, p. 121.
2. Emerson, *Letters*, vol. 3, pp. 262–3.
3. Bronson Alcott, *Letters*, pp. 114–15.
4. In *New Age*, vol. 1, xx (August 1, 1844), pp. 262–3, 264.
5. John Epps, *The Diary of the Late John Epps*, pp. 241–3.
6. Bronson Alcott, [MS] autobiographical fragment; Emerson, *Journals*, vol. 9, p. 145.
7. Bronson Alcott, *Letters*, p. 117.
8. Lane, [MS] letter to Abigail Alcott (February 22, 1845), Fruitlands.
9. Matteson, *Eden's Outcasts*, p. 173.
10. Bedell, *The Alcotts*, p. 235.
11. Abigail Alcott, letter to Samuel May (June 8, 1845), in [MS] family letters.
12. Abigail Alcott, letter to Samuel May (August 9, 1845), in [MS] family letters.
13. Sanborn, *Memorabilia*, p. 42.
14. Abigail Alcott, letter to Samuel May (August 9, 1845), in [MS] family letters.
15. See Sanborn, *Memorabilia*, pp. 48–9.
16. Louisa May Alcott, *Journals*, p. 56.
17. Abigail Alcott, letter to Samuel May (September 19, 1845), in [MS] family letters.
18. See Matteson, *Eden's Outcasts*, p. 183.
19. Bronson Alcott, *Letters*, pp. 125–6.
20. Bronson Alcott, diary (January 1846), in [MS] various papers, 1841–2 [actually 1841–6].
21. Lane, letter to Alcott (February 1846), in Bronson Alcott, [MS] letterbook, 1836–50.
22. Harland, "Bronson Alcott's English Friends," p. 39.
23. Lane, [MS] papers, Fruitlands.
24. Lane, letter to Emerson (May 20, 1846), in [MS] letters to Ralph Waldo Emerson.
25. Sanborn, *Bronson Alcott in Alcott House*, p. 98.
26. See Bedell, *The Alcotts*, p. 257.
27. Bronson Alcott, "Eighty-Six Letters," pt 2, p. 197.
28. Latham, *Search*, p. 226.
29. William Oldham, letter to Alcott (December 16, 1866), in Bronson Alcott, [MS] letterbook, 1865, 1866.
30. Oldham, [MS] letter to Alcott (March–September 1870), Fruitlands.
31. According to Sears, *Bronson Alcott's Fruitlands*, p. 137.
32. Quoted Sears, *Bronson Alcott's Fruitlands*, p. 142.
33. Lane, [MS] letter to Thomas Palmer (September 16, 1851), Fruitlands; Volmar, *Freelands*, no page numbering.

34. Carter, "Newness," pp. 130–1.

35. Swift, *Brook Farm*, p. 126.

36. Bronson Alcott, *Letters*, p. 127.

37. Bedell, *The Alcotts*, p. 261.

38. Bronson Alcott, in [MS] letterbook 1836–50. Susan Cheever, in *American Bloomsbury*, attributes the Skimpole remark to Margaret Fuller (p. 81), but this is impossible as Fuller died in 1850, and Dickens did not begin writing *Bleak House* until 1852.

39. Bronson Alcott, *Letters*, p. 127.

40. Bronson Alcott, [MS] journal excerpts, Fruitlands.

Conclusion

1. http://www.60sfurther.com/communes.htm (visited March 1, 2010).

2. http://www.architectmagazine.com/community-projects/sweet-earth-experimental-utopias-in-america (visited March 1, 2010).

3. Bronson Alcott, *Journals*, p. 281.

4. Wallace Stevens, *Collected Poems*, p. 67.

5. Thoreau, *Walden*, p. 323.

Sources

The main source of material for this book is the huge collection of MSS by Bronson Alcott and his family held by the Houghton Library of Harvard University. The other valuable holding belongs to the Fruitlands Museums of Prospect Hill Road, Harvard. This site (which in recent years has been the subject of detailed archaeological study by Michael Volmar and others) consists of the original farmhouse where the experiment took place, along with an art gallery, a Native American museum, and a collection of Shaker artefacts and documents. It was set up by Clara Endicott Sears, who published a collection of source materials, *Bronson Alcott's Fruitlands with Transcendental Wild Oats*, in 1915. Sears's book includes the Fruitlands journals of the two oldest Alcott children as well as Louisa's fictionalized sketch of life at the community. New material from Louisa's childhood diary that has since come to light is available in the edition of her journals edited by Joel Myerson and Daniel Shealy.

Selections from Alcott's journals were published by Odell Shepard in 1938, though his book contains only a fraction of the sixty-two MS volumes in the Houghton Library. Shepard compensates for the loss of Alcott's diaries of the early 1840s by including selections from those of Abigail Alcott during that period. Richard L. Herrnstadt published Alcott's *Letters* in 1969. More material from the journals and further letters discovered in recent years have been published in various scholarly outlets.

The most important source of material by Charles Lane is included in William Harry Harland's article, "Bronson Alcott's English Friends." Harland was a British journalist who had collected a large archive of letters by Lane and the other English Transcendentalists (now lost, alas). A number pertaining to Fruitlands are transcribed in his article, which he sent to F.B. Sanborn in 1906. Sanborn told him his article was not interesting enough for publication, rather disingenuously perhaps as he made use of it for his own disappointingly short and slight book, *Bronson Alcott at Alcott House, England, and Fruitlands, New England* (1908). The Harland typescript was acquired by Clara Sears and is still deposited at the Fruitlands Museums. It was finally edited and published by Joel Myerson in 1978. Lane's newspaper articles on *A Voluntary Political Government* were republished by a small anarchist press in 1982.

Odell Shepard wrote a pioneering biography of Bronson Alcott in 1937, though he devotes surprisingly little space to the Fruitlands experiment (about twenty pages in a book of over 500). More recently Frederick Dahlstrand has written a useful intellectual biography of Alcott. Other helpful contributions are Madelon Bedell's well-researched book about the Alcott family, and John Matteson's joint biography of Bronson Alcott and his daughter Louisa May.

The only biography of Greaves is by J.E.M. Latham, an oddly focused but valuable study. Roger Cummins wrote a well-researched PhD thesis on Charles Lane in 1967, but for some reason it has never been published.

A few years ago Larry Carlson wrote an article giving a general account of the Fruitlands experiment, and I devoted two chapters to the ideas behind it in my book *Transcendental Utopias*. This, however, is the first full-length treatment of the community.

MANUSCRIPT REFERENCES

Fruitlands Museums

Alcott, Amos Bronson, [MS] journal excerpts
Amos Bronson Alcott, [MS] Still River 1844
Alcott, Louisa May, [MS] letter to Mr. Wiley (May 13, 1873)
Greaves, James Pierrepont, [MS] "Notes and Sentiments expressed by James Pierrepont Greaves, Esq, in Conversation with R.W. Birch, of Derby in 1834."
Greely, Samuel Sewall, [MS] letter
Lane, Charles, [MS] letter to Abigail May Alcott (February 22, 1845)
Lane, Charles, [MS] letter Henry David Thoreau (June 9, 1843)
Lane, Charles, [MS] letter to Henry David Thoreau (December 3, 1843)
Lane, Charles, [MS] letter to Thomas Palmer (September 16, 1851)
Lane, Charles, [MS] papers
Oldham, William, [MS] letter to Amos Bronson Alcott (March–September 1870)
Pratt, Anna [Alcott], [MS] letter to F.B. Sanborn (September 21 [no year])

Houghton Library, Harvard University
I have followed the Houghton Library's citation preferences. The holdings are large but can readily be searched using the library's electronic finding aids, particularly by means of the full descriptions in OASIS.
[MS] Christopher Pearse Cranch, "Illustrations of the New Philosophy" (MS Am 1506)
[MS] Letters to Ralph Waldo Emerson (MS Am 1280)

[MS] Alcott Family Additional Papers 1707–1904 (MS Am 1130.14–1130.16)
Abigail Alcott, diary, 1841–4
Abigail Alcott, fragment of an autobiography
Amos Bronson Alcott, autobiographical fragment

[MS] Amos Bronson Alcott Papers (MS Am 1130.9–1130.12)
Family letters
Abigail Alcott, diary, in memoir, 1878
Amos Bronson Alcott, "Psyche, An Evangele"
Amos Bronson Alcott, autobiographical collections, 1834–9
Amos Bronson Alcott, autobiographical collections, 1840–4
Amos Bronson Alcott, autobiographical index
Amos Bronson Alcott, autobiography, 1843
Amos Bronson Alcott, journals
Amos Bronson Alcott, letterbooks, see those for 1836–50 and for 1865, 1866
Amos Bronson Alcott, various papers, 1841–2 [actually 1841–6]
Anna Alcott, journal, 1839

BIBLIOGRAPHY

A Prospectus for the Establishment of a Concordium; or an Industry Harmony College (London: Strange, 1841)
Alcott, Amos Bronson, "Bronson Alcott's Autobiographical Index," ed. David P. Edgell in *New England Quarterly*, vol. 14, iv (December 1941), pp. 704–15
Alcott, Amos Bronson, "Bronson Alcott's Journal for 1836," ed. Joel Myerson, *Studies in the American Renaissance, 1978* (Boston: Twayne, 1978), pp. 17–104
Alcott, Amos Bronson, "Days from a Diary," *Dial*, vol. 2, iv (April 1842), pp. 409–43
Alcott, Amos Bronson, "Eighty-Six Letters of A. Bronson Alcott," pt 2, ed. Frederick Wagner in *Studies in the American Renaissance, 1980* (Boston: Twayne, 1980), pp. 183–228
Alcott, Amos Bronson, "Orphic Sayings," *Dial*, vol. 1, i (June 1840), pp. 85–98
Alcott, Amos Bronson, *Record of Conversations with Children on the Gospels*, 2 vols (Boston: James Munroe, 1836–7)
Alcott, Amos Bronson, *The Journals of Bronson Alcott*, ed. Odell Shepard (Boston: Little, Brown, 1938)
Alcott, Amos Bronson, *The Letters of A. Bronson Alcott*, ed. Richard L. Herrnstadt (Ames, Iowa: The Iowa State University Press, 1969)
Alcott, Anna, "Diary," reprinted in Clara Endicott Sears, *Bronson Alcott's Fruitlands*, pp. 86–105
Alcott, Louisa May, *Little Men: Life at Plumfield with Jo's Boys* (Boston: Roberts Brothers, 1872)
Alcott, Louisa May, *Little Women or, Meg, Jo, Beth and Amy* (Boston: Roberts Brothers, 1868)
Alcott, Louisa May, *The Journals of Louisa May Alcott*, ed. Joel Myerson and Daniel Shealy (Boston: Little, Brown, 1989)
Alcott, Louisa May, *The Selected Letters of Louisa May Alcott*, ed. Joel Myerson and Daniel Shealy (Boston: Little, Brown, 1987)

Alcott, Louisa May, "Transcendental Wild Oats," reprinted in Clara Endicott Sears, *Bronson Alcott's Fruitlands*, pp. 145–74

Alcott, Louisa May, *Transcendental Wild Oats and Excerpts from the Fruitlands Diary*, ed. William Henry Harrison (Harvard, MA: Harvard Common Press, 1975)

Barthes, Roland, *Sade/Fourier/Loyola*, trans. Richard Miller (New York: Hill and Wang, 1976)

Barton, Cynthia H., *Transcendental Wife: The Life of Abigail May Alcott* (Lanham: University Press of America, 1996)

Bedell, Madelon, *The Alcotts: Biography of a Family* (New York: Clarkson N. Potter, 1980)

Boston Quarterly Review, The (Boston: Benjamin H. Greene, 1838–42)

Bower, Samuel, *A Brief Account of the First Concordium, or Harmonious Industrial College* (Ham Common: The Concordium, 1843)

Bower, Samuel, *A Sequel to the Peopling of Utopia; or, the Sufficiency of Socialism for Human Happiness* (Bradford: C. Wilkinson, 1838)

Bower, Samuel, *The Peopling of Utopia; or the Sufficiency of Socialism for Human Happiness: Being a Comparison of the Social and Radical Schemes* (Bradford: C. Wilkinson, 1838)

Broderick, John C., "Thoreau, Alcott and the Poll Tax," *Studies in Philology*, 53 (1956), pp. 612–26

Cameron, Kenneth Walter, "Junius S. Alcott, Poet and Transcendentalist," *Emerson Society Quarterly*, vol. 1, xiv (1959), pp. 57–75

Carlson, Larry A., "The Inner Life of Fruitlands," in *Lives out of Letters: Essays in American Literary Biography*, ed. Robert D. Habich (Madison, NJ: Fairleigh Dickinson University Press, 2004), pp. 93–113

Carlyle, Thomas and Ralph Waldo Emerson, *The Correspondence of Emerson and Carlyle*, ed. Joseph Slater (New York: Columbia University Press, 1964)

Carpenter, Helen Graham, *The Reverend John Graham of Woodbridge, Connecticut, and his Descendants* (Chicago, 1942)

Carter, Robert, "The Newness," *Century Magazine*, vol. 39, n.s. 17, i (November 1889), pp. 124–31

Channing, W.H., *The Life of William Ellery Channing D.D.* (Boston, 1880)

Cheever, Susan, *American Bloomsbury: Louisa May Alcott, Ralph Waldo Emerson, Margaret Fuller, Nathaniel Hawthorne, and Henry David Thoreau: Their Lives, Their Loves, Their Work* (New York: Simon & Schuster, 2006)

Cheney, Ednah Dow, *Louisa May Alcott: Her Life, Letters, and Journals* (Boston: Roberts Brothers, 1889)

Child, Lydia Maria, *Selected Letters 1817–1880*, ed. Milton Metzler and Patricia G. Holland (Amherst: University of Massachusetts Press, 1982)

Child, Lydia Maria, *The Letters of Lydia Maria Child* (Boston: Houghton Mifflin, 1883)

Clark, Annie M.L., *The Alcotts in Harvard* (Lancaster, MA: J.C.L. Clarke, 1902)

Coleridge, Samuel Taylor, *Biographia Literaria*, in *Collected Works*, vol. 3 (New York: Harper and Brothers, 1868)

Cummins, Roger William, *The Second Eden: Charles Lane and American Transcendentalism*, (doctoral dissertation, University of Minnesota, 1967)

Dahlstrand, Frederick C., *Amos Bronson Alcott: An Intellectual Biography* (Rutherford, NJ: Fairleigh Dickinson University Press, 1982)

Dial, The: A Magazine for Literature, Philosophy, and Religion, vol. 1 (Boston: Weeks, Jordan, 1841); vols 2, 3 (Boston: E.P. Peabody, 1842, 1843); vol. 4 (Boston: James Munroe, 1844)

Elliott, Walter, *The Life of Father Hecker* (New York: Columbus Press, 1891)

Emerson, Ralph Waldo, "English Reformers," *Dial*, vol. 3, ii (October 1842), pp. 227–47

Emerson, Ralph Waldo, "Fourierism and the Socialists," *Dial*, vol. 3, i (July 1842) pp. 83–97

Emerson, Ralph Waldo, "Samuel Hoar," in *Lectures and Biographical Sketches* (Boston: Houghton Mifflin, 1884), pp. 405–18

Emerson, Ralph Waldo, *Essays: First Series*, ed. Alfred R. Ferguson et al. (Cambridge, MA: Belknap Press of Harvard University Press, 1979)

Emerson, Ralph Waldo, *Journals and Miscellaneous Notebooks*, ed. William H. Gilman et al., 16 vols (Cambridge, MA: Belknap Press of Harvard University Press, 1960–82)

Emerson, Ralph Waldo, *Journals*, ed. Edward Emerson, 10 vols (Boston: Houghton Mifflin, 1909–14)

Emerson, Ralph Waldo, *Nature, Addresses and Lectures*, ed. Alfred R. Ferguson et al. (Cambridge, MA: Belknap Press of Harvard University Press, 1971)

Emerson, Ralph Waldo, *Poems*, ed. J.E. Cabot (Boston: Houghton Mifflin, 1884)

Emerson, Ralph Waldo, *Selected Letters of Ralph Waldo Emerson*, ed. Joel Myerson (New York: Columbia University Press, 1997)

Emerson, Ralph Waldo, *The Letters of Ralph Waldo Emerson*, ed. Ralph L. Rusk, 6 vols (New York: Columbia University Press, 1939)

Epps, John, *The Diary of the Late John Epps M.D. Edin.*, ed. Mrs. Epps (London: Kent & Co., 1875)

Feverel, Austin (pseudonym of William Harry Harland), "The Concordists of Alcott House," pt 1, December 23, 1905; pt 2, December 30, 1905; pt 3, January 20, 1906; pt 4, March 31, 1906, *Surrey Comet*

Francis, Richard, *Ann the Word: The Story of Ann Lee, Female Messiah, Mother of the Shakers, The Woman Clothed with the Sun* (New York: Penguin Books, 2002)

Francis, Richard, *Judge Sewall's Apology: The Salem Witch Trials and the Forming of an American Conscience* (New York: Harper Collins, 2005)

Francis, Richard, *Transcendental Utopias: Individual and Community at Brook Farm, Fruitlands, and Walden* (Ithaca: Cornell University Press, 1997)

Fuller, Margaret, "The Great Lawsuit. MAN versus MEN. WOMAN versus WOMEN," *Dial*, vol. 4, i (July 1843) pp. 1–48

Fuller, Margaret, *The Letters of Margaret Fuller*, ed. Robert N. Hudspeth, 4 vols (Ithaca: Cornell University Press, 1983–7)

Gove [Nichols], Mary S., *Mary Lyndon or, Revelations of a Life. An Autobiography* (New York: Stringer and Townsend, 1855), published anonymously

Graham, Sylvester, *Lectures on the Science of Human Life*, 2 vols (Boston: Marsh, Capen, Lyon and Webb, 1839)

Graham, Sylvester, *New Experiments: Means without Living* (Boston: Weeks, Jordan, 1837)

Greaves, James Pierrepont, *Letters and Extracts from the MS writings of James Pierrepont Greaves*, ed. Alexander Campbell, vol. 1 (Ham Common, Surrey: Concordium, 1843); vol. 2 (London: John Chapman, 1845)

Greaves, James Pierrepont, *New Theosophic Revelations from the MS. Journal of James Pierrepont Greaves* (London: John Chapman, 1847)

Greaves, James Pierrepont, *The New Nature in the Soul* (London: John Chapman, 1847)

Greaves, James Pierrepont, *Triune-Life Divine and Human* (London: Elliot Stock, 1888)

Greaves, James Pierrepont, *Three Hundred Maxims for the Consideration of Parents in Relation to the Education of their Children* (London: Darton & Clark, 1837)

Greene, Christopher, "Marriage," *Plain Speaker*, vol. 1, vii (December 1841), p. 27

Gura, Philip, *American Transcendentalism: A History* (New York: Hill and Wang, 2007)

Harland, William Harry, "Bronson Alcott's English Friends," in "William Harry Harland's 'Bronson Alcott's English Friends,' " ed. Joel Myerson, *Resources for American Literary Study*, vol. 8 (1978), pp. 24–60. Harland also wrote under the name of Austin Feverel

Hawthorne, Nathaniel, *The American Notebooks,* ed. Claude M. Simpson (Columbus, Ohio: Ohio State University Press, 1972)

Hawthorne, Nathaniel, *The Blithedale Romance and Fanshawe,* ed. Fredson Bowers (Columbus, Ohio: Columbus University Press, 1965)

Hawthorne, Nathaniel, *The Letters,* vol. 1 (1813–43), ed. Thomas Woodson et al. (Columbus, Ohio: Columbus University Press, 1984)

Healthian, The: A Journal of Human Physiology, Diet, and Regimen (London, 1842–3)

Hecker, Isaac T., *The Diary: Romantic Religion in Ante-Bellum America,* ed. John Farina (New York: Paulist Press, 1988)

Heraud, John A., *The Educator* (London: Taylor and Walton, 1839)

Higginson, Thomas Wentworth, *Cheerful Yesterdays* (Boston: Houghton Mifflin, 1898)

Holyoake, George Jacob, *The History of Cooperation,* 2 vols (London: Fisher Unwin, 1906)

Lane, Charles, "Transatlantic Transcendentalism," *Union,* vol. 1, v (August 1, 1842), pp. 166–8

Lane, Charles, "A Day with the Shakers," *Dial,* vol. 4, ii (October 1843), pp. 165–74

Lane, Charles, "A. Bronson Alcott's Works," *Dial,* vol. 3, iv (April 1843), pp. 417–54

Lane, Charles, "Brook Farm," *Dial,* vol. 4, iii (January 1843), pp. 351–7

Lane, Charles, "James Pierrepont Greaves," *Dial,* vol. 3, ii (October 1842), pp. 247–56; vol. 3, iii (January 1843), pp. 281–97

Lane, Charles, "Life in the Woods," *Dial,* vol. 4, v (April 1844), pp. 415–25

Lane, Charles, "Millennial Church," *Dial,* vol. 4, iv (April 1844), pp. 537–40

Lane, Charles, "Shakers," *The New Age, Concordium Gazette and Temperance Advocate,* vol. 1, viii (August 1, 1843), p. 75

Lane, Charles, "Social Tendencies," pt 1, *Dial,* vol. 4, i (July 1843), pp. 65–87; pt 2, *Dial,* vol. 4, ii (October 1843), pp. 188–205

Lane, Charles, *A Voluntary Political Government: Letters from Charles Lane,* ed. Carl Watner (St. Paul, MI: Michael. E. Coughlin, 1982)

Lane, Charles and Amos Bronson Alcott, "Fruitlands," *Dial,* vol. 4, i (July 1843), p. 173

Lane, Charles, review of *Dial,* in *Union,* vol. 1, viii (November 1842), pp. 356–60

Lane, Charles, *The Third Dispensation* (London, J. Davey: 1841); "The Third Dispensation," *Present* (November 15, 1843), pp. 110–21

Latham, J.E.M., "Fruitlands: A Postscript," *Studies in the American Renaissance, 1995* (Boston: Twayne, 1995)

Latham, J.E.M., *Search for a New Eden: James Pierrepont Greaves (1777–1842)* (Madison, NJ: Fairleigh Dickinson University Press, 1999)

Lewes, George Henry, "Spinoza," *The Fortnightly Review,* vol. 4, xii (April 1, 1866), pp. 385–6

"Literary Intelligence," *Dial,* vol. 3, iv (April, 1843), pp. 545–8

Liberator, The (Boston: W.L. Garrison, 1831–65)

Marshall, Megan, *The Peabody Sisters: Three Women Who Ignited American Romanticism* (Boston and New York: Houghton Mifflin Company, 2005)

Martineau, Harriet, *Society in America,* 3 vols (London: Saunders, Otley, 1837)

Matteson, John, *Eden's Outcasts: The Story of Louisa May Alcott and her Father* (New York: W.W. Norton & Co., 2007)

McCuskey, Dorothy, *Bronson Alcott, Teacher* (New York: Macmillan, 1940)

Melville, Herman, *Moby-Dick; or, The Whale* (New York: Modern Library, 2000)

Myerson, Joel, *The New England Transcendentalists and the* Dial (Rutherford, NJ: Fairleigh Dickinson University Press, 1980)

New Age, Concordium Gazette and Temperance Advocate, The (London: W. Strange, 1845)

New Moral World, The (London, 1834–45)

Newcomb, Charles King, "Dolon," *Dial*, vol. 3, i (July 1842), pp. 112–23

Officer, Lawrence H. and Samuel H. Williamson, "Purchasing Power of Money in the United States from 1774 to 2008," MeasuringWorth, 2009, http://measuringworth.com/ppowerus/

Officer, Lawrence H., "Purchasing Power of British Pounds from 1264 to Present," MeasuringWorth, 2009, http://measuringworth.com/ppoweruk

"On Association," *New Age*, vol. 1, xvi (April 1, 1844), p. 195

Peabody, Elizabeth Palmer, "Fourierism," *Dial*, vol. 4, iv (April 1843), pp. 473–84

Peabody, Elizabeth Palmer, *Record of Mr. Alcott's School, Exemplifying the Principles and Methods of Moral Culture*, 3rd edn (Boston: Roberts Brothers, 1874)

Peabody, Elizabeth Palmer, *The Letters of Elizabeth Palmer Peabody*, ed. Bruce A. Ronda (Middleton, CN: Wesleyan University Press, 1984)

Plain Speaker, The (Providence, RI, 1841)

Present, The (New York: W.H. Channing, 1843–4)

Reasoner, The (London: G.J. Holyoake, 1846–61)

Reisen, Harriet, *Louisa May Alcott: The Woman behind* Little Women (New York: Henry Holt & Co., 2009)

Sanborn, F.B., *Memorabilia of Hawthorne, Alcott and Concord*, ed. Kenneth Walter Cameron (Hartford, CN: Transcendental Books, 1970)

Sanborn, F.B., *Bronson Alcott at Alcott House, England, and Fruitlands, New England (1842–1844)* (Cedar Rapids, IA: The Torch Press, 1908)

Sears, Clara Endicott, *Bronson Alcott's Fruitlands with Transcendental Wild Oats* (Boston: Houghton Mifflin, 1915)

Shepard, Odell, *The Life of Bronson Alcott* (Boston: Little, Brown, 1937)

Spirit of the Age, The (New York: W.H. Channing, 1849–50)

Stevens, Wallace, *The Collected Poems* (London: Faber, 1955)

Stoehr, Taylor, *Nay-Saying in Concord: Emerson, Alcott, and Thoreau* (Hamden, CN: Archon Books, 1979)

Swift, Lindsay, *Brook Farm: Its Members, Scholars and Visitors* (New York: Macmillan, 1900)

Thoreau, Henry David, *The Correspondence of Henry David Thoreau*, ed. Walter Harding and Carl Bode (Washington Square: New York University, 1958)

Thoreau, Henry David, *Reform Papers*, ed. Wendell Glick (Princeton, NJ: Princeton University Press, 1973)

Thoreau, Henry David, *Walden*, ed. J. Lynton Shanley (Princeton, NJ: Princeton University Press, 1973)

Union, The (London, 1842)

Volmar, Michael and Mary Fuhrer, *Archaeological Site Reconnaissance and Locational Survey for the Fruitlands Museums Historic District, Harvard, Massachusetts* (Amherst, MA: University of Massachusetts Archaeological Services, 1999)

Volmar, Michael, *Archaeological Excavations at the Willard-Atherton Site (HA-197) Fruitlands Museums Historic District, Harvard, Massachusetts* (Harvard, MA: Fruitlands Museums, 2000)

Volmar, Michael, *Freelands* (Harvard, MA: Fruitlands Museums, 2009)

Wright, Henry Gardiner, "Diary," *New Age*, vol. 1, xiii (January 1, 1844), p. 152

Wright, Henry Gardiner, "My First Interview with James Pierrepont Greaves," *New Age*, vol. 1, xii (December 1, 1843), pp. 135–8

Wright, Henry Gardiner, *Educational Establishment, Alcott House, Ham Common, Richmond, Near London, conducted by Mr. and Miss Wright* (1842)

Wright, Henry Gardiner, *Marriage and its Sanctions* (Cheltenham: Willey, 1840)

Wright, Henry Gardiner, *Retrospective Sketch of an Educative Attempt at Alcott House, Ham Common, Near Richmond, Surrey, by Mr. & Miss Wright* (London: V. Torrus & Co, 1840)

Wright, Henry Gardiner, *What, When, Where, and How; or Subjective Education* (London, 1842)

Index